THE POETRY
OF
DEREK MAHON

ULSTER EDITIONS AND MONOGRAPHS
General Editors
Robert Welch
Joseph McMinn

ULSTER EDITIONS AND MONOGRAPHS
ISSN 0954–3392

THE POETRY
OF
DEREK MAHON

Edited by
Elmer Kennedy-Andrews

Ulster Editions and Monographs: 11

Copyright © 2002 by Elmer Kennedy-Andrews, Edna Longley, Gerald
Dawe, Bruce Stewart, Jerzy Jarniewicz, Eamonn Hughes, Michael Allen,
Richard York, Hugh Haughton, Frank Sewell, John Goodby, Neil Corcoran,
Stan Smith and Patrick Crotty

First published in Great Britain in 2002
by Colin Smythe Limited, Gerrards Cross, Buckinghamshire

British Library Cataloguing in Publication Data

A catalogue record for this book
is available from the British Library

ISBN 0–86140–425–4

Distributed in North America by Oxford University Press
198 Madison Avenue, New York, NY 10016

Produced in Great Britain
Typeset by Art Photoset Ltd., Beaconsfield, Buckinghamshire
Printed and bound by T.J. International Ltd., Padstow, Cornwall

CONTENTS

ACKNOWLEDGEMENTS

The editor would like to thank the Research Committee and the Dean and Faculty of Humanities of the University of Ulster for financial support towards the present volume. Thanks are also extended to the Arts Council of Northern Ireland and the Community Relations Council for grants towards the 1998 Ulster Symposium on which this book is based. Particular thanks are due to Professor Robert Welch, the General Editor of the Series for his invaluable advice and support.

The quotations from the work of Derek Mahon are included by permission of The Gallery Press, Loughcrew, Oldcastle, County Meath, Ireland, publishers of *Collected Poems* (1999) and Derek Mahon's other works.

ABBREVIATIONS

NC   *Night-Crossing* (London, Oxford University Press, 1968).
L   *Lives* (London, Oxford University Press, 1972).
TSP   *The Snow Party* (London and New York, Oxford University Press, 1975).
P   *Poems 1962–1978* (London, Oxford University Press, 1979).
THBN   *The Hunt By Night* (Oxford, Oxford University Press, 1982).
A   *Antarctica* (Dublin, Gallery Press, 1986).
SP   *Selected Poems* (Oldcastle, Gallery Press, 1991; Harmondsworth, Penguin Books, 1991).
THL   *The Hudson Letter* (Oldcastle, Gallery Press, 1995).
TYB   *The Yellow Book* (Oldcastle, Gallery Press, 1999).
CP   *Collected Poems* (Oldcastle, Gallery Press, 1999).

J   *Journalism: Selected Prose 1970–1995,* edited by Terence Brown (Oldcastle, Gallery Press, 1996).

INTRODUCTION: THE CRITICAL CONTEXT

ELMER KENNEDY-ANDREWS

This volume contains the proceedings of the University of Ulster's fourth Ulster Symposium, which was held on 17th-19th September 1998. In choosing Derek Mahon to be the featured poet, the Symposium aimed to redress a conspicuous critical deficit. A part of the remarkable flowering of Northern Irish poetry since the 1960s, Derek Mahon has not received anything like the amount of critical and media attention that his fellow Northern Irish poet, the Nobel laureate Seamus Heaney has attracted over the years. This is partly due to the differences between the two poetries: Heaney's poetry of rural experience and sensuous recreation of the physical world had a more immediate popular appeal than Mahon's poetry of 'the unreconciled, in their metaphysical pain' (CP 14).[1] It is also partly due to Mahon's reticence about promoting himself or his work. He has given relatively few interviews, rarely takes part in poetry readings, refuses to explain or introduce his poems. For him the artist is always an outsider, art always an art of failure: 'Artistic success', he once said, 'is the only kind that matters and it eludes us all'.[2]

Nor surprisingly, in comparison with Heaney, Mahon has shown relatively little interest in memorialising his childhood and family background, or explaining how he sees these as having shaped his poetry. Born in Belfast in 1941, he was an only child of Protestant parents. Both his father and his grandfather worked as engineers in the Protestant-dominated Belfast shipyards, his mother in the York Street Flax Spinning Company. Raised in Glengormley, a dreary suburb of new postwar estates about five miles outside Belfast, he was a Church of Ireland choirboy, and attended the Royal Belfast Academical Institution where he met Michael Longley and began writing poems for the *School News*. After Inst. he followed Longley to Trinity College Dublin which, Mahon recalls, 'wasn't much about work, though quite a lot of

reading got done' (*J* 222). This reading was mostly of contemporary poets, especially American poets such as Hart Crane,
Wallace Stevens and Richard Wilbur. Trinity and Dublin were
indisputably important influences on his life. The shift to Dublin
represented an escape from the industrialised North with its
Protestant ethic and lack of karma,³ and an entering upon new
freedoms. Trinity was where Wilde and Beckett were educated. It
was redolent of Anglo-Ireland. It was cosmopolitan and exciting.
He shared digs with Longley, lived in Bohemian squalor in
Merrion Square and contributed to *Icarus*, the Trinity magazine.
Longley recalls their Trinity years in his memoir *Tuppeny Stung:
Autobiographical Chapters*:

> We smoked and drank too much . . . A need to undermine
> Northern Irish middle-class respectability seemed to be at the core
> of our humour. Although pieties of any kind were fit targets . . .
> Unionism invariably focused our hilarity. But these were fulfilling
> rather than happy times. . . . I admired Mahon's disenchanted
> vision, but was less attracted to the role of *poète maudit*.⁴

The poems themselves provide some further autobiographical
insights. The early 'Glengormley' (*CP* 14) articulates his
ambivalent feelings towards the place and time in which he grew
up. The opening assertion of man's vast potential ('Wonders are
many and none is more wonderful than man') is immediately
followed by an image of suburban life in Glengormley offered as
the culminating achievement of human civilisation ('Who has
tamed the terrier, trimmed the hedge / And grasped the principle
of the watering can'). But irony modulates into a more expansive,
relaxed sense of the triumph of civilised domesticity: 'Clothes-
pegs litter the window-ledge / And the long ships lie in clover;
washing lines / Shake out white linen over the chalk thanes',
suggesting a more complex poetic attitude. The poet proceeds to
congratulate mankind on cleansing himself of atavism and
violence: 'Now we are safe from monsters, and the giants . . ./ . . .
No saint or hero, / Landing at night from the conspiring seas, /
Brings dangerous tokens to the new era -'; but there is also a
suggestion of a displacement of heroic energy into language and
text, a note of nostalgia for a lost time: 'Their sad names linger in
the histories'. In the sanitised world of 'the new era' reality has
emptied itself out into the simulacrum of the word. Words have
become more real than the real: 'Only words hurt us now'.
Alienation becomes the blight of modern man, and the poet
speaks elegiacally of 'The unreconciled, in their metaphysical

pain'. The last stanza begins: 'I should rather praise / A worldly time under a worldly sky -', 'should' ambiguously poised between its senses of 'choice' and 'necessity', a tension which is at least partially resolved in the poem's final line: 'By / Necessity, if not choice, I live here too'.

In a later poem, 'Courtyards in Delft' (*CP* 105), the speaker recognises in the world of the seventeenth-century Dutch painting an image of his own Ulster Protestant childhood: 'I lived there as a boy . . .'. De Hooch's painting is an image of 'trim composure' and 'chaste / Perfection'. Again, the speaker senses a troubling absence or suppression: 'No spinet-playing emblematic of / The harmonies and disharmonies of love, / No lewd fish, no fruit, no wide-eyed bird / About to fly its cage'. The politicisation of 'Glengormley''s terrier-taming, garden-watering rage for order in terms of an oppressive colonialism intensifies the dissociation between poet and people.

> I must be lying low in a room there,
> A strange child with a taste for verse,
> While my hard-nosed companions dream of fire
> And sword upon parched veldt and fields of rain-swept gorse.

'Lying low', as Edna Longley and others have noted, suggests a poetic situation 'well placed to subvert'.[5] It is the position of outsider, an oblique point of view in relation to dominant social, familial, communal and professional values and expectations. And it is that displaced angle of vision which conditions the speaker's response to the world of the painting. The tone of the poem is a finely balanced combination of admiring identification and detachment. In the occasional fifth stanza, that balance is lost and detachment spills into outright repudiation: the poet fantasises about an apocalyptic eruption of dark, pagan, female energy in the form of the Maenads, to overthrow the oppressive, patriarchal, Protestant order.

As John Goodby notes, Mahon's 'impulse to self-disclosure has increased' (see p. 196) in the two recent volumes, *The Hudson Letter* and *The Yellow Book*, where we find more discursive, anecdotal reference to family – his ex-wife, son and daughter – as well as to friends and his new love. 'Bangor Requiem' (*CP* 260–1), the only one of his poems to refer to his mother, is written on her death, but this 'cold epitaph' contrasts markedly with Heaney's elegiac tribute to his mother in 'Clearances', full of filial piety and tender reminiscence. Mahon can find little that is positive to say about his mother or her life-style. She epitomises the 'little soul' of a narrow, philistine Ulster Protestantism which he detests.

> I thought of the plain Protestant fatalism of home.
> *Remember 1690; prepare to meet thy God.*
> I grew up among washing-lines and grey skies,
> pictures of Brookeborough on the gable-ends,
> revolvers, RUC, B-Specials, law -'n'-order . . .

He recalls her preoccupation with 'appearances', presiding over a debased 'Dutch interior', 'your frantic kitsch decor designed for you / by thick industrialists and twisted ministers / . . . / with your wise monkeys and euphemistic "Dresden" figures / your junk chinoiserie and coy pastoral scenes'. Yet, for all the vulgarity, she is still 'a kind of artist, a rage-for-order freak'. But even as he tries to affirm some kind of connection or affinity ('Rage for Order' is the title of an early poem in which he self-deprecatingly figures himself as the alienated poet 'indulging his / Wretched rage for order -/ . . . / a dying art'), he indicates the distance that he is travelling away from his mother's world: 'but something of you, perhaps the incurable ache / of art, goes with me as I travel south', towards the 'blue skies of the republic . . .'

After Trinity and a year spent as a *libre auditeur* at the Sorbonne in Paris, he co-founded, along with Seamus Deane and W.J. McCormack, *Atlantis* (1970–4). From 1970 he worked as a journalist in London. He married Doreen Douglas from Portballintrae in North Antrim, and had two children, Kate and Rory. The marriage was not to last. His period as writer in residence at the New University of Ulster, 1978–9, was an unhappy time, as reflected in poems such as 'The Sea in Winter' and 'North Wind: Portrush', and in a 1979 prose piece, 'The Coleraine Triangle' (J 216–9), which he wrote for *Magill*. In the early 80s he lived in London, adapted the fiction of Jennifer Johnston, John Montague and Elizabeth Bowen for television, translated Molière for Field Day (1984) and completed a translation of Gérard de Nerval's *Les Chimères* (1982). In 1986 he was a writing fellow at Trinity. In the same year he moved to Kinsale, where he lived for two years and became a regular reviewer for the *Irish Times*. After the publication of *Antarctica* in 1985 there was a long ten-year silence (apart from the appearance of the *Selected Poems* in 1992, and not counting his version of Euripides' *The Bacchae* and a translation of poems by Phillippe Jaccottet) before the next collection of new poems appeared. Giving the lie to those who believed he had exhausted his poetic resources, he re-invented himself in two remarkable volumes, *The*

Hudson Letter (1995) and *The Yellow Book* (1997), in which he experiments with different perspectives and new experiences. *The Hudson Letter*, as the title implies, is Mahon's letter from America, the work of a 'resident alien' (*CP* 190) 'a recovering Ulster Protestant' (*CP* 218) – 'recovering' not only from his Ulster Protestantism but also his alcoholism – on lower Manhatten. In *The Yellow Book*, he ironically characterises himself as one of the new breed of poets who 'nod to you from the pastiche paradise of the post-modern' (*CP* 231). To some, these volumes represent a new lease of poetic life; to others, the high point of his achievement is still the short-lined, short stanza, highly wrought poems of *Night-Crossing*, *The Snow Party*, *Lives* and *The Hunt By Night* rather than the long-lined, discursive free verse of the recent two volumes. Since the publication of *The Yellow Book* he has settled in Fitzwilliam Square, Dublin.

What follows is an attempt to establish a critical context for the essays included in the present volume through a brief account of Mahon's literary outlook as articulated in his own essays and journalism, along with an overview of the main currents in Mahon criticism since the appearance of his first published poems in the mid-sixties.

* * *

Derek Mahon is generally credited with significantly extending the range and idiom of Irish poetry, away from both Yeats's national and Hewitt's regionalist ideals of rootedness and community, and away from Kavanagh's and Heaney's parochial and tribal concerns. Readers of the early volumes were struck by the 'whiff of cosmopolitanism', the suggestion of the 'foreign and exotic',[6] the way the diverse versions of Irish pastoral developed by Yeats, Kavanagh, Hewitt and Heaney give way to bleak North coast seascapes, desolate landscapes littered with the detritus of modern civilisation, frozen wastes, the depressed conditions of urban and suburban life which Mahon himself recognised as 'the final anathema for the traditional Irish imagination': 'Whatever we mean by "the Irish situation", he said, 'the shipyards of Belfast are no less a part of it than a country town in the Gaeltacht'.[7] As fellow Trinity poet Eavan Boland recalls, Mahon, coming from the Black North, had 'the outsider's suspicion of cultural monopoly'[8] and regarded 'the privileging of the Irish historical experience with deep suspicion'.[9]

In his essay, 'Poetry in Northern Ireland' (1970), Mahon draws a line between Northern and Southern Irish poetry:

> Like Ireland itself (and I intend no sneer), the (Southern) 'Irish' poet is either unwilling or unable to come to terms with 'the twentieth century'. . . to the extent that the Northern poet, surrounded as he is by the Greek gifts of modern industry and what Ferlinghetti called 'the hollering monsters of the imagination of disaster', shares an ecology with the technological societies his rulers are so anxious to imitate, he must, to be true to his imagination, insist upon a different court of appeal from that which sits in the South. [10]

Mahon's definition of 'Northern' poetry as the universalist, modern product of an industrialised, fragmented society and 'the imagination of disaster' closely reflects the character of his own internationalist and apocalyptic poetics. In the South, Mahon argues, the last court of appeal for the Irish writer is 'the plain people of Ireland', and this has had the effect of perpetuating a ruralist, revivalist, nationalist poetry. Contrastingly, Northern poets have been shaped by a wide variety of influences – 'a diffuse and fortuitous assembly of Irish, British and American models, not necessarily in that order' – which have helped the Northern poet to develop a more internationalist, less narcissistically provincial aesthetic capable of responding to the 'cultural fragmentation of our time'.[11] Even Northern Catholic poets, 'by reason of their Northernness', have been able to inflect their ancestral voices in ways which would allow them to speak to a wider world beyond Ireland. Though he shows none of Edna Longley's interest in defending the integrity of the North as a region, the highly controversial opposition which he elaborates in his 1970 essay between a supposedly insular tendency in the South and the 'diffuseness' and 'dissociation' of Northern poets such as Michael Longley, James Simmons and himself prefigures Edna Longley's apologia for the uniqueness of the North as a privileged site of poetry in *The Living Stream* (1994) :

> Both Irish nationalism and Ulster Unionism must accept the reality of the North as a frontier-region, a cultural corridor, a zone where Ireland and Britain permeate one another. The republic should cease to talk so glibly about 'accommodating diversity' and face up to difference and division. This would actually help the North to relax into a genuinely diverse sense of its own identity: to function, under whatever administrative format, as a shared

region of these islands. At which point there will definitely be no
such person as Cathleen Ni Houlihan.[12]

In later pronouncements Mahon seems to move away from the
concept of Northern Irish poetry as a distinct category. In the
preface to *The Sphere Book of Modern Irish Poetry* (1972), for
example, he presents Northern Irish 'difference' as the sign of an
evolving, dialogic rather than monologic concept of Irishness.
Doubtless thinking of himself, he describes 'Northern poets' as
'Protestant products of an English educational system, with little
or no knowledge of the Irish language and an inherited duality of
cultural reference', and goes on to say: 'They are a group apart,
but need not be considered in isolation, for their very difference
assimilates them to the complexity of continuing the Irish past.[13]
More recently still, in the introduction to the 1990 *Penguin Book of
Contemporary Irish Poetry* which he co-edited with Peter Fallon, he
remarks: '(T)he Northern phenomenon remains, in Kinsella's
phrase, "largely a journalistic entity". There was never, contrary to
received opinion, a Northern "School" in any real sense, merely a
number of individual talents'[14] How much of this view is Mahon's
and how much Fallon's is impossible to tell, but taken together the
three statements of 1970, 1972 and 1990 may be seen as indicative
of the progressive 'greening' of Mahon's cultural politics.

There is definitely no such person as Cathleen Ni Houlihan in
Mahon's poetry, yet his continued Yeatsian formalism disqualifies
him as a truly modern poet in the eyes of some English critics such
as Peter Porter. Observing none of the careful distinctions which
Mahon had sought to draw between Northern and Southern
poets, Porter sees all Irish poets (and mentions Mahon and
Heaney specifically) as marooned 'outside time':

> Reading it (*The Hunt by Night*) feels like time-travelling, even if the
> poetry is full of details from our own age. It is this that separates
> Irish poets like Mahon and Heaney from an audacious formalist
> like Auden, who for all his crustiness and Anglican high jinks is
> firmly lodged in the twentieth century. The Irishmen seem outside
> time, to be playing up to some committee preparing a Pantheon.
> 'Irish poets learn your trade, / Sing whatever is well made', wrote
> Yeats. They have learned it too well, they are banishing from their
> verse whatever parts of experience and necessity pose a problem
> to the shaping spirit.[15]

Edna Longley has already replied to Porter's criticisms in *Poetry in
the Wars*, and Gerald Dawe, in the present volume, again rises to

Mahon's – and Irish poetry's – defence against Porter's alleged libel (see pages 26–7) by insisting on both its universalism and its modernity.

Mahon had no more enthusiasm for Ulster regionalism than for Irish cultural nationalism. In a 1988 *Irish Times* review of John Hewitt's selected prose, *Ancestral Voices*, he wrote:

> The Ulster writer, says Hewitt, 'must be a *rooted* man. He must carry the native tang of his idiom like the native dust on his sleeve; otherwise he is an airy internationalist, thistledown, a twig in the stream ... He must know where he comes from and where he is; otherwise how can he tell where he wishes to go?' This is a bit tough on thistledown; and, speaking as a twig in a stream, I feel there's a certain harshness, a dogmatism, at work there. What of the free-floating magination, Keats's 'negative capability'?, Yeats's 'lonely impulse of delight'? Literature, surely, is more than a branch of ethics. What about humour, mischief, wickedness? 'Send war in our time, O Lord!' (*J* 94)

Mahon argues for a principle of self-delighting playfulness and creative freedom, for a sceptical, subversive poetry that unsettles rather than confirms, a poetry that explores doubts and uncertainties, and values aesthetics above ethics. As he himself says in 'Beyond Howth Head':

> And who would trade self-knowledge for
> A prelapsarian metaphor,
> Love-play of the ironic conscience
> For a prescriptive inocence?
>
> (*CP* 53)

With Mahon, Hewitt's 'airy internationalism' is turned into a valuable poetic resource, a necessary counterbalance to what Mahon considered a deadening Irish parochialism. *Atlantis*, the small Dublin magazine with which he was associated as both contributor and editor in the early 1970s, proclaimed an unashamedly internationalist agenda: 'The magazine will be published in Dublin, but not exclusively in Dublin. The range of contributors will be wide. Part of our aim is to see Ireland in an international perspective, to lift its drowsy eyelid and disturb it into a sense of relationship and awareness' (*J* 16). No 'rooted man', Mahon accepted deracination as the essential condition of modern life and found it importantly creative. His is, as Terence Brown has said, 'a peregrine imagination' (*J* 18), an 'emigrant sensibility, perhaps most in exile when actually at home' (*J* 18). Or, as Declan

Kiberd has it, Mahon is 'a poet of Belfast, but often by way of disavowal'.[16] He's also, of course, a poet of such diverse places as the 'Coleraine triangle', Rathlin Island and the Aran Islands, New York, San Francisco, North Carolina, lower Manhatten, Kyoto and Antarctica. Occupying marginal or interstitial positions, he favours imaginative locations such as strands, sea shores, river banks. He writes about night-crossings, vacations. departures and returns. Through his translations and his range of allusion he moves from one time or place or text or art work to another, always conscious of the wider cultural forces circulating through European history, art and literature and, more recently, through postmodern Americana. Even his constant revising of his poems testifies to a preoccupation with change and process, a resistance to fixity and completion. These are also central themes in his work. 'Lives' constructs the speaker out of a series of historically projected, trans-cultural events, roles and narratives which refuse categorisation within any ontological system; 'Preface to a Love Poem' is based on the assumption that the poem does not have a single unequivocal meaning corresponding to, or straight-forwardly mirroring, the reality it reflects.

One could mention Yeats, Graves, Auden, Crane, Beckett, Stevens, the French symbolists, but the undisputably most important influence on Mahon was Louis MacNeice, with whose sceptical vison and touristic persona (at least as far as his relations with his homeland were concerned) Mahon aligns himself:

> 'A tourist in his own country', it has been said, with the implication that this is somehow discreditable; but of what sensitive person is the same not true? The phrase might stand, indeed, as an epitaph for modern man . . . (*J* 25)

To understand the nature of MacNeice's influence, one might turn to Paul Muldoon's introduction to *The Faber Book of Contemporary Irish Verse* (1986), which consists of an excerpt from a 1939 discussion between MacNeice and Yeats's friend and protégé, F.R. Higgins. Here Higgins champions a monolithic, homogenous, unified culture, and a poetry expressive of a sense of place, history and 'belief' – 'a belief emanating from life, from nature, from revealed religion, and from the nation. A sort of dream that produces a sort of magic . . . blood-music that brings the racial character to mind'.[17] Reacting against Higgins' nationalistic, visionary conception of poetry, MacNeice speaks for a cosmopolitan, detached, 'common sense' view of poetry. In his essay, 'The Pre-Natal Mountain: Vision and Irony in Recent

Irish Poetry', Seamus Heaney explains the importance of MacNeice as an exemplary poet of 'displacement and unrest'[18] to the younger generations of Mahon and Muldoon (Muldoon's own affinity with MacNeice is reflected in the generous representation which he affords MacNeice's work in the anthology). MacNeice was the kind of poet who, instead of serving an ideal of tribal or national purity, responded to a world perceived as 'flux', as 'incorrigibly plural'. And yet, one must be wary of over-simplification. As Heaney notes, for poets of 'the ironical and distancing sort',[19] questions of identity, community, history and politics will not go away. Referring to Northern Protestant poets, he says:

> Mahon, like MacNeice, like Longley, cannot totally identify with the pieties and refusals of the group they were all three born into ... These poets, who share an origin in the Northern Unionist majority, are in natural communion withn that Irish culture of which the unionist ideology is chronically if understandably suspicious. As poets, they comprehend both the solidarities of their own group and the need to subvert them.[20]

Such poets, in Heaney's view, have not only managed to breathe new life into traditional themes and styles but worked towards a broader and more comprehensive notion of Irish identity.

From the beginning, what many readers have found most striking about Mahon's poetry is its stylishness, its formal perfection and musical quality. In her essay, 'The Singing Line: Form in Derek Mahon's Poetry', Edna Longley praises Mahon for his 'extraordinary formal achievement'. Mahon's poetry, she argues, 'constitutes a residual faith in form amid circumstances which offer nothing else'.[21] 'Metaphysical unease' and social turmoil generate a compensatory strict formal control. With no secure sense of belonging, background or identity, Mahon becomes a voice for the dispossessed and abandoned, the existential boulevardier desperately attempting to invent himself and a world on nothing but style. As well as citizen of the world, Mahon comes to epitomise a particular kind of *Irish* poet which Declan Kiberd calls 'the dandy in revolt':

> For the dandy's tragedy turns out to have been the story of the bards who woke up to find themselves wandering *spailpini*, and of gentry who were reborn as tramps. All such nomads know the truth of Wilde's aphorism: that the first duty of life was to adopt a pose, a style, a way of being in the world. [22]

But also from the beginning the very brilliance of Mahon's formalism has been questioned. To what extent do the aesthetic satisfactions of formalist perfection represent an escape from intense cultural confusion? What imaginative nourishment has been foregone in renouncing myth and atavism? How significantly has he contributed to the development of a late twentieth-century language of poetry given his preference for traditional 'well-made' forms? To Peter Porter's strictures quoted above (p. xvii), we might add Eavan Boland's reservation that while Mahon may be 'a dark, witty and adventurous formalist' capable of producing poems of 'clarity' and 'wonderful sophistication of cadence', his modernist obsession with the authority of the poet has inhibited him from doing justice to the complexity of his experience:

> Too often the authority of the life is predicated upon the ability of the poet to give it grace or interest. Therefore the experience is promoted or demoted according to its ability, like a clever child, to find a winning expression for itself.[23]

Stan Smith, in his book, *Inviolable Voice: History and 20th Century Poetry* (1982), takes an even sterner tone. Writing from a Marxist-structuralist point of view, Smith sees Mahon as representative of a whole generation of Northern Protestant poets who, he says, retreated from the public world into a privileged, but panicked, middle-class privacy which found expression in the complacencies of the 'well-made poem':

> a poetry that looks back to the sceptical Protestant tradition of Louis MacNeice takes up a worried, disapproving but finally uncomprehending stance towards an experience with which it feels no sense of affinity. In accents familiar from 'The Movement' such a poetry performs its civic duties equitably, by reflecting, in an abstracted kind of way, on violence, but its hands are indubitably clean. It speaks, at times, with the tone of a shell-shocked Georgianism that could easily be mistaken for indifference before the ugly realities of life, and death, in Ulster. . . .
>
> Mahon's poetry repeatedly returns to this interface, where a guilty but finally secure consciousness abstracts itself from its contingent world even as it concedes its implication in that world.[24]

Seamus Deane is also uneasy about Mahon's formal conservatism. In his 1977 *Crane Bag* interview with Heaney, Deane raised the issue of the ideology of form: 'Do you not think that if some political stance is not adopted by you and the Northern poets at large, this refusal might lead to a dangerous strengthening of earlier notions of the autonomy of poetry and corroborate the recent English notion of the happy limitations of a "well-made" poem?'[25] In his chapter on Mahon in *Celtic Revivals* (1985), Deane echoes Smith's disquiet at the division between poet and history that he sees running through Mahon's early poetry. Mahon, Deane says, wants to be 'through with history'. For Deane, there is a necessary connection between violence and art: 'contact with violence is regarded by some as a stimulus to the deep energies of creation . . . avoidance of it is regarded as a form of imaginative anaemia'.[26] In this respect, Heaney's poetry is exemplary, emanating as it does from the tension between rational condemnation of the violence and understanding of 'the exact/and tribal, intimate revenge': 'Heaney's dilemma is registered in the perception that the roots of poetry and of violence grow in the same soil; humanism, of the sort mentioned here, has no roots at all'.[27] But Mahon's first two volumes are characterised, in Deane's view, by an 'urbanity' that 'helps him fend off the forces of atavism, ignorance and oppression which are part of his Northern Protestant heritage'.[28] This is, in Deane's opinion, a bad thing, because it suppresses the 'uncivilised', instinctual and irrational elements of both the self and the culture. Mahon's early work, says Deane is an 'ultimately "protestant" poetry',[29] witty, sophisticated and knowing, resistant to the traditional image of Ireland, founded on the notion of disengagement, and expressive of 'his "protestant" ethic of the independent imagination'.[30] Mahon's primary loyalties are to 'the abandoned', to 'a maverick individuality',[31] to those rebels haunted by a metaphysical dread; his most deeply felt poems derive from his sympathy for the isolation and decline of his Northern Protestant community rather than from outright condemnation. The Troubles, Deane argues, forced him to turn towards 'the very history which he had so successfully deflected in his first two books'.[32] In this process, Mahon is impelled to interrogate his own (ahistorical) liberal sentiments and to register his contempt for the modern socialist, the professional visitor, the political tourist and other 'middle-class cunts' who have no understanding of the dark forces of the instinctual life. 'In allowing for the dark gods', says Deane, Mahon 'stays clear of and yet in contact with their tribal communities'.[33] Thus, his poetry, like de Hooch's or Uccello's paintings, incorporates history's force into its stillness, the formal control of the poems an expression of a kind of moral stoicism, a mark of grace under pressure.

Where Deane's discussion of Mahon is part of a larger project of re-politicising Irish criticism, Edna Longley has sought to rescue and protect poetry from politics, claiming the existence of a transcendent, ideologically-free poetic zone. Her empirically based criticism is resistent to totalising theories and the kind of narrativisation of Irish culture which she takes Deane's *Field Day Anthology* to represent (and scathingly refers to as the 'Derry metanarrative'[34]). From her New Critical 'close reading' perspective, she reacts sharply against Porter's and Smith's criticisms, reminding us that it is the musicality of a poem which determines whether it is worth attending to or not in the first place. Implicit in her essays is an affirmation of the primacy of aesthetic vision and a belief in the autonomy of the poetic artefact:

> Poetry and politics, like church and state, should be separated. And for the same reasons: mysteries distort the rational processes which ideally prevail in social relations; while ideologies confiscate the poet's special passport to *terra incognita* ... Ulster poets today are sometimes the victims of improper expectations. Whatever causes they may support as citizens, their imaginations cannot be asked to settle for less than full human truth.[35]

Mahon is Longley's kind of poet. She is his most prolific and admiring commentator. Their ideas about poetry and politics chime harmoniously together. His first book of poems, *Night-Crossing*, was dedicated to 'Michael and Edna Longley'. She, in turn, takes as epigraph for her essay 'Poetry and Politics in Northern Ireland' a notable formulation of Mahon's – 'A good poem is a paradigm of good politics'. This remark occurs in his 1970 essay, 'Poetry in Northern Ireland', in which he discusses the proper role of the poet in time of war:

> The war I mean is not, of course, between Protestant and Catholic but between the fluidity of a possible life ... and the *rigor mortis* of archaic postures, political and cultural. The poets themselves have taken no part in political events, but they have contributed to that possible life, or the possibility of that possible life; for the act of writing is itself political, in the fullest sense. A good poem is a paradigm of good politics – of people talking to each other, with honest subtlety, at a profound level. It is a light to lighten the darkness; and we have darkness enough, God knows, for a long time.[36]

Like Longley, Mahon carefully marks off the fields of poetry and politics from one another. Poetry constitutes a transcendent realm that must be protected from the contaminations of politics and ideology. The poetic consciousness occupies a privileged position above and beyond language and history, even though implicated in both, revolving serenely in its own autonomous world, influencing politics without being influenced by them, capable of revealing the 'fluidity of a possible life' (Mahon), grasping 'full human truth' (Longley). Poetry can provide a space beyond politics where the usual divisions of everyday life in Northern Ireland can be magically resolved in the self-contained, transcendent poetic symbol. The 'good poem' is opposed to fixity, entrenchment and political dogmatism; it demonstrates the possibility of fluidity, balance and resolution. Clearly, this is a position which comes under severe pressure in a period of political upheaval and social breakdown. Poetry's claim to transcendental expression of 'full human truth' beyond the merely political not only presupposes an essentialist, immutable 'human nature' but is interpreted by critics such as Deane as a refusal of history, conflict and politics, a middle-of-the-road, middle-class acceptance of the status quo. In the end, however, Longley's concept of the poem as an ideal or transcendent space where opposites may be resolved is not unlike the Field Day concept of the 'Fifth Province', which Patrick Hederman defined in his *Crane Bag* essay, 'Poetry and the Fifth Province' (1985)[37] as a free space of the imagination, a kind of no-man's land, a neutral ground, detached from all partisan and prejudiced connection. Hederman explicitly acknowledges the similarity between his concept of the 'fifth province' and Longley's *terra incognita*. While both Field Day and Longley are agreed on the priority of culture over politics, and on the 'transcendent quality' of the 'fifth province', the difference between them is that the Field Day apologists believe the 'fifth province' can be reached only *through* the historical world, and that our experience of the 'fifth province' crucially conditions our continued existence *in* the historical world.

Mahon's image of the poem as 'a light to lighten the darkness' invokes an Arnoldian concept of literature as a substitute religion in a secular age, fulfiling an urgent social need to 'Hellenise' or cultivate the benighted philistines. Longley shares Mahon's belief in poetry as a liberal, humanising pursuit, capable of providing an effective antidote to political bigotry and ideological extremism, a vehicle of timeless, universal human truth, the means of inculcating larger human sympathies and the right moral values. Significantly, Longley discusses Mahon's poetry in religious terms. In her essay, 'Derek Mahon: Extreme Religion of Art' (1995), she writes: 'The religious dimension of Ulster Protestant culture – devolved into aesthetics and metaphysics – counts for much in Mahon's poetry and conditions its extremity'.[38] Arguing that Mahon takes a 'predominantly religious view of history',[39] she discounts Deane's insistence that in his early poetry Mahon 'successfully deflected' history. As far as Longley is concerned, 'Mahon had been writing autobiography and history together from the outset'.[40] In his best-known poem, 'A Disused Shed', she says, the oppressed/victims represented by the mushrooms are the maimed and silenced casualties of history, longing for transcendence, not (as they are for Deane) lost lives longing for re-integration, recognition and fulfilment 'in history'.[41] Where Deane sees 'A Disused Shed' as representing that point in Mahon's career where the poet is saying 'that the only life which can produce art is one that is engaged with history, even (especially?) if it is the history of the victims, the lost, the forgotten',[42] Longley sees the poem (and poetry) as history's redemption. Mahon's poetry, Longley claims, is generated out of Protestant guilt, identifies with the outcast and the damned, pursues a despairing dream of innocence, and meditates on the possibility of 'atonement' or 'retribution' (sometimes in apocalyptic terms). All the time the poet is conscious of his own ambiguous relationship with his people, who still expect his 'ministry'[43] ('The Sea in Winter', 'Dowson and Co.', 'Ovid in Tomis', 'The Poet in Residence'). The Mahon persona, threatened by chaos, which is both elemental (symbolised by sea, wind, cosmic apocalypse) and man-made (destructive technologies, cultural impoverishment), struggles to affirm a willed order, but there is only minimal confidence in the possibilities of renewal. The poet's 'redemptive epiphanies' [44] are mere 'reliefs of the spirit, brakes on entropy, remission in a terminal illness'. [45]

The relationship between Mahon's poetry and his Northern Protestant origins has been one of the central points of interest for his commentators and critics. The poet and academic, Brendan Kennelly, whom he first met as a student at Trinity, sees Mahon's 'protestantism' as the source of his 'shrewd, reticent humanism' (143),[46] 'a form of intelligent loneliness' (143).[47] Where Deane thinks Mahon's pose of ironic detachment inhibits the poet from tapping the deep instinctual energies of creation, Kennelly regards it as wonderfully enabling and productive. For Kennelly, Mahon is 'the ironic romantic outsider who is not subject to the delusion of self-pity' (144).[48] Protestant humanism, in Kennelly's view, 'involves the habitual workings of a conscience and/or consciousness which seem interchangeable'(143).[49] It produces a poetry of scrupulous self-examination, and a poetic language which Kennelly describes in the terms Mahon used to describe MacNeice's poetry: 'words at war with themselves, or at least in argument with each other, ironical, loving, wild, reticent, fragile, solving'.[50]

Peter McDonald has also written extensively and influentially on Mahon's so-called 'Protestantism'. In his book, *Mistaken Identities: Poetry and Northern Ireland* (1997), he argues against the totalising ambitions of identity-politics, showing how Northern Irish poetry, by making an issue of poetic form, subverts political analogies in terms of 'identity'. An advocate of 'close reading', McDonald argues 'for the significance and value of poems as discrete achievements ... things which possess, so to speak, identities of their own'.[51] Thus, Mahon's poems, he believes, assert the freedom of the poetic voice by complicating the political stereotypes of Protestant identity, projecting them beyond cliché into extreme metaphysical realms of meaning. Mahon's poetry, McDonald claims, has always 'gravitated towards a cold and unpeopled area which exists generally before, or after, anything ordinarily recognizable as historic process'.[52] In contrast to Heaney's sense of 'belonging', McDonald argues, Mahon's 'apocalyptic projections'[53] beyond human history and the human self subvert the idea of belonging to anywhere.

* * *

The essays included in this volume update, extend or challenge the critical paradigms established by the critics surveyed above. In an authoritative essay, which formed the key-note lecture of the symposium, Edna Longley identifies 'five literary points of reference' which represent basic co-ordinates of Mahon's entire poetic *oeuvre*: *fin-de-siècle* aestheticism, French Symbolism, the British 1930s, (especially the example of MacNeice and Auden); American poetry (especially Wallace Stevens, Hart Crane and Robert Lowell), and Anglo-Ireland. Reprising her earlier view of Mahon's 'extreme religion of art', she demonstrates the ways in which religion conditions Mahon's poetry in terms of its sounds and rhythms, its symbolism, its response to modernity, its longings for transcendence. She concludes with the assertion that '"Cultural Protestantism" or post-Protestantism (as with Yeats,

MacNeice and Beckett) ramifies into aesthetic, psychological and metaphysical zones until it becomes virtually the ground of modern literature'. This arresting declaration, on a par with the William Drennan quotation – 'The Catholics may save themselves, but it is the Protestants must save the nation'[54] – with which she closes an essay on three other 'dissenting' Protestant writers, MacNeice, Hewitt and Butler in *The Living Stream*, demonstrates the large claims Longley is willing to make in constructing a tradition of (post-) Protestant dissent, arrogated above class or gender or any other social, economic or political category as the most meaningful and productive ground of criticism. Her book, *Across a Roaring Hill: The Protestant Imagination in Modern Ireland* (1985), which she co-edited with Gerald Dawe, may be seen as part of the same controversial project. Not all critics approve W.J. McCormick, for example, deplores what he calls Longley's 'sectarian sociology of art'[55] which would appear to contradict the universalist, humanistic premises of her literary philosophy.

One of the essays in *Across a Roaring Hill* was Gerald Dawe's '"Icon and Lares": Derek Mahon and Michael Longley'. In that essay Dawe identified Mahon and Longley not only as exemplars of the MacNeicean tradition of Protestant dissent but of the way this tradition meshes with the modernism of Lawrence, Joyce and Pound, writers who, in the words of Edward Said (quoted by Dawe), 'present us with the breaking of ties with family, home, class and country, and traditional beliefs as necessary stages in the achievement of spiritual and intellectual freedom . . . invite us to share the larger transcendental . . . or private systems of order and value which they have adopted and invented'.[56] Dawe distinguishes between Michael Longley's concern to 'embrace History, to restore the ties of family, home, class and country', and Mahon's rejection of his Northern Protestant past and attempt at 'discovering in the imagination an alternative home that transcends what he perceives as the failed filiative bonds'.[57] It is no surprise therefore to find Dawe in the present volume identifying the influences of Beckett, Camus and MacNeice in Mahon's poetry and lauding its 'existential clarity', in the face of Peter Porter's dismissal of Irish poetry as archaic and fatally restricted by its 'concentration on the narrow concerns of Irishness'.

In his essay '"Solving Ambiguity": The Secular Mysticism of Derek Mahon', Bruce Stewart aims to show the inadequacy of the usual terms such as 'ironic conscience', 'tough scepticism' and 'disenchanted liberalism' to describe Mahon's essential quality, and, in seeking to advance a more comprehensive understand-

ing of Mahon's poetic persona, recommends the avowedly
oxymoronic term 'secular mystic', a phrase which Mahon himself
applied explicitly to Jaccottet and implicitly to Brian Moore, and
which Douglas Dunn and Terence Brown have both already used
in reference to Mahon's poetry. By situating Mahon in a tradition
of Ulster 'secular mysticism' deriving from MacNeice, Stewart
wishes to identify a poetic voice which is celebratory as well as
sceptical, which recognises the 'deeper energies of mysticism and
religion' as well as 'metaphysical unease'.

Jerzy Jarniewicz, a Polish poet and critic, joins the debate about
Mahon's relationship with history, challenging those who argue
that Mahon, like his Fire King, simply wishes to be 'Through with
history'. Jarniewicz shows that Mahon, in recognising that history
is a constructed and inevitably selective narrative, devotes himself
to redeeming the 'mute phenomena' which have been silenced by
history and written out of the 'grand narratives' of the past. While
recognising Mahon's distrust of history and desire for transcendence, Jarniewicz, following Deane, demonstrates Mahon's
understanding that value and meaning are possible only in the
historical world: only in the human world of history, time and
consciousness can the victims of history be retrieved and saved in
human memory.

Eamonn Hughes, in his essay on Mahon's treatment of place in
this volume, identifies another kind of anti-essentialism in
Mahon's writing. Acknowledging the importance of Hugh
Haughton's 1992 essay, 'Place and Displacement in Derek Mahon',
Hughes alludes to Haughton's emphasis on the cosmopolitanism
of Mahon's poetry. But while holding on to Haughton's sense of
Mahon's universal 'anywhere', Hughes wishes to combine it with
an equal recognition of Mahon's devotion to the local and the
specific, his insistence on the 'weird haecceity' of all locales.[58] The
truly original thrust of Hughes' discussion of place becomes
apparent when, in moving to consider Mahon's principles of
organising space, he uncovers the existentialist emphasis in
Mahon's writing. Mahon's 'weird haecceity', Hughes remarks,
always declares difference, and this makes his places resistant to
any rational ordering or relationship. Thus, Hughes argues,
metamorphosis – transformative process – becomes 'the major
relationship between places', with the result that the Mahonian
persona is never an exile ('there is an essentialism at the heart of
exile'), but continually in transit as tourist or commuter,
continually subject to metamorphosis in a world which is itself
subject to 'the strange poetry of decay'.

Michael Allen's essay demonstrates the potential of New Critical 'close reading'. In returning to the vexed question of Mahon's revisions, which Peter Denman had addressed in his 1994 essay, 'Know the One? Insolent Ontology and Mahon's Revisions', Allen deduces significant changes that occur between the mid-sixties and the mid-nineties in Mahon's work. Where in the early work the poet is an alienated artist, he becomes a spokesman or representative of his situation, group or culture; where the sixties poem is a 'medium of the artist', the later poem is an 'act of communication'; where the early poem deals in linguistic density, irony, ambiguity and paradox, with 'negative capability' at a premium, the later poem deals in clarity and strength of utterance, with 'bardic authority' at a premium; where the 'I' persona of the early poems is to be read as a fictional construct, it becomes in the later work a more obviously transparent figure of the poet himself. These changes, Allen shows, represent a movement away from a poetry of uncertainty and marginality and towards a more 'brutally confident' poetry of frequently ampler forms.

Richard York's essay on 'Derek Mahon and the Visual Arts' is also based on a formalist analysis of both poems and paintings, and reflects on Mahon's meditations on the paradoxical nature of art – its simultaneous mimetic and estranging capabilities; its combination of movement with permanence, the arrested moment with a sense of time and history; the challenge offered to the aesthetic by suffering and violence. Just as Mahon has used the cultural artefacts of de Hooch, Munch and Uccello to focus his own artistic vision, he has also used earlier poems, which he has translated and adapted, to comment on the contemporary situation. In his essay, Hugh Haughton emphasises the ways in which Mahon has been 'open to and energised by ideas of and from elsewhere', and demonstrates the extent to which Mahon's *oeuvre* takes the form of a creative intertextual re-writing of earlier poems. Following on from Bill Tinley's discussion of Mahon's 'Francophile Poetics' (1994) and John Kerrigan's examination of Mahon's Ovidian connections (1995), Haughton considers Mahon's treatments of Baudelaire, Laforgue and Corbière, of the Provençale poet Macabru, of the Irish MacGhiolla Ghunna, of Renaissance Italian poets such as Ariosto and Michelangelo, and twentieth-century Italians such as Pasolini and Saba, as well as his classical translations of Ovid, Juvenal and Sappho.

While Longley and Dawe have defended Mahon against Peter Porter's criticism that Irish poets have excluded themselves from becoming truly modern poets by continuing to concentrate on 'the narrow concerns of Irishness', Frank Sewell takes issue with Peter McDonald who, in a 1998 review of *The Yellow Book*, accused Mahon of having 'chosen to work hard at sounding like an Irish poet'. Sewell's essay is devoted to the questions of 'if and when "Irishness" possibly *could* become counter-productive to art', and whether or not Mahon really does 'sound less like himself and more like an "Irish poet" these days'. Sewell's answer to the first question is simple: 'Irishness" is a liability when it is 'put on' rather than 'lived or let alone to look after itself'. In answering the second question, he returns to a comment Mahon made in 1970 wherein he regretted that Michael Longley and other Northern poets seemed to deprive themselves of 'the benefits of the "Irishness" at their disposal'. Mahon, in Sewell's view, does not so deprive himself, but is, rather, a kind of cosmopolitan provincial who has throughout his career drawn productively on the Irish literary tradition as well as world language and literature.

John Goodby's mobilisation of the new critical paradigm of 'Men's Studies' re-inflects the category of gender politics to produce a powerful critical position capable of complicating other more traditional interpretations of Mahon's poetry. The question of gender was originally broached by Eavan Boland, in her 1994 memoir, 'Compact and Compromise: Derek Mahon as a Young Poet', where she delimited the radicalism of a poetry in which the sexual self 'remains conservative, exclusive and unquestioning of inherited authority'. Goodby notes in Mahon's work the evolution in the mid-70s of a more 'feminine' subject position, a relaxation of the 'hieratic' modernist pose of the earlier work, which coincided with the emergence of postmodernism and the 'normalisation' of the Ulster Troubles. However, even in the recent work, Goodby shows, Mahon's scepticism towards the notion of a unified self and cultural practice does not extend to his poetic constructions of masculinity which remain bound to the reactionary sexual ideology of high modernism.

In his essay in the present volume, Stan Smith offers a stimulating redress of his earlier Marxist disapproval of what he regarded as the poet's middle-class detachment from history and politics by concentrating on Mahon's postmodern, neoplatonic awareness of how the world of consciousness, constructed in language, is always necessarily at a remove from the real, a mere simulacrum of authentic being which has always already absconded. Mahon's poetry, is thus, in Smith's view, a poetry of lack, exile, absence, loss. The past exists only as traces: but, says

Smith, the idea of afterlives, ghosts, is pervasive, and is associated with writing itself, which stands in for the always absent original event, and is subject to the intertextual hauntings of other writers. Yet, Smith insists, it is the very lack of wholeness which is the precondition of poetry. Mahon's neoplatonic awareness of generic paradigms co-exists with devotion to 'all passing and particular experience' – Smith's conclusion echoing that of other critics such as Deane and Hughes.

Smith's ideas, premised on his view of the Mahonian subject as 'stranded on the shore of postmodern disenchantment', might be placed alongside certain associated insights offered by other essayists in this volume: for example, Crotty's analysis of Mahon's postmodern 'apocalypse' in *The Yellow Book*; Hughes' and Jarniewicz's emphasis on Mahon's poststructuralist rejection of 'essentialism' in the poet's constructions of 'self', 'place' and 'history'; Haughton's discussion of the rich intertextuality of Mahon's poetry and its status as simulacrum – its 'self-conscious culture of mimicry', its penchant for translation as 'a form of virtual originality'; Corcoran's description of *The Hudson Letter* as 'testimony to the way a contemporary postmodern consciousness is itself a textualised subjectivity, already written as well as writing'; Goodby's analysis of Mahon's commitment to modernism (and an associated masculinism), and the extent to which he embraced the radically destabilising modes of the postmodern. All these critics recognise in Mahon's work a site of tension, a struggle to hold on to a (modernist) concept of formalist coherence, self-sufficiency and autonomy, grounded in a metaphysics of rational humanism, in the face of a (postmodern) meltdown of the modes of cultural legitimation. Perhaps Mahon's poetry illustrates the way the 'postmodern' has always inhabited the 'modern'.

Displacement, dispossession, disconnection, discontinuity, exile, migrancy: these are central themes and conditions of Mahon's poetry. Timothy Kearney's statement in his 1979 *Crane Bag* essay, 'The Poetry of the North: A Post-Modernist Perspective' – 'When we come to consider the main body of poetry which has been written in the province of Ulster since Yeats, we cannot omit consideration of this feature of all Post-Modernist literature – the alienation of the individual from his community'[59] – is perfectly illustrated by Mahon's poetry, and Mahon's 'alienation' is more comprehensive than anything suggested by Kearney. 'Matthew V, 29–30' is a satirical allegory on the absurdity of the quest for ever-elusive sources, cores or 'essences'. The *Collected Poems* opens with 'Spring in Belfast' which presents the poet's conflicted and ambiguous relationship with his Protestant Ulster origins. The tone is one of detachment and distaste mixed with a sense of guilt and obligation.

> One part of my mind must learn to know its place.
> The things that happen in the kitchen houses
> And echoing back streets of this desperate city
> Should engage more than my casual interest,
> Exact more interest than my casual pity.
>
> *(CP 13)*

The later poem, 'Afterlives', indicates that, though 'the hills' around Belfast may offer some sense of continuity ('We could *all* be saved by keeping an eye on the hill / At the top of every street' – 'Spring in Belfast'), not only has the poet never learnt to know his place, but 'his place' – taken in its sense of Belfast – has changed beyond all recognition:

> And I step ashore in a fine rain
> To a city so changed
> By five years of war
> I scarcely recognize
> The places I grew up in,
> The faces that try to explain.
>
> But the hills are still the same
> Grey-blue above Belfast.
> Perhaps if I'd stayed behind
> And lived it bomb by bomb
> I might have grown up at last
> And learnt what is meant by home.
>
> *(CP 59)*

"Should' ... 'Perhaps' ... 'might have': Mahon's is a poetry of hypothetical scenarios, alternative states, virtual realities, afterlives, roads not taken, imagined futures. Yearning for some kind of re-connection or wholeness pervades the entire work. 'Nostalgias' is a poem of displacement and yearning for a return to origins in which the poet speaks, with near-religious pathos, out of the Protestant sense of loss and abandonment: 'In a tiny stone church / On the desolate headland / A lost tribe is singing "Abide With Me"'(*CP* 75). But the very idea of a return to origins is ironised as well as intensified by the juxtaposition of human yearning with that of chair, kettle and soap: 'The chair squeaks in a high wind, / Rain falls from its branches, / The kettle yearns for the / Mountain, the soap for the sea' (*CP* 75). 'A Disused Shed' is another poem which foregrounds discontinuity and disconnection – between speaker and mushrooms, owner ('expropriated mycologist' (*CP* 89)) and property, past and present, interior and exterior worlds, light and darkness, desire and reality, poetry and history. Discontinuity scores even the poem's central signifiers, producing a sense of continually unstable, kaleidoscopically changing identities and scenarios. As Eamonn Hughes shows, the mushrooms metamorphose into images of distinctly different, unrelated kinds of victimage/ oppression/ suffering; time and locale shift and dissolve; the speaker slides between identification with, and separation from, his own people. 'The Studio' resembles 'Nostalgias' in beginning with the hypothetical longing of inanimate objects in a room. The speaker imagines these objects – 'deal table', 'ranged crockery', frail oilcloth' – as desperate to break free of their alienated 'haecceity' and enter the public arena of history outside the window:

> You would think with so much going on outside
> The deal table would make for the window,
> The ranged crockery freak and wail
> Remembering its dark origins, the frail
> Oilcloth, in a fury of recognitions,
> Disperse in a thousand directions,
> And the simple bulb in the ceiling, honed
> By death to a worm of pain, to a hair
> Of heat, to a light snowflake laid
> In a dark river at night – and wearied
> Above all by the life-price of time
> And the failure by only a few tenths
> Of an inch but completely and for ever
> Of the ends of a carefully drawn equator
> To meet, sing and be one – abruptly
> Roar into the floor.
> > But it
> Never happens like that. Instead
> There is this quivering silence
> In which, day by day, the play
> Of light and shadow (shadow mostly)
> Repeats itself, though never exactly.
> > > > > > (*CP* 36)

The poem rehearses the familiar tensions – between imagination ('You would think . . .') and reality ('"But it/Never happens like that . . .'), interior and exterior, subject and object, poet and history. These failed connections are dramatised in Mahon's broken, enjambed phrasal units and irregular rhyming, and imaged in the reference to the light bulb filament which never quite touches but derives its generative power from this very condition of incompleteness.

The process of the poet's displacement from origins, from family and community, also involves displacement into the linguistic, discursive and ideological systems in which he is inscribed. The early 'In Carrowdore Churchyard' declares that meaning exists ambiguously, riddlingly; that there is no simple correspondence between subject and object, text and world; that indeterminacy pervades our actions, ideas, interpretations, indeed constitutes our world. 'Love Poem' (originally entitled 'Preface to a Love Poem' in *Night-Crossing*) expresses awareness that language is not transparent, allowing direct access to meaning. There is no possibility, even for the autobiographical or lyric poem, of finding some pure and originary point of consciousness which pre-exists the symbolic order of codes and discourses. An ineradicable gap exists between subject and object. The earlier title indicates the partial and provisional nature of the poem, unsettling any notion of poetic authority. The poem is, the poet goes on to say, 'a circling of itself and you', 'A form of words, compact and compromise', 'a blind with sunlight filtering through', 'at one remove, a substitute' (*CP* 18) – a play of signifiers that constantly elude any single centre, essence or meaning. Obsessed with the condition of loss, difference and absence out of which any poetry is written, the speaker longs for silence, for a return to a pre-verbal pre-history of 'mute phenomena'.

History is always a construct, a text. 'Tithonus' declares the inevitable selectivity of historical narratives:

> I forget nothing
> But if I told
> Everything in detail -
>
> Not merely Golgotha
> And Krakatoa
> But the leaf-plink
>
> Of raindrops after
> Thermopylae,
> The lizard-flick

In the scrub as Genghis
Khan entered Peking
And the changing clouds,

I would need,
Another eternity,
Perish the thought.
(*SP* 169–70)

Poems such as 'The Early Anthropologists' and 'Lives' intimate
that it is impossible to recover or to know the past: it is always
pre-figured. However, as 'Lives' illustrates, the poet can delight in
the variety of modes by which he can attempt to recover it, and
play with reality in the very act of constituting it. The poem
cannot restore reality, but it does give us a pleasureable awareness
of the artifice of all poetic constructions. The speaker, refusing to
be trapped within any given identity, assumes a Whitmanian
plurality of identities, a multitude of selves. This infinitely
dispersed subject, a kind of free floating signifier, exists – like the
past – in a verbal space beyond or before all codes and categories:

I know too much
To be anything any more;
And if in the distant

Future someone
Thinks he has once been me
As I am today,

Let him revise
His insolent ontology
Or teach himself to pray.
(*CP* 45–6)

For Oscar Wilde, 'The real life is the life we do not lead'[60]: Mahon
wishes to give a voice to the multiple lost 'lives we might have
led' (*CP* 60), those virtual lives of the imagination which exist
outside definition, as unfulfilled desire, and to which the poet
refers in the polyvalent term (and poem) 'Leaves'. The unitary,
imperial self is always haunted by 'an infinite/Rustling and
sighing' of the 'dead leaves' of other selves, other lives, which
clamour for recognition with the same poignant yearning as the
mushrooms in 'A Disused Shed'. As Mahon puts it in the
companion poem, 'A Garage in Co. Cork', 'We might be anywhere

but are in one place only' (*CP* 131).

Mahon's interest in translation and adaptation, and the rich intertextuality of the later work, testify to a subject constituted out of a proliferation of cultural codes. 'The Hudson Letter' has the poet displaced and isolated in an apartment in Manhattan, attempting to re-construct himself and his world in the aftermath of marital failure and alcoholic breakdown, rather like Saul Bellow's Herzog, withdrawn from the world to his run-down house in the Berkshire Mountains of New England. Like Herzog, the poet writes letters, conducting his own analysis of self, family, society, the past. By incorporating the diverse discourses of popular culture, Mahon loosens his hold on modernist notions of aesthetic autonomy. Posing as decentred *bricoleur* he manipulates disparate cultural phenomena, wishing to give the impression of absorbing the undifferentiated dreck of modern America, a world of flux and broken forms. Any purely aesthetic significance is wryly undermined: the Inca tern and Andean gull in Part VI, 'like Daisy's Cunard nightingale ... belong in another life' (*CP* 196). Yet, 'The Hudson Letter' still rests on an aesthetic ideology, and turns out to be another modernist text about art and the aesthetics of composition: 'Never mind the hidden agenda, the sub-text;/ it's not really about male arrogance, "rough sex"/ or vengeful sisterhood, but about art/ and the encoded mysteries of the human heart' (*CP* 199). For all the poet's going out into the 'real world' of history and people, he invariably retreats into a closeted aesthetic world of high culture. As John Goodby remarks: 'The poems (in *The Hudson Letter* and *The Yellow Book*) often begin with a New York scene but appeal, in seeking fit closure, to the likes of Glenn Gould, George Herbert, Confucius and Racine. The irony is all at the expense of the present'. The pervasive and corrosive postmodern scepticism concerning subjectivity, identity and representation does not erase from the poetry a central core or structure of meaning; nor does it cancel the possibility of renewal and redemption, which 'The Hudson Letter' rises to affirm so powerfully in its exquisite lyric close. The poignant yearning of 'Spring in Belfast', 'Nostalgias' and 'A Disused Shed' continues to animate a poetic quest for home and wholeness:

> I think of the homeless, no rm. at the inn;
> far off, the gaseous planets where they spin,
> the star-lit towers of Nineveh and Babylon,
> the secret voice of nightingale and dolphin,
> fish crowding the Verrazano Bridge; and see,

even in the icy heart of February,
primrose and gentian. When does the thaw begin?
We have been too long in the cold. – Take us in; take us in!

(*CP* 222)

By necessity, if not choice, he inhabits an entropic, decadent world. The title of his last major volume, *The Yellow Book,* is taken from the name of a notorious literary magazine which, because of its associations with moral decadence, folded around the time of Oscar Wilde's trials for homosexual behaviour. The epigraph to *The Yellow Book* is taken from Palinurus: 'To live in a decadence need not make us despair; it is but one technical problem the more which a writer has to solve'. Mahon's 'solution' is, characteristically, a 'solving ambiguity' (*CP* 17), a reponse which combines Juvenilian satire of the cynical materialism and moral vacuity of the times, elegiac feeling for lost civilised values, MacNeicean celebration of life's crazy variousness, and a minimal confidence in the 'afterlives' of art.

LOOKING BACK FROM *THE YELLOW BOOK*

EDNA LONGLEY

This essay will be a tour of the Mahon horizon with *The Yellow Book* as my tour-guide. Of course, looking back from *The Yellow Book*, touring his own horizon, is precisely what Mahon does in *The Yellow Book*: the collection of twenty-two intertwined verse-epistles or soliloquies or dramatic monologues or self-styled 'eclogues' (their genre is not clearcut) that he published in 1997. Mahon's backward look takes in the origins of modern literature, the advent and fate of modernity. Thus he also looks back to *The Yellow Book*: to the house-journal of Aubrey Beardsley, Oscar Wilde and Decadence. In the text's autobiographical time-frame the Mahon-figure himself becomes historical. He recalls 'growing up among washing lines and grey skies', 'Smokey Joe's café a generation ago', Trinity College in 'the demure 1960s', London in the 1970s, his 'New York time/ spying for the old world in the new'. And, in the text's literary time-frame, he assumes the voice of Elizabeth Bowen in 1940 (the year before he was born) and quotes, mimics, translates or mentions scores of writers as the gyre spools back to 'Schopenhauer's Day', to Wilde in 'the humid side-streets of the Latin quarter', to Baudelairean dusks, to Juvenal's 'modern Rome'.

The Yellow Book accurately calls itself a 'forest of intertextuality'. But this is self-irony, too, given the speaker's distaste for 'the pastiche paradise of the post-modern'. Similarly, Mahon distrusts the literary self-consciousness induced by the academy. This may explain why he did not attend his own party/ symposium. It certainly explains the title he gave to his selected critical prose. *Journalism* echoes Philip Larkin's *Required Writing* as a studied denial of grand design. Among the significant affinities between Larkin and Mahon is a sense – ultimately aesthetic – that the poet should not pander to academic modes and audiences. Thus

29

Mahon deplores 'the deconstructionist racket' (*J* 136); or, reviewing Seamus Heaney's *The Government of the Tongue*, hints that
a poet-critic should not become 'excessively professorial' (*J* 112).
So if *The Yellow Book* is, in part, a work of literary criticism, it takes
its cue from the Horatian epistle rather than the Research
Assessment Exercise, its tone from Audenesque play rather than
Eliot's macaronic or mandarin. Mahon's 'forest of intertextuality'
yields its richest meanings where it is witty, where it is inner-
directed, or where it is both together as in XV 'Smoke' which
begins with some quizzical self-quotation: 'must I stand out in
thunder yet again/ who have *thrice* come in from the cold?' That
the speaker deprecates the therapeutic poetic modes of Yeats and
Coleridge, preferring a cigarette, actually serves to align his
reverie with Romantic introspection:

> I climb as directed to our proper dark,
> five flights without a lift up to the old
> gloom we used to love, and the old cold.
> Head in the clouds but tired of verse, I fold
> away my wind-harp and my dejection odes . . .
> Skywards smoke from my last Camel rises . . .

Mahon's credentials as a modern reinventor of Romanticism
(credentials which he underlines in that passage) suggest that the
intertextuality of *The Yellow Book* contributes to the autobiography
of an imagination, a post-dated *Prelude*. The sequence reflects on
the composition of a poetic self viewed both in retrospect and as
work in progress. The 1890s or 1960s finally merge into the 1990s.
Meanwhile, artistic autobiography merges into aesthetic manifesto: an apology for poetry in brutal times. And, as with the last
fin de siècle, the retro may be the radical.

   Considered as a manifesto, *The Yellow Book* obliquely resists
some over-familiar terms in which Mahon's poetry has been
discussed. In *Mistaken Identities: Poetry and Northern Ireland* (1997)
Peter McDonald attacks the substitution of 'identity-discourse' for
literary criticism where poets from Northern Ireland are
concerned. In Mahon's case, the reductive traps are obvious.
Themes like 'cosmopolitanism' or modern 'displacement' slide
back into *a priori* labels. I have been guilty myself of what I am
about to parody:

> Derek Mahon's profound sense of alienation from his Ulster
> Protestant background has produced an ironic poetry of exile,
> expiation, absence, aporia and apocalypse. Haunted by visions of a

'lost tribe' in a twilit, terminal no man's land, he writes – to quote
Seamus Deane – 'for posterities'. In contrast, Seamus Heaney's
profound sense of affiliation to his Ulster Catholic background has
produced a celebratory, richly rooted, glowingly epiphanic poetry
of presence and triumphant transcendence.

To fend off this kind of language (which also reflects the
distortions produced by taking Heaney as the supposed aesthetic
norm) I will postpone Mahon's local connections until I have
discussed five literary points of reference that bind *The Yellow Book*
to the matrix of Mahon's poetry. These are: *fin-de-siècle*
aestheticism, French symbolism, the British 1930s, American
poetry, Anglo-Ireland.

1

Apart from wanting to get in on the millennial act, why *The Yellow
Book*? Mahon's powerful feelings of attraction-repulsion towards
the *fin-de-siècle* were signalled thirty years ago in *Night-Crossing*.
The poem originally called 'Dowson and Co' castigates the
English poetic decadents or aesthetes by highlighting the
contradiction between the 'religion of art' and the lives of its poet-
acolytes: 'frustrated rural clergymen/ Nobody would ordain'. Yet
Night-Crossing itself embraces aestheticism, if more vigorously.
The belief that art has its own ends, independent of the social
order, can be radical as well as escapist. Thus 'A Portrait of the
Artist' (originally 'van Gogh among the Miners') approves the
sterner religion of art associated with the self-ordained van Gogh.
The 'fierce fire' of van Gogh's pictures is seen as transmuting his
evangelical religion and rekindling 'the dying light of faith'. The
fact that Mahon already likes to assume a painter's persona, and
to appropriate painterly images, continues the aesthetic doctrine
of solidarity between the arts. Later poems such as 'The Last of the
Fire Kings' and 'The Snow Party' renew modern literature's
dialectic between the aesthete's 'cold dream/ Of a place out of
time,/ A palace of porcelain' and the 'boiling squares' where
history burns 'witches and heretics'. Here Mahon specifically
revisits Yeats's 'Lapis Lazuli': a poem in which the 1890s come up
against the 1930s. Mahon, too, asks how the imagination should
comport itself when the times 'Pitch like King Billy bomb-balls in'.

And his answer, like Yeats's, often seems to be perfection of the
work: i.e., by translating aesthetic principles into formal practice.
When Yeats reflects on the poetic creed of the *fin-de-siècle*, he

invokes life 'at its intense moments', poetry freed from rhetoric and impurities, the 'ice or salt' of traditional metres.[1] What happened to this creed? Did it dissolve into the Celtic Twilight ether? Or it was revised rather than replaced by the rhetoric that history forced back into Yeats's structures? In lyric poetry aestheticism survives as formal concentration. To cut out impurity became to cut out the inessential: a decision made deeply within the process of formal shaping. Mahon's early poem 'Recalling Aran' is a concentrated hymn to concentration:

> A dream of limestone in sea-light
> Where gulls have placed their perfect prints.
> Reflection in that final sky
> Shames vision into simple sight -
> Into pure sense, experience.
> Four thousand miles away tonight,
> Conceived beyond such innocence,
> I clutch the memory still, and I
> Have measured everything with it since.

Mahon reasserts aesthetic values by renewing their Yeatsian liaison with visionary western landscape. The dream-Aran thus 'recalled' is not only the Aran that Mahon visited in 1965 but also a perennial resort of the spirit. (Mahon's title-change to 'Thinking of Inis Oírr in Cambridge, Mass.' misses some of his poem's point.) Aran takes on aesthetic properties: perfection, purity, finality. Here nature does not so much imitate art, in Wildean style, as identify with it. Yet their fusion casts us back upon the world. It offers a way of sensing and experiencing which acts as a measure for all things: vision shamed into 'simple sight'. This corresponds to the deepest aesthetic doctrine – that 'the values of art should be the directing values of life itself'.[2] The poem's own effects are measured carefully: 'perfect prints' of assonance, four beats to the line, three rhyme-sounds strategically distributed, octosyllabics maintained until the more expansive rhythm and emotion of the last two lines, the poignant placing of 'And I', the ambiguously chimed 'pure sense, experience'. ('Pure sense', an oxymoron that pivots on the point where art meets life, is resolved into 'experience': an implied totality.) Mahon is one of the few poets who have absorbed and modified the Yeatsian architectonic of syntax and stanza. Sometimes, for instance, he reworks *fin-de-siècle* cadences as if to subvert the muscular rhetoric of the later Yeats. When the ten-line stanza of 'A Disused Shed in Co. Wexford' moves between diminuendo and crescendo, it seems to repeat the discovery of new energies in Decadence:

> Even now there are places where a thought might grow -
> Peruvian mines worked out and abandoned
> To a slow clock of condensation,
> An echo trapped forever, and a flutter
> Of wild-flowers in the lift-shaft,
> Indian compounds where the wind dances
> And a door bangs with diminished confidence,
> Lime crevices behind rippling rain-barrels,
> Dog-corners for bone-burials;
> And in a disused shed in Co. Wexford,
>
> Deep in the grounds of a burnt-out hotel,
> Among the bathtubs and the washbasins
> A thousand mushrooms crowd to a keyhole . . .

As compared with the masterful tones of some Yeatsian soliloquy, this voice is inflected by the residual images it tentatively introduces. There is a sense of the poet, like John Cage, orchestrating faint echoes, flutters, bangs and ripples. In Mahon, sounds that just break silence figure poetry; a louder 'roar' figures history. But here, of course, he also orchestrates the rumours of history. And the delicacy that links disparate historical moments – 'Magi, moonmen' – is most profoundly a delicacy of rhythm and assonance. A pleasurable aspect of 'A Disused Shed', as of other Mahon poems, is the *brio* with which it plays monosyllable against polysyllable: 'a slow clock of condensation', 'the rooks querulous in the high wood'. Mahon makes ordinary words numinous again – not only 'star' but 'clock' and 'wood'. He also makes polysyllables flamboyant rather than pompous, as in 'the gravel-crunching, interminable departure/ Of the expropriated mycologist'. Whatever else this may be, it is dandyism, high style, high camp, aesthetic display. It defies critical orthodoxies (to quote Auden's 'The Truest Poetry is the most Feigning') that prefer 'Plain cooking made still plainer by plain cooks'.

In *The Yellow Book* Mahon defiantly relishes ivory towers, high windows, Baudelaire's 'white fountains weeping into marble courts' – all of which amounts to nostalgia for nineties nostalgia. Besides the obvious centrality of Wilde, Pater and Yeats, there are nods to congenial aesthetes from later generations: Robert Graves, white god of Mahon's early lyric; the Larkin who wrote 'Beyond the light stand failure and remorse'; Cyril Connolly, who also provides the epigraph: 'To live in a decadence need not make us

despair; it is but one more problem the artist has to solve.'
Reviewing a biography of Connolly, Mahon praises his
'magnificent prediction: "It is closing time in the gardens of the
west, and from now on an artist will be judged only by the
resonance of his solitude or the quality of his despair"' (*J* 200). In
VIII 'Remembering the Nineties' (altered to 'Hangover Square' in
the *Collected Poems*) the Mahon-figure claims with bravado: 'I keep
alight the cold candle of decadence'. And he clings, however
futilely, to 'rhyme-sculpture against the entangling vines of
nature'. Mahon has written several villanelles – that French
'rhyme-sculpture' which epitomises the ritualistic and formalist
extreme of emergent 'modern poetry'. His villanelle 'Dawn
Chorus' also echoes Yeats's cadences of desire in *The Wind Among
the Reeds*:

> It is not sleep itself but dreams we miss,
> Say the psychologists; and the poets too.
> We yearn for that reality in this . . .
>
> Listening heart-broken to the dawn chorus,
> Clutching the certainty that once we flew,
> We yearn for that reality in this.
>
> Awaiting still our metamorphosis,
> We hoard the fragments of what once we knew,
> It is not sleep itself but dreams we miss.
> We yearn for that reality in this.

In 1991 Mahon agreed to call a poem an 'act of faith', and
declared:

> After many years of beating about the bush, the fact is, I am an
> out-and-out traditionalist. That's the way it is, and that's the way
> it's going to stay. I find that certain poets want to express certain
> things, want to be truthful about their emotions, about the nature
> of the world as they understand it . . . They are full of liberal
> intentions, they are admirable people; but they are not poets, not
> to me they're not. They're writing free verse . . . without any
> specific talent for poetry – to express themselves, to deliver
> narrative, to state opinions. But they are not doing the thing that
> poetry does, as far as I'm concerned. Formally, that is. I remember
> talking to Richard Pevear about this, and the three principles that
> we found ourselves agreeing on were Soul, Song and Formal
> Necessity – the Coleridgean sense of formal necessity that the

poem should 'contain within itself the reason why it is thus and not otherwise'.[3]

2

'Remembering the Nineties' internalises the neurosis, excess and tragedy that characterised some literary lives at the end of the nineteenth century. Mahon's impatience with Dowson and Co argues his deeper affinity with the French symbolists they tried to imitate. In the first section of *The Yellow Book* the protagonist instructs himself and the reader:

> Never mind the new world order and the bus tours,
> you can still switch on the fire, kick off your shoes
> and read the symbolists as the season dies.

In Mahon, perfection of the work more continuously faces imperfections of the life than in Yeats. Or perhaps their proximity points to different imperfections: those darker elements of the Decadence on which Yeats missed out ('Twas wine or women, or some curse', as Yeats discreetly puts it in 'The Grey Rock'). Mahon finds Yeats finally 'consolatory' as compared with the experience of reading Baudelaire. Here, he says, 'No masterful heaven intervenes to save us.' (J 129) 'Landscape' (after Baudelaire) prefaces *The Yellow Book*. Here Mahon-Baudelaire is to be found self-ironically and self-referentially 'extracting sunlight as my whims require/ my thoughts blazing for want of a real fire'. XIII 'Dusk', also after Baudelaire, salutes 'Night now, bewitching night, friend of the evildoer' and disturbing haunt of 'some of us (who) have never known the relief/ of house and home, being outcast in this life'. In *Night-Crossing* France and French poetry, both read from their symbolist apotheosis, help to inaugurate the nomadic psychodrama that will characterise Mahon's work. This features solitude, despair, guilt, the unavailability of consolation, withdrawal *from* others, withdrawal *of* others. It also expresses a wholesale resistance to the bourgeois 'pandemonium of encumbrances' which necessitates, as for Malcolm Lowry, 'a round-the-cosmos trip with the furious Muse'. The now-sober Mahon still associates 'morning-after lucidity' with 'revelation', and the 'original bohemian idea' with the conditions for writing poetry.[4]

Mahon claims that there is 'no exact English equivalent' for Baudelaire's *mal* 'any more than there is for *triste* or *mélancolie*, two more of his favourite words' (*J* 130). But even without exact synonyms (though Mahon's 'bleak' might do) he translates this ethos into many effects: 'With wise abandon/ Lover and friend have gone'; 'and the years, the years/ Fly past anti-clockwise/ Like clock-hands in a bar-mirror'; 'Its mourning faces are cracked porcelain only quicker'. In *Night-Crossing* Baudelairean night-thoughts are juxtaposed with the more robustly scapegrace poetics of Villon's 'Shorter Testament'. Here I disagree with Bill Tinley's useful article on Mahon's 'Francophile Poetics', which finds dissonance between Mahon's Villon voice – 'sharp-tongued, worldly' – and his lyrical voice.[5] Mahon's 'French' poems, whether they tend to *tristesse*, *mal* or ironic wit, negotiate existential crisis in interconnected ways. The Villon of 'Legacies' is a poet just holding on despite his perkiness: 'Done at the aforesaid time of year/ By Villon, of such great repute/ He wastes away with cold and hunger,/ Thin as a rake and black as soot'. Mahon's underworld of drunks, tramps, travellers conflates the Bohemian and picaresque into a composite outsider. Graham Robb notes that Rimbaud's 'Bohemian' sonnets, which 'endeared him to later generations of literary vagrants . . . seem to lead French poetry out of the library and the furnished room for the first time since Francois Villon'.[6] It is interesting that Mahon should attach his Beckettian 'Exit Molloy' (France and Ireland meet in Beckett's literary vagrancy too, of course) to his 'Breton Walks' sequence. This speaker holds on – and holds out – in a different key of gallantry to Villon's:

> Now at the end I smell the smells of spring
> Where in a dark ditch I lie wintering -
> And the little town only a mile away
> Happy and fatuous in the light of day.
> A bell tolls gently. I should start to cry
> But my eyes are closed and my face dry.
> I am not important and I have to die.
> Strictly speaking, I am already dead,
> But still I can hear the birds sing on over my head.

'Reading the symbolists' focused, exoticised and universalised Mahon's psychodrama.

But what about symbolism in a more technical sense? Tinley argues that Mahon is not ultimately a symbolist, because 'Baudelaire's correspondences are primarily sensory, his symbolism an endeavour to rekindle our capacity to take pleasure in the world. Mahon's metaphysic, on the other hand, is philosophical and political insofar as his metaphors keep their correlatives in view'.[7] Yet there are different kinds or degrees of symbolism, and Baudelaire with his 'vast cloud formations dreaming about eternity' ('Landscape') may also be more transcendentally inclined than Tinley makes out. Mahon's affinity with Baudelaire includes not only the psychology of *poète maudit* but also its structures of compensation. The Baudelairean aesthetic encompasses both the aspirational, utopian thrust of a *poésie de départs* and the nihilistic extreme from which life appears 'an oasis of horror in a desert of ennui'. Mahon can do both aspiration and ennui, and views the poetic 'act of faith' as a 'defiance of nihilism'.[8] He can also traverse a symbolist spectrum from correspondence to transcendence. He approaches the transcendental pole in his translation of Rimbaud's proto-symbolist 'Le Bateau Ivre', which pulls back from the poem's 'crescendo of sensations' to highlight its quest for cosmic order:

> Delirious cape! Strewn archipelagoes!
> Do you nurse there in your galactic foam
> The glistening bodies of obscure flamingoes
> Tranced in a prescience of the life to come?
>
> Meuse of the cloud-canals, I would ask of you
> Only the pond where, on a quiet evening,
> An only child launches a toy canoe
> As frail and pitiful as a moth in spring.

By compressing Rimbaud's concluding quatrains, Mahon illuminates the mix of aspiration and pathos that drives the whole phantasmagoria.

Where Mahon's symbolism differs from Yeats's may imply his fuller sense of the complexities stemming from the French symbolist tradition. Hence the lightness of touch, depth of 'suggestion' – that key symbolist term – in 'A Disused Shed' with its mix of local and over-arching symbolism. The mushrooms/shed never settle into a stable field of 'correlatives' as does, for example, 'the holy city of Byzantium'. Even where the voice steps in to interpret, it hardly claims authority – 'They are begging us, you see, in their wordless way,/ To do something, to speak on their behalf'. In a sense this is where symbolism itself came in: as an effort to get beyond words and discursiveness, to figure a dimension beyond tangible reality. Yet symbolist *poetry* had to confront the contradiction of its very medium. Mahon, in so finely mediating between the wordless and the tangible, may solve a

problem which 'modernist' poetics evaded by abandoning
symbolism as a means of organising a poem. 'A Disused Shed'
also mediates between the psychological and spiritual desires
whose interaction drove the symbolist enterprise. Finally,
Mahon's engagement with French symbolism and Yeatsian
symbolism has wider importance. It suggests that Irish poetry did
not necessarily forsake symbolism (incorporating 'Soul, Song and
Formal Necessity') for its 'modernist' derivatives. And Mahon's
practice shows that if symbolism is a means of unifying a poem, or
at least a conduit of belief in artistic unity, this need not imply an
orderly universe.

3

The theory of Mallarmé took transcendental symbolism to an
abstract extreme. Mallarmé claimed that poetry itself conjured the
unknown reality into being – 'Words alone are certain good' in
Yeats's version. Mahon draws the line at this as he does at
deconstruction. In 1986 he referred to 'Mallarmé's noxious belief
that the world came into existence in order to finish up between
the covers of a book' (*J* 193). Perhaps the best poets have a touch of
both the 1890s and the 1930s in their make-up. When we start
remembering the thirties rather than the nineties, the socio-
political – and Enlightenment – dimension of Mahon's poetry
comes into view. The artistic relation between Mahon and
MacNeice has already been much canvassed. Mahon's response to
MacNeice has Irish as well as 1930s contexts, and is not bounded
by the pressures exerted on poetry by that 'low, dishonest decade'.
Nonetheless, 1930s Britain and Europe crucially tested the modern
movement. Mahon absorbed from MacNeice scenarios whereby
poetry met history in challenging new contexts: in urban settings,
urban demotic, leftwing politics, the threat of fascism and war. All
these elements come together in *Autumn Journal*. Mahon does not
reproduce MacNeice's struggle with political and historical
imperatives. Rather, he distilled its meaning – an *engagé* but
unillusioned liberalism – and moved on. Hence the fact that the
poems in which Mahon alludes to the Northern Troubles are
closer to the Yeats of 'Lapis Lazuli' than to any kind of
'committed' poetry. The 'silence' of 'The Snow Party' laments and
rebukes the impotence of art. Yet, the poem remembers the thirties
because it implies that inadequate or tendentious art adds insult to
injury. And, remembering the Holocaust, it implies that all
masterful images are suspect. Mahon, then, has also absorbed

Beckett's postwar critique of the sin of being born into history. To take the long view, the religious view, is not necessarily to evade. Hence the powerful sorrow of 'Lost People of Treblinka and Pompeii!'

At the same time, to write discursively as Mahon does in *The Yellow Book* and elsewhere is to invoke more immediate horizons, a more immediate audience. It is to put communication as well as history back into symbolism. The 1930s revived that quintessentially social mode, the verse-epistle, most notably in Auden's and MacNeice's *Letters from Iceland* (1937). In a slightly moralistic article, John Redmond finds Mahon's epistles guilty of too much 'wilful inconsistency'. He says: 'Mahon was trying to elaborate . . . a casual voice of the kind which we associate with Auden . . . [and] to avoid . . . a more consistently grand and insistently authoritative voice of the kind which we associate with Yeats'.[9] I have already suggested that Mahon successfully modifies Yeatsian registers: this also applies to his first verse-letter 'Beyond Howth Head' (1970) written at the age when MacNeice and Auden wrote *Letters from Iceland*. The Troubles were just beginning, the swinging sixties just ending. The poem may thus rediscover, rather than inadequately imitate, a particular chemistry between poetry and history. Its verbal play, promiscuity of reference, cheeky rhymes and switches of register are (as in *Letters from Iceland*) consciously, but also strategically, on holiday from more pressing concerns:

> I woke this morning (March) to hear
> church bells of Monkstown through the roar
> of waves round the Martello tower
> and thought of the swan-sons of Lir
> when Kemoc rang the Christian bell
> to crack a fourth-dimensional
> world-picture, never known again,
> and changed them back from swans to men.
>
> It calls as oddly through the wild
> eviscerations of the troubled
> channel between us and North Wales
> where Lycid's ghost for ever sails
> (unbosomings of sea-weed, wrack,
> industrial bile, a boot from Black-
> pool, contraceptives deftly tied
> with best regards from Merseyside)

and tinkles with as blithe a sense
of man's cosmic significance
who wrote his world from broken stone,
installed his Word-God on the throne
and placed, in Co. Clare, a sign:
'Stop here and see the sun go down'.
Meanwhile, for a word's sake, the plast-
ic bombs go off around Belfast . . .

Critics stress Mahon's debt to Auden's epistolary idiom and to the
Marvellian Robert Lowell of 'Waking Early Sunday Morning' and
'Fourth of July in Maine'. But perhaps his discursive verse is most
deeply charged by a *tension* between the precedents of Auden and
MacNeice. To take Auden first: when Mahon diagnoses, and
prescribes for, the ills of the modern condition he leans towards
Audenesque generalisation. 'Beyond Howth Head' anticipates
didactic aspects of *The Yellow Book*, as well as characterising its
own tilt, when Mahon describes himself as 'rehearsing for the *fin
de siècle*/ gruff Jeremaids to redirect/ lost youth into the knacker's
yard/ of humanistic self-regard'. The humanistic politics of *The
Yellow Book* do, indeed, resemble the later Auden's. They are
religious and aesthetic rather than socialist in their critique of late
capitalism. Thus II 'Axel's Castle' ends:

The fountain's flute is silent though time spares
the old beeches with their echoes of Coole demesne;
foreign investment conspires against old decency,
computer talks to computer, machine to answering machine.

This is also the cry of the Celtic Twilight against the Celtic Tiger.

MacNeice's most achieved discursive mode differs from the
Auden epistle. In *Autumn Journal* he adapts the socio-political
themes of the 1930s verse-letter to an autobiographical, interior
and latently lyrical voice. The poem's structural grid is laid out in
the lines: 'Time is a country, the present moment/ A spotlight
roving round the scene'. The roving soliloquies directed from
MacNeice's London flat underlie the soliloquies directed from
Mahon's New York apartment in 'The Hudson Letter' and from
his Dublin flat in *The Yellow Book*. The generic and structural
template of *Autumn Journal* allows public and private worlds to
interpenetrate – the 'quarrel with others' and 'the quarrel with
oneself'. Such quarrels, and the richly diverse language in which
they are conducted, entangle commentary with reportage,
generalisation with concreteness. Thus MacNeice's precedent can

prevent Mahon from slipping into the shallower 'authorial monologue' that some critics detect in his last two books[10] – as in gestures like 'We are all tourists now'. 'Waterfront' in 'The Hudson Letter' takes its epigraph from MacNeice in the 1930s: 'We shall go down like palaeolithic man/ Before some new Ice Age or Genghiz Khan'; and associates a line in *Autumn Journal* ('Sunlight dancing on the rubbish dump') with the homeless of 1990s New York: 'The sun shines on the dump, not on the *côte d'azur*/ and not on the cloistered murals, to be sure'. Yet Mahon's latterday resort to 1930s discursive modes may still harbour unresolved conflict between the models of Auden and MacNeice: between 'slick and easy generalisation' (to quote Auden's self-criticism in 'Letter to Lord Byron') and more profound public quarrels with oneself.

4

Section XVI of *The Yellow Book*, 'America Deserta', evokes the ethos which attracted Mahon to the US, and led him to live there and in Canada between 1965 and 1967. This was 'an older America of the abrasive spirit/ *film noir*, real jazz and grown-up literate wit'. Mahon has said of his period in Cambridge, Mass.: 'There was this enormous poetic energy in America at that time, and I was very conscious of it around Harvard Square'.[11] But now the speaker of 'America Deserta' prophesises cultural doom: 'not long before/ the pharaonic scam begins its long decline/ to pot-holed roads and unfinished construction sites'. I have written elsewhere of the 'Atlantic' dimension in the early poetry of Mahon and Michael Longley. Their enthusiasm for Wallace Stevens, Hart Crane and Robert Lowell had a historical and material basis in the mix of trade and Protestantism that once produced the culture of Atlantic cities (Belfast, Liverpool, Glasgow, New York, Boston). Christopher Harvie has stressed the pan-Atlantic currency of Whitman's 'Sea Drift' poems, and 'the technology they projected'.[12] In this sense 'Waterfront' can be called an Atlantic poem, albeit a poem of Atlantic post-industrial change. Yet it retains a visionary sense of the shipping history shared by the Hudson River and Belfast Lough, of the sea hubristically challenged by technology and the *Titanic*. Mahon imagines 'the blind Atlantic snow ... Smoky and crepitant, glacier-spiky, rough/ in its white logic'. Back in 1970 Mahon wrote of Crane's 'Brooklyn Bridge' sequence: 'Reading Hart Crane's "All afternoon the cloud-flown derricks turn;/ Thy cables breathe the North Atlantic still", it was possible to endow the shipyards of Belfast with an immanence of poetic life they had never had before'.[13] (Mahon's version of the quotation, in a layered Freudian slip, substituted the more usual Belfast word 'gantries' for Crane's 'derricks'.) There are deliberate allusions to Crane in 'The Hudson Letter', but his influence more crucially reaches into the very foundations of Mahon's poetry. 'Landscape' sounds more like Crane than Baudelaire, and perhaps more like old Belfast than new Dublin, when it invokes the city as Muse: 'I can see workshops full of noise and talk,/ cranes and masts of the ocean-going city'.

Mahon is a notable sea-poet in the Atlantic tradition. His introduction to his translations from Philippe Jaccottet links Jaccottet's tendency to exclude 'the abrasive surfaces of the modern world', to refine his poetry out of existence, with there being '(almost) no *sea*'.[14] Mahon's own 'soul landscape' habitually features sea and storm beating against fragile human constructions: an interiorisation of the Antrim coast. This connects with the influence of Stevens, Crane and Lowell, as we can track it in *Night-Crossing*. Besides the 'glacier-spiky' Atlantic, Mahon and these American poets share a similarly unstable metaphysical locus where varieties of Romanticism mingle with varieties of Protestantism. The sea in American poetry not only symbolises the formless energy from which the imagination derives and upon which it works. It also figures psychic and spiritual 'voyages', to cite the title of Crane's most famous work. Mahon's early poem 'In the Aran Islands' significantly if reluctantly identifies his own aesthetic with a gull 'Circling now with a hoarse inchoate/ Screaming the boned fields of its vision'. This contrasts with the aesthetic personified by an 'earthed' folk singer (possibly akin to Seamus Heaney) saluted as 'Hand-clasping, echo-prolonging poet'. Nevertheless, the poem ends with a seeming re-dedication to an oceanic Romantic extremity, to some insatiable and 'unearthly' quest:

> Unearthly still in its white weather
> A crack-voiced rock-marauder, scavenger, fierce
> Friend to no slant fields or the sea either,
> Folds back over the forming waters.

To scream the fields of your vision implies that verbal intensity is of the visionary essence:

> I like to be spoken to in the tone of voice of Robert Lowell's 'Waking Early Sunday Morning':

Pity the planet, all joy gone
From this sweet volcanic cone.

Then I'm hearing music loud and clear. I like the tenor of it. Here
is a voice that has committed itself to words without hesitation,
without irony, without fear. It's a form of giving yourself to life.
It's the ability to surrender; to walk into the water without a
lifebelt; to do the big thing.[15]

Lowell's earlier poetry ('A Quaker Graveyard'), as well as *Life
Studies*, influenced Mahon in the early 1960s. Reviewing Lowell's
Collected Prose in 1987 Mahon approves the fact that Lowell prefers
Crane to William Carlos Williams, and emphasises Lowell's 'life-
long love-hate relationship' with 'the New England puritan
tradition' (*J* 166). Clearly this is a strong point of identification.
The extent to which Mahon's critique of Ulster Protestantism, as in
'Ecclesiastes' ('the/ dank churches, the empty streets,/ the
shipyards silence, the tied-up swings'), was mediated by Lowell
has often escaped attention. 'Death in Bangor', Mahon's elegy for
his mother in *The Yellow Book*, represents her as a puritan amid
'the plain Protestant fatalism of home': 'your chief/ concern the
"appearances" that ruled your life/ in a neighbourhood of bay
windows and stiff/ gardens'. The counterpoint between 'Death in
Bangor' and an earlier familial elegy by Mahon, 'My Wicked
Uncle', suggests his multiple debt to Lowell. The former laments a
kind of death-in-life; the latter celebrates a kind of life-in-death.
Lowell was, first, a congenial anti-puritan spirit. Second, in *Life
Studies* he devised a poetic mode designed to break repressive
silences, appearances and taboos. 'That night I saw my uncle as he
really was'. And Lowell's 'music' (like Crane's) struck chords with
the more positive effects of Protestantism – the 'hymnology',
'words' and 'tunes' of Anglican liturgy – on Mahon's poetry.[16]

5

But I want to bring Mahon to Belfast – to the 'home' that 'terrifies'
him – by way of Dublin.[17] *The Yellow Book* is a Dublin book. It
contains several Dublins and literary Dublins between its covers.
Notable, however, is its nostalgia for Anglo-Irish Dublin and what
this implies about the locus of Mahon's poetry. Earlier I quoted
lines that link his current abode in Fitzwilliam Square with the
beech trees of Coole Park. Is Mahon obliquely reclaiming his
poetry's 'ancestral house' as he contrasts the Dublin of Yeats and

Wilde with the Dublin of computers and 'junk-film outfits'?
Speaking as Elizabeth Bowen 'At the Shelbourne', Mahon
positions her and himself in what 'is home really, a place of
warmth and light/ between the patrician past and the egalitarian
future'. Here 'home' is the precarious palace of art.

At one level Bowen's placing reproduces Mahon's own move
from Belfast to Dublin when he went to Trinity College in 1960 –
except that, in artistic terms, he travelled to the patrician past. He
recalls 'the struggle going on between a surly Belfast working-
class thing' and the persona or voice of a metropolitan 'flaneur'.[18]
In Trinity, subject to haunting presences from Burke to Beckett,
Mahon found 'a happy alternative to Belfast' and 'a very fertile
environment, very supportive'.[19] His poetic apprenticeship had
absolutely nothing to do with the later Belfast 'Group', which he
visited just once. Mahon's (and Michael Longley's) literary
nursery was the Trinity magazine *Icarus*. The presiding creative
spirit in the Trinity English department was Beckett's friend, Alec
Reid. And key relationships with contemporaries like Longley and
Brendan Kennelly were fully established in the context of Trinity
and Dublin. Trinity's significance needs to be reiterated against
the persistent and unexamined myth of the Belfast 'Group'. That
milieu undoubtedly fostered Seamus Heaney, but it was very far
from being the only begetter of 'Northern Irish poetry'. The myth
of the Group exemplifies the kind of lie that goes round the
academic world before the truth has got its boots on. In *The Yellow
Book* we can get a flavour of the truth from a much more loving
elegy than 'Death in Bangor': 'To Eugene Lambe in Heaven'.
Lambe (to whose memory the whole collection is dedicated) first
appears as a civilising flaneur in Belfast: 'your manner that of an
exiled Stuart prince'. Then he arrives in the apter milieu of Trinity:

> Next year you appeared
> in the same gear and spread Tolstoyan beard,
> our ginger man in Trinity's front square
> you called the 'playground' once; and it was here
> in pub and flat you formed the character
> we came to love, colloquial yet ornate,
> one of those perfect writers who never write,
> a student of manners and conversation straight
> from the pages of Castiglione or Baudelaire . . .

Lambe, clearly an *alter ego*, persisted in a Bohemian lifestyle
through the 1960s and 1970s until the Thatcher years when 'the
new harshness must have wounded you to the heart'. As Mahon

says: 'Before the bohemian clichés, there were bohemians who were originals'.[20] A fusion of old-style Trinity, Bohemia and Yeats's ideal Renaissance prince, 'Eugene Lambe' points to the mutuality between the symbolist and Anglo-Irish strains in Mahon's sensibility.

Perhaps architecture is implicated in all this. Lambe – shades of Robert Gregory – was the aesthete as interior decorator: 'an indolent perfectionist on a chaise-longue'. Dublin (now desecrated by tourists) and Trinity were beautiful as well as liberating. We do not usually think of Mahon as a Big House poet. We think of him as a little house, kitchen-house, disused shed, ditch-lying poet. But 'Penshurst Place' revisits the original 'Big House' poem:

> The bright drop quivering on a thorn
> in the rich silence after rain,
> lute music in the orchard aisles,
> the path ablaze with daffodils,
> intrigue and venery in the air
> *à l'ombre des jeunes filles en fleurs*,
> the iron hand and the velvet glove -
> Come live with me and be my love . . .

Ambiguous as this may be, like Mahon's Ford Manor poems it imagines a plenitude, a rich flowering, that contrasts with another scenario (from 'A Refusal to Mourn') with which it shares two words:

> All day there was silence
> In the bright house. The clock
> Ticked on the kitchen shelf,
> Cinders moved in the grate,
> And a warm briar gurgled
> When the old man talked to himself,
>
> But the door-bell seldom rang
> After the milkman went . . .

'A Refusal to Mourn', an elegy for his grandfather, is perhaps Mahon's most positive 'Belfast poem'. Obviously different subject-matter mainly accounts for the differences between the two poems. Nonetheless, it seems significant that Mahon represents his grandfather's life-style and house-style as without any animating civilisation which might connect the disparate objects that define them. Here silence and brightness are not replete with tradition, creativity and promise. Of course, Mahon's

poem supplies as well as notices the lack. I have discussed Mahon
as a Bohemian sensibility (not an 'exile') who writes a poetry of
no fixed abode, a poetry that questions fixed abodes. But houses
do play a part in his work: the disused shed has not quite given
up on the architecture of the burnt out hotel, the former Big
House. Insofar as houses figure social architecture, poetic
architectonic and literary tradition Mahon's imagination moves
between a utopian elaboration and abundance, which has
something to do with Dublin or Anglo-Ireland, and a dystopian
lack – sometimes a salutary minimalism – which has a lot to do
with Belfast.

'Eugene Lambe in Heaven' prefers the Dublin to the Belfast
milieu of Mahon's Northern Protestant generation. The North
does no better in 'Death in Bangor' whose very title implies that
death in Venice has more glamour. Peter McDonald criticises
Mahon for revisiting Northern Ireland with 'a cartload of clichés
and prejudices'.[21] Yet the prejudices are internalised – 'this is a
cold epitaph from your only son' – and therefore more
interesting. Mahon's inability to forgive the North signifies his
inability to forgive his mother. Her presence in his poetry is
marked by washing-lines, a pathological cleanliness next to
Godliness. She presides over 'Courtyards in Delft' where
'Houseproud, the wives/ Of artisans pursue their thrifty lives/
Among scrubbed yards, modest but adequate'. (In 'A Refusal to
Mourn', an equally meagre interior is suffused with Mahon's love
for his grandfather.) 'Scrubbed yards, modest but adequate'
explains why the 'strange child with a taste for verse' took the
bateau ivre and left home. Yet although 'Courtyards in Delft'
indicts a repressive culture ('We miss the dirty dog, the fiery
gin'), it concedes something incipiently artistic to the houswifery
that produces 'The ceiling cradled in a radiant spoon'. 'Death in
Bangor' is more explicit: 'you too were a kind of artist, a rage-for-
order freak'. But overall we receive a subtextual message that the
child was less warmly 'cradled' than the ceiling, that a fraught
boyhood and adolescence underlies Mahon's poetry.

Mahon's imaginative relation to his Protestant background is
too often seen in exclusively cultural and political terms – or seen
as the cultural and political terms. But the psychological basis of
his critique is what gives it force – and gives it bias. Nor does the
critique stop short at any border. Interior conflicts, conditioned
but not determined by cultural Protestantism, have generated
images and insights that apply more broadly to modern life: 'The
poignancy of those/ Back yards'. One representative conflict is

that between aesthete and philistine. Like Matthew Arnold, Mahon regards nonconformism as the enemy of beauty and karma: 'Elsewhere the olive grove/ *Le Déjeuner sur l'herbe'*. Brought up in the Church of Ireland, a choir boy no less, Mahon never directly suffered the theological severities of fundamentalism. Yet something in him appears at once frightened and fascinated by the intuition of a more rigorous faith that would question his 'taste for verse'. Thus a further conflict is that between the repercussions of Anglicanism and Calvinism, between form and ferocity: what Mahon himself calls the 'hissing chemicals inside the well-wrought urn'.[22] This conflict is dramatised in those partly satirical, partly self-punishing poems where neither humanity nor poetry is deemed worthy to survive.[23] 'Cultural Protestantism' or post-Protestantism (as with Yeats, MacNeice and Beckett) ramifies into aesthetic, psychological and metaphysical zones until it becomes virtually the ground of modern literature, the ground revisited in *The Yellow Book*. Protestant Ulster, so to speak, provided exactly the kind of bourgeoisie that the symbolists originally set out to *épater*. The (not exhaustive) literary points of reference toured in this essay, and absorbed into something different from the sum of their parts, show Mahon now deploying those creative sources against his background, now finding them expressive of it.

I began with the religion of art, and I have ended with the art of religion. This essay has implied that religion conditions Mahon's poetry in various ways – not all negative. It shapes his sounds and rhythms, his symbolism, his response to modernity, his pleas for the spirit to re-enter history, his signposts to a 'home' for 'lost people'. He readily assumes the mask of supplicant, preacher or evangelist; and the word 'god' occurs surprisingly often – if minus a capital letter. Derek Mahon's poetry has to be called religious when it sighs with 'a nameless hunger', when it prophesies the revelatory colour that will 'shine in the rainbow', when it speaks like Christ on the Cross: 'Let the god not abandon us/ Who have come so far in darkness and in pain.' And, of course, Mahon's interest in endings is millennarian as well as millennial: he imagines apocalypse, rebirth, poetry beginning again too. *The Yellow Book*, so conscious of the Book of Revelation, itself ends with a vision of genesis:

> I dreamed last night of a blue Cycladic dawn,
> a lone figure pointing to the horizon,
> again the white islands shouting, 'Come on; come on! . . .

HEIRS AND GRACES:
THE INFLUENCE AND EXAMPLE OF
DEREK MAHON

GERALD DAWE

This essay is based upon two non-poetic sources. One is a letter
Derek Mahon wrote to the *Irish Times* on 16 July 1987 and the
other text is a fascinating, and rarely quoted interview between
Mahon and the literary historian and critic, Terence Brown,
published in *Poetry Ireland Review* in the autumn of 1985, a couple
of years before the *Irish Times* letter. Now before I turn to these
two critical points of reference, I'd like to sketch in very roughly
what is in the back of my mind.

I think Derek Mahon is a magnificent poet. Like many others, I
have followed his books of poetry with a keen eye, particularly, I
have to say, those early volumes which seemed to parallel, in
some almost subconscious way, the experience of a generation
growing up (and out) of Northern Ireland. From *Night-Crossing*
(1968) with the photograph of Mahon on the cover looking
somewhat like a jazz-man through *Lives* (1972) with the black-and-
white-print of the famous Titanic and shipyard scene and the tram
advertising Inglis Bread, through to *The Snow Party* (1975) and the
Munch lithograph of 'The Lady with the Brooch' to *The Hunt By
Night* (1982) and its cover illustration from Paolo Uccello, it might
be truer to say that reading Mahon was closer to collecting the
next album. The point of this is simply that Mahon was very much
part of the inner life of this particular reader and I have found it
very difficult to detach myself from the immediate circumstances
of the time in which those early volumes started to appear,
beginning thirty years ago. Mahon's poetry represents a kind of
singular, challenging history. What I want to try to do is suggest
my sense of what that singularity consists (the 'graces') but also
offer a few comments on the history – those influences (or 'heirs')
which Mahon's poetry embodies and which he has, in turn, made

available to other writers through his own example.

First things first. I want to quote from an expert witness who has described Derek Mahon's verse as 'a disenchanted vision'. In his little masterpiece of a prose memoir, *Tuppenny Stung: Autobiographical Chapters* (1994), Michael Longley recalls:

> We smoked and drank too much. If not in Number Sixteen, our seminars were held in O'Neill's Bar, Suffolk Street. From time to time we breakfasted on pints. Mahon embodied for me the spirit of Pan or Puck when he played the tin whistle in Victor Blease's rooms and walked up and down the furniture as weightless. We laughed a lot. A need to undermine Northern Irish middle-class respectability seemed to be at the core of our humour. Although pieties of any kind were fit targets, a posh Cherryvalley accent which caricatured the wobbly vowel-sounds of the more complacent brands of Unionism invariably focused our hilarity. But these were fulfilling rather than happy times. Our friendship and our abilities were often stretched as far as they could go. I admired Mahon's disenchanted vision, but was less attracted than he to the role of *poète maudit*... Mahon's verve and edginess helped to keep me sane.[1]

The 'disenchanted vision', 'verve and edginess' are of course characteristics of Mahon's poetry as is the role of *'poète maudit'* with which Mahon has played, mockingly and in a more complex way since, for instance, 'The Poets Lie Where They Fell':

> No rest for the wicked -
> Curled up in armchairs
> Or flat out on the floors
> Of well-furnished apartments
> Belonging to friends of friends,
> We lie where we fell.
>
>   (NC 34)

A reading of Mahon's books of poems reveal an extraordinary range of worldly authoritative figures and figures of authorising presence: Malcolm Lowry, Cavafy, Brecht, Pasternak, Hamsun, Rilke, Rimbaud, Ovid, Pound, Madox Ford, Van Gogh, MacNeice; more recently, Kavanagh and Clarke. The over-riding presence is, however, the singular Samuel Beckett, with whom Mahon has expressed 'a great affinity' – 'a friendlier, a matier kind of voice speaking in my ear . . . hilariously funny', 'one of my writers'. One need only cite the following examples to get the briefest of impressions of just how important Beckett is to Mahon: 'Exit Molloy' 'in a dark ditch . . . wintering' (*SP* 17), 'An Image from Beckett' (*SP* 34–5), 'The pros (which) outweigh the cons that glow/ from Beckett's bleak reductio' (*SP* 45); the verse letter, 'Beyond Howth Head', 'where once Molloy uncycled, heard/thin cries of a surviving bird' (*SP* 47), and 'The Sea in Winter' where the poet is 'trapped . . . in my own idiom': 'One day,/ perhaps, the words will find their mark/ and leave a brief glow in the dark' (*SP* 117). Beckett's writing lives inside Mahon's poems in an afterlife of intertexuality: from direct quotations from *The Unnameable* (*SP* 168), and reference to Echo's bones (*SP* 171), to 'Burbles: after Beckett' in *The Hudson Letter* (21), the presence of Beckett is simply everywhere.

For it seems to me that Mahon's singularity consists of the manner in which he has single-mindedly made of poetic self-consciousness a subject continuously contested in his poems and in what he called his *Journalism* (1996). From the earliest of those poems which dramatised poets and artists, forgers and fugitives, Mahon has established a critical and (almost) misanthropic eye on a whole series of cultural and social developments in contemporary life. The extent to which he has taken on this critical, dramatic role in later books like *The Hudson Letter* and *The Yellow Book* demonstrates the consistency at the core of Mahon's artistic personae. In a sense the under grad' *poète maudit* has found a true vision and (dare I say it) a role.

There are two sides to this story to which I want to turn. Firstly, Mahon has stood outside the literary history of 'Northern Poetry' and the cultural homing which conventionally goes along with the term. He has rebuked, to quote from *The Irish Times* letter, those who critically enlist him in the category and has shown little mercy when making a 'forlorn attempt to set the record straight about that damned "Group"' and the foolhardy recycling of 'errors of fact' and 'irritating falsehoods'. This is an edited reading of the main points of that letter:

> 1. I was never a student of Hobsbaum: I took my degree at Trinity, in a very different climate. Philip Hobsbaum imparted an English 'Movement' aesthetic to his students in Belfast, via the 'Group' which used to meet there under his guidance. This may well be true. I can't be absolutely sure, since I was never a student of Hobsbaum.

> 2. By our alleged acceptance of Hobsbaum's 'anti-mondernist line'

we found 'commercial, academic success' whatever that means. I have found neither; not that I'm complaining. Artistic success is the only kind that matters, and it eludes us all. I do, however, agree that Irish 'modernist' poets like MacGreevy and Devlin have received less than their due; and I, for one, rate both of them higher than any 'Movement' poet.

3. The 'Group' story has a pleasing symmetry, and nobody wants to hear the more complex truth. The critics have decided we were all (Heaney, Longley, Mahon) Belfast students together, happily anti-modernist at Hobsbaum's feet, when at least one of those mentioned was sitting in Dublin reading Graves, Crane and Beckett, unaware that irritating falsehoods about him would one day appear in a national newspaper.[2]

The significance of this letter is not merely the irritation that Mahon clearly felt about historical inaccuracies and critical stereotypes – all important as these may be. It is those names which Mahon identifies as part of 'the more complex truth' – Graves, Crane and Beckett, for a start – and also the acknowledgement of two lesser-known poets, Thomas MacGreevy and Denis Devlin which should be noted. Fifteen years earlier, Mahon had included both poets in what he later referred to as 'a terrible piece of hack work', namely his edition of *The Sphere Book of Modem Irish Poetry* (1972). It were as if Mahon was establishing for himself, publicly, once and for all for the record, a different imaginative space and literary context from the supposedly dominant 'anti-modernist' one of what I suppose we should call critical folk customs. This edginess finds a further expression in what I think is the most astute of the handful of interviews Mahon has given over the years. Mahon is alert to the social specifics of the North without endorsing its literature with culturally burdensome priority:

Not having been in the war (World War 2) shunted Ireland to the sidelines, and I think she's been forced back into the twentieth century by events in the North, by the forgotten North. The nastiness reared its head as it had to sooner or later; the poet from the North had a new thing to say, a new kind of sound to make, a new texture to create. Looking back on it, there's a sort of inevitability that the new energy should have come from the North.[3]

Mahon goes on to dismiss, alongside the notion of Northern

poetry, the possibly privileged relationship between 'the fruits of industrialism' as a factor which can move the Ulster poet 'closer to making a new and fundamental statement':

> The fruits of industrialism are ruination and waste, ugliness. Also the so-called Ulster poetry that ill-informed people in England are so excited about, I don't see it lasting much more than another generation and then probably it'll never happen again.

Responding to Terence Brown's suggestion that the North is represented in his world 'as a kind of cultural deprivation ... a place that has no magic, no karma perhaps, no poetic possibility', Mahon states:

> I think the Protestant ethic has made it its business to dispel any karma that there might have been. In so far as I have written about the North what I have been about, one doesn't always know what one is doing, but in retrospect I may have been trying to put back in some of the karma that bad Protestants over the generations have removed.

It is the next step which Mahon takes which is the most telling and, I guess, the most influential:

> All the better for poems ... if they issue from a feeling of cultural deprivation. They issue from a feeling that's very widespread ... Most people live with deprivation of some kind, so if one writes out of a deprived and depressed culture, wondering what there is to turn to, you're not only writing about Northern Ireland, you're writing about a much more widespread phenomenon.

Mahon's deconstruction of what he was to call 'pleasing symmetry' discounts also the idea of a 'belief system' and opts, somewhat modestly, for seeing himself as 'what is now a very old-fashioned term ... an existentialist with a small "e". . . I would call myself an existentialist, an open-minded existentialist'. In 'Dawn at St. Patrick's', Mahon ironises this condition from a hospital bed:

> Next-door, a visiting priest
> intones to a faithful dormitory.
> I sit on my Protestant bed, a make-believe existentialist,
> and stare at the clouds of unknowing. We style,
> as best we may, our private destiny; or so it seems to me.
>
> (*SP* 105)

We need only cite 'Death and the Sun' (*SP* 192–4) to realise just how much the existential austerity of Albert Camus exercised its influence on Mahon. Alongside the key influence of MacNeice in the young Mahon's writing life, both of these writers played a defining part in giving confidence to Mahon's sense of *writing* and artistic *independence*. The profile of disenchantment is, even in this most cursory of looks, definitive. A writing 'career' is set against a writing 'life' and I would make the guess that Mahon's artistic presence, in Ireland, Britain and the U.S. is all about the latter rather than the former. For Mahon's writing seems to carry with it a kind of anger or unease, an 'edginess' (to quote Michael Longley) and questioning of present-day social and cultural values which is rare in poetry of the first order. As cultural history changes, or dumbs down, Mahon records the shifts as they take place; his poems are implicated in the process of the changes. And this makes Mahon's graceful use of English so shocking because he reveals through the urbane, sometimes chilly, yet often humorous and uncompromising voice of his poems a rebuttal to a widespread notion, recently articulated by Peter Porter in a largely hostile review of Seamus Heaney's *Opened Ground: Poems 1966–1996* that poetry in Ireland (with a few exceptions: Paul Muldoon, Ciaran Carson and Paul Durcan) is doomed to exempt itself 'from the 20th-century dilemma of discovering a contemporary language for poetry'. Porter goes on to complain that:

> Ireland enjoys the luxury of retaining a diction derived from pre-industrial society, the privilege of seeing the world in pastoral, even agricultural terms. [So much for Belfast!] Irish poetry . . . has chosen to follow the feudal Yeats, not the urban and demotic Joyce. It is Heaney's concentration on the narrow concerns of Irishness which is restricting: we want more of life in its wide-ranging social, artistic and spiritual dimensions than we are given in his poetry.[4]

I cannot think of a more simplistic line of argument than this but even accepting the terms of reference it is perfectly obvious that 'among contemporary Irish poets' Mahon preeminently does not live in 'a Wordsworthian landscape' and that his language is demonstrably 'urban', if not overtly 'demotic'. The old trick of wheeling out Mutt and Jeff, Yeats and Joyce, in the interest of creating what Mahon called (in another context) a 'pleasing symmetry', crumbles when Beckett joins the fathering figures because the whole critical business of what comes next begins to look much more complicated, much more like 'the more complex truth' which nobody wants to hear. In effect one can look to Mahon's poetry as an ongoing conversation with all of the founding fathers – Yeats and Joyce, Beckett and MacNeice, with Austin Clarke and Patrick Kavanagh in more recent times, getting their dues. Under which distorted critical dispensation must Mahon stand in for these claustrophobically 'narrow concerns of Irishness' that Porter sees as the 'privileges of an Irish poet'? I would suggest that Mahon has scuppered these concerns for good.

Addressing the 'intentions and procedures' of Samuel Beckett's poetry, as well as 'reaching an understanding of his failures', Mahon suggested in his review of Beckett's *Collected Poems in English and French* (1977) that Beckett 'extend(ed) the possibilities of English poetry, the more so since his work owes its beginning to a quite different set of premises from that to which the English poet is accustomed'.[5] I think that, notwithstanding some important reservations, this statement holds true for much of Mahon's own poetry, particularly in terms of those influences Mahon assimilates from European literary sources as much as the distinctive Irish consciousness at play in his work. In the creation of an existential clarity, with its verve, edginess and artistic self-awareness, the critical direction of Mahon's writing points a way ahead, 'from the burnt match to the farthest star'. But perhaps the most startling influence which Mahon brings to bear on contemporary poetry in English notwithstanding the well-documented critical respect with which his graceful, meditative poems are held – is the doubting, questioning voice 'in' the poems, a chastising artistic presence which is fast becoming a thing of the past.

Peter Ansorge in the Epilogue to his collection of essays, *From Liverpool to Los Angeles: On Writing for Theatre, Film and Television* (1997) makes the following point, summarising over twenty-five years of creative and editorial experience:

> The assumption that art is anger – that it is in opposition – appears to be far more problematic today. It exists hardly anywhere within the media. The younger writers and directors who pass through my office do not appear to be particularly angry. In fact they are all too eager to please – both audiences and the broadcaster. But then no one is asking the young to be angry. Even seemingly controversial work like *Trainspotting* appeals to a targeted young audience who share the writers' and directors' relish for Tarantino and the drug culture. As plays and films, they are not at heart truly challenging. Some would argue that this speaks for a fundamental change in the taste of the audience. But I can only see it as a failure of nerve.[6]

Whatever one may think of the specific points of reference here,

Ansorge raises a crucial point about the challenge to writer and audience alike of what actually constitutes art, opposition and anger in the shifting sands of current fashion. Mahon kept his nerve in this regard and it shows, as in the Swiftian 'At the Chelsea Arts Club', canto XI of Mahon's most recent collection *The Yellow Book* (1997):

> Everything aspires to the condition of rock music.
> Besieged by Shit, Sperm, Garbage, Gristle, Scum
> and other 'raucous trivia' we take refuge
> from fan migrations, police presence, road rage,
> narcotics, Abrakedabra, festive rowdytum,
> from Mick and Gazza, Hugh Grant, paparazzi,
> TOP TORIES USED ME AS THEIR SEX TOY
> and Union-jacquerie at its most basic
> in shadowy, murmurous citadels like this.

'SOLVING AMBIGUITY': THE SECULAR MYSTICISM OF DEREK MAHON

BRUCE STEWART

'It's old light, and there's not much of it. But it's enough to see by Margaret Atwood, *Cat's Eye*.[1]

In 1970 Derek Mahon wrote: 'Like Ireland itself (and I intend no sneer), the Irish poet is either unwilling or unable to come to terms with the "twentieth century".'[2] By this he was widely taken to mean that Irish poets had refused to acknowledge the dominant framework of modern culture – liberal, secular, agnostic – or to reject the privileged status conferred on nationality since the literary revival or, finally, to engage with a poetics that reflected the fragmentary nature of the individual and the prevailing relativities of culture and society. In short, they had chosen to follow the example of Yeats and Kavanagh in preference to that of Auden and MacNeice or the American and European moderns.[3] At about that date, his own poetry became a beacon to younger writers who took no keep of traditional pieties in culture, politics and religion.[4] By professing to be 'through with history' (*CP* 64), the title-character of 'The Last of the Fire Kings' became something of an emblem for all this. Colm Tóibín later wrote of the impression this made: 'I understand that to be the whole point of revisionism'.[5] In such a climate, Mahon was a by-word for scepticism and sophistication:[6] his models were Baudelaire, Camus, Beckett and the continental writers as well as the Graeco-Roman classics. Yet, much as his work was admired, his intellectual stance attracted warm discussion for reasons not unconnected with the Northern Irish conflict. For Edna Longley he was an example of 'the poet serving humanity on his own terms' while resisting 'the contrary pressure that would make him in the image of the people'.[7] For Seamus Deane his 'urbanity helps him to fend off the forces of atavism, ignorance and oppression which are part of his Northern Protestant heritage'; at the same time he was 'doomed by his disengagement from feeling as is atavism by its surrender to feeling'.[8] While one side treated Mahon as a pretext to pour scorn on Ulster Protestant culture the other set him up as a bulwark against cultural nationalism.

Mahon's Fire King challenged conventional Irish wisdom in more ways than one. In it, for instance, the unnamed speaker declares that he 'want(s) to be like the man / Who drops at night / From a moving train // And strikes out over the fields / . . . Not knowing a word of the language' (*CP* 53). In other words he does not wish to be tied by the umbilical cord of language that was standard issue for nationalists since the literary revival. Raised in Belfast and educated at Trinity College, Dublin, Mahon identified the true artist as an outsider, and with this stroke he repudiated the autochthonous version of Irish culture associated with the theme of 'sense of place' soon to be expounded magisterially by Seamus Heaney.[9] On that occasion, Seamus Heaney identified 'visionary desolation'[10] as the characteristic mark of Mahon's work. Ten years later he argued that the 'dominant mood' was one of 'being on the outside (where one had laboured spiritually to arrive) only to end up looking back nostalgically at what one knows are well-nigh intolerable conditions on the inside'[11] – a benign version of Deane's analysis. Clearly, matters would have been easier if Mahon had simply been a Nationalist or a Unionist – in either case a little more like John Hewitt whom Heaney was able to greet as 'another poet of our places'.[12]

Mahon's answer is given in an interview of 1981:

> Seamus is very sure of his place; I've never been sure of mine. My home landscape, and here I mean North Antrim where I spent most of my childhood holidays, and not Belfast where I was born, figures largely in my poems. Aside from these poems the place that the poetry occupies is not a geographical location; it's a community of imagined readership.[13]

What is striking here is the placatory tone. Not only does Mahon dissociate himself from his native city but he espouses the vocabulary of Irish literary criticism ('sense of place' being Heaney's and 'imagined communities' Benedict Anderson's hallmark contributions). A certain bending before the wind of nationalist rhetoric was to be characteristic of his writing in the future. Mahon is not, by temperament, a refuser and things that another modernist might object to have often provided him with his most effective themes: *metempsychosis*, 'spirit of place', and apotheosis of female divinity amongst them. For Heaney, at any rate, it became increasingly easy to laud Mahon's work in terms better-suited to his own. In a pre-publication notice for *The Hunt by Night* (1982), he wrote:

> This is Mahon's most exuberant and authoritative single volume to date. Some creative tremor has given him deepening access to his source of power; it is as if the very modernity of his intelligence has goaded a primitive stamina in his imagination.[14]

The nationalist trope of repressed chthonic forces emerging from the past, albeit *via* the extreme point of modernist alienation – the existentialist outsider turned nostalgic exile – similarly governs his account of 'A Disused Shed in Co. Wexford':

> This could be called visionary or symbolic: it is about the need to live and be known, the need for selfhood, recognition in the eye of God and the eye of the world, and its music is cello and homesick. A great sense of historical cycles, of injustice and catastrophe, looms at the back of the poems mind.[15]

In spite of wide differences in temper and development, both these Ulster poets share a good deal in common. What they share, in the first place, is a poetic dialogue. Just as Mahon's poem 'Lives' is dedicated to Heaney, so Heaney's *Seeing Things* (1991), a collection concerned with after-images and after-lives – elegies, in fact – is dedicated to Mahon. If this seems unremarkable in a literary ambience where dedications are so commonplace, it can also be taken to show that, where 'Lives' was conceived as an answer to the essentialist argument of Heaney's 'Bog Poems', *Seeing Things* (1991) goes through a door opened by Mahon in so many poems addressing time and being, the staple of his art.

The literary colloquy between Heaney and Mahon entered an acute stage after the publication of 'Bogland' and 'The Tollund Man' between 1968 and 1972.[16] The cultural politics of those poems have been discussed so often that it may be well to turn instead to a notice Heaney wrote for the painter T. P. Flanagan's water-colours 1971:

> The pictures are the afterlife of experience. . . . Occasionally the manifestations are dramatic and yearn openly back towards their local habitation, more often it is the name that reminds us that the ghosted forms once possessed the lineaments of place.[17]

The image of ghosts 'yearning back' towards the landscape they

had inhabited presented here implies a supernatural conception of
the relation between man and his environment of the very kind
that pervades Heaney's 'Bog Poems'. Heaney composed the first
of these, 'Bogland', on his return from a visit to Flanagan's home
in 1968. Much has been written about the way he sought to
establish a 'congruence' – as he once put it – 'between memory
and bogland', on the one hand, and 'for the want of a better word,
our national consciousness',[18] on the other. Not everyone
considered this a good thing: reviewing the collection *North*
(1975), for instance, Ciaran Carson called Heaney a 'laureate of
violence'.[19] By contrast, Mahon offered a series of witty responses
addressing philosophical rather than political aspects of the matter
and in particular the notion that the archaeological treasures of
Ireland are receptacles of national memory or conduits for the
national spirit. Put in other terms, he derided the idea that Irish
history concerns a metaphysical entity ('Irishness') and that the
national territory ('Ireland') has a greater regard for that entity
than any others living in it, whether the humble anemone or an
Ulster planter.

Mahon visited the topic of privileged relations between the
niche and its inhabitant numerous times, often revealing his
own ambivalence about the metaphysical questions involved no
less than his mistrust of romantic antiquarianism. In 'The
Archaeologist' he envisages a helicopter ride during which a
Neolithic hunter is spotted in an ancient landscape. On returning
by land, we are told, the scientists will find him dead, 'unkempt,
authentic, and furnace-eyed' – or else encounter a more modern
figure 'in tweeds and a hunting hat . . . out for a walk', who will
tell them, 'You must be mad to suppose that this rock / Could
accommodate life indefinitely' (*L* 12). The poem casts doubt upon
the notion that landscapes are sentient in the way suggested by
the 'Bog Poems'; at the same time, it proposes the idea that the
walker is a metamorphosis of the stone-age man while
entertaining the possibility that the archaeologists have mistaken
one for the other in their silly scientific way. (A further confusion –
intentional or otherwise – concerns the identity of the
archaeologist and may explain the change of title in reprints of the
poem.)[20] 'Entropy' is cast in the same intellectual mould: the
'earth-inheriting dandelions' and 'ditched bicycles', together with
'bronze shards of the monumental sculptor' and sundry survivors
'holing up' in 'terminal moraines' all bespeak the indifference of a
dying star to the denizens of its surface (*L* 30, *P* 49). It is the sheer
contingency of things rather than their connections that gives to

Mahon's early poems such driving energy and wit.

A studied argument for contingency is framed in the title-poem of the collection *Lives* (1972). For the most part this entails an extended parody of the idea of national revenants and reincarnated spirits, beginning:

> First time out
> I was a torc of gold
> And wept tears of the sun.
> (*CP* 44)

In the ensuing stanza Mahon's pointedly Celtic torc is unearthed and sold by a labourer in Newmarket-on-Fergus (an impertinent invention catching the ethnic mix of Ulster). Next, the 'I' who speaks the poem returns as a Greek oar – possibly the one that marks the unquiet grave of Palinurus – and after that a 'bump of clay / In a Navaho rug', to be followed by other metamorphoses in Texas and Tibet before finally appearing as an anthropologist equipped with dictaphone and credit card. With these incarnations behind him, the speaker challenges the ontological supposition that transmigrating souls retain their national identity from incarnation to incarnation. What is more, the sheer numbers of cultures involved in an anthropological perspective – and that perspective is the manifest subject of several poems – has the effect of evacuating the idea of cultural identity of any essential meaning:

> I know too much
> To be anything anymore . . .

This leads on directly to a philosophical injunction:

> And if in the distant

> Future someone
> Thinks he has once been me
> As I am today,

> Let him revise
> His insolent ontology
> or teach himself to pray.
> (*CP* 45–6)

'Lives' is dedicated to Seamus Heaney and may read – as one critic has said – as a riposte to the religious intensity with which Heaney presses his self-identifications.[21] True as this may be, it does not quite explain the call to prayer with which the poem ends. Here the speaker seems to take the moral high-ground in proposing that those who espouse the essentialist outlook associated with romantic nationalism are victims of a defective notion of spirituality as compared to those who address their prayers to a *deus absconditus* or the existentialist *Néant*. They are mistaken about their own grounds in being: hence the advice to 'revise (their) insolent ontologies'. By corollary Mahon seems to suggest that the very condition of rootlessness that informs his poetry constitutes a *via negativa* by means of which the only valid metaphysics can be framed.

That the word 'metaphysical' has a definite meaning for Mahon can be judged from his introduction to *The Sphere Book of Irish Verse* (1972). Here he reflects on the older Irish poets in terms that might be thought to embrace Seamus Heaney in some measure also:

> Their assumptions and credulities were those of the Irish country people of the time: and the Irish, for many years, returned the poets' reverence with reverence for a poetry which evaded the metaphysical unease in which all poetry of lasting value has its source.[22]

'Metaphysical unease' may be taken as expressing an affinity with the critical outlook enunciated by Samuel Beckett when he condemned the Irish poets' characteristic 'flight from self-awareness' in a review-article of 1934.[23] For further light we may turn to Mahon's early (and in many ways defining) poem 'Glengormley', where he wrote in ironic celebration of his native Belfast suburb:

> The unreconciled, in their metaphysical pain,
> Dangle from the lamp-posts in the dawn rain;
>
> And much dies with them . . .
>
> (*CP* 14)

The 'unreconciled' are those who cannot accept the life of 'terrier-taming, garden-watering days' which defines the existence of modern urban man. Among these are the kind of poets Mahon most admires, yet the speaker opts for reconciliation, ending on an apparently pessimistic note: 'By / Necessity, if not choice, I live here too' (*CP* 14). Elmer Andrews has offered a credible appraisal of Mahon's quicksilver rhetoric in this poem: 'With convoluting irony, he invokes the unreconciled and the damned as the only element in these diminished circumstances with which he can identify'.[24] The irony is underscored by the fact that metaphysical pain is precisely the source of 'poetry of lasting value' in Mahon's distinctly self-referential account, as we have seen.

In all of this Mahon has a mentor, as his *New Statesman* essay of 1977 on Samuel Beckett makes clear:

> In early articles and reviews Beckett spoke of a rupture and of poetry as the only way out of 'the tongue-tied profanity'. This rupture isn't the social and cultural phenomenon so often adumbrated by English poets, but rather a *metaphysical disjunction* between 'subject' and 'object', between the perceiving sensibility and everything external to it, from the burnt match to the farthest star. (Italics mine.)
>
> (*J* 56)

This locates poetic energies along the axis that extends between the noetic and noematic poles of perception (as phenomenologists in the tradition of Edmund Husserl have seen it). It further suggests that poetry is the product of the interaction between human consciousness and what Mahon calls 'mute phenomena'[25] – though Mahon's phenomena are curiously articulate, their utterances less indicative of issueless misery than the vanity of human wishes: 'Already in a lost hub-cap is conceived / The ideal society that will replace our own' (*CP* 82). In this context metaphysical pain can be seen to have two related sources: a gap between subject and object that gives consciousness its riven structure and secondly the knowledge that the self is limited in space and time, as Blaise Pascal famously observed (*le silence éternel de ces espaces infinis m'effraie*), and ultimately doomed to be extinguished along with matches, civilisations and stars, as Ovid portends (*tempus edax rerum*).

Mahon adds a third and more conventional reason for man's metaphysical plight in speaking of the death of God:

> (T)hat tongue-tied profanity has less to do with economic conditions than with, in Pascal's phrases, '*la misère de l'homme sans Dieu*'. Beckett himself, writing about the Irish poet Thomas MacGreevy, coined the phrase 'the existential lyric', and his own best poems come under this heading
>
> (*J* 56)

Beckett's adumbration of a world without God co-opts the sense of loss and separation recorded by the philosopher of Port Royale while leaving the theological burden where he found it. This sense of God as absent (*deus absconditus*) is part and parcel of the

Protestant tradition and it is easy to see why Mahon should relish finding it in Beckett. What is more, it secularises well: the principal actor may leave the stage but the theme persists to become, *inter alia*, the central matter of Beckett's *En attendant Godot* (1952) and many a Mahon poem. In this respect Mahon's best work often answers to that epithet 'existential lyric' though rarely stripped of rhyme, stanza, setting, theme and closure as Beckett's or MacGreevy's are. In this he displays a large indebtedness to the poetic craft of which Louis MacNeice was the past master whom Mahon expressly adopted as a model.[26]

Mahon has noted that what MacNeice 'latches on to is the existential tingle of the passing minute' (*J* 27), illustrating the point with some lines from 'London Rain':

> Whether the living river
> Began in bog or lake,
> The world is what is given,
> The world is what we make
> And we only can discover
> Life in the life we make.
>
> (*J* 27)

This sounds a little like existentialism, a movement with which MacNeice had no connection. Mahon's connection was never much stronger though he employs the word itself with some frequency – e.g., 'the existential, stark face of the cosmic dark' ('North Wind: Portrush', *CP* 100) and once called himself a 'make-believe existentialist' ('Dawn at St Patrick's', *CP* 170). In summarising the precepts of the movement in his review of Ronald Hayman's life of Sartre, he did so with dismissive blitheness:

> Same for everybody: choose your life, and don't be frightened of your freedom. You exist before you become, as a contingent blob, to be transformed or not as you wish. (Sartre) called this existentialism; to some it may seem like common sense. It is humanistic, but it must also be humane. When you choose, said Sartre, remember that your choice takes place in the human arena and is of necessity political; so make the right choice, Marx not God. He never got it quite clear why one should necessarily choose Marx, except that Marx was his own choice.
>
> (*J* 46–7)

On the question of influence more generally, Mahon offers a *caveat* within a *caveat* in writing of Beckett's literary and philosophical antecedents:

> (J)ust as it would be misleading to suggest that Beckett's long
> think is a sort of comic mime of the history of Western philosophy
> from the pre-Socratic to the Existentialist, so it would be a mistake
> to make too much of literary influence.
>
> (J 60)

Clearly, then, existentialist is the wrong term for Derek Mahon. In
the last analysis his intellectual outlook is equally remote from
Jean-Paul Sartre's as it is from Samuel Beckett's, as he lets us know
in 'Beyond Howth Head':

> The pros outweigh the cons that glow
> From Beckett's bleak *reductio* -
> And who would trade self-knowledge for
> A prelapsarian metaphor,
> Love-play of the ironic conscience
> For a prescriptive ignorance?
>
> (CP 53)

The 'ironic conscience' memorably cited here is not a frame of
mind that readily admits of close identification with literary
schools or movements. Mahon has always stood peculiarly alone
in that regard. At the same time he has consistently honoured
those writers who influenced or impressed him – amongst whom
Philippe Jaccottet, a selection of whose poems he published in
1988. Mahon wrote of Jaccottet in the introduction: 'he is a secular
mystic, an explorer of *le vrai lieu* ("the real place")', and went on to
explain:

> Nabokov, in *The Real Life of Sebastian Knight*, says of Clare Bishop
> that she possessed that real sense of beauty which has less to do
> with art than with the constant readinesss to discern the halo
> round a frying pan or the likeness between a weeping willow and
> a Skye terrier. They might have been speaking of Jaccottet.
>
> (J 19)[27]

Quoting this characteristically readerly comparison, Terence
Brown instances the 'Light Music' sequence and 'A Garage in Co.
Cork' as poems by Mahon where 'his own secular mysticism finds
expression' (J 19).

The rapport between Derek Mahon and Terence Brown is long-
established – they were near contemporaries at Trinity and Mahon
supplied an article in the volume on MacNeice which Brown
edited with Alec Reid in 1974.[28] It was, in addition, Brown's

coinage 'sceptical vision' that passed into critical currency as a
term for Protestant Ulster writers in a tradition including signally
(if not exclusively) Louis MacNeice and Derek Mahon.[29] Michael
Longley lent authority to this in his memoir of the Royal Belfast
Academical Institution where he 'encountered that tough
scepticism and disenchanted liberalism with which many
educated and moderate Protestants who cannot accept either
Nationalism or die-hard Unionism fill the vacuum which was',
he attests, 'most deeply articulated in Louis MacNeice's
imagination'.[30] Yet, as Mahon's career proceeded, it began to be
felt that scepticism was but one aspect of his poetic mind – a
systole requiring the diastole of visionary thought that Heaney
identified with him. Here the idea is not so much that the poet's
sight is troubled by visions in the Yeatsian sense as that he has
tapped into instinctual forces that lie closer to the region of
mysticism and religion than that of liberal agnosticism. Adrian
Frazier exemplified this new critical perspective in writing that the
title-poem in The Hunt by Night (1982) displayed 'a faith in the
midst of scepticism, hope through despair, and trust com-
mensurate with terror', especially where 'Night is accepted as the
Goddess of both our annihilation and our salvation'.[31]

'Mysticism' is certainly in some sense apposite to describe the
quality of sharpened perception and metaphysical awareness
irradiated by the fragmentary poems of 'Light Sequence', where
Mahon's hermeneutic attitude towards the natural order invites
just such an epithet, if deeply metaphorical in its application to an
agnostic poet. The compound term, 'secular mystic' though clearly
oxymoronic – since the frying-pan has no halo (unless viewed
short-sightedly in oblique light) is designed to bridge that gap.
The obvious thrust is that Mahon's perception of phenomena
resembles that of a religious mystic though shorn of the usual
theological associations: closer to William James than St. John of
the Cross. Yet mysticism implies something more than a sharpened
phenomenal awareness or even the 'theoptic' perspective to be
met with in the later poems (CP 141).[32] It imports a sense of the
presence or co-presence of a spiritual world along with the
physical world in which the poet lives. It is not clear how deeply
Mahon shares in this or whether his sense of the place of human
life in the universe admits of this interpretation. Indeed, his direct
engagements with the subject indicate a provisional rather than a
true-believer relation with the state of mind invoked by such an
epithet.

In the early poem 'The Mayo Tao' we are told:

> There is an immanence in these things
> which drives me, despite my scepticism,
> almost to the point of speech —
> like sunlight cleaving the lake mist at morning
> or when tepid water
> runs cold at last from the tap.
>
> (CP 69)

It is notable in these lines that 'immanence' and 'scepticism' are presented as mutually exclusive: a conflict has occurred and scepticism has come off worse – or 'almost' so. What Mahon attempts to show us here corresponds to the Aristotelian term *entelechy* – beloved of Joyce – denoting the way in which things reach their completed form in time.[33] Applied to inanimate objects, the idea is distinctly pantheistic. At the same time, it speaks cogently of an ontological whatness inhering in structures and ultimately touches on the idea of Pure Being in a larger metaphysical sense.[34] This might be seen as a mystical revelation but is better taken as the poetical expression of an acute perception of a kind familiar enough to those who are perceptually self-aware. By contrast, the coinage 'secular mystic' implies a synthesis of enspirited and inert conceptions of reality (unless 'secular' merely means non-denominational, anti-clerical, &c.). The speakers in a Mahon poem generally remain within the conventional parameters of theological debate: they are doggedly agnostic rather than merely secular – that is, atheist – being furnished with a full panoply of eschatological and teleological ideas, however those aspirants to eternity may be disappointed by the post-mortal vistas that they meet.

It is easier, in the main, to read those scenarios (including 'The Hunt by Night') as tokens of historical disappointment than as expressions of mystical enlightenment, albeit of the darker kind. In many cases the scenarios verge on the burlesque, as in 'The Apotheosis of Tins', where discarded objects give voluble utterance to their hopes and fears:

> Deprived of use, we are safe now
> from the historical nightmare
> and may give our attention at last
> to things of the spirit, noticing for example
> the consanguinity
> of sand and stone,
> how they are thicker than water,
> and the pebbles shorter than their shadow.
>
> (CP 69)

Here, as elsewhere, Mahon registers the strange allure of abandoned objects (more *pour soi* than *en soi*), cast adrift and forced to 'spend the night in a sewer of precognition' or wake 'amid shoe-laces . . . raw wind and the cries of gulls' (*CP* 69) – not unlike Beckettian tramps. The verses are crammed with *trouvailles* of no small ingenuity and interest, not least things of the spirit which hover between earnestness and jest: if tins have souls, spirit is ubiquitous; if spirit is ubiquitous, then this is prayer; if not, despair. The title of the poem itself reflects such ambiguity, while the ending affords a similarly double-edged interpretation: 'We shall be with you as long as there are beaches', the tins say in their ecological grief, while the museum guide enjoins us nobly to 'Think . . ./ what saintly / devotion to the notion of permanence / in the flux of sensation / and crisis' they exhibit. Tins are products of our incomparable ability as waste-makers but also autonomous creations with a spiritual value above our own. The first of these positions is certainly satirical, taking modern man as its butt; the second hovers between a joke at the expense of the credulous museum-trotters and a celebration of a real element of transcendence in the *detritus* that we strew around us. But these are rhetorical alternatives native to the poem and not mystical postulations in any extrinsic sense.

Next to 'A Disused Shed in Co. Wexford', the most favoured example of a visionary lyric in Mahon's *Collected Poems* in probably 'A Garage in West Cork', already cited by Terence Brown. The inner movement of this poem corresponds to what Brown has said in general of the poet's vision: 'For Mahon too is absorbed by the way light falls on the visible world to invest it with numinous presence and an impression of inherent relationships'.[34] The radiance of so many epithets ('rainbowed with oil-puddles . . . phosphorescent trail'), together with the eclectic glee of its narrative sallies '(the old pumps . . . / Antique now . . . squirting juice into a chrome / Lagonda') and, finally, the gravity of the social subject-matter ('Where did they go? South Boston? Cricklewood?' (*CP* 130)) serve to intensify the sympathy which the 'outsider' status of the speaker might be expected to diminish. To this Mahon adds a strand of reflection concerning a special quality to be met with in so many ghost-towns:

> Left to itself, the functional will cast
> A death-bed glow of picturesque abandon.
> The intact antiquities of the recent past,

> Dropped from the retail catalogues, return
> To the materials that gave rise to them
> And shine with a late sacramental gleam.
>
> (*CP* 131)

Here 'late' denotes tardiness in historical time as well as lateness in the day for these remainders. Yet 'late' also catches the sense of 'now extinct', as if to say that sacraments as a feature of our lives are now 'late lamented' in the undertaker's phrase. (There is a touch of 'Protestant magic' about this.)[36] Taken together, these hints suggest a diffuse elegy bearing on a world from which the spirit has been abstracted – though perhaps, too, a world in which the spirit is about to be released by the phosphorescent processes of decomposition. While 'sacrament' has obvious religious implications it serves here to capture the luminance of phenomena in their 'whatness' (*quidditas*) rather than the theology of transubstantiation.[37]

Not transubstantiation, indeed, but transmigration (or rather metamorphosis) is the dominant trope in the poem; for, at this point, Mahon ventures a mythological sally that introduces a very different kind of divinity to the scene. It seems that a Greek god who spent the night here once has rewarded the old man and his wife's 'natural courtesy' with eternal life by turning them into petrol pumps while the daughter who escapes 'his dark design' gets turned into a 'prickly shrine' (*CP* 131) (i.e., a rural grotto to the Virgin Mary). What follows directly after this, however, switches to quite another key:

> We might be anywhere but are in one place only
> One of the milestones of earthly residence
> Unique in each particular, the thinly
> Peopled hinterland serenely tense
> Not in the hope of a resplendent future
> But with a sure sense of its intrinsic nature.
>
> (*CP* 131)

From a sociological standpoint this might mean that the denizens of Co. Cork, faced with the haemiplegia of emigration (Celtic Tigers being still unheard of), must content themselves with a nutrifying 'sense of place' based on Seamus Heaney's well-known literary prescription when he wrote: 'The landscape was sacramental, instinct with signs, implying a system of reality beyond the visible realities'.[38] It is not that Derek Mahon has not followed this prescription: his distinguished poetry of place relates to venues as disparate as Cork, Achill, Kensington, Paris, Naxos and Manhattan. In 'Brighton Beach', for instance, Belfast flats and a Donegal fishing-quay are neatly juxtaposed with the place named in the title. Here, indeed, the underlying question is expressly faced. 'Now, in this rancorous peace, / Should come the spirit of place', the poet hopes, but then accedes to pessimism on the matter: 'Too late . . . for already / Places as such are dead / Or nearly' (*CP* 155). Notwithstanding the final phrase with its faint prevarication – Irish places an exception? – the effect is to suggest that the modern world has no time for suppositious connections between spirit and place, *geist* and matter: how, then, can the particular milestone in man's sublunary trek which is a disused petrol station-*cum*-homestead in Co. Cork possess an 'intrinsic nature' to comfort and console? Or the surrounding countryside either, notwithstanding its place in Irish history and legend?

Critics have been universally severe in their estimate of this stanza while Mahon himself has implied that he regards it as a failed attempt to reproduce the ending of 'A Disused Shed in Co. Wexford'.[39] Elmer Andrews holds it to exemplify 'a slackening of tension, lack of unity, a tendency to reduce and to simplify, a yielding to didactic resolutions which dogs Mahon's later lyrics'.[40] John Constable considers that the poet has 'distanced the images in a moralising conclusion'.[41] Both seem to feel that the difficulty of sustaining an essentially non-thetic apprehension of the place eludes the poet at the last moment. It might equally be guessed that the shift in gear to mythopoeic fancy, magnificent though it is, held uneasy company with talk of Irish emigration. There is a distinct air of diplomacy in a conclusion that concedes so much to the place-centred ideology of cultural nationalism.[42] William Wilson has wondered about 'what degree we should credit the priority of place over history in Mahon's poetry'.[43] Yet Mahon's alienation from community and place has never been as extreme as critics (including those who see it as a forte) have suggested. Places may be dead, but this is an elegiac theme, not a cause for post-modernist satisfaction. Mahon is not the enemy of a 'sense of place' any more than he is the enemy of transcendence: he is their elegist. Occasionally, he evinces a distinct yearning as when, in an interview, he said, 'I suppose home for me would be a little place in County Antrim called Cushendun, where both my children were baptised.[44] (The self-confessed sentimentality of the assertion that the Glens of Antrim are a little bit of 'real Ireland' which follows reveals the effects of homesickness on the poet in America.)

The 'spirit of place' made its way into an earlier review of Brian Moore's novel *Catholics* (1972) where Mahon offered an enthusiastic eulogy of the Belfast-born novelist – a Northern-Irish Catholic whom he saw as eschewing the formulas of organised religion to return to essential spirituality in the later novels:

> Having lost interest in Catholicism as such, whilst retaining an interest in the Catholic church as a determining influence in the social and psychological backgrounds of his Irish characters, he now moves into an area we associate with Catholic writers like Bernanos and (in a different way) Greene. Is he going back to the fold? I think not. His new-found interest in religion is less theological than poetic, and intimately bound up with the spirit of place.
>
> (*J* 65)

Clearly Mahon was fascinated by the novel with its meditation on the consequences for Catholicism of surrendering the idea of miracles – and especially the eucharistic miracle (that 'God is . . . actually present, there in the tabernacle') – in favour of a symbolic interpretation involving the more provisional idea of 'an unbeliever's faith'.[45] The effect, presumably, would be a form of 'secular mysticism'.

In 1976 Mahon published a much fuller account of Moore's fiction – actually longer than any other critical piece from his hand except his essay on 'MacNeice, War and the BBC'. On this occasion he wrote:

> Although a lapsed Catholic, he retains, like Joyce, the sacramental sense. An object, for Moore, is more than the sum of its atoms; it contains within it a racial memory of its raw material.
>
> (*J* 69)

Once again, Mahon focuses upon Moore's relation to the spiritual. He now digresses to cite David Jones's remarks in *Anathémata* on the limited value of water without the sacrament of baptism before resuming: 'Repeatedly in Moore's work food and water are associated with spiritual well-being and their absence or perversions with "the hell of metaphysicians"' (*J* 70). Adverting next to *Fergus* (1970) – a novel in which the central character, a writer, escapes from the oppressive religion of his youth into the imaginative freedom through intense hallucinatory encounters with family, girlfriends and others from his past – Mahon retales

Moore's aesthetic *credo*:

> The novelist as God, as creator of that supreme fiction, the world
> imagined, now puts his cards on the table. We are to understand
> that, in a universe without God, the religion of art is the only hope
> of salvation from the hell of metaphysicians.
>
> (J 73)

In rejecting existentialism ('hell is other people') while embracing
'metaphysical unease', Mahon shows what a thin line he walks in
regard to Christian and post-Christian metaphysics. In welcoming
sacramentalism as an artistic impulse without embracing it as a
theological doctrine, he could be said to rub agnostic salt in the
metaphysical wound. This puts the modernist poet in an
ambiguous position: as with Joyce's *alter ego* Stephen Dedalus, it
might be thought that his religion has been injected the wrong
way. The forms of faith are present but not the content. His
scepticism tortures him with belief, his belief with scepticism,
producing the amalgam that Terence Brown has called 'secular
mysticism'.

There is a certain futility in trying to decide whether Derek
Mahon is or is not a' secular mystic'. There are also dangers in
the term: how it serves the critics is one thing, how it serves
the poet is another. Every admirer of his work must welcome
the acknowledgement that his art is not merely sceptical but
celebratory also and this is a positive merit of the term. In this
Mahon is the poetic son of Louis MacNeice whose Church of
Ireland origins (like his own) have served Irish literary criticism in
just this way in recent years. In a somewhat melodramatic reading
of the case, John F. Deane has argued that MacNeice's upbringing
in a 'zealot faith' induced him to 'despair of any form of
humanism' with the effect that his poetry 'charts his personal
decline from faith into gnawing emptiness'.[46] On a truer note,
Gerald Dawe and Terence Brown have drawn on MacNeice's
autobiography to show how extensively his mind was formed by
early religious experience and, throughout his adult life, how he
continued to associate the country of his birth with spirituality in
spite of demurs about its record in the present (chiefly rendered in
Canto XVI of *Autumn Journal*).

MacNeice himself had much to say about the place of mysticism
in modern culture, chiefly in the context of his brilliant study
of W. B. Yeats where the tone may be judged from his remarks
on Walter Pater's influence: 'Pater supplied Yeats with a belief
in the importance of passion, a belief in the importance of

style, a distrust of the vulgar world, and a curious sort of aesthetic pantheism'[47] – the last-named another term that might easily stand in for the currently fashionable 'secular mysticism'. In debating the question of mysticism so dear to Yeats, MacNeice departed from a series of intellectual strictures about the pervasively secular ethos of modern society – liberal, or socialist or otherwise:

> Man cannot live by courage, technique, imagination – alone. He has to have a sanction from outside himself. Otherwise his technical achievements, his empires of stocks and shares, his exploitation of power, his sexual conquests, all his apparent inroads on the world outside, are merely the self-assertion, the self-indulgence, of a limited self that whimpers behind the curtains, a spiritual masturbation.[48]

He believed, in other words, that wherever God fails to exist, Man must invent him – or at else some transcendent power to motivate and underpin our value-system.

> Man is essentially weak and he wants power; essentially lonely, he creates familiar daemons, Impossible Shes, and bonds – of race and creed – where no bonds are. He cannot lie by bread or Marx alone; he must always be after the Grail.[49]

The tone is sceptical – grails are imaginative constructs and no more – yet MacNeice has obvious regard for the life-blood of religion: 'Mysticism, in the narrow sense, implies a specific experience which is foreign to most poets and most men, but on the other hand it represents an instinct which is a human *sine qua non*.[50] Moreover,

> (b)oth the poet and the 'ordinary' man are mystics incidentally and there is a mystical sanction or motivation for all their activities which are not purely utilitarian (possibly, therefore, for *all* their activities) as it is doubtful whether any one does anything purely for utility.)[51]

It is generally understood that MacNeice espoused no particular ideology or creed. While sharing 'the generalised left-wing tendencies of his Oxford and Cambridge contemporaries' – as Mahon himself has put it – 'he was apprehensive about the rise of Fascism, conventionally dubious about Communism, hostile to capitalism, and indifferent to formal religion – the very model, in fact, of a liberal intellectual' (J 24). According to D. B. Moore, his agnosticism was central to his poetic talent: 'MacNeice could find neither spiritual faith, political belief, or personal love and understanding to form the basis of his poetry, but relied instead on conflicts and indecision'.[52] At the same time, it is certain that the childhood loss of a mother together with the grim evangelism of his father's household produced a psychological trauma that shaped his sensibility. Michael Longley has expressed it thus: 'The autobiographical writing indicates that he was terrorised by a precocious sense of sin and feelings of guilt which were connected with early encounters with death and mental illness'.[53]

In examining MacNeice's attitude towards the places of his childhood, Terence Brown professed a view which was destined to become orthodoxy: 'The dark shadows of that County Antrim rectory remain to haunt a mind ready to salute an Ireland that could now somehow represent psychological release and spiritual intimations'.[54] The effect is to provide recent Ulster poets in the Protestant tradition with a precursor who is no less mystical – and, one might add, no less Irish – for being an agnostic. MacNeice's latent mysticism can be seen to shine through such poems as 'Snow' and 'Train to Dublin', but also 'Bagpipe Music' and in 'Prayer Before Birth' whose 'vivid anarchy' Mahon has specifically applauded (*J* 34). Yet, in listing these, Mahon characteristically eschews any attempt to define the philosophical outlook to which they bear witness beyond identifying them with the values whose loss [MacNeice] imagines in the following lines from 'An Eclogue for Christmas':

> We shall go down like Palaeolithic Man
> before some new Ice Age or Genghiz Khan.
>
> (*J* 34)

The interest of these lines is greatly amplified by their probable role as an inspiration for the many poems in which Mahon himself strikes a similarly chiliastic note – poems such as 'Girls in their Seasons' ('. . . keep me warm / Before we go plunging into the dark for ever' (*P* 24)), and 'Bruce Ismay's Soliloquy' ('I . . . hear . . . my costly / Life go thundering down in a pandemonium of /Prams, pianos, sideboards, winches' (*P* 32)), or even 'Ghosts', set in Pompeii ('we found an old hotel . . . where, with a squeal of seagulls far below, / white curtains blew like ghosts into the room' (*CP* 271)). In 'An Unborn Child' Mahon emulates MacNeice in theme if not in treatment ('I . . . produce in my mouth the words, I want to live!' (*CP* 27)), but devised an eschatological framework of his own for such poems as 'Consolations of Philosophy' where stout middle-class citizens enjoy an after-life of second thoughts in the grave ('There will be time to live through in the mind / The lives we might have lived and get them right' (*CP* 50)). It is here that the metaphysical thread in his poetry – always something less than belief in resurrection – seems to emerge from the mesh of ironies to suggest that consciousness of its very nature refuses demolition. Yet Mahon also recognises (what he must recognise) that life is circumscribed by time and, even if alternative existences can be imagined, the one we have is finite: hence the quick glimpse in 'Glengormley' of Finn McCool and St. Patrick, those 'heroes who have struggled through the quick noose of their finite being' to live on (*CP* 14).

The finite nature of individual lives is a subject that lends itself particularly well to dramatic treatment in the context of the Graeco-Roman classics – itself an elegiac strategy in regard to literary history. 'Heraclitus on Rivers' provides an opportunity to rehearse the theoretical situation. 'Nobody steps into the same river twice' (*CP* 114): this is so because of the nature of water and equally because of our changing metabolism which ensures that 'you are not longer you' (*CP* 114). The impact on romantic love is dealt with briskly: 'the precise configuration of the heavenly bodies' when the lover professes her love 'will not come again in this lifetime'. In the realm of art, too, the bronze monument (pace Horace's *aere perennis*) is ultimately perishable, and even

> The very language in which the poem
> Was written, and the idea of language,
> . . . will pass away in time.
> (*CP* 114)

Mahon explores the caducity of human institutions and those who inhabit them in 'Tithonus', taking as his vehicle the legend of a beautiful Trojan youth who asked the god for immortality but omitted to ask for youth, and was mercifully changed by Eros into a cricket. The only inmate of the classical dictionary whom he envies in this state is Endymion '(w)hom Selene fixed up / With eternal youth // And placed in a coma / To obviate insomnia' (*SP* 171). Perhaps it is the coma that he envies. Having outlived Man and even nature, he inhabits a world devastated by the wars of civilisation – listed in profusion – and awaits in no great confidence a personal 'transfiguration' (*SP* 168). These mordantly facetious verses are offset by solemn epigraphs from the Book of Kings ('. . . and after the fire a still small voice') and Beckett's *Unnamable* ('Worm will see the light in the desert'). On this showing, then, there is something that survives our transitory condition. 'Ovid in Tomis', written to the same poetic template,

offers an even saltier montage combining classical lore with all the
bric-a-brac of our own prolificly wasteful civilisation; yet it ends
up with a very definite mythopoeic postulation. Having scouted a
future in which his sojourn at Tomis is commemorated in 'a statue
of *me*' amid the 'Martini terraces' of a Black Sea resort, the exiled
Roman poet lays claim to an insight consonant with his standing
as the author of *Metamorphoses*.

> I have a real sense
> Of the dumb spirit
> In boulder and tree;
> . . .
> the infinity
> Under our very noses
>
> The cry at the heart
> Of the artichoke,
> The gaiety of atoms.
>   (*SP* 184, 186)

'Pan is dead' (*SP* 185), the poet tells us; yet, in an access of
pantheistic feeling, he concludes his poem: 'Better to contemplate
/ the blank page / And leave it blank seeing that it is woven of
wood-nymphs' (*SP* 186). Those wood nymphs are the kin of
Syrinx whose 'keening' at the vision of her 'certain future' as
'cording / For motor-car tyres' provides a tingling imaginative
sally mid-way through the poem. Paper with such magical origins
– Syrinx was turned into a reed – 'speaks volumes / No-one will
ever write'. Yet the contrary of this sentiment lies under the
reader's hand though that does not preclude the possibility of
those words themselves participating in the nature of the mythical
and divine. (Is not the poem itself an example of *metempsychosis*?).

Mahon's engagement with time and being compasses the
decline and fall of individuals no less than societies and types. The
personal elegies are devoid of consolation as regards a Christian
after-life but they often celebrate a more tenuous – and more
imaginative – kind of spiritual persistence in the legacy of
remembrance and art. Mahon's elegy at the grave of Louis
MacNeice ('In Carrowdore Churchyard') assures the elder poet
that his 'plot (is) consecrated . . . To what lies in the future tense'
(*SP* 11), and identifies his literary posterity with the coming of
spring like an all-clear after times of war. Mahon's monument to
his grandfather, in the poem of that title, incorporates a crucial
play on words which suggests that human personality eludes any

attempt to confine it ('Nothing escapes him; he escapes us all' (*SP* 13)), while the deceased grandparent in 'A Refusal to Mourn' is similarly promised a ludic form of immortality when 'his name (is) mud once again' (*CP* 87). For, in spite of that reduced condition, 'the secret bred in the bone' will be perpetuated in

> Other times and lives
> Persisting for the unborn
> Like a claw-print in concrete
> After the bird has flown.
> (CP 88)[55]

The levity of that final verse cannot undo the finality of death or dissipate the grimness of decomposition but it does transcend the fear of sheer annihilation with its suggestion that something actually escapes the wreck to live again in whatever form. This is, of course, the common consolation of secular society: genes and memes are the only form of post-mortal survival we are entitled to look for any longer.

The demise of parents can produce intense poetical meditations on the metaphysical questions that death raises: Seamus Heaney's *Seeing Things* (1991) gives warm testimony to that. By contrast, Mahon's poem on his mother's death, 'A Bangor Requiem' can hardly be called an elegy at all. Its dearth of compassion or involvement suggests an uncomfortable degree of alienation from familial background, class, caste, and even native place. In common with 'The Sea in Winter' (*CP* 115–7) and its prose counterpart 'The Coleraine Triangle' (*J* 216–9), it reads like a stock-taking of the petty-bourgeois society that drove the unreconciled to hang themselves (or be hanged) from the Glengormley lamp-posts. Paradoxically, the sentiment directed towards the mother is magnificent in articulation of emotional failure (unlike mawkish passages in 'The Hudson Letter'):

> Little soul, the body's guest and companion
> this is a cold epitaph from your only son,
> the wish genuine if the tone ambiguous.
> Oh, I can love you now that you're dead and gone
> to the many mansions of your mother's house . . .
> (CP 261)

'(A)ll artifice stripped away, we give you back to nature' (*CP* 261): and there the matter seems to end for the *anima parvula* of Hadrian's song, except that the poet admits his share in her posterity: 'something of you, perhaps, the incurable ache / of art, goes with me as I travel south . . . all the way (to) the blue skies of the republic' (*CP* 261).

A more ancient republic mentioned elsewhere in the poem evokes Plato's ideal world in which transitory beings are lodged in an eternity of pure form. Mahon recalls his mother, in her later years, 'wool-gathering by Plato's firelight / a grudging flicker of flame on anthracite' (*CP* 260), and then imagines her returning to her kitchen, its 'bread-bin and laundry-basket awash with light', as if some such kind of immortality awaited her as a quiet revenant in her own home. Sombrely the poet concludes that her neurotic involvement with 'nylon and bakelite' and 'frantic kitsch decor' during the anxious time that was her life precludes that kind of apotheosis. On this reckoning she is unlikely to be counted among the angels who inhabit the 'Dutch interiors' where 'cloud-shadows move' (*CP* 260) – a kind of Protestant heaven in the idiom of 'Courtyards in Delft'. (Mahon has said that his poem 'Courtyards in Delft', which centres on the Dutch interiors of Pieter de Hooch, is 'about Protestantism'.[56]) On this reckoning, the slender mead of eternity assured for Mrs. Mahon is her son's ambivalent remembrance and an exiguous place in his art. Yet, in one of the more pointedly self-reflexive ironies of this poem, Mahon allows his mother to possess a share of his own artistic temperament: she is an 'artist', if only in a pathological sense that finds expression in 'junk chinoiserie and coy pastoral scenes' (*CP* 260). Her kitsch aesthetic is the distaff side of a 'man's aesthetic of cars and golf' (*CP* 260). In her attention to the ornaments and breakable stuff she proves herself to be 'a rage-for-order freak' (*CP* 260), and in this we are reminded of the poem of that title in which the claims of art are presented in an uncharacteristically emboldened form:

> Watch as I tear down
>
> To build up
> With a desperate love,
> Knowing it cannot be
> Long no till I have need of his
> Terminal ironies.
>   (*CP* 48)

The final phrase has been subjected to notoriously frequent alteration, appearing in successive printings as 'germinal ironies' (*L* 1972), 'desperate ironies' (*P* 1979) and 'terminal ironies' (*CP* 1999).[57] To some readers the shift from 'germinal' to 'desperate' has suggested a failure of nerve on the poet's part. For Andrew Waterman – a poet unreasonably hostile to Ulster writing though occasionally formidable in criticism[58] – an 'adjective intimating connection and growth' in the first version has been replaced by another that seems 'gloomy, merely personal'[59] in the *Poems 1962–1978* (1979). From this he infers: 'Mahon's talent, which has blazed a lonely track in Ulster poetry and created some fine unique poems, seems now in a state of critical fatigue, with little among the ingredients of his recent writings to suggest direction along which decline might prove reversible'.[60] It is hardly necessary to remark that the astonishing series of strong poems gathered in the 1981 pamphlet *Courtyards in Delft* (including 'The Hunt by Night' which gave its title to the highly-acclaimed 1985 collection) refutes this necromantic assessment as completely as any literary forecast has ever been refuted. More to the point, Waterman failed to grasp the true import of the brilliant coinage 'eddy of semantic scruple' which justly drew so much attention when it appeared in 'Rage for Order', a poem not without excesses as regards the self-adulation of the poets' guild. Semantic *scruple* means precisely that: an epistemological instability which not only admits to uncertainty and change in the linguistic fabric of the poem but positively enjoins the task of continual revision. *Not* to revise, under such circumstances, might be the greater dereliction.

It may be noted that the phrase 'secular mystic' which Mahon applied to Jaccottet and which Terence Brown applied to Mahon by returns, was applied to Mahon by Douglas Dunn, as William Scammell recalls.[61] Mahon's response to the point-blank question posed by Scammell in that connection is worth citing:

> I am not any kind of mystic, though I can think of worse things to be ... but I do believe poetry and religion *are* related, at least in origin, as are theatre and dance. When Plato banished the poets what he was banishing was the subversive Dionysian spirit, which is lyrical and unamenable to rational explanation and control.[62]

Mahon moves between the Apollonian and the Dionysian in highly conscious, though by no means artificial, ways. In spite of some of the names he mentions in illustration of the mystic strain ('Yeats, Dylan Thomas, Pound and Graves – even Eliot'),[63] his own method is tentacular without being in any sense vatic. His ample vocabulary of metaphysical ideas is the stuff out of which the poems are made not the transcendental reality they reveal. This is by no means a demeaning conclusion. On the contrary, one measure of Derek Mahon's achievement is the fact that he has succeeded in combining a heightened sensitivity to phenomenal impressions and their traditional counterparts in mythology and religion – all conveyed with extraordinary lexical resourcefulness without blunting the edge of his philosophical scepticism.

Again and again it is the 'existential tingle' of some moment, whether given in immediate experience or mediated by cultural awareness, that provides the signature in his poems. Often this involves a definite ambiguity of ideas. By way of example, 'A Swim in Wicklow' – first collected in 1999 – ends with this resonant sentence: 'But today you swirl and spin . . . as if . . . life were a waking dream / and this were the only life' (*CP* 281). On the surface the poet seems to take the existence of another life for granted, yet the poem only begins to make sense when we adopt the view that he actually believes the contrary: this *is* the only life (there is no 'as if' about it). The allusion to Keats's 'waking dream' confirms this: among discrete presences in the poem are the 'hungry generations' who tread us down in 'Ode to a Nightingale'. It is the perceptual effect of immersion in a numinous-seeming landscape that engenders the metaphysical impression of a more real world elsewhere. Intimations of mortality have rarely been better caught, yet it is *intimations* rather than *immortality* that remains in our minds. In case the point is missed Mahon supplies an epigraph from Montale that argues how irrelevant the debate between matter and spirit, world and eternity, agnosticism and religion, really is: 'The only reality is the perpetual flow of vital energy' (*CP* 280). 'A Swim in Wicklow' presents the reader with an irresolvable ambiguity: either an after-life exists or it does not; yet, in the poem it both exists and doesn't, while its existence and non-existence are simultaneously savoured and lamented. Ambiguity is indeed the way the poem works so far as its thetic contents are concerned. Early in his career, Mahon arrived at the notion of resolving ambiguities which he posited as an ordering principle to put alongside the supreme fiction postulated by Wallace Stevens.[64] The idea that ambiguities *solve* anything is paradoxical as regards the incompatible meanings involved in them, yet they can give rise to fertile connections in poetry (as William Empson showed) and thus embody the liberal-humanist outlook in an exemplary form.

It is notable that Mahon himself owns contradictory ideas, as we know from a revealing interview where he spoke frankly as an atheist about the reality of experience, plotting his position in terms of a comparison with W. B. Yeats whose *Autobiographies*

(1955) tell how he was deprived of faith by his father's scepticism and so turned to the occult. Mahon continues:

> I don't think I have a religious nature in that sense but I have a consciousness of things over and above, beside and below human life. I am deprived of belief in God, if deprivation it is, by my own rationalistic habits of mind, my own education, and yet there is . . . I make room for the numinous, for the unexplained.[65]

As regards the numinous, Mahon's position is not perhaps very different from that of Brian Moore's novel *Fergus* (1972) as he described it in 1988: 'As the work proceeds (. . .) the reader is presented with the real possibility of spiritual significance; however this remains no more than a possibility giving rise to these alternative interpretations: either the world may be alive with messages, or the book may be no more than a semiotic puzzle' (*J* 79). The contrasting spheres of spirituality and semiotics, mysticism and scepticism, metaphysics and cultural relativity are conventionally opposed, yet Mahon succeeds in making them mesh like gears in poem after poem. Is this what is meant by *secular mysticism*? If so, it may be the right name for his intellectual temper. In the last analysis, Mahon's poetic universe comprises 'everything that is the case, imaginatively' – nothing more and nothing less, as he tells us in a revised version of Wittgenstein's apothegm ('Tractatus', *CP* 120). To suppose otherwise may be a case of wishful thinking on the part of literary critics. How far the poet shares in that is another question.

DEREK MAHON: HISTORY, MUTE PHENOMENA AND BEYOND

JERZY JARNIEWICZ

In his free translation of Gérard de Nerval's poem 'Mute Phenomena', Derek Mahon departs from the traditional distinction between the physical world, subject to time, and the ideal, noumenal world that transcends sensory experience. This distinction, rooted in Platonic dualism, gives place in the poem to the characteristically Mahonian opposition between the world of humankind and the world of inanimate objects. What differentiates the two worlds is their relation to time and voice.

Though both human beings and mute phenomena exist in a temporal reality, in each case we are dealing with a different understanding of time. Human time, exclusively *human*, is known as history. It is characterized by the linearity that links birth with death, creation with apocalypse, and hence it is the realm of destruction and decay, where noise, arbitrariness and chaos reign. By contrast, the time of mute phenomena is a time beyond history – it is cyclic and, in a special sense which I shall define later, paradoxically eternal.

History is one of the key terms in the criticism of Derek Mahon's poetry. It appears in numerous articles and reviews, functioning as a starting point for analysis of other aspects of Mahon's work, such as his sense of belonging, his aestheticism, the theme of metamorphosis, the question of identity and Irishness. It is significant, and I think not at all surprising, that Peter MacDonald's essay despite its title, 'History and Poetry',[1] for the first half a dozen pages deals not with history as such, but with place, linking the two, later on, with the idea of community.

'History' is an ambiguous and emotionally charged noun. In one of its meanings it is synonymous with time. In that sense anything that exists in the phenomenal world, both human beings and inanimate objects, is subject to history: everything begins,

83

transforms itself, and terminates. In Platonic dualism, history in this sense is the realm of illusion; true knowledge can be gained only by transcending it. It should be observed here that Mahon does not identify history with time.

In another, narrower and more popular sense, history is a series of past events formed into a narrative. This type of history is a particularly human phenomenon, endowed with its own voice.

But there is also another meaning of history, defined by Raymond Williams as a continuous process due to which 'products of the past are active in the present and will shape the future in knowable ways'.[2] History emerges here as a powerful determining factor, synonymous with fate, the mechanism of relentless, inescapable continuity.

It seems to me that it is primarily with the third meaning that Mahon's poetry is concerned. And it is with that type of history that Mahon conducts his polemical dispute, or as some critics would have it, it is from that type of history that he seeks to escape. Edna Longley, in her essay '"When Did You Last see Your Father?" Perceptions of the Past in Northern Irish Writing 1965–1985', noticed that in Irish literature 'the past as continuum looms larger than the past as mortality'.[3] Irish writers, she adds, 'are obsessed with the irreversible presentness of the past'. Mahon takes issue with this understanding of history. The past to him means mortality, i.e. it is a closed chapter which cannot be read again. That is why he prefers to project his visions into the future, rather than look back at the irretrievable past.[4] It can be argued that Mahon's suspicious attitude towards visions of history as a continuum, linking past, present, and future, is the attitude of someone who remembers that historians (in the words of Kenneth McLeish) have often worked 'as cultural nationalists, constructing epic narratives of the origins, tragedies and triumphs of their nations'.[5] The linear ordering of events into a narrative creates an illusion that it is possible to turn back and return to past events, which by virtue of their continuity in the *hic et nunc* acquire the status of mythical origins. Mahon opposes this view of time in an ironic poem called 'Lives', dedicated to Seamus Heaney, which engages in a polemical dialogue with the author of *North* and his vision of the continuity of history.

Another reason for Mahon's distrust of history, apart from the fact that it is the foundation of essentialist thinking, is its highly selective character. History excludes more than it includes, and in this sense it is an annihilating force, leaving behind it numerous lost tribes, the subject of a number of Mahon's poems. Thus history, rather than imposing order on chaos, offers us a perspective which impoverishes the world and blinds us to the 'drunkenness of things being various'. The poet tries to redeem the phenomena that have been marginalized by history and ignored by grand narratives. Never too far from the Romantic paradigm, Mahon takes on the role of a truly Promethean figure, who challenges a force greater than the gods: history. He gives a voice to those mute phenomena which have not been incorporated into any narrative, phenomena like the mushrooms in 'A Disused Shed in Co. Wexford' which belong to the temporal world, but have been exiled from history and consequently deprived of the capacity to speak for themselves. And yet Mahon, the sceptic, is aware of the impossibility of the task he sets himself. A history that includes all the events that have ever occurred is a purely theoretical construct; it cannot be reproduced, nor for that matter even imagined. Non-selective history is impossible; it has always been and always will be a dispossessing, discriminating force. This contradiction between the will to include everything that has ever existed, the attempt not to forget a single phenomenon, and the impossibility of such an attempt is dramatized in Mahon's poem 'Tithonus':

> I forget nothing
> But if I told
> Everything in detail -
>
> Not merely Golgotha
> And Krakatoa
> But the leaf pink
>
> Of rain-drops after
> Thermopylae,
> The lizard-flick
>
> In the scrub as Genghis
> Khan entered Peking,
> And the changing clouds,
>
> I would need
> Another eternity,
> Perish the thought.

In his attempts to transcend history, Mahon does not invoke the Platonic world of ideas that exists outside the categories of space and time. Remembering that history is an exclusively human dimension, Mahon abandons the human world and confronts the world of mute phenomena. The muteness of these things is the effect of their exclusion from great historical narratives. To be sentenced to exist outside history (which is the territory of voice) is to be dispossessed of speech. Yet the voice of history is often a mistaken or misleading voice, if not a simple noise whose only function is to cover the vested interests of those who write historical narratives. If then the voice of history is corrupt and suspect, silence stands for the true, undistorted reality, or in fact – the state of innocence. Silence embodies the only reliable knowledge; it is also the only adequate reaction to reality. In 'The Banished Gods' Mahon writes:

> thought is a fondling of stones
> And wisdom a five minute silence at moonrise.

All Mahon's epiphanies are born of silence, all his soul landscapes where mind meets the real are invariably silent.

I have not come across any information that would lead me to think that Mahon has read any Polish poets, apart perhaps from a remark that he made years ago in a conversation with his Polish translator Piotr Sommer.[6] Mahon admitted then to having been influenced by Romantic poets, Keats particularly, but also by the Polish poet Adam Mickiewicz, whose poem 'Mushroom Picking' in Donald Davie's translation was supposedly one of the sources for 'A Disused Shed in Co. Wexford'. Yet although Mahon, unlike Heaney or Paulin, does not admit to any knowledge of Polish poetry, his interest in mute phenomena, which results from his resentment of history, may be seen as analogous to, though by no means identical with, similar concerns in the works of Zbigniew Herbert, Wislawa Szymborska and Czeslaw Milosz. These poets all turned towards mundane, degraded objects, seeing them as the only reality which in the falsified world of the twentieth century remains authentic, simple, undistorted, and real, and as such can serve as a foundation on which morality and metaphysics can be rebuilt. 'Only what is human can truly be foreign. / The rest is mixed vegetation, subversive moles, and wind'. This is not Derek Mahon, but Szymborska, though it seems the words might have been written by Mahon himself. Zbigniew Herbert in his poem 'The Knocker' writes:

> my imagination
> is a piece of board
> my sole instrument
> is a wooden stick

I strike the board
it answers me
yes-yes
no-no[7]

And in the poem entitled 'The Pebble' Herbert depicts a truly
Mahonian mute phenomenon, albeit in a non-Mahonian abstract
diction:

The pebble
is a perfect creature

equal to itself
mindful of its limits

filled exactly
with a pebbly meaning

with a scent which does not remind one of anything
does not frighten anything away does not arouse desire

its ardour and coldness
are just and full of dignity

I feel a heavy remorse
when I hold it in my hand
and its noble body
is permeated by false warmth

– Pebbles cannot be tamed
to the end they will look at us
with a calm and very clear eye[8]

The silence of such objects as the pebble or the knocker is the
language of undistorted wisdom, too easily discarded, ignored
and rejected as non-language. In contemporary Polish poems, as
well as in Mahon's, objects are not mute in themselves; they are
mute to us. It is only humans who do not listen to them, humans
who do not hear 'their revolutionary theories'. Yet they speak the
language of silence, like the stone on the road in Mahon's 'The
Mayo Tao' which tells its sob-story: 'the best, most monotonous
sob-story I have ever heard'.

Let me now briefly compare Seamus Heaney's interest in mute
phenomena with Mahon's. Both poets, just like their Polish

counterparts, turn towards concrete objects in a situation of
political upheaval and historical pressures. In a society in which
history is, in Tom Paulin's words, 'an unescapable condition',[9]
objects offer them a standpoint free from the havoc of noisy
everyday politics, a reliable solid ground in the world of
unreliable, conflicting ideas and ideologies. They offer relief,
release and what Philip Hobsbaum in his essay on Mahon called
'*claritas*'[10].

And yet Heaney's objects remain comfortably well within the
realm of history; they function as arguments in Heaney's historical
discourse. They are immutable centres around which the sense of
belonging and the sense of communal identity can be built.
Heaney needs objects in order to create his versions of history:
clear-sounding narratives, purified but petrified, stone-like in their
solidity, permanent and inevitable as myths. His interest in objects
is an attempt to provide a vulnerable sense of identity with firm
foundations, since objects link us with our past – that is, they
maintain the sense of history – and with place – that is, they
maintain the sense of belonging. Heaney's objects become
emblems of rootedness, anchoring us in time and in space. They
are not only evidence of one's identity, but they are indeed the
symbolic guardians of that identity. It is thanks to such objects as
the sofa in *The Spirit Level* that we know who we are, that the
burden of uncertainty, the burden of identity in crisis is suddenly
lightened.

Mahon's poetry presents an entirely different case. His objects
for one are mute: they do not offer seductive narratives of memory
and belonging. And since history is founded on these two pillars,
on memory and belonging, on past as continuity and on place as
home, they exist outside history. And if they speak of anything in
their silent tongue, it is only of the ultimate vast void which
testifies to the absence of any still points or immutable centres.
The world of Mahon's mute phenomena is the domain of the
always open possibility. If Heaney's objects point to the past and
by linking it with the present discover there the origins that define
us, then Mahon's objects are directed towards the future: to the
permanent existential potentiality. If they promise anything it is
existence without any given meaning, without any inherited
identity. Heaney's garrulous objects have their private history;
they belong to particular places and particular narratives; they are
the legacy of those who lived in the past, left to those who live in
the present. Mahon's objects, on the other hand, are essentially
rootless, they belong nowhere. They are discarded, useless

materials, tossed into the void. They could be anywhere: in the back streets of Belfast or on the strands of Portrush. Mahon's poem 'Nostalgias' dramatizes this state of uprootedness; the objects' yearning for their origins is as futile as the lost tribe's waiting for God. They do not guarantee human identity, because they themselves have no identity, no origins; they can change into anything. They are the roaming gypsies of the phenomenal world – mute, mutilated, mutable, existing in a world where everything must change, except the fact of change (see 'The Globe in North Carolina').

Much has been said about Mahon's religious concerns. According to this poet, if there is any transcendent meaning to the world, or, for that matter, if there is any God, He can be found under a stone ('Mute Phenomena'). Significantly: under, rather than above. This is a paradoxical statement of Mahon's immanent religion, or – if one may use an apparently even more disjunctive oxymoron – immanent transcendence. Here I disagree with Tom Paulin, who once wrote of 'Mahon's rejection of sense experience' and called him 'an intransigent aesthete who rejects life almost completely'.[11] I think these phrases do not do justice to Mahon, as they would not do justice to John Keats, one of the poets with whom Mahon shares the ambivalence of the desire to escape combined with a simultaneous devotion to the real. Sean O'Brien is closer to Mahon's stance, when he writes: 'Mahon's imagination seeks, or is driven, to the margins of the social and the human'.[12] The difference is crucial: it is the *social* and the *human* that Mahon seems to resent, and not life or sensory experience as such. What Mahon seeks to transcend is the human world of history, its web of established meanings, ossified categories, and repressive definitions, which falsify and disrupt, as much as they explain and order.

It has been noticed by many critics writing about Mahon that the poet's greatest problem is not so much time, nor the sensory world in a continuous Heraclitean flux, as human society. Whether Mahon's rejection of the human world originates in the Irish predicament and particular historical circumstances, or whether the rejection stems from his metaphysics, is a matter of pure speculation. I would venture to say that the two aspects, the historical / biographical one and the metaphysical one, do not have to be mutually exclusive: Mahon's disengagement from history may be essentially an effect of his philosophical stance, whose validity is supported by contemporary political events. History, and particularly Irish history, proves the reasonableness of Mahon's metaphysical intuitions.

In these intuitions Mahon seems to share Pascal's dark view of human beings. This 'make-believe existentialist', as he called himself in 'Dawn at St. Patrick's', would, I imagine, agree with the French proto-existentialist that within human beings one can find 'a series of dramatic contradictions', that 'man is a unique creature, but condemned to die in an infinite, impersonal universe'.[13] In Mahon's poetic anthropology, human beings are doomed to belong to a particular place; they are confined to one place, and one time, though simultaneously they seek to go beyond these limitations, yearning for other places, dreaming of the beyond, endeavouring to transcend their unsatisfying immediate circumstances. Humans 'might be anywhere but are in one place only' wrote Mahon in 'A Garage in Co. Cork'. One answer to this dilemma which most religions would offer is to ignore the sensory world as only transient and to focus on the other, ideal reality, in which time is replaced by eternity, and the relativity of things disappears in the Absolute. But Mahon writes in a world that has witnessed the death of God. He cannot accept the possibility of a positive transcendent world. If there is any beyond, it is the eternal silence of infinite space that so horrified Pascal.

The human historical world does not satisfy man's metaphysical need. Its contingency, noise, and blind destructiveness make man look for another world, a world that can satisfy the human appetite for the real. The human world is unable to do this, because it has lost any contact with the real, like modern anthropology, the science of mankind of which Mahon writes: 'Once it studied man, Now it studies the study of man, Soon it will study. . . Like the baking soda tin, inside the baking soda tin, inside the baking soda tin'. This could be said of course of any branch of learning that builds its metalevels: metaethics, metapsychology, metasociology. Probably this is also the reason for Mahon's choice of silence: words no longer have any relationship with the real. Once they referred to reality, now they refer to other words, soon they will refer to words referring to words . . .

It may be that the same intuition about the insignificance of words lies at the source of Mahon's ten-year silence. In the interview with Piotr Sommer he declared (I am translating from the Polish text of the conversation): 'I do not think that poetry itself has any special significance. The poets that I admire are those who stopped writing, because they realized that it is impossible to construct things out of words'. And in the later part of the same interview Mahon speaks about the insufficiency of poetry: 'I'd like to write poetry that goes beyond poetry'. The discovery of the widening gap between language and reality may have been the reason of Mahon's silence.

In speaking of the real, it is worth pointing out that the word 'ideal' appears to my knowledge only twice in Mahon's poetry, and in both cases it is linked with the word 'society' – there is no ideal 'world' or ideal 'reality'. The phrase 'ideal society' emerges in 'The Mute Phenomena' and 'The Facts of Life', both of which are incidentally versions of other poets' work. The ideal society in 'The Mute Phenomena' is the miserable world of discarded objects, such as lost hub-caps ignored by arrogant humanity, blinded by its spurious hegemony. The speaker of the 'Facts of Life', speaks confidently about his foreknowledge of the future world, the ideal society in which he will be reborn and which will offer him freedom 'denied by the life we know'. If the poet invokes the concept of an ideal society, the implication is that the existing ones disappoint him. Another poem from the same volume, 'Mathew V.29–30', offers a sarcastic commentary on the dream of the ideal society. By reducing the idea of perfection/purity to absurdity, Mahon seems to suggest that imperfection is part of this world; the consistent urge to purify life may only result in total annihilation. Read as an ironic parody, the poem finally comes to accept the life we know, and reveals the dangers of fanatical hostility towards it. The title turns the poem into a scene of confrontation between religious belief and common sense, revealing the inadequacy of rigorous idealism. The concluding line of the poem adds further irony to the argument, by referring not as might be expected to the promised other world, but to human society. Instead of saying that the fulfilment of rigorous religious demands will make him worthy of God's grace, the speaker lowers his sights and looks at his neighbours, the fellow human beings among whom he lives. In this masterly way the eschatological dimension which initially seemed to underlie the poem is downgraded to the prosaic level of the social and the political. Mahon's resentment of human society can be observed in other poems, such as 'Grandfather' or 'My Wicked Uncle', in which he celebrates outlawry and presents enthusiastic, vivid descriptions of individuals who wilfully rejected the straightjacket of a repressive society and by extension – the straightjacket of history.

In Mahon's poetry the human world, the aftermath of the Fall, is a world of noise; its landscape is the city, which is often metonymically described as noise. In the poem 'Teaching in Belfast' the city is identified with the 'cries of children, screaming of bells, the rattle of milk bottles, footfall echoes of jails and hospitals'. In contrast to this cacophonic urban landscape, the place beyond, Mahon's 'elsewhere' is always a depopulated area entirely immersed in silence. The contrast is perhaps nowhere more evident than in 'The Early Anthropologists' which concludes with an image of an old man torn between the roaring machines and silent nature, exemplified here by a mute, wordless sunset: 'The sun sets in the west without remark'. The seemingly redundant adverbial phrase of place, 'in the west', may suggest the permanent order in which natural phenomena exist. The peasant, like Pascal's human being, the thinking reed, exists between the silent eternity of the universe and the noisy linear progression of history.

The contrast between the man-made world and the world of mute phenomena is emphasised by an analogous opposition of two sets of elements: civilisation is usually associated with earth and fire, the two apocalyptic forces, whereas the world of the mute phenomena is consistently associated with water and air. The latter pair of elements, apart from being characterized by transparency – an ethereal quality that makes it possible to look through, to see beyond, to get beyond the surfaces – comes perhaps from observing the sea horizon, the imaginary line where the visible world ends and water meets air, the sea meets the sky. No other place can be further from human society, no other approximates more conspicuously the idea of the beyond. A whole series of Mahon's poems single out these two elements: 'Let rule the wide winds and the long-sailed seas' ('The Death of Marilyn Monroe'), 'Towards sleep I came/ Upon the place again,/ Its muted sea and tame /Eddying wind', and 'And night I walk beside the river/ So that the elements of air and/ Water are not lost' ('Bird Sanctuary'), 'Redemption in wind or a tide' ('April on Toronto Island'), 'overtures to the vindictive wind and rain' ('Day Trip to Donegal').

It should be noticed that Mahon's landscapes of the soul are depopulated territories, deprived of any meaning that could be reduced to human categories, or articulated in words. These landscapes thus lack the transparency of water and air, but are evoked by means of highly sensual concrete imagery. In Mahon's verse those who want to be 'through with history' choose depopulated regions and a basic elemental life; they search for detachment from the madding crowd, but they hardly ever escape from time and life as such.

In the non-historical world, time is the element of change which however does not exclude eternity. It is interesting how often Mahon speaks of eternity in his poems about the phenomenal, ie. temporal, world. In 'A Garage in Co. Cork', an old man and his wife are rewarded for their courtesy with eternity – by being changed not into angels, or spirits, but into petrol pumps, as if eternity rested in these humble corroded objects. In 'The Studio' Mahon says: 'Things immerse in the play of light and shadow (shadow mostly) which repeats itself, though never exactly'. It is this repetition of things that again evokes the idea of eternity, which however is only an aspect of time, and not a triumphant victory over time. The eternity which the poet encounters in the cyclic mutability of things is like everything that exists – far from ideal, far from perfection. It is never exact.

In 'Breton Walks' Mahon includes a surprising sentence: 'birds fly away at my approach as they have done time out of mind'. The sentence, with its skilfully ambiguous syntax, plays about with the idea of eternity. If 'time out of mind' means 'a time that goes back further than human memory', in other words a time that exceeds history, then the human being at whose approach birds fly away, the mortal speaker entrapped in time, belongs to the eternal order of things. As the sentence allows us to conclude, he has been scaring the birds away from time out of mind, before history started.

Mahon's phenomenal world changes, but does not die – as if death, the fruit of the original sin, were truly attached only to human, i.e. historical beings. Even the seemingly obvious disappearance of temporal phenomena is never complete: there is a persistence in the phenomenal world of which the human world cannot boast. In 'The Apotheosis of Tins' human beings admire 'their saintly devotion to the notion of permanence in the flux of sensation'. In 'A Refusal to Mourn', the phenomenal world remains like a 'claw print in concrete' which persists 'after the bird has flown'. The claw print is both an evocation of absence which underlies all there is, and a sign of the permanence of the mute phenomena: the fragile bird did not disappear, but changed in one of Mahon's Ovidian metamorphoses into a claw print.

Mahon's eternity of the phenomenal world may sound like a contradiction in terms: by very definition phenomena are transient and temporal. And yet in 'The Spring Vacation' Mahon writes about a hill that is 'eternally, if irrelevantly, visible'. Here again, as in 'Breton Walks', Mahon skilfully disrupts a simple statement.

His casual insertion of another adverb ('irrelevantly'), allowing for a moment of hesitation or doubt, a condition and a sense of relativity, separates the word 'eternally' from the word 'visible'. In this way the syntax makes the hill eternal, if only for the moment that it takes the reader to reach the concluding adjective. It is only then that eternity is qualified, and given its proper limits. WHENEVER YOU LOOK, IT WILL BE THERE. If this is eternity, then this is unashamedly *relative* eternity, eternity written into the human historical world, another paradoxical, seemingly contradictory concept in this poem about the divided self. All mute phenomena, like that hill in Belfast, are eternal from the point of view of human beings only when they are seen; but then this is the only vantage point available in the phenomenal world. It is the human perspective that can grant the mute phenomena eternal life, but is there any other eternity? An eternity – as in 'Dream Days'- from the first milk van to the latest shout in the night. Beyond the realm of history lies the world of the mute phenomena, and beyond it – history again.

In 'A Disused Shed in Co. Wexford' Mahon invokes the Platonic parable of the cave, yet he turns it upside down. The mushrooms, standing for the mute, muted and mutilated people of Treblinka and Pompeii, exist in the world beyond history, from which they have been excluded by historical processes. They are exiles from history. The date of their banishment is specified: the owner of the shed was expropriated during the Irish civil war, and with him these mushrooms, the mute phenomena. In Plato's parable, the chained slaves live in the cave, with their backs to the light, without realizing that the real world is outside. In Mahon's poem the mushrooms, like the slaves, live in darkness, but they remember history, from which they have been banished, and yearn for it: we are confronted here with an ironically reversed Platonic anamnesis. In Mahon's vision, history, riddled with contradictions and paradoxes, is a destructive force but it also shows itself as a necessarily human element. The mushrooms should have been content to live in this perfectly Mahonian place, cut off from the meaningless noise of the world, the accumulating junk of civilization, but they are not.

Mahon's controversial universalization of the Holocaust in this poem can be defended only when we remember that the mushrooms are exiles from history. Treblinka and Pompeii as the two catastrophes of history are comparable only in the dark world of the disused shed, in the limbo of the forgotten. The meaning of the Holocaust, its uniqueness which makes it impossible to compare it with any other event, can be regained only in history. It is only in history that the victims of history can be saved; their uniqueness can be redeemed only in human memory.

In Mahon's poem history is associated with light, however trivial this light might be – it is in fact a tourist torch. The ironic ambiguity of the unexpected salvation which promises to take the lost tribes back into history, is voiced also in the image of the firing squad, signifying here perhaps not so much death as pain, the preamble to what it means to live in history. The world of the wordless mushrooms is that of silence. But it is not the silence of de Nerval's mute phenomena: the cutlery, the turnip or the hubcap. Their muteness meant wisdom and dignity. The mushrooms are not mute, they are muted – they have been silenced by history, deprived of the right to speak – their muteness is the sign of their deprivation. All the time they are in the shed they can hear the noise of the outside world ('the rooks querulous in the high wood', 'trickle of masonry, a shout from the blue, or a lorry, changing gear at the end of the lane'). They may regain their voice only when they are returned to history, brought back into its light. It is then that they will be able to speak – if only vicariously through the words of the poets. The mushrooms wait for the imposed silence to be broken, and so when history invades their shed it is announced by a series of noises: the cracking lock and creak of hinges. This noise means the end of their painful exclusion from history. It also means the new beginning of their equally painful presence in human memory. With a creak of hinges the mute phenomenal world ends. History begins.

'WEIRD/HAECCEITY'[1]: PLACE IN DEREK MAHON'S POETRY

EAMONN HUGHES

> The idea of 'place' is only a rough practical approximation: there is nothing logically necessary about it, and it cannot be made precise.[2]

Bertrand Russell's words provide a useful way of unsettling the sense that place is to be easily understood. The centrality of place in Irish writing, particularly poetry, has long been recognised. Indeed, we can talk about what amounts to geographical determinism but despite some new conceptualisations of place in recent years[3] much Irish criticism dealing with place remains locked into an increasingly worn set of oppositions: the parishioner versus the cosmopolitan; the rooted man versus the airy internationalist; fidelity versus betrayal; belonging versus alienation; fixity versus possibility. Derek Mahon is certainly aware of, indeed has contributed to this kind of critical discourse, as the introductions to his two anthologies of Irish poetry make clear. In the solo-authored 'Introduction' to *Modern Irish Poetry* (1972), although the major thematic concern is with history and time, geographical images arise at significant moments: thus, Clarke and Kavanagh are seen as having introduced a 'rougher, terrestrial idiom' in the wake of Yeats, and Ireland is defined in terms of the variety of its places: 'Whatever we mean by the "Irish situation", the shipyards of Belfast are no less a part of it than a country town in the Gaeltacht'. The 'Introduction' then culminates with the hope that 'Irish poetry is at last freeing itself from the parochial self-content it once enjoyed'[4] and seems therefore to be saying a farewell to the obsession with place as Mahon also seemed to do at the beginning of his 1974 essay 'MacNeice In Ireland and England' which begins with the statement that 'The time is coming fast, if it isn't already here, when the question "Is So-and-So really an Irish writer?" will clear a room in seconds'.[5]

However, by 1990 and the 'Introduction' to *The Penguin Book of Contemporary Irish Poetry* (co-authored with Peter Fallon) it seems that what we might call topomania has set in. Not only does it dwell thematically on place (with reference to the North versus the South, Kavanagh's parish, and the uncertainty about 'home') it is also permeated by, sometimes awkward, geographical images while once again hoping (though less resoundingly) that place is becoming less important:

> Among the *contours* of modern Irish poetry . . . Yeats is *Everest* . . . The commanding *features in the landscape* of more recent Irish poetry are Louis MacNeice . . . and Patrick Kavanagh . . . Somewhere between 'the mountains and the gantries' of MacNeice's Belfast and the 'black hills' of Kavanagh's Shancoduff, contemporary Irish poetry has its figurative source . . . These poets are tied less to particular places – or parishes – than ever before. The notion of exile has for centuries permeated the Irish consciousness and while it was true of writers like Joyce and Beckett in the recent past, it is hardly true in the same sense for young poets . . . who spend most of their lives outside Ireland . . . You might say these writers *commute* . . . The word most frequently dwelt on in this selection, though, is probably 'home', as if an uncertainty exists as to where that actually is. This book tries to suggest the *map* of achievement . . .[6] (my emphasis)

In all of this it is difficult to avoid the feeling that we are being teased by excess. This is the mark of Mahon's poetry too. Even more than his contemporaries he is a toponymic poet, though the very excess in naming places immediately suggests a form of anxiety rather than any settled or possessive relationship to place. Not surprisingly, the debate about the centrality or marginality of place in Mahon's poetry has been a constant in the criticism, where it takes two broad forms: there are those who try to locate him securely, if at times reductively, while others are happier to cast him out upon the world.[7] Of course as the incomplete list of oppositions around place above indicates it is possible to both place and displace him positively and negatively.

Such arguments tend to centre on specific, actual places and as I've indicated there are plenty of those in Mahon's poetry; his Dedalean address could read Glengormley, Belfast, Dublin, the West, Ireland, England, France, Europe, America, the Globe without even coming close to beginning, much less exhausting the possibilities. In what follows some attention will be paid to actual places, but I am more interested in place from a conceptual and abstract angle rather than from the geographical or topographical one which would concentrate on actual places.

Partly, I'll want to argue that this chimes with Mahon's own approach. He is not a country poet like Seamus Heaney, a nature poet like Michael Longley,[8] nor yet a *flaneur* like Ciaran Carson, to take examples of three writers whose approach to place and landscape concentrates on its actualities at a variety of levels. Mahon's rural places and landscapes are usually composed of a few, scant topographical features – more often than not hills, rocks and beaches, sometimes coloured (in a muted range of greys, greens and blues)[9] and often overshadowed (literally as well as figuratively) by changeable weather. Indeed, it is arguable that Mahon is more of a meteorological poet than a geographical one. (He is probably the only contemporary writer who could have a particular type of day named after him.) If his urban landscapes – particularly Belfast are more detailed then that's because they are filled with some stock properties, mostly borrowed from MacNeice: 'Boiler-rooms, row upon row of gantries' ('Grandfather', *SP* 13), which are placed alongside a few maternal washing lines.[10] What is more important is the 'wet/ Stone' (*P* 4) to which he turns; as Peter McDonald says: the 'material, mineral reality outfac(es) the human scenes played before it'.[11] If the 'figurative source' of contemporary Irish poetry lies 'between "the mountains and the gantries" of MacNeice's Belfast and the "black hills" of Kavanagh's Shancoduff', then it seems that many of the details of place in Mahon's poetry come from the same source. This use of what amounts to poetic stock properties in Mahon's treatment of place indicates a lack of concern with circumstantial details and a consequent tendency towards the abstract and conceptual in his treatment of place which, though other writers treat of place conceptually, still sets Mahon apart. It is this difference that I want to try to examine.

Given what I have just been saying about the lack of detail in Mahon's poems of place it may seem somewhat paradoxical to start by agreeing with Terence Brown (and Richard York, see pp. 101–114) about the visual emphasis in Mahon's poetry.[12] However, in the face of the strong tendency in Irish poetry to figure place as text, it is the visual emphasis in Mahon's work which most immediately marks him as different. While it is true that places for Mahon frequently have literary associations – from Ovid to Auden, from Tomis to St Mark's Place – he does not fit into that predominant mode of Irish writing about place which figures it as primarily literary and linguistic, there to be read or to be inscribed.

It is through the figure of the singer in 'Aran' that Mahon comments most directly on this traditional association of the land and language:

> He is *earthed* to his girl . . .
> Singing the darkness into the light.
> I close the pub door gently and step out
> Into the yard, and the song goes out,
> And a gull creaks off from the tin roof
> . . . Circling now with a hoarse inchoate
> Screaming the boned fields of its vision.
> . . .
>
> Scorched with fearful admiration
> Walking over the nacreous sand,
> I dream myself to that tradition,
> Fifty winters off the land -
>
> The long glow springs from the dark soil, however -
> No marsh light holds a candle to this.
> *Unearthly* still in its white weather
> A crack-voiced rock-marauder, scavenger, fierce
> Friend to no slant fields or the sea either,
> Folds back over the forming waters.
>   (*SP* 31, my emphasis)

Here, his avowed 'admiration' for the folk singer who sings the 'darkness into the light' (an implicit reference to Heaney?) is 'fearful' and he ends by endorsing the 'hoarse inchoate/ Screaming' of a gull, 'A crack-voiced rock-marauder, scavenger, fierce/Friend to no slant fields or the sea either . . . '. This is not just the exchange of one song for another but also a transition from the auditory to the visual; as the singer 'listens,/ An earphone, to his own rendition' (an image, surely, of 'parochial self-content') so Mahon leaves, but it is the song that goes out (like a light). As the doubly 'unearthly' flight over water of the gull displaces the 'earthed' quality of the singer, so the singer's audition is displaced by the 'boned fields of . . . vision.' This is not without its ambiguity, however. The syntax and punctuation of the start of the third stanza make it impossible to know if 'this' refers back to 'that tradition' or forward to the final vision of the gull in flight. In 'Glengormley', a poem about Mahon's own tradition, 'Only words can hurt us now' precisely, it seems, because this suburban place is devoid of the literary, having been stripped of its relationship to the sagas and epics in which the 'heroes' lived. 'Ecclesiastes' could be taken as a companion piece to 'Aran'. (It was originally collected as the title poem of the volume in which (the then) 'In the Aran Islands', a title more redolent of Synge, appeared.) Again, this is more directly about Mahon's own place, and again in the figuration of that place the textual is seen as threatening because it is associated with distorted vision: 'to speak with a bleak/ afflatus' (the very opposite of the visionary), to 'stand on a corner stiff/ with rhetoric' all the speaker must do is to 'close one eye and be king' (*SP* 28). In all three poems, though I think particularly in the energy and sheer rhetorical gusto of 'Ecclesiastes', 'fearfulness' and 'admiration' are in balance as Mahon is tempted by this textual way of relating to and representing place.

These three poems, in particular 'Glengormley' and 'Ecclesiastes', are most often seen as part of Mahon's poetry of departures but it is not so much the case that he is departing from particular places as that he is saying farewell to a particular way of conceptualising and representing place in poems such as these. The aim of such poems is to achieve or preserve vision, what could be called an existential vision, which is 'not deceived by scenery' ('Brecht in Svendborg', *SP* 130), that is, by the circumstantial actualities of place. As is nearly always the case in Mahon's work, however, he will not let us overstate: his yardstick in 'Thinking of Inis Oírr in Cambridge, Mass.' 'Shames vision into simple sight' (*SP* 25) and if we begin to think of Mahon as a visionary voyager, he reminds us that ' . . . I failed the eyesight test/ When I tried for the Merchant Navy' ('Father-in-Law', *SP* 55). With these reservations in mind, the centrality of 'vision' in Mahon's scheme of things is best exemplified by what strikes me as his equivalent of Beckett's curse on God: 'The bastard, he doesn't exist'. In Mahon's case this becomes in his version of de Nerval's words:

> Striving to catch the eye of God, I faced
> An empty socket beaming its black night
> Over the world with ever-thickening rays.[13]

To paraphrase: 'The bastard, he doesn't see'. It is the poet's task, even duty, to see and to attempt to do so without being distracted by the existing narratives. It is for this reason that the function of place in Mahon's writing, as Hugh Haughton acknowledges, has 'proved strangely difficult for critics' and in the face of this the usual move is to define the writer as cosmopolitan. Haughton has this to say about Mahon:

Mahon's poetry always works with that sense of 'larger ground' beyond the 'local', 'regional', and personal . . . and nearly all his poems take an avowedly comparativist stance or are about a kind of 'crossing' between different places . . . There is *no purely local world* in Mahon, whose poetry reminds us that . . . poetry is part of 'global community' . . . In this sense all of Mahon's poems are maps of the world, instances of a cultural frame in which *particular places have no privileged part*. You are always aware of an elsewhere, or a universalist's cold and rueful sense of *anywhere* in Mahon's work. Like Camus, he is a kind of unhoused universalist for whom the local detail, the detailed locality, is always an instance of a larger condition.[14] (my emphasis)

I've quoted Haughton's essay at some length because it has, rightly, become the more or less standard account of the place of place in Mahon's writing, though Haughton's stress on the cosmopolitan is partly to counter Seamus Deane's potentially reductive reading of Mahon as a world citizen defined by Belfast.[15] I would not be foolish enough to argue against the idea of the larger condition, but I do want to say that the cosmopolitanism of Mahon's work does not necessarily preclude attention to the local and its specificity. Mahon's admiration for and influence by Samuel Beckett is well-known, but I am intrigued by an anecdote he tells about this apparently most placeless and universalist of writers. 'A Tribute to Beckett on his Eightieth Birthday' begins with an account of meeting Beckett which is worth quoting at length:

> . . . we met by appointment in the Hotel St Jacques . . . The St Jacques surprised me. A soulless, Hiltonesque place with piped muzak and revolving racks of thrillers, it seemed a far cry from what legend had led me to expect. A corner cafe, perhaps, where the great man would be on first-name terms with the proprietor and Jameson's Irish whiskey mysteriously available. Instead he went unrecognised, an erect athletic figure with a cliff of white hair, and a Tunisian tan, the famous gull's eyes, grey-blue behind granny glasses . . .[16]

This seems to me to be an odd story for the allegedly placeless and cosmopolitan Mahon to tell about the allegedly placeless and cosmopolitan Beckett. His complaint about the St Jacques is, in effect, that 'it might be anywhere' ('A Lighthouse in Maine', *SP* 142–3 – the phrase is repeated; 'A Garage in Co. Cork', *SP* 153), whereas what he wants Beckett to have is a 'home from home' ('Dawn at St Patrick's', *SP* 106; 'Brecht in Svondberg', *SP* 131). This seems to me to be an expression of a preference for some kind of locale and a denial of the idea of universality (the St Jacques as a universalist place is fit, in Mahon's description, only for the barbarians). Apart from anything else Beckett is rendered, his tan apart, as a typical Mahon landscape, reminding us that 'it might be anywhere', a phrase used in two poems which insist (as so many of Mahon's poems do) on their setting, is countermanded by 'but we are in one place only'.

The mention of Beckett's 'gull's eyes' is another instance of how birds (often with a residual Pentecostalism still associated with them) frequently figure as images of the artist in Mahon's poetry. Beckett is dissociated from the local just as the gull in 'Aran' is flying from it. However, we must remember that in 'Craigvara House' where he 'sat down and began to write once more' (*SP*, 157) the thrush which entrances him with 'a new air picked up in Marrakesh' is 'practising on a thorn bush' which is an image of the artist, no matter how influenced by the cosmopolitan, being hurt into poetry by the local. Therefore, 'let me never forget the weird/ haecceity of this strange sea-board' is Mahon's secular prayer in 'The Sea in Winter' (*SP* 117) as he attempts to find 'the narrow road to the deep/ north the road to Damascus' ('The Sea in Winter', *SP* 117). An authentic existential vision may require the 'road to Damascus' but it becomes inauthentic and futile if it cannot recognise the 'deep north', and both Damascus and the deep north are characteristically for Mahon being journeyed to and as such are on an equal footing. The point here is that Mahon's poetry seems to me to be neither 'comparativist' nor 'universalist' (and I suppose therefore not properly cosmopolitan). Rather the world of his poetry is one in which all locales retain an identity, it is a world in which the 'weird haecceity' of all locales must be respected.

If we reject comparativism and universalism as organising principles, we need to think about the organisation of space, about the ways in which places are constructed and related to each other, especially in the Irish context. Mahon has insisted on several occasions that the Belfast shipyards and suburbs should be a part of the Irish imagination, that they should contribute to our imagining of the place called Ireland. This is both a challenge to, and a refusal to be complicit with, the general presumption that Irish places are related to each other

within an idea of the nation. In this refusal and challenge
Mahon is like Louis MacNeice and Tom Paulin; like Paulin this
is something he has learned from MacNeice. Paulin also follows
MacNeice in thinking about the organisation of space in terms
of the state, rather than the nation. Mahon, MacNeice and
Paulin are also alike in being sea-obsessed poets and while for
all three the sea can function as a symbol of the Protestant
conscience (all it takes, after all, is one bird sitting on a mast to
remind us of 'The Ancient Mariner'), sea-crossings in MacNeice
and Paulin are often related to their responsibilities as citizens
on the ship of state. Mahon diverges from them on this count;
the one avowedly political term in his poetry for the
organisation of space is 'empire', with its connotations of
grandeur and endurance. However, even empires are 'fugitive'
('A Kensington Notebook, IV', *SP* 94, 'Brighton Beach', *SP* 179),
they come and go ('Another Sunday Morning', *SP* 141). The
world that Mahon inhabits is not 'a world with method in it.'
('As It Should Be', *SP* 40) and the forms of organisation that
obtain for him are not those of the state, or nation. As Elmer
Andrews has said: '(Mahon's) anthropological habit of mind
does not discover a landscape instinct with meaningful signs,
but one littered with meaningless rubble'.[17] There are, however,
numerous moments when meaning, some form of organisation,
seems to be implicit in his landscapes. How then are places
related within Mahon's work? Kathleen Shields's phrase from a
discussion of 'A Disused Shed in Co. Wexford' is useful here:
she talks about the 'dissolving analogies'[18] in the poem to
describe what happens when Wexford, Treblinka, Pompeii are
placed together. We see these places put side by side and
assume that an analogy exists, but what universalism could
unite them; what is the basis of comparison between them? Any
connection we might devise will be ethically troubling,
something which is deliberate. Similarly, in 'Tithonus' in which
place names run through and support the poem like vertebrae,
what sense can we make, what narrative can we construct that
would explain 'Golgotha ... Krakatoa ... Thermopylae ...
Peking ... Dresden ... Hiroshima ... Ethiopia'? (*SP* 168–172).
Some linkage might seem to be implied, but the 'weird/
haecceity', the rebarbative specificity of each place re-asserts
itself; the 'angel' of Dresden is opposed to the 'bas-relief' of
Hiroshima in a characteristic Mahon opposition of light and
shade which distinguishes places rather than bringing them
together. Insofar as there is a narrative or a set of relationships

between the places in Mahon's poetry, we would have to characterise them as happening within evolutionary or geological
frames in which even rocks have only a

> Shuddering endurance,
> Their dreams of holding fast
> In the elemental flux.
> ('Rocks', P 35)

No wonder that even empires are fleeting, futile gestures towards
organisation.

Given this we can then return to the sea, or rather to the sea-
boards, beaches, strands, and riverbanks which are among the
most characteristic of Mahon's places. The sea can, as in MacNeice
and Paulin, have the conventional function of symbolising the
Protestant conscience (cf. 'the redemptive enterprise of water',
'The Sea in Winter', SP 115), but there is nothing in Mahon of
Paulin's Auden-derived 'maritime pastoral'.[19] Mahon's sea-board
is a marginal zone, a proper place for the artist, but we must
remember that its marginality is two-fold. As well as being
marginal to the land, he is also, in evolutionary terms, now
marginal to the sea which was once 'procreant' and 'forming'
('Aran', SP 31). In 'The Sea in Winter' the speaker's attempt at
teaching is made futile by the conflation of quotidian and
evolutionary time-schemes with which the poem ends: 'a new day
crawls up the beach' (SP 118). But that is in the past for a now
'land-minded' humanity which would be 'mindless in the sea'
('Day-Trip to Donegal', NC 22). The sea has therefore changed
from its original nurturing, forming, procreant role to become
'esurient' ('Courtyards in Delft', SP 120) as humanity is
transformed.

Whether the sea has metamorphosed, or the poet's vision, his
'metamorphic eyes' ('The Woods', SP 155) have allowed him to
see it as changing as our relationship to it changes. The sea, like
the weather, recurs in Mahon's poetry as a reminder of the
metamorphic nature of the world. And I want to suggest that
metamorphosis is the major relationship between places in
Mahon's work. In stressing metamorphosis in this way, I am
opposing it to its Ovidian counterpart 'exile'.[20] Exile, as Mahon has
acknowledged, has played its part in the Irish imagination (and in
other imaginations) but it no longer seems to fit the case. We
should remember that he has written a number of poems about
gypsies (the exact number being difficult to judge[21]) being too alert
and empathetic a writer to assume that there was a time when

everyone lived a settled life in which the security of place
authenticated their identity; *some* of us may once have had 'house
and home/ And books against the cold./ We are all gipsies now -'
(*NC* 24). However, let us suppose for the moment that the
condition of exile does apply to Mahon. In that case we would
have to ask: where is he exiled from? I can think of poems of
return and homecoming to Glengormley, Belfast, Coleraine, and
Dublin. (Exile from one place may be a misfortune; this looks like
carelessness.) We should also remember that Mahon has applied
the terms 'commuters' and 'tourists' to poets and defended
MacNeice against the charge that he was a 'tourist in his own
country' by claiming this as the condition not just of the poet, but
of modern man.[22] The successive title changes of 'Poem in Belfast',
'In Belfast', and finally 'The Spring Vacation' mark a change in
Mahon's relation to the place[23] which alters the poem from one of
homecoming to one of tourism. This is after all a world in which 'I
have no choice but to go/ And cannot vouch for my return' ('The
Condensed Shorter Testament' after Villon, *P* 21) and in which
being forced to stay in one place is a form of 'House arrest' ('Jail
Journal', *P* 16) Commutation and tourism are alike in relating
places to each other on the basis of their difference rather than
their similarity, though Mahon is alert to the ways in which
tourism can falsify places, as in 'Night Thoughts' (*TYB* 12–13).
However, as Neil Corcoran has said 'The poet, like the tourist (in a
'A Disused Shed'), is inevitably an accidental intruder on
sufferings which are not his own.[24] And I want to insist that the
toponymic quality of Mahon's poetry is in the service of
difference, rather than likeness, and that exile runs counter to
this.[25] Exile is always exile *from*, by implication the nation-state,
and only ever exile *to*, or exile *in*. There is an essentialism at the
heart of exile: the exile is transplanted but not transformed;
likewise there is an un-existentialist motivation to exile, a reason
for the exile's new circumstances which overwhelms the
circumstances themselves. Insofar as we are all exiles – poor
banished children of Eve – we are enjoined to ignore the haecceity
of our world: to ignore the accident in favour of the substance (to
make use of another kind of Roman vocabulary). Metamorphosis
on the other hand is metamorphosis into, a transformative process
which denies essence in favour of haecceity. We are not exiled sea-
creatures – we have metamorphosed from 'sea-minds' into 'land-
minds' ('Day-Trip to Donegal', *NC* 22) – any more than we are
exiled from our mothers' wombs ('An Unborn Child', *SP* 223). We
may carry features from one state into another, but we have to

make sense of those continuities in the here-and-now, not looking back to the there-and-then. History, as the change from there-and-then to here-and-now, is ignored by those who see it as exile, but not by those, like Mahon, who see it as a constant metamorphosis. I am, of course, taking this opposition of exile and metamorphosis from Ovid via Mahon, and it is worth pointing out that his translations and versions are themselves a part of this process, as he draws on and transforms writings from other places (without alienating them from those places, it should be said) to produce an existentially authentic tradition for himself, rather than accepting a necessarily inauthentic inherited tradition. If his bigots are those who, seeing themselves as exiles, refuse to change from a pre-destined tradition (cf. 'Ecclesiastes'), his tragic figures are those, like 'Tithonus' or the mushrooms of 'A Disused Shed', for whom metamorphosis has stopped while the world keeps changing from Golgotha to Krakatoa, from Pompeii to Treblinka. It is the sense of the world as metamorphic that stops Mahon's metaphysical unease from becoming vacuously solipsistic, mere self-indulgence. His sense of the metamorphic grounds his work in the processes of a materiality in which crockery remembers its 'dark origins' ('The Studio', *SP* 30), in which 'an oar ... thought/ Of Ithaca but soon decayed' ('Lives', *SP* 36), to take just two examples of a major feature of the poetry. In such a world, where everything is subject to 'the strange poetry of decay' Mahon 'must effect mutations of dead things/ Into a form that nearly sings' ('The Sea in Winter', *SP* 114, 117). That 'nearly' is a characteristically clear-sighted acknowledgement by Mahon that while the process of metamorphosis may be preferable to fixity (whether of exile or tradition), metamorphosis does not necessarily lead to anything better, and if gain is involved so too is loss. The challenge to the writer in such circumstances is that he too is part of this process, and must therefore realise that:

> Your best poem,
> you know the one I mean,
> The very language in which the poem
> Was written, and the idea of language,
> All these things will pass away in time.
> ('Heraclitus on Rivers', *SP* 112)

Which necessarily raises a question that Mahon himself constantly returns to: what is the place of the poet in such a scheme? What is it that keeps Mahon writing in the face of a metamorphic world which will sweep away the best of his writing, as it sweeps aside

everything else? In such circumstances writing is an irrational
activity. And that is its very point. The Protestant tradition from
which Mahon comes values 'order, law, stability and rationality',[26]
but the 'world with method in it' that such a tradition would
produce is anathema to Mahon precisely because it denies the
absurdity and irrationality of the world. The value of writing lies
in its very irrationality, its ability to pit 'desperate ironies' ('A
Rage for Order', *P* 44) against the apparently rational, and
certainly methodical actions of others. The poet is then like the
'Mythological Figure' whom the gods curse, because of 'an
implied inkling of their random methods', always to sing, 'But her
songs were without words, Or the words without meaning – ' ('A
Mythological Figure', *P* 10). In this the poet is necessarily set aside
from others and not surprisingly, in this light, one of the
commonly referred to places in Mahon's work is the 'high
window' ('A Rage for Order', *P* 44), or the attic 'Up here under the
roof' ('The Attic', *SP* 102). 'Why am I always staring out/ of
windows, preferably from a height?' ('The Sea in Winter', *SP* 115)
Mahon later asks and his answer has to do with 'distance' being
the 'vital bond', the necessary space within which transformations
can be effected. If this seems finally to suggest that the poet is
removed, reserved to his own specific place as if in 'a house of
artifice neither here nor there' ('At the Shelbourne', Elizabeth
Bowen, Nov. 1940, *TYB* 17), then we must bear in mind the
relationship that Mahon establishes between such heights and the
depths over which he looks.

In *The Yellow Book* attics feature so frequently as to amount to a
self-mockery of the idea of the ivory tower in which the poet is
selfconsciously garretted. However, in the first poem in the
volume 'Landscape' (after Baudelaire) (*TYB* 11) the short distance
between the attic and the 'grave hymns' is an irresistible reminder
that the first poem in Mahon's first pamphlet collection, *Twelve
Poems*, similarly juxtaposes a poet's 'high ground' with the grave.
'In Carrowdore Churchyard' (at the grave of Louis MacNeice) was
deposed from its pole position in *Poems, 1962–1978* but was re-
instated in the *Selected Poems* of 1991. It has therefore a primary
place in Mahon's work, and it is not an exaggeration to say that it
is also about the primary place in his work. The 'play of shadow'
and the lines 'these hills are hard/ As nails, yet soft and feminine
in their turn' ('In Carrowdore Churchyard', *SP* 11) are instances of
continuing metamorphoses rather than of a final resting place. The
poet at the graveside is also aware of that which survives ('All we
may ask of you we have') as is also the case with 'A Refusal to

Mourn' where 'the secret bred in the bone/ . . . survives/ In other times and lives' (*SP* 61).

The poet at the graveside is also, unlike the poet at his window, in dialogue. Indeed, in two poems spoken *d'outre tombe* there is either a movement from 'I' to 'we' and 'our' ('An Image from Beckett', *SP* 34–5) or a use of 'we' from the outset ('Consolations of Philosophy', *SP* 42) which provide unusual instances of community in Mahon's poetry. In both of these cases the grave is also a rather jolly, jokey place, (as in the 'querulous complaining' of the neighbours in 'Consolations of Philosophy') partly because the speeded-up, evolutionary or geological sense of the brevity of human lives allows for a relaxed view ('past tension') of human endeavour and achievement, in which an Arnoldian view of culture ('Sweetness and light') is handled dismissively. The repetition of Arnold's phrase serves only to underscore its futility in a scheme of life in which 'grave/ Cities' are the pinnacle of human achievement. This phrase and the self-enfolding, self-cancelling quality of the poem's last lines:[27]

> To whom in my will,
>
> This I have left my will.
> I hope they have time,
> And light enough, to read it.
> ('An Image from Beckett', *SP* 34–5)

make no allowance for distance (either spatially or temporally), and thus reveal how Mahon's absurdism, based as it is on a sense of the non-human scale within which humanity operates, disdains the idea of distance. His more recent work, notably *The Hudson Letter* and *The Yellow Book*, may still have a sense of the folly of human endeavour but it is expressed in a more topical and even journalistic manner in which irony and satire displace absurdism. Where absurdism functions on a non-human scale, irony and satire depend precisely on the measurable distance between endeavour and achievement. The earlier Mahon should not however, be taken as a misanthrope as the tenderness of 'A Refusal to Mourn' (*SP* 61) makes clear.

To conclude, I want to turn from places of the dead to dead places in these lines from 'Brighton Beach':

> Now, in this rancorous peace,
> Should come the spirit of place.
> Too late though, for already

> Places as such are dead
> Or nearly . . .
>
> (*SP* 179)

In the light of Mahon's respect for the haecceity of place I think we must understand these lines not as an absolute statement, but rather as a compressed narrative of a continuing metamorphosis. There are two statements here, to the effect that it is the nature of the world that already places are dead, and that places are nearly dead. In typically Mahonic fashion 'place' is pitched between the assonantly and near-anagramatically linked 'already . . . or nearly', one looking to the past, the other to the future, the one metamorphosing into the other, leaving 'place' its brief moment of stability. In such circumstances too much piety accorded to any necessarily, relatively-fleeting spirit of place will leave us washed up on the shores of history and not knowing where we are.

RHYTHM AND REVISION IN MAHON'S POETIC DEVELOPMENT

MICHAEL ALLEN

. . . musicalisation pluralises meanings.[1]
Julia Kristeva

Mahon's most interesting revisions come to light in association
with changes in his rhythms. (If, as Kristeva says, poetry is '. . . a
rhythm made intelligible by syntax' and the poet follows '. . . the
instinct for rhythm that has chosen him'[2] this is exactly what we
might expect.) These revisions are nearly all carried through
between *Night-Crossing* (1968) and *Poems 1962–78* (1979) though
one or two are not fully rounded off until *Selected Poems* (1991). A
second set of significant revisions to which I will briefly refer later
crops up between *The Snow Party* (1975) and *Selected Poems*: these
occur, I think, more because the older Mahon came to agree with
Auden that '. . . a poem must not be "dishonest", must not express
beliefs that a poet does not actually hold'.[3] Finally, throughout the
work there tend to be emendations which we could almost call
cosmetic and which need little attention.

In the *Night-Crossing* version of 'Day Trip to Donegal', vigorous
speech-rhythms play against the iambic beat in the second and
third lines to dramatise the speaker's nervous irritability about
social obligations:

> We reached the sea in early afternoon,
> Climbed stiffly out. There were urgent things to be done -
> Clothes to be picked up, people to be seen. . .

> (*NC* 22)

This is like George saying to Martha at the beginning of *Who's
Afraid of Virginia Woolf?* 'Where *are* these people. Where are these
people. . . .'.[4] The protagonist's complementary response to the
reassuring solace of 'the . . . hills' and the implacable gravity of
'the sea' is communicated in underlying iambic regularities picked

111

up from the first line:

> . . . as ever, the nearby hills were a deeper green
> Than anywhere in the world, and the grave
> Grey of the sea the grimmer in that enclave.

But the irritability persists and heavy consecutive stresses in the second line of stanza 2 convey how it has coloured the quayside details in the speaker's mind:

> Down at the pier the boats gave up their catch -
> Torn mouths and spewed-up lungs.

He is still driven to project his own malaise on (or locate it within) the scene.

In contrast, the version emerging in *Poems* and rounded off in *Selected Poems* straightens out the metre throughout to give dignity and courtesy to a representative human speaker, 'the poet', in what is clearly a more public poem,

> We reached the sea in early afternoon,
> Climbed stiffly out. There were things to be done,
> Clothes to be picked up, friends to be seen.
> As ever, the nearby hills were a deeper green
> Than anywhere in the world, and the grave
> Grey of the sea the grimmer in that enclave.
>
> Down at the pier the boats gave up their catch,
> A writhing glimmer of fish . . .
>
> > *(SP* 21)

Notice that there is now no psychological justification for the speaker's extravagant empathy with the mutilated fish. No need either, therefore, for the 'metaphysical' conceit which originates in the chafing sensibility of the 'I' persona and claims our startled attention as future readers of the poem:

> How could we hope to make them understand?
> Theirs is a sea-mind, mindless upon land
> And dead. Their systematic genocide
> (Nothing remarkable that millions died)
> To us is a necessity
> For ours are land-minds, mindless in the sea . . .
>
> > *(NC* 22)

So this stanza (stanza 3 of the 1968 version) is deleted in both *Poems* and *Selected Poems*. The effect of these changes on the two versions of closure is striking:

> At dawn I was alone far out at sea
> Without skill or reassurance (nobody
> To show me how, no earnest of rescue),
> Cursing my mindless failure to take due
> Forethought for this, contriving vain
> Overtures to the mindless wind and rain.
> 1968 (*NC* 23)

> At dawn I was alone far out at sea
> Without skill or reassurance – nobody
> To show me how, no promise of rescue -
> Cursing my constant failure to take due
> Forethought for this; contriving vain
> Overtures to the vindictive wind and rain.
> 1991 (*SP* 21)

Without the forward-looking associative word-play of the deleted stanza ('land-minds' sounding ominously close to 'land-mines') there would be considerable semantic slackness to the parallel rhythms of lines 4 and 6 in the early version here and the repetition of 'mindless' would seem rhetorical. So in 1991 the speaker's steady and stable discursive identity is confirmed ('constant') while the wind and rain are melodramatised ('vindictive'). We are now reading a rather different poem. In particular, the irony about the speaker's belated attempt to acquire the good manners he had lacked earlier ('contriving vain overtures') has been dissipated by the changes to the first two stanzas. Notice, though, that while the 1968 speaker may have been socially maladroit, he did, in the deleted stanza, strike up an almost contractual relationship with the reader: 'How could we hope to make them understand?' Other *Night-Crossing* poems, 'The Prisoner', 'First Principles', 'The Poets Lie where they Fell', also construct or imply such a contrast which depends upon a recognition of the speaker as 'poète maudit', as gifted victim of artistic temperament.

The convention goes back to the English (and Irish) 'nineties (but is here tinged with a 'metaphysical' wit that was still just viable in the 1960s by courtesy of Geoffrey Hill). The complicity wrung stylistically from the sender by the conceit of the original stanza 3 was clinched by the wry archaism 'earnest' (literally, money given in part-payment, a pledge or guarantee). While no such guarantee of normal human reciprocity and ease can be given to the *poète maudit* (so the convention says), with closure he had been gifted with a different concrete pledge, the poem as text, which is passed on to the reader. The poem is our surety: It gives us aesthetic reasons for extending our sympathy to the speaker and recognizing him as poet. In the later version, of course, with the substitution of 'promise' for 'earnest', this whole layer of meaning is removed: the speaker/poet has been a trustworthy communicator all along. And he is no longer asking for a preferential treatment which in 1979 might be seen as not ideologically correct. Rhythmically too the placing of the three substituted words, 'promise', 'constant', 'vindictive', results in the rhythmical transformation of a cajoling voice displaying flair and panache into one of restraint, sobriety and honesty.

In the adjacent table I have set out in two columns some tenets of the Anglophone poetics of the last fifty years or so. Those listed in the left-hand column were dominant in the poetry that Mahon and his peers, Heaney and Longley were writing in the mid-sixties. Those on the right are dominant in the poetry they write in the mid-nineties. Movement from a predominance of the qualities on the left to a predominance of the qualities on the right seems to govern Mahon's revisions. Looking at the left-hand column it is apparent why we were invited by the early version of 'Day Trip to Donegal' to forgive the speaker his irresponsibility for the sake of his language-gift. And the lilting variations on the iambic which open 'In Belfast' (1968) make a similar appeal, intensified by the metrical urgency of the sustained conceit in lines 3-4 as the speaker tries to come to terms with his own endemic evasiveness:

> Walking among my own this windy morning
> In a tide of sunlight between shower and shower,
> I resume my old conspiracy with the wet
> Stone and the unwieldy images of the squinting heart.
> Once more, as before, I remember not to forget.
>
> There is a perverse pride in being on the side
> Of the fallen angels and refusing to get up.
> We could all be saved by keeping an eye on the hill
> At the top of every street, . . .
>
> (NC 6)

Like the 'maudit' of 'Day Trip . . .' his condition is dysfunctional: but unlike him, this protagonist is confronting a society which is equally dysfunctional, but with which, thanks to his origins within

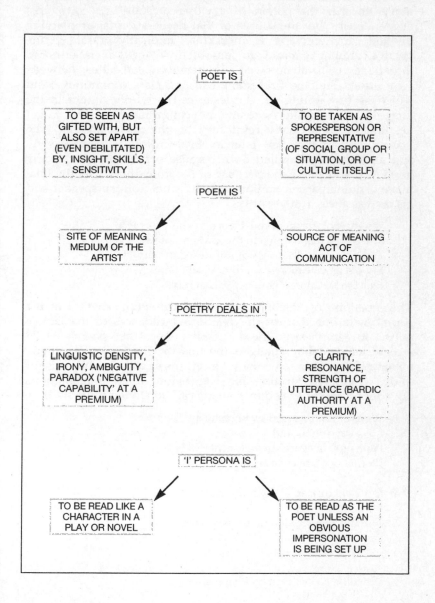

it, he is sometimes at one. Through various contortions he does move towards the notion of a closer acquaintance with 'this desperate city' but the source of that desperation (an implacably divided community) is no more than implicitly present in the poem's cumulative innuendo: 'among my own'; 'remember not to forget' (i.e. 1690); 'all be saved'. The renewed 'conspiracy' between *poète maudit* and the Protestant working class community from which he has sprung (cf. 'Ecclesiastes') is wittily caught in the image of one of Milton's cosmic nonconformists 'refusing to get up', a note contextually reinforced by the insouciance of 'The Poets Lie where they Fell' later in *Night-Crossing*. Closure is slyly and ambiguously handled both because only '[o]ne part of my mind' is volunteered and because of the irony thrown by the final moneylending conceit on both the city's hold on the speaker and his own aesthetic ruthlessness:

> One part of my mind must learn to know its place
> The things that happen in the kitchen-houses
> and echoing back-streets of this desperate city
> Should engage more than my casual interest,
> Exact more interest than my casual pity.

The repetition of 'interest' and the sharp speech-rhythm of the penultimate line disrupt the reassuring cadences of the iambic norm to emphasise these *caveats*. For the poem's 1979 republication Mahon changed the title to 'The Spring Vacation', making his speaker someone who returns as an occasional visitor to his childhood terrain; this suggestion of an unambiguous outsider role is confirmed by a single revision to the poem itself:

> We could *all* be saved by keeping an
>   eye on the hill
> At the top of every street, for there it is -
> Eternally, if irrelevantly, visible -
>
> But yield instead to the humorous
>   formulae,
> The spurious mystery in the knowing
>   nod.
>   1968
>
> We could *all* be saved by keeping an
>   eye on the hill
> At the top of every street, for there it is,

Eternally, if irrelevantly, visible -

But yield instead to the humorous
    formulae,
The hidden menace in the knowing nod.

            1979 (*P* 4)

The immediate effect of 'hidden menace' is flat, melodramatic and inauthentic; the language is that of a different period (that of the 'troubles') and a different poem. The 'desperate city' in the original poem is not as explicitly sinister as this, the poetic emphasis never as moral, and despite the changed title the words read as a journalistic intrusion. Mahon seems to have been tempted (at a time when he identified himself with Northern Irish poetry[5]) to try out the role of 'spokesperson' for that troubled region alongside the Heaney of *North* (1975) and the Longley of *An Exploded View* (1973). But what is needed to play this role as Clair Wills points out is an ability to 'root public statement in personal experience, from which it derives its authenticity and hence the authority to speak of more communal concerns'[6]; and unlike Heaney and Longley, Mahon found the combination difficult at that traumatic time. (He is, of course, triumphantly successful with such a combination in *The Hudson Letter* (1995) and *The Yellow Book* (1997) where he looks back from an achieved vantage point as the relaxed cosmopolitan spokesperson for culture[7] itself).

When we look closely it is apparent that the clumsiness of this particular revision is basically a matter of rhythm. In the original version the two key lines imitate a street exchange, the flutter of syllables at the end of the first line echoed almost to the point of internal rhyme in the first half of the second line to catch a jauntiness and confidence which the speaker knows to be meretricious (while he partly shares it and clearly capitulates to it):

. . . But yield instead to the humorous formulae,
The spurious mystery in the knowing nod.

            (*NC* 6)

How this cultural defeat comes to figure as central to an aesthetic victory (the poem) hinges precisely on the way an inversion of metrical patterning in the two four-beat lines jells with a moment of mimetic authenticity. And this effect is lost in the later version without any compensatory rhythmical reformulation (neither version of this piece passed muster for *Selected Poems* while the revised version of 'Day Trip . . .' did).

Both of the poems I have discussed show Mahon reshaping iambic verses at a time when his deeper creative energies were being drawn in quite different rhythmical directions. The emendations he made give one a sense that the resolving resonances of the iambic staple might themselves be coming to seem unearned or inappropriate. The changes of emphasis I formulated above for Heaney, Mahon and Longley involved their response as a literary generation[8] to a number of things: the growing ascendancy of American culture and American poetry; the impact of Eastern European poetry in translation; alterations in the dominant critical frameworks which influenced the reception of their poems; and, of course, the changes in Irish society and culture *vis-a-vis* England which had come to a traumatic focus in the North. (It seems to me that it is the way they engage with the tension among these various forces that has nudged into canonical conspicuousness the talents of these Northern writers and the generation which follows them.) Some or all of these factors can usually be felt distorting or transforming the original impulse of Mahon poems at their point of emendation: Edna Longley, interestingly, spoke of Mahon's revisions (with 'Day Trip to Donegal' as her example) as 'like literal translations[9] in their flatness and coldness. But the most important influence is probably the first I mentioned. Alongside the internationalising of poetry (and a pluralising of literary-critical norms) had come an urge to get rid of the assumption of abiding ('English') continuities implicit in the iambic under-pinning of Anglophone rhythmical expression. And the shift of the centres of cultural influence across the Atlantic brought into play American distrust of '"closed" verse'[10] (Charles Olson), 'a tribal magic against a real threat of upset and things not keeping their place'[11] (Robert Duncan) both directly and through closer models like Plath, Hughes and Gunn.

Social and cultural change is always reflected in poetic rhythms at two levels – one which is widespread, bland and conventional and the more important one we detect in our chosen canonical poets as we identify them and go on to confirm and affirm our judgement. Rhythmical development in them seems intense and deeply felt at a psychological level which is almost physiological. And in response to social and cultural changes between the middle nineteen-sixties and the late nineteen-seventies, Heaney, Mahon and Longley were all deeply and tensely engaged in the effort, in Robert Lowell's words, to 'break metre'.[12] (Pound's original formulation perhaps gives more sense of the felt energies involved in such deep rhythmical change: 'to break the pentameter, that was the first heave'.[13]) Between 1970 and 1976, Heaney, Mahon and Longley (each publishing two major collections) seem to have accomplished this shift. All three found a curtailed free verse useful in this respect as a way of opening up the possibility of a variety of ampler forms. Longley has left the clearest impression[14] of the contingent tension, the creative seizures, freeze-ups and dry spells: and though the rhythmical transition through the early poems in *Wintering Out* to the later poems in *North* seemed less troubled for Heaney, I remember as a colleague and confidante at the time his displaying some of the same symptoms. It may be, then, that Mahon's rhythm-related revisions in the seventies were a response to the strain of transition, falling back on an earlier poem and recreating it in response to some kind of felt threat to his originative identity. On the other hand, carried through as they mainly were in the preparation of a seemingly exclusive collection (*Poems 1962–78*), one might see them as more extravert than the Longley model suggests and Mahon himself as 'strengthening' his 'textual authority' in the course of what Harold Bloom calls 'an act of imposition, a declaration of property'.[15] (As Peter Denman says, 'If nothing else, the revisions assert [Mahon's] continuing right as the author of the poems'.)[16] It is my contention that we should not lose sight of either of these ways of interpreting Mahon's revisionary behaviour, although the two examples studied so far smack more of the second.[17]

Movement through the strain of rhythmic development to its freedom is illustrated by the two lyrics I treat next: 'A Dark Country' (1972) is painfully engaged with breaking the iambic; 'Afterlives' 2 (1975) displays a newly restored regularity of line-length which has nevertheless freed itself from the iambic straitjacket. Both raise again the issue of Mahon's 'place' and his engagement or non-engagement with it. The first presents an attempt to reopen an intimate relationship with his native region in the metaphorical terms of love-making after long separation: '... a coming/ Into a dark country ...'; '... now move – / Circumspectly at first ... '; ' ... Among these / Signs, these wild declivities ...' (*L* 18). (Note the Jacobean innuendo of the first quotation and the echo of middle Yeats in the third, demonstrating, perhaps, a still equivocal attitude to movement from left to right across my earlier table.) It is through this 'metaphysical' mode that the arrival of the cross-channel ferry in

Belfast Lough is given its erotic charge:

> Starting again
> After a long patience.
> A long absence, is a slow
> Riding of undertow,
> A ship turning among buoys in dawn rain
> To slide into a dockyard fluorescence; . . .
>
> (*L* 18)

As a whole, the second lyric in question ('Afterlives', 2) is not a revision of the first: it is a recasting of its subject (returning 'home') and its argument (it might be / might have been possible to understand the place) in a way which reanimates that ferry image:

> At dawn the ship trembles, turns
> In a wide arc to back
> Shuddering up the grey lough
> Past lightship and buoy, Slipway and dry dock
> Where a naked bulb burns;
>
> (*TSP* 2)

'[T]rembles' and 'Shuddering' impart a different but still nervously physical and intimate implication so that the way the ship backs into dock, its arrival a preparation for departure, illuminates the speaker's similar stance as he arrives already aware of the futility and pain of the attempt to 'go home again':[18]

> . . . a city so changed
> By five years of war
> I scarcely recognize
> The places I grew up in,
> The faces that try to explain.
>
> (*TSP* 2)

The two lyrics are contrasting examinations of the 'mind', part of which, according to 'In Belfast' should 'know its place', and the rhythmical balance of the later poem is inseparable from its paradoxical discovery that the only way to be a spokesperson for the troubled region is to explain why he can't be:

> Perhaps if I'd stayed behind
> And lived it bomb by bomb
> I might have grown up at last
> And learnt what is meant by home.

But it is the rhythm with which 'A Dark Country' broached the possibility of intimate return which is most germane to my argument here. Each stanza follows the pattern of the first one (quoted above) in its self-impeding progress from a three or four syllable line to a painfully reclaimed or restored iambic pentameter. In stanza 3 this relentless breaking and rebuilding of 'metre' recognises itself and the emotional prospect as an impasse:

> But now move -
> Circumspectly at first
> But with a growing sense
> Of the significance,
> Crippling and ordering, of what you love,
> Its unique power to create and assuage thirst - . . .
>
> (L 18)

Desire and impediment are opposite and equal for two more stanzas but the self-reflexive awareness results in a closure which fails to clinch the proposed return either rhythmically, erotically or regionally speaking:

> Recognizing,
> As in a sunken city
> Sea-changed at last, the surfaces
> Of once familiar places.
> With practice you might decipher the whole thing
> Or enough to suffer the relief and the pity.

What I called earlier the threat to Mahon's originative identity is obviously not far away in the four beats of that almost despairing last line. When one reassembles 'Afterlives' (I have looked at its second lyric section in isolation until now) it is apparent that the association of the erotic with 'elsewhere' and with insistent light[19] in 'Afterlives' 1 and the separate presentation of the local and the familial in comparative gloom in 'Afterlives' 2 while involving a stylistic dilution of 'A Dark Country' has made possible the simultaneously rhythmic and discursive development into more extrovert modes. The deletion of 'A Dark Country' in *Poems* is no more than a kind of authorial confirmation that 'Afterlives' has taken its place. Of course, the poised relationship between the two parts of 'Afterlives' is itself dialectical and ironic, disclosing like so many of Mahon's divided settings the incompleteness at the core of each possible locale;[20] but there is a deeper dialectic to be seen when 'Afterlives' 2 is set against 'A Dark Country', one situated at the heart of the poet's development.

The use of unconfident rhythms to present a numbed and insecure consciousness had emerged in various post-Pound technical experiments as a way of 'breaking metre' and responding to the stress of cultural change, most influential for the sixties and seventies in Lowell's *Life Studies*. The earliest version of 'An Image from Beckett' (*Lives*, 1972) uses this device; but comparison with the later versions (1979, 1991) shows again how Mahon's revisionary rhythms point to a movement away from the articulation of uncertainty and marginality (as well as from regional self-identification). The left-hand column of my parallel quotation below simulates fear, hesitation and loneliness through a sequence of unstressed line-endings; the revised text on the right, removes them, transforming the speaker's idiom into something much tougher — sardonic, elegant and ruthless:

In that instant	In that instant
There was a sea, far off,	There was a sea, far off,
As bright as lettuce,	As bright as lettuce,
A northern landscape	A northern landscape
(Danish?) and a huddle of	And a huddle
Houses along the shore.	Of houses along the shore.
Also, I think,	Also, I think, a white
A white flicker of gulls and	Flicker of gulls
Washing hung to dry -	And washing hung to dry -
The poignancy of those	The poignancy of those
Back yards -	Back yards -
1972 (L 8)	1991 (*SP* 34)

One response to the phrase 'The poignancy of those / Back yards –' when one meets it in the later version would be Martha's response to George in *Who's Afraid of Virginia Woolf?*: 'Phrasemaker!'[21] (Which would also, it is true, be an appropriate response to a Beckett character.) The identical line and a half in the earlier version does not carry itself with such assurance precisely because of those unstressed endings: '. . . huddle of / Houses . . .', ' . . . I think,/ A white . . .', '. . . gulls and / Washing . . .', which construct a quite different speaker.

As the two versions proceed the speaker in the first is more and more readily identifiable with the *poète maudit* of *Night-Crossing* (who subsequently, in *Lives* turns out to be also a novelist *manqué*):[22]

. . . and the gravedigger	. . . and the gravedigger
Putting aside his forceps.	Putting aside his forceps.
Then the hard boards	Then the hard boards
And darkness once again.	And darkness once again.
Oh, I might have proved	But in that instant
So many heroes!	I was struck by the
Sorel, perhaps, or	Sweetness and light,
Kroger, given the time.	The sweetness and light,
For in that instant	Imagining what grave
I was struck by the sweetness	Cities, . . .
and light,	1991
The sweetness and light,	
Imagining what grave	
Cities, . . .	
1972	

In the earlier version, too, the conjunction 'For' renders dramatically an ecstatic shift in awareness, followed in the next line by a spontaneous gulping leap into experience. The alliteration and the word's central placing in the line makes the first 'sweetness' Yeatsian in its intensity: the further Arnoldian intertextuality is subsidiary to this dramatic impact, working as a corrective to the speaker's naivety. Contrast the abstract resonance of the phrase in the later version. It is clearly to the latter that a comment like this one from Eamonn Hughes (see p. 79 above) refers:

> the speeded-up, evolutionary or geological sense of the brevity of human lives allows for a relaxed view ('past tension') of human endeavour and achievements, in which an Arnoldian view of culture ('Sweetness and light') is handled dismissively. The repetition of Arnold's phrase serves only to underscore its futility in a scheme of life in which 'grave / Cities' are the pinnacle of human achievement. This phrase and the self-enfolding, self-cancelling quality of the poem's last lines make no allowance for distance (either spatially or temporally), . . .[23]

And this abstract effect is even more apparent when a second deletion

(... what lasting monuments,   ... what lasting monuments,
Given the time.   Given the time.

But even my poor house   They will have buried
I left unfinished;   My great-grandchildren, ...)
And my one marriage   1991 (*SP* 34)

Was over as soon as it started,
Its immanence so brief as to be
Immeasurable.

They will have buried
My great-grandchildren, ...
          1972 (*L* 8–9)

removed the domestic dimension which melded with '[w]ashing' and '[b]ack yards' to root the speaker in a world not entirely separate from that of 'In Belfast' and 'Glengormley' from *Night-Crossing*.

The direction of Mahon's scheme of revision is signalled in his wider development, as Peter Denman has pointed out,[24] by the way a book called *Lives* is followed by a book (*The Snow Party*) whose first poem is called 'Afterlives'. It is announced thematically in a key phrase from 'The Last of the Fire Kings', ' ... my cold dream / Of a place out of time ... ' (the speaker's alternative being to remain the 'creature' of 'the fire-loving / People') (*TSP* 10). Behind the mythological terms one detects a reluctance to retain either the self-immolating stance of *poète maudit* or a vestigial relationship to an intolerant and atavistic regional community. The final touch to the transformation of 'An Image from Beckett' appears only in its 1991 republication:

They will have buried   They will have buried
My great-grandchildren,   My great-grandchildren,
    and theirs,   and theirs,
Beside me by now   Beside me by now

With a subliminal   With a subliminal batsqueak
Batsqueak of reflex lamentation.   Of reflex lamentation.
Our hair and excrement   Our knuckle bones

Litter the rich earth   Litter the rich earth
Changing, second by second,   Changing, second by second,
To civilizations.   To civilizations.
          1979 (*P* 38)   1991 (*SP* 34–5)

The replacement of the sixth line here changes the viewpoint (with implacable logic) from that of those who lived the life at the time to that of posterity, with a consequent total change in the meaning of 'civilizations'.

A similar transformation of the central persona is effected in the dramatic lyric 'Rage for Order' (also from *Lives*). It is done almost entirely by rhythmical means:

Somewhere beyond	Somewhere beyond the scorched gable
The scorched gable end	end and the burnt-out buses
And the burnt-out	there is a poet indulging
Buses there is a poet indulging his	his wretched rage for
Wretched rage for order -	order—or not as the case
	may be; for his is a dying art, ...
Or not as the	1979 (*P* 44)
Case may be, for his	
Is a dying art,	
1972 (*L* 22)	

Restraint, reticence and even a certain deference to the 'high culture' he castigates are attributed to the paramilitary speaker by the hesitant line-endings on the left: on the right he is given a ruthless and indomitable energy by the expansive free verse. But the searing scorn for the poet's ineffectuality, which is brought to life in the original version by the internal rhyming throughout line four is submerged by the new arrangement. And the way that scorn modulates into momentary compassion and back towards sarcastic parody, all achieved through line-end words, 'far', 'as', 'is', has disappeared in the sweeping dismissiveness of the later version:

He is far	He is far from his people,
From his people	and the fitful glare of the high window
And the fitful glare	is as nothing to our scattered glass.
Of his high window is as	
Nothing to our scattered glass.	His posture is grandiloquent and
	deprecating, like this, ...
His posture is	
Grandiloquent and	
Deprecating, like this, ...	

One could argue that the no-nonsense ruthlessness of the later characterisation is more realistic. And that, in pursuit of such realism Mahon has sensibly replaced an eruditely ambiguous word in the poem's last line:

. . . his is a dying art.	his is a dying art
Now watch me	
As I make history,	Now watch me as I make history. Watch as
Watch as I tear down	I tear down
	to build up with a desperate love,
	knowing it cannot be
To build up	long now till I have need of his
With a desperate love,	desperate ironies.
Knowing it cannot be	1979
Long now till I have need of his	
Germinal ironies.	
1972	

But lacking the halting earnestness conveyed by line-endings in the earlier version and the antithesis there engineered across the stanza-gap, we cannot believe in the speaker's 'desperate love' on the right as we can on the left. The placing of this phrase at the end of two breathlessly long lines suggests instead a combination of incoherence and hypocrisy, an impression not mitigated by the final loose repetition of the word 'desperate'. The possibility raised in the earlier version of a rapprochement between poet and Yeatsian man of action seems less likely in the later version; the intertextual reference of the title phrase when it reappears in the poem seems more abstract and, as with the Arnold phrase in the 1991 'An Image from Beckett', consciously dehumanised. This is because Mahon's original line-break ('. . . his / Wretched rage for order -') caught and parodied the Stevens rhythm ('Oh! Blessed rage for order . . . ')[25] rather than deadening it. The result is to replace a reactive antipathy to the figure of the 'nineties poet and his 'high window' with an ironic detachment. So, again, responding appropriately to the genre 'as if making a given kind of movement or a given kind of effort',[26] one is virtually reading two different poems. Even more striking is the case of 'Matthew V, 29–30' (where the revisions are entirely rhythmical:

Lord, mine eye offended	Lord, mine eye offended, so I plucked
So I plucked it out.	it out.
Imagine my chagrin	Imagine my chagrin
	when the offence continued.
	So I plucked out
When I plucked out	the other; but the offence continued.
The other but	
	In the dark now, and working by
	touch,

<table>
<tr><td>The offence continued.</td><td>I shaved my head.</td></tr>
<tr><td>In the dark now and</td><td>(The offence continued.)</td></tr>
<tr><td>Working by touch, I shaved</td><td>Removed an ear, . . .</td></tr>
</table>

My head, the offence continued	But now, the thing finding its
Removed an ear . . .	own momentum,
	the more so since
But now, the thing	the offence continued,
Finding its own momentum,	I entered upon a prolonged course
The more so since	of lobotomy and vivisection, . . .
	1979 (*P* 69–70)

The offence continued,
I entered upon
A prolonged course

Of lobotomy and vivisection . . .
1975 (*TSP* 13–14)

The halting stanza-breaks and unstressed line-end syllables are again replaced by a brutally confident, frequently longer-line free verse. And the contrast is just as ferocious when the culture which conditions and identifies the persona is seen as requiring the same treatment (note the respective placings of the word 'deletion'):

. . . A scalpel	. . . a scalpel
For the casual turns	for the casual turns of phrase engraved
Of phrase engraved	on the minds of others;
On the minds of others,	an aerosol for the stray thoughts
	hanging in air,
A chemical spray	for the people who breathed them in.
For the stray	
Thoughts hanging in the air,	Sadly, therefore, deletion of the
	many people . . .

For the people
Who breathed them in.
Sadly, therefore, deletion

Of the many people . . .

The hesitant left-hand column articulates a diffident and well-meaning urge towards ideological correctness which gets out of hand, the right, something hypocritical ('Sadly, therefore, deletion of the many people . . . ') and totalitarian.

Because of the rhythm, one's response is quite different in the two cases (although in both cases it is full human and social identity that is the victim). Fully appreciating Mahon's mordant humour, one still sees much more in the early version why Steven Tuohy found at the heart of his poetry 'a doomed gesture of appeasement of extraordinary pathos';[27] reading the later version one is instead tonally reminded of Mahon's Weberian account of the seventeenth century Protestant ruthlessness of his forebears (at the end of one version of a still unstable text);[28]

> For the pale light of that provincial town
> Will spread itself, like ink or oil,
> Over the not yet accurate linen
> Map of the world which occupies one wall
> And punish nature in the name of God.
>
> *(HBN* 10)

In the two versions of 'Rage for Order', Mahon had found he could use the same regional materials to express progressive detachment from both the regional community and the outdated aesthetic he wanted to break with. Now, in these two versions of 'Matthew V, 29–30', he achieves something similar with regard to the religion which permeated that community and acquired for him a perverse kinship with that aesthetic. Note how the dour pulpit ring of the title is poised against the repeated Gallic shrug of 'Imagine my chagrin'. It is no coincidence that the other set of significant Mahon revisions I mentioned earlier all turn on different possible attitudes to religious belief.[29] What is most striking about this very powerful poem, however, is that its first version seems to carry prophetically and its second self-reflexively complementary commentaries on the revisionary practice itself. It seems, then, almost a piece of the purest logic, almost part of Mahon's *meaning* that the later version of 'Matthew V, 29–30' should subsequently be excluded from *Selected Poems*.

Mahon's admirers will surely be rewarded sooner or later with a *Variorum* or a volume which does for Mahon's early versions (and earlier work in general) what *The English Auden*[30] does for Auden's ('An Ulster Mahon'? 'Mahon *Maudit*'?) The latter would ideally be published in tandem with a *New Selected Poems*, so that *The New Selected* could pursue (as the *Selected Poems*[31] does) Mahon's project of subsuming 'historical difference and rupture into an aesthetic continuum'.[32] Meanwhile the anthology of early texts and versions would reveal how Mahon's creative processes are bound up with the society he was born into and the traditions he inherited and would offer us the opportunity to read his developing work 'as a symbolic meditation on the destiny of community'.[33] As for the *Variorum*: there, a pair of rhythmically contrasted versions like the two of 'Matthew V 29–30' I've discussed could be read as a dialectical entity, a kind of disjunctive 'dialogue of soul and self'. (Both Mahon and Longley had experimented with this kind of contrapuntal representation of the poles of imaginative growth, the systole and diastole, waiting on rhythm and dominating it.)[34] At the same time such rhythmical transformations could be seen with all the other revisions, deletions and relegations as part of Mahon's wider development ('So one must move forward / Into the space left by one's conclusions'.)[35] There is no way round the fact that Mahon's conscious poetic enterprise seems intent on frustrating such editorial projects and we may have to wait a long time for these books. But as W. K. Wimsatt says, 'The poem is not the critic's own and not the author's (it is detached from the author at birth and goes about the world beyond his power to intend about it or control it). The poem belongs to the public.'[36]

DEREK MAHON AND THE VISUAL ARTS

RICHARD YORK

This is a topic which has aroused a considerable amount of critical interest. One must specially refer to Terence Brown's very sensitive account in an article in *Irish University Review* in 1994[1], but references are made by many of Mahon's critics. And quite rightly so; it is an unusual aspect of Mahon's work that so much of it is concerned not just with art, but specifically with quite precise accounts of specific works of art and of the careers of particular painters. It is of course far from rare for poetry to concern itself with such subjects; in the twentieth century one thinks perhaps first of Rilke (with whom Mahon has shown himself to be familiar) and more directly of Auden's 'Musée des Beaux Arts', which contains a detailed account of a Brueghel painting. But in general there does seem to be some general expectation that poetry should deal with such matters as personal relationships, nature or religion, and there may be some suspicion that the topic of art is a way of dealing with the same things at a distance. The recent critical view that there is no such thing as direct experience, that nature and society are always perceived through some sort of mediation, should perhaps reassure us that the topic is not a perverse one; and we shall certainly see that Mahon himself is very conscious of what is involved in writing about something that is already an interpretation of life.

Mahon's knowledge of art appears to be quite wide ranging. I note references in his verse or his journalism to the following artists: Botticelli, Uccello, Tiepolo, El Greco, de Hooch, van Meegeren (the Vermeer forger), Chardin, van Gogh, Monet, Whistler, Munch, Klimt, Schiele, Ernst, Wyndham Lewis, Orpen, Dufy, Mondrian, Jack B. Yeats and his less well-known father John B. Yeats, and Paul Henry. They are not, of course, all mentioned with the same degree of seriousness or approval. There are also several references to types of painting or schools or periods of painting without specific identification. The sense we get, I think it is reasonable to say, is not that of an academic or professional critic, but of a person of wide and genuine culture, who finds art to be a normal point of reference in discussing other aspects of culture or in defining the sense of certain impressions or emotions.

This sense of a personality is particularly important, of course, in the verse. It is part of the picture of the speaker or of the implied author that the poems communicate to us. Mahon speaks as (or implies himself to be) a person not unlike most of his readers, or not unlike what his readers might wish to be: not an expert, not a scholar, but someone who is cultured and well-educated, who is observant, and in particular who observes things that we are not all conscious of all the time, such as the quality of light and of colour, who is not afraid to use his imagination (as art-critics perhaps are and perhaps should be), and who, above all, feels that there are important aspects of our life that can be conveyed through the visual world but which are not in their nature wholly visual. This means, put negatively, that Mahon is avoiding certain registers which are otherwise considered appropriate to the discussion of art: the review, the historical explanation, the critical analysis, and this has implications about the relationship of speaker and audience in the poems, since the speaker is not claiming to be an authority.

The list of painters I mentioned goes some way to indicating the kind of painting that interests Mahon. It must obviously be far from a complete indication of his taste, and we cannot draw much significance from the omissions; there is, for instance, no English art, little of Chardin or the like, little of the Impressionists, and we may think of artists we would expect to appeal to him who do not explicitly appear. I suspect that the absence of very recent art is not accidental; the reference in *The Yellow Book* to 'snuff sculptures' may give a clue to this absence. I suspect, more seriously, that we can find the absence of certain categories of painting significant and hazard a guess at the reasons for Mahon's lack of concern with them. Except for the passing reference to Mondrian, there are no non-representational artists: Mahon is not interested in paint, shape and colour for their own sakes, but as a means of formulating some vision of life. There are no landscapes: Mahon is interested in 'the human presence', in what art shows of human life either directly in images of people or in images of the objects of daily human use, the settings of daily life. There are no paintings of heroic or religious subjects, since Mahon is interested in the normal current of life and not in the great transcendent moments. He commends John B. Yeats for his concern with 'the poetry of life' his sense of 'the priority of the real'. He seems to find this priority of the real especially in Uccello, de Hooch, van Gogh and Munch, painters to whom a poem (or more than one) is dedicated and on whom I shall be concentrating in these remarks.[2] These artists differ greatly from each other in visual style. Butthere is something they have in common. They depict the ordinary, the domestic, the everyday. Uccello may seem to be an exception, but is less so than one might think: his 'Hunt by Moonlight' is thought to represent a hunt organised by the Medici as a courtly entertainment. So, while the work may be remote from us in time and in social context, it is nevertheless a depiction of a social and sporting occasion which is not totally alien to the life we know. One notes that Mahon did not choose to consider Uccello's battle scenes, his St George or his 'Profanation of the Host'. It is strange, of course, that the hunt does take place by night (so that at least one critic has erroneously doubted the nocturnal character of the scene), and the pictorial expression of this strangeness is the intense glow of colour, both nocturnal and radiant, that seems to transform the occasion. And something similar is true of the later artists Mahon considers: de Hooch with his domestic middle class courtyard scene, Munch with his studio and his girls in the evening light, van Gogh with his boots, chairs, sun-flowers, all show the everyday transfigured or heightened by colour. The draughtsmanship is what varies most, from the meticulous precision of de Hooch to the bold, almost slapdash energy of Munch, and this is what Mahon does not comment on; he seems to accept the various styles of painting as apt to various kinds of devotion to the real.

And he brings to the paintings a similar sense of devotion, indicated by the sheer accuracy of much of his description. In Uccello's painting, for instance, Mahon notes the lemon-blue air (an acute colour sense: presumably the kind of blue is to a more typical blue what lemon-yellow is to primary yellow), the 'sombre trunks', the 'slim dogs', and we get the painter's handling of these things, with the recession to a vanishing point which is itself obscured by the dark paint: a selection of pertinent details and an economical suggestion of the painter's craft, Uccello having been one of the first masters of perspective. In the Munch, we get a much fuller evocation of the details of the painting: the house, the bridge (or jetty), the dusty road, the position of the girls, their long hair (in fact only one has long hair, though Munch produced other versions of the picture in which all three have long hair), the dark waters, the 'ghastly sun' (sometimes taken to be a moon, understandably enough). The most attentive to detail is, aptly enough, the poem on de Hooch, as the canvas itself is rich in detail: the brick and tile, the water tap (which the casual viewer may have to search to find), broom and wooden pail, the foliage and the trees, the girl waiting by the 'sunlit railings' of the houses opposite, the cracked out-house door: again there is a sense of one of the specific artistic forms of the painting, de Hooch's much admired use of perspectives leading onto a different space with different lighting, and there is an acute sense of the implications of a house-proud and thrifty society, and an acute vision of a society that distinguishes radically front and back, public and private.

But there is a curious set of absences in these descriptions as well, a strange negativity in Mahon's recreations. In the Uccello, for instance, why are there no references to people? Why is there nothing on the delicate colour contrasts brought about by the figures in red? What of the extraordinary perspective effect brought about by the horses which are turned almost directly away from the viewer and into the depth of the image? What of the stags, already caught in the midst of the hunt? The Munch poem seems very thorough, but one might be struck by the absence of any reference to one of the largest masses of colour in the canvas, the huge dark green tree beside the house (analysed by one critic as a mass of three linden-trees growing together). Most extraordinarily of all, in the de Hooch, we have the young woman with her back to us, waiting, according to Mahon, but we don't have the two figures who are mentioned in the usual title of the work, the woman and child. These people are beautifully prominent in the painting, delicately placed just off centre, the white headdress capturing the highlight of the whole picture, the line down from the woman's face to the child's balancing the uprights that slant the other way on the left, their eyes meeting so as to make them into a self-contained emblem of care for each other in what is otherwise an image of cleanly orderliness and solitude. But they don't get into Mahon's poem, which thus becomes oddly empty, comprising apparently various bits of humdrum decor and someone turning her back to us. The 'Hunt by Night' is about a vanishing point, the 'Courtyard' appears to be about vanishing people.

This is all the stranger as in these poems of description there is a strong implied address to the reader, who is treated as a fellow viewer of the work. The point is least clear in the Uccello poem, where it is suggested only by the definite articles, 'the glade aglow', 'the slim dogs', which imply the reader's familiarity with the scene; Mahon will go on to refer to 'our hunt by night', but the 'our' may refer to humanity in general and throughout history. More clearly in the 'Girls on the Bridge', as early as line 4 we get 'the house there', and then a sudden shift of time scale which includes a reference to 'the scream we started at'; the reader is involved in the poem. And so, curiously, are its subjects, as the girls are apostrophised at some length: 'grave daughters of time, you lightly toss your hair . . .'. The poem, apparently, has poet and reader side by side addressing the remote – and now dead – girls; there is a drama, but a manifestly fictitious one, in which the imagined interaction is essentially an assertion of absence and loss. 'Oh you may laugh', the poet warns them – and the colloquial menace of the tone goes further to insist on a strangely hollow familiarity – 'but wait'. . . Just you wait: the moment shared by poet, reader and subject is essentially impermanent. Similarly in 'Courtyards in Delft' we get a very strong placing of the reader as viewer: 'that / Water tap, that broom and wooden pail' ('that' strengthened by the line ending, which allows it to rhyme, rather tangentially, with 'adequate'); and the poet returns to the same perspective in the third stanza, which has 'That girl with her back to us' and then the definite articles on 'the outhouse door' and 'the sunlit railings' and 'the houses opposite'.

In each of these cases, as I have been attempting to conceal up to this point in my comments, the poem places the actual description of the work of art in the context of a shared knowledge of other things. There is none of the structuralist or formalist concern with the work itself about Mahon. In Uccello, we have a rather hasty history of art, comprising the cavemen and Uccello (they were both interested in hunting) and some general reflections on 'our hunt by night' which, with its dark cave, sounds oddly platonic, and becomes a half-frivolous account of 'what we do for fun not food' or, more solemnly put, for culture rather than natural necessity; in 'Girls on the Bridge', we get two other paintings of the same artist, the very well-known 'Scream' and a picture of people who 'wander in the dazzling dark/ Amid the drifting snow', which I suspect is his 'Avenue in Snow, Koesen' of 1906. This is the kind of effect referred to by Haughton as 'double vision';[3] the poem sees not only the painting placed before it, but other, absent paintings as well. And the introduction of these things is complex in effect. First, of course, the references appeal to the reader's knowledge of the actual world of art, and reinforce his sense of a public culture. No doubt for many readers the 'Scream' reference is almost blatant in its obviousness, while the snow picture is much more elusive, and may force us, individually, to recognise the limits of our artistic culture. And this difference corresponds to a difference in the handling of the two: the scream is presented as an event synchronous with the scene of the bridge picture: 'a mile from where you chatter, somebody screams'; the speaker, that is, is turning from the actual picture to fabricate a link with another, so inventing a mythical world of peace and horror. But then he shifts the time frame substantially: 'The girls are dead/The house and pond have gone'; we move into a modern world of steel and concrete; and this then modulates through the wandering in the snow back to the girls, who now however exist as a past. The reader's engagement, very full at first, is gradually loosened, and becomes elegiac.

In 'Courtyards', we get a whole range of other works of art, which the reader is assumed to have some idea of, though they are not specifically identified; Hugh Haughton identifies them as other works of de Hooch.[4] These, moreover, are emphatically said to be what is not there: 'We miss the dirty dog, the fiery gin'. What we have left is 'the chaste perfection of the thing and of the thing made' – the scene depicted and the work of art made by de Hooch are both works of chaste perfection; the random, the accidental is absent – and we miss it. And in fact the poem ends by a turn from this impersonal purity to a personal memory, a memory of childhood in Northern Ireland. (More recently, in the very fine 'Death in Bangor' Mahon has spoken of his mother as 'a kind of artist, a rage-for-order freak'.) The effect is a very complex one: there is an obvious break in the continuity of the poem (anticipated, however, by the anachronistic refererence to tea in stanza 3) with the phrase 'I lived there as a boy'; the poet turns from the painting to what appears to be a fantasy of living in a work of art; this then rapidly turns into a very precise visual memory of what is obviously presented as a similar way of life, the thriftiness and cleanliness of Northern Ireland enhanced by the poet's visual sense akin to that of Dutch art, by his sense of lambency, reflections and containment. And this then shifts again, into a second-rate adventure fiction, as the child's companions 'dream of fire/And sword upon parched veldt and fields of rain-swept gorse': the veldt of the Netherlands' South African colony and the gorse of Ireland. And this creates a fantasy of the poet himself as concealed within the picture and, it would seem, thereby alienated: 'I must be lying low in a room there,/ A strange child with a taste for verse'. The work of art, in its glowing perfection, is an excuse for imagining one's own absence.

These have been poems which describe specific works. The other form of poem in which Mahon reflects on art is the monologue attributed to an artist: the examples are van Meegeren and van Gogh. The van Meegeren poem, 'The Forger', makes almost no reference to actual works of art (and, of course, the van Meegeren pictures are not well known, though it is possible to trace reproductions[5]); it concerns a view of what art means. The poem therefore depends on an appeal from speaker to reader, directed against an opponent, thus asserting the private, personal character of art: van Meegeren had been accused of betraying his nation by selling real Vermeers to the occupying Germans, and defended himself on the grounds that they were actually fake Vermeers. A paradoxical enough situation, since it required him to boast of his dishonesty as well as his skill and use his guilt as a proof of innocence. But that is not the whole of the the point Mahon makes:

> To hell with the national heritage
> I sold my soul for potage

He mocks the experts, and presents himself as a martyr to art; his work is, despite everything, a form of creativity which surpasses the experts' conception of technique; he works 'beyond criticism' and the pun is an important one: he is in fact solitary, not normally exposed to criticism at all; he claims to work at a level of effectiveness too high for critics to assess; and he arrogantly asserts the inherent superiority of the artist. This then makes him virtually Christlike:

> And I too have suffered
> Obscurity and derision
> And sheltered in my heart of hearts
> A light to transform the world.

These poems are full of the transforming power of light; the irony is that this redemption is the work of a forger, and the reader has to restrain his respect for the speaker. He or she may well admire the speaker's sense that art is not a matter of skill but is an integration of technique and vision (I wonder incidentally whether Mahon was recalling Proust's remark that style is a question not of technique but of vision), and he may admire his assertion that his art arises from love; but he should balk at the reference to 'my genius', and at what appears to be the implication that genius is

proved by hunger. The reader is distanced from the speaker, he is
'at one remove' from the works: art becomes a matter of heroic
self-congratulation which is also a matter of self-betrayal.

The van Gogh poem, 'Portrait of the Artist', which follows in
the *Selected Poems* is also elusive in its relationship with the reader.
The speaker ends by referring to works the reader will recognise
without difficulty and doing so in terms of light and fire that the
reader will have no difficulty in recognising as characteristic of the
extraordinary intensity of colour and application of paint in the
late van Gogh:

> A meteor of golden light
> On chairs, faces and old boots,
> Setting fierce fire to the eyes
> Of sun-flowers and fishing boats.

But the final line forces the tone: these boots, sunflowers and so on
are claimed to be 'Each one a miner in disguise'. Mahon seeks to
teach us that there is darkness hidden in this light. We feel the
strain of the interpretation: the visual alone gives us no grounds
for believing the speaker's claim, and indeed the word 'disguise'
precisely points out the poet's rejection of appearance – which
may well appear startling, since we most obviously would regard
art precisely as a fascination with the appearance of things. The
rhetoric is conceivable only because this celebration of one of the
familiar high achievements of European art arises from a more
obscure background. It is in fact presented as a prophecy: van
Gogh as a young man is prophesying what he will paint when he
has seen it. Fortunately van Gogh proves to be a reliable prophet –
or more precisely, proves to exist outside time, as both the young
man in the Belgian coal-fields and the mature artist in the South
of France. van Gogh, the true artist, suffers obscurity as van
Meegeren, the forger, purports too; he has none of the arrogance
of van Meegeren, but a firm confidence in his recreation of a
world which is both one of vitality and one of deathliness and
frustration. The early parts of the poem are carefully documented,
as far as the events of van Gogh's life are concerned: the reference
is to the time in 1879 when he was a lay preacher in Wasmes and
was dismissed for excess of zeal and for inappropriate clothing.
The church authorities are the opponents, philistines who are
blind to the speaker's real intensity of feeling. And this is
reinforced by a close quotation from a letter to his brother Theo
(the 'Portrait' is presented precisely as one of these letters) in
which he speaks of his sense of captivity: 'A caged bird in spring

knows quite well that he might serve some end: he feels well enough that there is something for him to do, but he cannot do it'. This is then conflated with his quotation from a terribly sentimental guide book to the Borinage: 'The Belgian miner has a happy disposition, he is used to that kind of life, and when he descends the shaft, carrying on his hat a little light that is designed to guide him in the darkness, he trusts himself to God ...'.[6] Darkness and captivity are then depicted and transcended in van Gogh's paintings of the time:

> light
> Refracted in a glass of beer
> As if through a church window
> Or a basin ringed with coal dust
> After the ritual evening bath.

What one needs to realise is that these are the very first paintings of van Gogh's career; Mahon is obviously right in biographical fact in seeing this as the crucial moment in his life, the one that made him an artist. The problem for most readers is that these paintings are very little-known; convincing, observant and symbolically apt as Mahon's description appears to be, it does not touch the same note of recognition as the final stanza does; these works are, for most of us, at one remove, and might almost be fictional.[7]

'In time', van Gogh is made to say,' I shall go South'. And here lies one of the vital issues in Mahon's view of art. Art may seem to be timeless, in two senses. Firstly, works of art depict a moment in space, which has no duration; secondly, the work itself, as an object, survives (in principle) without change throughout the centuries: the bust survives the city, in the famous line of Gautier. What we have already been seeing is that Mahon seeks to place the work in a perspective of personal or historical change: the mere fact of the clearly delineated period quality of some of the works reminds the reader of the gap between ourselves and the creation of the painting; the 'courtly' hunt, the pageantry and the hunting horn (more precisely the echoes of the hunting horn: one more remove), the wooden pail in Delft. The poems also deliberately depict changes in time: van Gogh's youth and later life, van Meegeren's crime and punishment, the cave paintings and the Renaissance. But more than that, Mahon writes change into the pictures, either by reading the temporal implications of the scene depicted or by introducing details that are not and couldn't have been in the paintings, because they are not visual details. In Uccello, there are the 'pungent prey' and the sound of the dogs' cries. There is the man coming home for tea in the de Hooch; in Munch there are a vast number of imagined details: starting, very conspicuously, with the 'Audible trout', and going on to the 'notional midges' and then the things inside the house, beds, lamplight and crisp linen; then there is sound and movement in the conversation of the girls, their laughter, and the tossing of their hair. There is a negative in de Hooch, where no breeze disturbs the trees. There are speculations: the road in Munch is 'perhaps' the road to the south. There are metaphors: God himself becomes a metaphor in 'Portrait of the Artist'; in 'Girls on the Bridge' the sun 'watches in pale dismay' and the lake is, one may take it, not just literally reflective, though it is that, but also a symbol of reflectiveness. Most obviously the account of Munch's 'Studio' painting is essentially comprised of metaphor and of fantasy, recalling Mahon's interest in the French Romantic view of the life of objects:

> You would think with so much going on outside
> The deal table would make for the window.

There are literary echoes (as there are throughout Mahon; he has recently noted his 'forest of intertextuality'): the unplumbed lake of Munch, the daughters of time in the same poem. Painting, for Mahon, is not only about what you can see: it is about what you need to add to make a total significance: details that give the concrete depth of sensation lacking in the visual, feelings apt to the characters or to the viewer. The poem, it might be said, usurps the painting; it completes what is lacking in the painting and reveals to us how far the painting abstracts from the multiplicity of the real.

   And the observation of implicit change does the same; by careful attention to time of day and to gesture or pose, Mahon shows how far the paintings isolate a moment and how far that isolation is not only artistic but artificial. The hunting dogs 'go/wild with suspense'; they actually appear in the painting to be suspended above the ground, because of their elegant gravity-defying leaps, but they also illustrate a suspense in the painting which has selected a moment in their motion; similarly in the same poem 'midnight hints at break of day'; on the one hand, the strange quality of luminosity in the painting, what Mahon calls in another poem 'a partial dark/ Stage-lit by a mysterious glow', suggests day as well as night; on the other, the passage of time inevitably brings morning after night. The girl in Delft is waiting, and

> Will wait till the paint disintegrates
> And ruined dikes admit the esurient sea;

the outhouse door is already ruined and bears witness to a past, as the girl bears witness to a future; time is both a force that threatens the work of art and the nation and also an element inscribed in the painting, which thus combines an Apollonian stability and completeness with a recognition of change and contingency. Mahon is specially sensitive to the evening atmosphere of the girls on the bridge, with the long shadows, the dark waters, the pale sun. The suggestion is that the adolescents will age, will be subject first of all to 'the peaceful increment of your lives', and then to bad dreams which will scatter this peaceful domestic order (the reference may be to traumas in private life, or it may be to the wars which have scarred the twentieth century, the painting being dated 1900); and so change in time is a move towards insecurity and death. A picture of stillness is, by its very precariousness, a threat of transience.

And here, I think, one has to turn for a moment from the visual content of the poems to think about their rhythmic form. The painting organises space; the poem organises words in time, and one might wonder whether there is any parallel between the two kinds of artistic organisation. I particularly refer to 'Girls on the Bridge', which has an unusual rhythmic pattern, which it shares with 'The Hunt by Night' and 'St Eustace' (a poem based on Pisanello's painting of the theme, and strongly visual but not clearly related to the actual form of Pisanello's work). In this form in each stanza the lines gradually lengthen and then shorten; this makes a pulsation of contractions and dilations, as Elmer Andrews has put it,[8] and it also makes an interesting pattern of lozenges on the page, adding to the visual sense of the whole; the syntax is then superimposed in a virtuoso instance of what Edna Longley has called 'stanzaic skill'[9] on this undulation of sounds. The total effect is of a constantly delayed search for conclusiveness. I quote the first three stanzas:

> Audible trout
> Notional midges. Beds
> Lamplight and crisp linen wait
> In the house there for the sedate
> Limbs and averted heads
> Of the girls out

Late on the bridge.
The dusty road that slopes
Past is perhaps the highroad south
A symbol of world-wondering youth,
of adolescent hopes
and privileges;

But stops to find
The girls content to gaze
At the unplumbed reflective lake
Their plangent conversational quack
Expressive of calm days
And peace of mind.

The poem starts with tiny details that arouse our curiosity, which
is then heightened by the apparent shift of scale with the beds
and linen; we soon discover that the poem is going to be about
waiting, as we wait for the primary subject, but this is strangely
contradicted by the rhyme with 'sedate' and the apparent
symmetry of the third and forth lines; this is only apparent since
we are still being led on to the main figures, who appear in
truncated reference in the last syntactically incomplete line of the
stanza – 'the girls out'; the next line at last concludes the sentence
and the picture, but has started a new stanza and a new sequence
of rhyme and rhythm. These now prove to be concerned with
change; the stanza coherently articulates an interpretation of part
of the painting, namely the road, though it is a topic that leads on
to limitless change, and the rhyme pattern may leave us
somewhat disconcerted; the eye-rhyme of 'south' and 'youth', the
odd match of 'slopes' and 'hopes', the road apparently about to
slope off on some dubious errand, and the very imprecise echo of
'bridge' and 'privileges'. After all this uncertainty and shifting,
the third stanza stresses stopping, contentment, calm: the girls are
'content to gaze', as the viewer of a painting perhaps should be;
and this is aptly concluded with the full stop and stable rhyme of
'peace of mind'. There are still details that are elusive: the first
main stress in the stanza falls on 'stops', but the line doesn't stop
there, and the echo in 'stops' of 'slopes' and 'hopes' is rather
confusing; the sudden irony of the 'quack', unevenly answering
'lake', suggests that poet and reader may not yet have found
peace of mind. The same kind of study could of course be carried
out for the rest of the poem, and for the other poems; I hope this
is sufficient to show that the poet's voice is one that promises and

withholds satisfaction in the same way as, according to him, the painters of his choice do.

Overall then it seems as if Mahon finds in art a way of approaching various important dichotomies. Firstly, he sees art as reconciling acceptance of the given world with a sense of its strangeness, its remoteness, of the need for another level of living; it shows the laughter of the girls but shows it coming across dark waters; it shows them content to gaze, but it shows that beyond them is a life of pain; it shows the beauty of the sunlit railings, and the pride of the housewives, but it also shows the limitations of the trite, adequate, sparse and clinging world of the domestic, and accepts it in the context of the hints or anticipations of love, desire and disorder that appear elsewhere in the poem; it asserts the basin ringed with coal dust, as socio-historical fact, but shows it also in van Gogh's vision as a 'ritual bath', a sacrament – or more precisely the aftermath of a sacrament in a dying religion. Yeats is 'an exile and a stranger'; the sense of not belonging and of discontent with the ordinary seems integral to Mahon's view of art.

Secondly, art reconciles the moment with time; as people should be, according to *The Hudson Letter*, it is capable of 'prolonging the inconsequence of a gaze'. The hunt that symbolises culture – and so art itself – is tense and long pursued, it is a dimension of history; but it is a great spectacle, something tamed and displayed; (it is because Mahon is fascinated with art in history, and because he seeks to escape from 'era-provincial self-regard', that Lewis and Orpen can be presented as characteristic of the first world war period, and that Mahon has recently come to be concened with the Decadents, Klimt, Schiele and the *Yellow Book*). Van Gogh's meteor is sudden, but it is also an expression of a remembered past. A key concept here is calm, as when he speaks in the Schopenhauer poem ('Schopenhauer's Day', *The Yellow Book* V) of the conceivable satisfaction offered by 'the calm light of Dutch interior art'. A significant concept is that of the flicker, the 'flickering shades' of cave art, which combines movement with permanence, a concept most thoughtfully articulated in the poem on 'The Studio', where there is

> this quivering silence
> In which, day by day, the play of light and shadow (shadow mostly)
> Repeats itself, though never exactly.

Thirdly, art reconciles incompleteness with fulfilment. What is implicit in all that I have said is that the works are based on a profound love of art; Auden refers to 'intensity of attention, in

other words love', and that intensity of attention is precisely what
Mahon gives to his artists and what the artists, as he sees them,
have given to the world about them. The effect is perhaps best
summed up in the last lines of the 'Girls on the Bridge', which
refer to some

> lost evening when
> Our grandmothers, if grand
> mothers we had, stood at the edge
> Of womanhood on a country bridge
> And gazed at a still pond
> And knew no pain.

The grandmothers' attitude is an aesthetic one; they stand on the
edge, at a moment of preparedness, but also on an edge in space,
and they gaze in stillness, and they feel no pain. This is, in Terence
Brown's phrases, a 'luminous moment', a 'momentary significant
stasis'.[10] As usual irony is built into this: the grandmothers become
grand mothers, their existence is absurdly doubted, the
Scandinavian girls of Munch are confused with the poet's and
reader's own forebears, and above all the last line, superbly charged
with finality, implies its own reversal: most lives do know pain; in
'Shiver in your tenement' in *The Yellow Book* the poet will ask, not
wholly frivolously, 'Has art, like life itself, its source in agony?' The
moment of art is brief and provisional, but none the less real. But
this fullness of attention is not enough. The poet has entered into a
sort of contest with the work: he has added the midges and sheets,
he has subtracted the linden trees, he has reprimanded the girls in a
slightly hectoring tone for their juvenile insouciance, for their
innocence (like his van Gogh, he is capable of prophecy in
hindsight), he has turned his attention away to judge his own
generation, so that those last lines which I have quoted appear not
as the reality of the poem but as an ideal fiction constituted by art;
and it is constituted also by Mahon's sense of difference; art
becomes an image of what we are not. We have seen that Mahon
does indeed have an 'aesthetic doubt', as Brown points out, and
that he does recognise how far the aesthetic is challenged by
suffering and violence;[11] but part of the aesthetic doubt, I think, is
that the aesthetic is a sort of annihilation of the self and the known
world. 'It suggests alternatives to the world we know', as *The Yellow
Book* claims of tobacco, 'and is to that extent consoling'. Very
consoling indeed, perhaps, hinting at the 'redemption through the
aesthetic' of Schopenhauer; and yet never quite escaping what in
The Yellow Book is called 'the incurable ache of art' (*TYB* 53).

'THE IMPORTANCE OF ELSEWHERE': MAHON AND TRANSLATION

HUGH HAUGHTON

1

Mahon's recent *Collected Poems* (1999), like that of every original and large-scale poet, introduces us to a unique signature and a unique world. One of the most pleasurable things about Mahon's world, however, is the way it is inhabited by many other signatures and worlds. His poetic Baedeker resonates with literary allusions to other writers in other places. There are poems about Ovid in Tomis, Sappho in New York, Wilde in the Rue des Beaux Arts, and Raftery in New England. In addition there are translations giving us Pasternak on Moscow, Juvenal on ancient Rome, Pasolini on modern Rome, and Baudelaire on Paris. A garage in Co. Cork echoes with memories of Ovid, Kensington with memories of Pound. Literary allusion and translation reflect the poet's sense of the forest of intertextuality in which he writes but also, I suspect, his need to take his bearings from elsewhere, as part of a larger cultural history. The role of translation is particularly important in this respect. *Collected Poems* demonstrates the developing interplay between translation and poetic creation in his career, and its publication offers an opportunity to reflect on his role as translator, or rather the role translation plays for him.[1]

Translation can be seen as one aspect of Mahon's interest in cultural adaptation and transfer, a central preoccupation throughout his writing life. From the start he has been a poet acutely conscious of locality: 'By necessity,/ If not choice, I live here too', he wrote in 'Glengormley' (*CP* 14) and 'We might be anywhere but are in one place only', in 'A Garage in Co. Cork' (*CP* 131). On the other hand, he has also always chosen to look beyond the local, to locate himself within a wider cultural world, beyond Kavanagh's 'provincial' and 'parochial' values.

Philip Larkin wrote his poem 'The Importance of Elsewhere' in
Northern Ireland, and Mahon, as a poet from the North of
Ireland, has always, in response to what he has clearly
perceived as the insularity of Irish, in particularly Northern
Irish culture, been open to and energised by ideas of and from
elsewhere. 'Ovid in Tomis' laments that 'The Muse is
somewhere/ Else, not here/ by this frozen lake', and translation
is one form of making connection with that elsewhere. In earlier
versions of 'North Wind: Portrush' he wrote 'Elsewhere *le
déjeuner sur l'herbe*/ Blue skies and mythic love' (an idea that
incidentally gets muted in the *Collected*, where the French
phrase is itself translated to the lamer 'Elsewhere the olive
grove,/ Naked lunch in the grass'). In 'Craigvara House', set on
the same North Antrim coast, we witness the poet respond to a
thrush singing 'an air picked up in Marrakesh'. Airs picked up
from elsewhere, in particular France, renovate the air of
Mahon's characteristically terminal imagination.

Commenting on the development of Irish poetry after the
war, Mahon early in his career noted that 'side by side with a
renewal of interest in the old Gaelic poetry (evidenced by the
enthusiastic flurry of translation) went a new 'European'
orientation. For him 'the most striking exponent of this was
Denis Devlin, who turned to French and German poetry rather
than the English tradition in which Yeats worked'.[2] In this essay
I want to look at Mahon's translations as ways in which he too
has looked beyond English and Irish tradition.

In *Notes Towards the Definition of Culture*, T.S. Eliot wrote that
the 'ability to receive and assimilate influences from abroad',
was an essential condition for 'the possibility of each literature
renewing itself'.[3] In late nineteenth-century Ireland translation
from the Irish was seen as a crucial precondition for the
'renewal' or invention of a national literature, as exemplified
by the Irish Renaissance with its search for a distinct national
identity.[4] In the late twentieth-century, translation from Irish
has once again become an important resource and challenge to
Irish poets, but so, in a culture increasingly suspicious of
notions of exclusive nationalism, has translation from abroad.
Devlin, Beckett and Brian Coffey, all committed themselves to
the cross-cultural resurrection business of poetic translation,
and among contemporary Irish poets, so have many others,
including John Montague, Seamus Heaney and Ciaran Carson.
Terence Brown has given a vivid sense of why this might be
so:

> Translation as cultural metaphor is a sign of the degree to which in contemporary Ireland inherited definitions of national life . . . fail to account for much individual and collective experience. It is a sign also that the language we most usually speak and in which we write, with its history of British and (more recently of US) imperialism has not yet come to seem inevitable, wholly congruent with our world as we know it. So we turn to the Irish past, to Europe, and to the poetry of the other, whose accent is of antiquity or of a savage and complex present, seeking ways to speak of our own less than fully comprehended dilemmas. [5]

European literature has inflected Mahon's work with a cross-cultural air and provoked some of his most enduring poems.[6] Seamus Heaney has drawn attention to what he calls the characteristic bi-location of Mahon, among other poets from the North of Ireland – noting the way Mahon's poems thrive on alluding to other places while apparently set in 'one place only'.[7] A translated poem is a particularly intense form of cultural bi-location, a text in English but generated from another place and another language. Certainly reaching over the Irish Sea and La Manche for poems from French and other European languages has been a fertile resource for generating poems during most of Mahon's career. As the Collected Poems reveals, this is especially true of his work since The Hunt By Night (1982) where translation rather than being a separate activity has become an integral element in his own 'original' work. It is particularly clear of the two ambitious sequences of the 90s, The Hudson Letter and The Yellow Book, which integrate translation into his own work to an unprecedented degree.

Mahon has been a prolific translator, but the Collected embodies a strong sense of which translations as well as which poems he considers canonical. Some of Mahon's earliest poems were translations from the French.[8] 'Epitaph, from Tristan Corbière', published in Icarus as early as 1962, is a pungent version of the haunting mock-epitaph of the original poète maudit, while 'Elevation', one of two early Baudelaire translations, is notably better than any other I know, though neither were ever republished. His first book, Night-Crossing (1968), ended with a translation of Villon, 'Legacies', while both Lives (1972) and The Snow Party (1975) included versions of Cavafy, 'After Cavafy' and 'Cavafy'. These and the few other European translations included in the early books don't feature in the Collected, making his early investment in translation largely invisible. There is no great loss involved, but their absence makes it harder to perceive the young Mahon's investment in the figure of the *poète maudit* or the Cavafy-esque dimension of poems such as 'Rage for Order'.[9] The only early quasi-translation to figure, in fact, is 'I am Raftery' (*CP* 51), an ironic update of Raftery's autobiographical portrait of the Irish language poet at the end of his tether and tradition. In fact it is less a translation than a sardonic update of the earlier poem, a self-portrait of the artist as writer in residence playing to American audiences rather than to Irish ones, as in Raftery's poem, or English ones in the original version in *Lives*, where it was set in East Anglia rather than New England. The Gaelic poet introduces himself as 'Mise Rafteiri, an file, lán dóchas is grá' ('I am Raftery, the poet full of courage and love' in Kinsella's translation), and presents himself as blind, tired and playing his music to 'empty pockets.' Mahon's Raftery by contrast is 'hesitant and confused among the/ loud-voiced graduate students' and, facing 'another New England winter' plays not to empty pockets, or even pockets ringing with 'a bright inflationary music' (as in the *Lives* version) but 'with a bright imperious music'. The poet re-contextualises Raftery, updating his earlier self-portrait, and putting him in the situation of the archetypal modern Irish poet (most Irish poets, including for a while Mahon himself, seem to spend at least some of the year as writer in residence on a U.S. campus). Raftery's poem is given a new currency, translated from its original Irish language, form and context but also from its original context in Mahon's life when first published (he had been a writer in residence at the University of East Anglia), and given a new life in the *Collected* in the new representative cultural space Mahon sets him in. In this respect, it is typical of the translations included here.[10]

Mahon has done occasional translations throughout his career, and for a while in the later 80s seemed to be more occupied by translation than original work of his own. Since then, translation has become an increasingly integral dimension of his most ambitious work, as the 'cunningly contrived' canonic reshaping of his *oeuvre* represented by the *Collected* shows. His career now looks spectacularly different to that represented in his last retrospective collection, the Penguin/Gallery *Selected Poems* (1991). Instead of a career leading to the bleakly formalised poems of *Antarctica*, ending with the poet listening to Camus's 'rich despair', we see Mahon's work moving forwards into new territory, experimenting with mixed styles and more open, epistolary-style forms, and incorporating more of the débris of everyday life but also of translation into his verse. With the publication of *The Hudson Letter* and *The Yellow Book,* and then *Roman Script* and other poems about Italy and Ireland, the whole shape and intellectual direction of his work has changed. In this essay I want to look at the role of translation as revealed and concealed by this very deliberately shaped canonic collection, which includes the new work and concludes with it.

2.

Ezra Pound wrote that 'the translation of a poem having any depth ends by being one of two things. Either it is the expression of the translator, virtually a new poem, or it is as it were a photograph, as exact as possible, of one side of the statue'. In his essay on 'Guido's Relations', he distinguishes between 'interpretive translation', which is an 'accompaniment' to a foreign text, and 'the other sort' where 'the "translator" is definitely making a new poem.'[11]

Mahon has been a prolific and versatile translator and adaptor. Much of his translation work can be said to be interpretive translation. This includes the wonderful verse translations of Jaccottet, now collected in *Words in the Air* (1998), and de Nerval, *The Chimeras* (1982), both of which are published in the form of parallel texts facing French originals. In an early sonnet Jaccottet, faced with the repetitive 'seul cri' of a bull-finch, asks 'Mais qui peut dire/ quel est son sens? ('who can say its meaning?').[12] On the opposite page Mahon translates this as 'Who can translate its meaning?', as if Jaccottet had written 'traduire' not 'dire'. This says a lot about the meaning of translation of this sort. By advertising its semantic infidelity, it demonstrates the difficulty of fidelity to a work in another language. Beside these, Mahon has produced theatre adaptations of plays by Molière, Racine and Euripides, a television adaptation of Turgenev's *First Love*, and a prose translation of Raphaële Billetdoux's novel *Night Without Day*.[13] All these, in some sense, represent translation projects done for professional reasons, and for the specific purpose of giving a foreign text a new lease of life in the English language. Taken together, they would make up a sizeable supplementary volume of *Collected Translations*, comparable to Tony Harrison's or Denis Devlin's. These translation projects have a life of their own – as translations or adaptations into English of work from other languages. They don't, however, have the status of Mahon poems – or that seems to be the implication of the *Collected Poems*. None are represented in the *Collected Poems*.[14]

Though it includes translations from many sources and languages, including Irish, French, Russian, Greek, Latin and Italian, they are nearly all of Pound's 'other sort', instances of the poet 'definitely making a new poem' or incorporating translated material into a work of his own. Mahon as 'interpretative' translator is only glimpsed fleetingly in versions of Ní Dhomhnaill and Saba, Horace and Michelangelo (though even here his versions are aligned with the style and preoccupations of the surrounding poems rather than pointing outwards to work in a source language, 'An Orphan at the Door' being linked to the exploration of the 'homeless' in *The Hudson Letter*, 'The Siren' to Mahon's other Italian poems). More representative are poems like 'The Mute Phenomena', where Mahon takes off from a 'foreign' original and runs off in a direction of his own. Such poems do not aspire to 'fidelity' as a prime value, or even to provide conventionally fluent updated English versions of non-native texts in the normative way discussed by Lawrence Venuti in *The Translator's Invisibility*.[15] They follow the modernist model of Pound or Bunting, standing almost independently as Mahon poems, used to explore his own views of the world, albeit in a 'dialogical' relationship with a work of art from another cultural moment. Or to problematise the relation between a poem's source culture and target one.[16]

Mahon's approach is not unlike that of Robert Lowell in *Imitations*. Early in his career Mahon dismissed Lowell's 'swinging, contemporaneous versions of poems in several European languages' as 'very bad', seeing in them 'a literary arrogation of powers, a confusion of poetic and critical functions'.[17] Later, discussing the analogy between translating poems and adapting novels for the screen, he spoke of the American in a more positive way:

> Eschewing what he called 'taxidermy', the late Robert Lowell published a collection of Lowell-isations of various European poets under the title *Imitations*. His object was to take the letter and fly off after the spirit as he updatedly perceived it; and foreign literatures provide as rich a feeding ground for the predatory adaptor as for the blocked poet.[18]

Mahon quotes Lowell again in his introduction to his own *Phaedra*, and he must have recognised that many of his own translations are Mahon-isations.[19] 'The Mute Phenomena' is a striking example, being almost as much a spoof of de Nerval as a modernisation. In fact Mahon published what he called a 'respectful' version of the same de Nerval poem, suggesting a certain guilt about his earlier Mahon-isation of the poem may have helped trigger his translation of de Nerval's complete sequence *The Chimeras*.[20]

Mahon's 'The Mute Phenomena' is a jauntily sardonic, not to say downright satirical version of the last of *Les Chimères*, 'Vers Dorés'. Mahon recasts de Nerval's generous pantheism into a sardonic idiom utterly at odds with the romantic rhetoric of the original, giving a new polemical edge to the French poet's critique of the ruinous complacency of the human. De Nerval's opening is monitory, philosophical: 'Homme, libre penseur! te crois-tu seul pensant/ Dans ce monde où la vie éclate en toute chose?'[21] Mahon's is downright belligerent:

> Your great mistake is to disregard the satire
> Bandied about among the mute phenomena.
> Be strong if you must, your brusque hegemony
> Means fuck-all to the somnolent sunflower
> Or the extinct volcano. What do you know
> Of the revolutionary theories advanced
> By turnips, or the sex-life of cutlery?
> Everything is susceptible, Pythagoras said so.

Mahon cuts the address to 'Man' as 'free-thinker', turning the whole poem into a knockabout satire on the 'brusque hegemony' of humans, and their disregard of other life forms. At the same time, the 'brusqueness' of the poem's tone ironises de Nerval's Pythagorean intuitions too. De Nerval had spoken of each flower as a 'soul' and of the 'mystery of love' shown in the attraction of metals, affirming the principle that 'everything has feeling'. Mahon's 'everything is susceptible' is susceptible of different interpretations, and his talk of the theories of turnips and sex-life of cutlery gives a subversive interpretation to such claims. The biological life that 'explodes' in all things in de Nerval's poem explodes with dissident discursive energy in Mahon's. As a spokesperson for the mute phenomena, he insists on their voluble satire on mankind, their resentment of our 'politics and bad draughtsmanship'.

De Nerval's poem ends in an atmosphere of hushed admonition and pantheist mystery ('Souvent dans l'être obscur habite un Dieu caché/ Et comme un oeil naissant couvert par ses paupières,/ Un pur esprit s'accroit sous l'écorce des pierres'). Mahon, by contrast, imagines the hidden God in terms of a more recent universe of technological obsolescence, more J.G. Ballard than Symboliste

Bard: 'God is alive and lives under a stone./ Already in a lost hub-cap is conceived/ The ideal society which will replace our own'.

Mahon's updated version of de Nerval has huge gusto, but there is no question that he has subjected the French to what he calls in his second translation of the same poem ('Pythagorean Lines') in *The Chimeras* a certain 'base manipulation'. In fact, the reproach implicit in the opening of the second version ('Your urgent guile/ Works blithely on its raw material,/ But you ignore the spiritual perspective') might well have been addressed to himself as translator. In any case, while 'Pythagorean Lines' recasts it into tough contemporary English, this 'respectful version' is clearly much more faithful to the tone and logic of de Nerval's sonnet. At the close de Nerval's natural supernaturalism and Mahon's awe at human waste converge: 'Even now a God hides among bricks and bones- / And, like an eye closed in the womb, a pure/ Spirit evolves beneath the glaze of stones!'. Even having accomplished this 'respectful version' in his *The Chimeras*, however, it is his brazenly Mahon-ised 'The Mute Phenomena' which survives in the *Collected*.

Translation and adaptation – including the de Nerval book and the verse translations of Molière – took up a lot of Mahon's energies during the otherwise poetically lean late 1980s and early 1990s. Though they aren't represented here, the theatre work, the playful and stagey Molière adaptations in particular, helped loosen up Mahon's poetic idiom in general, giving him experience with working with longer lines and on a broader canvas, and encouraging him to think in terms of a chattier speaking voice. This bore fruit in the long autobiographical sequences of the 1990s. In fact in both *The Hudson Letter* and *The Yellow Book*, meditations on metropolitan post-modernity, translation generates a substantial amount of the text itself. These are not primarily 'interpretative' translations, but ways of reading the late twentieth-century decadence of New York or Dublin by generating a trans-historical dialogue between different texts and times, between source cultures and target culture, from an avowedly personal and modern angle. There is no pretence here of objectivity, of canonic accuracy, or classical dignity of the kind Venuti finds so suspect. Mahon has made a point across his career of either dis-integrating originals – he only translates an extract from Rimbaud's 'Le Bateau Ivre', only the first part of Pasolinis's *Cenere di Gramsci* – or of integrating them into his work as 'foreign' bodies as in the autobiographical rewrite of a fragment of the

Procne episode from the *Metamorphoses* in 'Ovid on West 4th', or the fragments of Laforgue in *The Yellow Book* or the use of the Metastasio in *Roman Script*.

Though Mahon makes no claim to be a linguist, the translations in *Collected Poems* come from many sources. There are translations from French – he includes versions of poems by Rimbaud, Baudelaire, Laforgue, Corbière, and de Nerval (though nothing from the brilliant Jaccottet book); from Provençale ('Domnei'); from German, Rilke's 'Night Drive' (though no longer the composite collage translation 'Brecht in Svenborg', sadly); from Latin, Ovid in particular (as represented in 'Ovid in Love', 'Galatea', 'Ovid on West 4th'), but also Horace ('How To Live') and Juvenal ('The Idiocy of Human Aspiration'); from the Russian of Pasternak (the two poems in 'After Pasternak'); from the Italian in 'Roman Script', 'Night and Day, 'Gramsci's Ashes', 'After Michelangelo', 'A Siren.' He doesn't claim knowledge of Irish, but there are two translations of Nuala Ni Dhomhnaill ('An Orphan at the Door', 'The Race') and the two autobiographical adaptations, 'I am Raftery' after 'Mise Raftery' and 'An Bonnan Bui' in *The Yellow Book*, a Mahonian version of Cathal Buidhe Mac Giolla Ghunna's 'Yellow Bittern' .

In *The Yellow Book*, Mahon advocates reading 'the symbolists as the season dies' (*CP* 225), and the strongest thread in all this is French. Mahon is part of the tradition of Irish writers, from Yeats and George Moore through Joyce, Beckett, Devlin, Montague and Ciaran Carson, who take their bearings from Paris. As for Beckett and Devlin before him and Ciaran Carson after him, translation from French holds a special place (Beckett, Mahon and Carson all try their hand at Rimbaud's 'Le Bateau Ivre', a perfect poem for the Francophile, alcoholophile). Mahon studied French at Trinity and spent some time as an *auditeur libre* at the Sorbonne during his undergraduate degree and he has proved an astonishingly versatile translator of French poetry and verse drama over his career. Though he makes no claim to be fluent in French, it has clearly provided him with the earliest and most far-reaching linguistic and cultural 'Elsewhere'. For Mahon, as for the writers and artists commemorated in *The Yellow Book*, and for the modernists Pound and Eliot, poetic modernity is bound up with the legacy of Baudelaire, Corbière and Laforgue. He translated poems by the first two at the onset of his career, and *The Yellow Book* contains versions of Baudelaire and Laforgue. *Collected Poems* includes his version of Corbière's 'Old Roscoff' (*CP* 98) between 'The Chinese Restaurant in Portrush' and the newly entitled

'Camus in Ulster' (a brutally truncated version of the earlier Camus poem 'Death and the Sun'), giving Corbière's Roscoff a distinctly North Antrim accent; 'the cannon pointing still/ At England' have a completely different inflection in British Northern Ireland than in French Brittany, as do the 'wild geese', an ornithological reference which acquires a distinctly political resonance in the Irish context. However Mahon banishes his truncated translation of Corbière's 'Le Poète Contumace', 'Beyond the Pale', nominally set in a 'ruined convent on the Breton coast' but which Mahon described as 'the *cailleach* of the countryside.' Its account of 'a feral poet' in a 'one-eyed tower', one of 'life's fugitives', writing a poetic letter within ear-shot of the sea, conjures up a recognisable Mahon *alter ego* – akin to the quasi-self-portraits in 'The Sea in Winter' and 'Beyond Howth Head'- but this is now one of the translations to be adjudged beyond the pale. Though it is an erratic poem, it revealed the continuity of his autobiographical as well as aesthetic dialogue with one of the original *poètes maudits*, one of the Symbolistes whom he first read when his season as a poet began. He has also banished his 'Burbles', after Beckett, which were originally included with the light verse in *The Hudson Letter*. Mahon's dialogue with Beckett from the early work of 'An Image from Beckett' and 'Exit Molloy' is never far away, but Beckett's presence is much more alive in 'Ovid in Tomis' or 'Antarctica' than in the discarded translated bagatelles. In *The Yellow Book* Mahon returns to Baudelaire, however, after over 30 years.

The poets Mahon choses to translate inevitably bear upon, indeed seem to translate, his own preoccupations. Characteristically the poets he has translated represent those he calls in his defining early poem, 'Glengormley', 'the unreconciled in their metaphysical pain.' He has also shown a predeliction for poems about the city by writers as different as Baudelaire, Laforgue, Pasternak, Brecht, Cavafy and Pasolini. Pasternak's Dr Zhivago writes that 'cities are the only source of inspiration for a truly modern contemporary art', a sentiment Mahon would find congenial, I suspect.[22] The Belfast poet's versions of 'White Night' and 'The Earth' (*CP* 138–40) from *Dr Zhivago*, are pure Mahon: Pasternak's Moscow is a setting for stoical urban epiphanies, but also lit up with a sense of political terror ('Outside and in, the same/ Mixture of fire and fear'), as in 'Derry Morning'. 'What a lot depends on the choice of metre', Zhivago says, and in both poems Mahon, as is his wont as translator, converts the more irregular Russian stanzas into his own regular, rhymed six-line units.[23] He is also drawn to poems about what he calls 'The Mute Phenomena' by writers like de Nerval himself, Rimbaud, Ovid, Rilke, Jaccottet and Ponge (though the last two aren't represented here). Despite the fact that Mahon is an unrepentant devotee of traditional form, he has drawn consistently on the poets Pound, Eliot, Yeats, Stevens and the modernists identified as their models – the French *Symbolistes* (including de Nerval, Baudelaire, Rimbaud, Corbière and Laforgue) – and also on Brecht and Cavafy (though neither figure in the *Collected*).

In *The Hunt By Night*, Ovid joins Mahon's informal pantheon of beleaguered marginalised poets, like Raftery, Brecht, Corbière and others, and from this point on classical poetry becomes a key source and resource for Mahon as much as French – as it has increasingly become for his contemporaries, Seamus Heaney and Michael Longley. Mahon's Ovid first appeared in person in 'Ovid in Tomis', published in *The Hunt By Night*, alongside the translation from Horace 'How to Live' (*HBN* 36–42). Though not exactly a translation, this was a witty, telegrammatic condensation of Ovid's *Tristia*. Later 'Ovid in Love', Galatea' and 'Ovid on 4th' confirm Mahon the Ovidian, and 'The Idiocy of Human Aspiration' his engagement with the classical satirist Juvenal. Mahon gives a further spin to the classical in his *Racine's Phaedra* and *The Bacchae*, a play which, like 'Ovid in Tomis' is about scepticism and belief.

Interestingly, Mahon pairs French and classical translations together in the first small cluster of translations in the *Collected*. They don't represent the order in which they were published but create a quasi-sequence in their own right, showing Mahon in the guise of classicist and *Symboliste* as in his recent work, *The Hudson Letter* and *The Yellow Book*. There's a pair of classical translations, Horace's 'How to Live' (from The *Hunt By Night*) with 'Ovid in Love' from *Antarctica* (1985), made up from versions of two of the *Amores*, followed by a pair of versions from the French *Symbolistes*, 'The Mute Phenomena', originally published in *The Snow Party* and a chunk now entitled 'from The Drunken Barge' (after Rimbaud), first included in *The Hunt By Night*. The shift from 'boat' to 'barge' looks a minor twitch, and with no obvious trigger in the 'bateau' of the French, but by invoking a usually inland craft it injects Rimbaud's bizarre oceanic fantasia with an added element of ironic incongruity. 'I thought of Europe and her ancient towers', we find in Mahon's fragmentary rendering of Rimbaud's *Symboliste* hymn to poetic travel, and the group of translations clearly has an implicit bearing on the poet's sense of the complex ties between England,

Ireland and Europe in the surrounding poems ('Penshurst Place' and 'The Banished Gods').

Of the Roman poets, Mahon has drawn only upon Horace and Ovid, being clearly more drawn to the latter. Mahon has a Horatian vein of his own, 'How to Live' is his only published Horatian adaptation, a cool version of Horace's *carpe diem* which translates Horace's eight Latin hexameters into eight polished English ones in rhyming couplets.[24] It begins drily: 'Don't waste your time, Leuconoé, living in fear and hope/ of the imprevisable future; forget the horoscope/ Accept what happens'. 'Imprevisable' has a certain unpredictable, pedantic oddity, otherwise the prescriptions are direct and forceful, with 'forget the horoscope' a pithy version of Horace's 'nec Baylonios/ temptaris numeros'. It ends with fine zest:

> decant your wine: the days are more fun than the years
> which pass us by while we discuss them. Act with zest
> one day at a time, and never mind the rest.

The two enjambements precipitate passing ambiguities that are akin to double-takes. 'The days are more fun than the years' sounds complete in itself, a smart aphoristic recipe with a cynical edge. It then turns into something more poignant and elusive with its second clause, as the voice slides over the line-break to read 'more fun than the years/ which pass us by while we discuss them' ('pass us by' plays on time passing but combines it with the idea of being overtaken by those who pass us by). 'As we discuss them' sets the poem in an urbane conversational framework, with the discussion covering what we do day by day but also philosophical discussion and not suggesting much difference between them. 'Act with zest' looks a good recipe for acting as well as living, but the continuation of the phrase 'one day at a time' gives it a new momentum. It makes the day the object of the verb, turning the day into a play and each performance into a one-day stand ('Act with zest one day'). The final phrase ('never mind the rest') then unobtrusively expands into a multiple Empsonian pun. It can mean 'never mind the rest' (of the days or years); but also 'never mind the rest'(i.e. other people or what they may say); and also, equally plausibly, and equally tellingly, 'never mind the rest', that is 'don't worry about resting, or the ultimate rest (death)'.

Louis MacNeice translated the same lines in 'Memoranda to Horace': 'While we chat, envious time gives us the/ Slip; so gather the day, never trusting an inch to futurity'.[25] The enjambement here seems lame, and the idiom wobbles uneasily between the conversational ('never trusting an inch') and the portentous ('to futurity'), not quite comfortable with the chattiness of 'chat'. Peter MacDonald has suggested that Mahon's poem takes on his predecessor in 'open competition', concluding that 'Mahon's contained and neat chattiness may well miss the purchase MacNeice's more intricate pacing and diction gain on the 'chat' that time overshadows.'[26] However, cool, worldly, and idiomatic as it is, Mahon's translation is a masterpiece of brevity – one of the finest versions of the *carpe diem* in the language.

John Kerrigan has written of 'Ulster Ovids' – identifying a recurring preoccupation of poets from the North, and proving prophetic of developments in the future – as Ovid has come to feature in subsequent collections of Heaney, Muldoon and Longley (whose 'According to Pythagoras' is a compendium of Ovidian lore).[27] He is certainly a more pervasive presence in Mahon than Horace (Ulster Horaces are thin on the ground), making his first appeared in person in 'Ovid in Tomis', (*CP* 157). Ovid is one of the many poets to figure in Mahon's poetry as a figure of the beleaguered marginalised poet, like Raftery, Brecht, Corbière and others. 'Ovid in Tomis' is not a translation but has its origins in Ovid's Tristia, a long autobiographical commentary on his political banishment to the Black Sea at the age of 50 (Mahon's age when he published his poem). 'Ovid in Tomis', a wittily telegrammatic condensation and modernisation of Ovid's epic series of letters of complaint, begins as a portrait of the artist in exile from the metropolis:

> Imagine Byron banished
> To Botany Bay
> Or Wilde to Dawson City
>
> And you have some idea
> Of how it is for me
> On the shores of the Black Sea.

We can see the poet's place of exile, Tomis, as an ancient equivalent of Mahon's Portstewart or Portrush, though he imagines it transformed in some future time into 'A handsome city,/ an important port,/ A popular resort' with 'a dignified/ Statue of Ovid/ Gazing out to sea/ From the promenade' (a posthumous literary metamorphosis of poet to statue, banished intellectual to civic monument).[28]

As the poem develops, Mahon's metamorphosis-haunted Ovid

comes to recognise a different kind of exile, not so much political and cultural as metaphysical. It occurs as a result of a fundamental metamorphosis of the relation of human to the cosmos of which we are part. 'Pan is dead, and already/ I feel an ancient/ Unity leave the earth', he declares, quoting Browning, and he comes to speak of something more like metaphysical exile, a banishment from the animated universe of Pagan theology. This banishment fundamentally changes the nature of the poetic for Mahon's belated and beleaguered poet: 'The Muse is somewhere/ Else, not here/ By this frozen lake', he says, before going on to ask: 'Are we truly alone/ With our physics and myths,/ The stars no more/ Than glittering dust. . .?' Mahon's Ovid, with his patent anachronisms, is speaking here of the situation of the modern intellectual, like Raftery a contemporary of Mahon rather than of Ovid. In this, paradoxically, he is part of a long tradition of Ovidian translation.[29]

Mahon is himself a poet of metamorphosis and exile, but his first Ovidian *translations* draw upon Ovid as poet of love. Under the title 'Ovid in Love', Mahon has translated two of the love elegies from *The Amores*, which he published in *Antarctica* (pp. 20–1)) and the story of the erotic artist Pygmalion whose story is told in the *Metamorphosis*, which Mahon published in *The Hudson Letter*, where it is complemented by his grotesque story of the Procne episode from *Metamorphoses* of domestic love turned to murderous hate.[30]

'Amores 1, v' shows how Mahon takes over Ovid's poem, licensed by its erotic licence, but free to adapt it to his own suave rhymed octosyllabic idiom. The Ovid has references to Phoebus, Semiramis and Lais, as well as the Corinna he makes advances to. Mahon strips away the names and mythological references, leaving a secular ethos permeated by the erotic, focused around the precise time-of-day effects Mahon is so good at:

> The open window to my right
> reflected woodland-watery light,
> keyed-up silence as of dawn
> or dusk, the vibrant and uncertain
> hour when a brave girl might undress
> and caper naked on the grass.

'Woodland-watery light' is a fresh, and freshly compounded translation of 'quale fere silvae lumen habere solent', as 'keyed-up silence as of dawn/ or dusk' is of the 'qualia sublucente fugiente crepuscula Phoebo' Ovid invokes. The 'uncertain hour' remembers T.S. Eliot's crepuscular effects in *Little Gidding* ('In the uncertain hour before the morning') but gives it a playful erotic turn. In the Latin the poem is in the third person, and addressed to Corinna; by contrast Mahon addresses the woman in the second person with arrestingly intimate effect, reminiscent of Wyatt's 'They flee from me':

> You entered in a muslin gown,
> bare-footed, your fine braids undone,
> a fabled goddess with an air
> as if in heat yet debonair.

The Latin tunic becomes a muslin gown, while the dignity of Semiramis is transferred to the more general 'fabled goddess' who manages to combine the animal energy of being 'in heat' with the flirtatious courtliness of being 'debonair' (a word that airily incorporates the word it rhymes with). Mahon plays down the reiterated erotic violence of the original, and 'I held you hard and down you slid/ beside me, as we knew you would' implies a more fully shared erotic experience than the Ovid (or in the Latin is only vouchsafed after consummation, 'lassi requievimus ambo'). By turning the poem into a second person address, the erotic is made altogether more reciprocal.

His adaptation of *Amores* Book 2, 11 is equally secular and *civilisé*. It condenses and transposes the poem, cutting down on the wealth of mythological allusions on which Ovid plays, once more recasting Ovid's expansive hexameters in unemphatic, glancing octosyllabic couplets. This is part of a more general lightening of the tone and heightening of the poem's playfulness. Mahon starts with a reference to Jason and the Argo as a reference point, retains the graceful references to Triton and Nereus as sea powers, but omits the original's heavy cargo of allusions to Boreas and other winds, preferring instead to invoke the 'frightening anecdotes/ of rocks and gales and splintered boats' told by 'those with real/ experience of life under sail' than the Scylla and Charybdis, Ceraunians and Syrtes mentioned by Ovid. The effect, like the earlier reference to Corinna going 'cruising upon the treacherous blue', is to suggest yacht-clubs rather than the Odyssey, Mediterranean beach resorts or Kinsale rather than classical ports. The classical poet's 'litora marmoreis pedibus signate, puellae;/ hactenus est tutum – cetera caeca via est' becomes the affectionately ludicrous, hyperbolically cautious 'Dance in the foam, but never trust/ the water higher than your waist.'

In the same spirit the poet addresses the prayer for his lover's safety to a more generalised and more idiomatic divinity than Ovid's Galatea ('Still if you're quite determined, God/ preserve you from a watery bed'). Mahon's Ovid is mischievously anti-nautical and his tone is genially downbeat, witness the jokey 'off rhymes' with which it is peppered:

> So much more comfortable ashore
> reading, or practising the lyre!
> Still, if you're quite determined, God
> preserve you from a watery bed. . .
> Think of me as your shrinking craft
> becomes a pinpoint in the aft-
> ernoon, and again when homeward bound
> with canvas straining in the wind.

'Think of me as your shrinking craft' conflates the poet's and the lover's views of each other, and the absurd rhyme of 'craft' and 'aft' is typical of the poet's own craft. He refuses to take either of their predicaments too seriously. Loeb gives Ovid's conclusion as saying 'all I shall take for truth, though you invent it all – why should I not flatter my own heart's desires', followed by a prayer to Lucifer to hasten the hour of her return. Mahon's ending dispenses with this last prayer and is more throwaway. It confirms the camp mock-seriousness of the whole thing, not only the lover's anticipated sailing yarns about the dangers of her trip but the poet's own performance, trying to dissuade her from the trip:

> Right there we'll make a bed of sand,
> a table of a sand-dune, and
> over the wine you'll give a vivid
> sketch of the perils you survived -
> how faced with a tempestuous sea,
> you kept your head and thought of me!
> Make it up, if you like, as I
> invent this playful fantasy. . .

These translations mark a new preoccupation with meta-morphoses of the classical, later explored more fully in his verse adaptations of the *Bacchae* of Euripides (1991) and *Racine's Phaedra* (1996). The specifically Ovidian returns in *The Hudson Letter*.

Most of these translations were grouped together in *Selected Poems* too. Given that Mahon frees himself from sticking to order of publication or compositional, their position tends to be revealing, a sign of their place in the Mahonian order of things. Here they are sandwiched between two related poems. The first of these is 'Penshurst Place' (first published in *Selected Poems*), a topographical poem which rewrites Christopher Marlowe's 'Come Live with Me and Be My Love' and conjoins an Elizabethan country house in England with a vision of 'The Spanish ships around Kinsale'. The second is 'The Banished Gods' (from *The Snow Party*), an epiphanic embodiment of 'The banished gods in hiding', sitting out the centuries down a dark lane at the back of beyond in what seems an Irish landscape. Both poems are in some degree about the survival of earlier cultural forms in the present – and about the intertwining of places from different cultures.

'After Pasternak', which in *The Hunt*, appeared in the company of 'How to Live' and 'from the Drunken Boat', now appears 50 pages later, though set, as previously, before 'The Globe in (originally North) Carolina', the poetry of 'The Earth' and 'The Globe' being clearly related. 'The Globe' is now followed by 'A Kensington Notebook', which in *Selected Poems* came 70 pages earlier but now sets up an intriguing subliminal parallel between the Kensington of Mahon's high modernists, Lewis, Ford and Pound, and the contemporary Moscow of Pasternak's Zhivago.[31] In their new context, the translations that survive are transformed once again by the company they keep in *Collected Poems*. 'Night Drive – St Petersburg 1900' (after Rilke) (*CP* 165) survives alongside other poems from *Antarctica*. Though alert to the glacial climate of so many of the *Antarctica* pieces, this is another in the series of Mahon's translations of European city poems – of a piece with his version of Pasternak's wintry Moscow, the Oslo of Knut Hamsun's 'Hunger', the versions of Baudelaire's Paris smuggled via translation into the Dublin of *The Yellow Book* (1998), and the Rome of Juvenal's *Idiocy of Human Aspirations* and Pasolini's 'Gramsci's Ashes'. Rilke's poem, with its flashing sense of a metropolitan milieu suspended before its imminent dissolution, is pure Mahon. The Mahon light-meter is alert to the 'thin/ half-light neither of earth or heaven' pervading the city, and the poem's conclusion captures his vertiginous sense of the precariousness of urbanity, as he watches 'a fixed idea in its Byzantine,/ varnished and adamantine shrine/ spin off from the whirling mind/ and vanish, leaving not a trace behind.' In two intricate, speed-conscious sentences Yeats's Byzantium and Mount Meru converge within Rilke's St Petersburg, retrospectively fraught with a sense of impending Revolution.

Mahon's next book, *The Hudson Letter*, appeared in 1995, ten years after *Antarctica*. His television and radio adaptations date from the years 1980 to 1986, and his sparkling *Buffo* versions of Molière, *High Time* and *The School of Wives*, from 1985 and 1986. If these were relatively sparse years for Mahon the lyric poet, they were years of productivity for Mahon the translator. The Jaccottet *Selected Poems* appeared in 1988, his most intensely realised exercise in lyric translation, and *The Bacchae* in 1991. The witty, knockabout verse of the Molière adaptations, with their street-wise colloquial irreverence, proved a great theatrical success, but *The Bacchae* which, perhaps unexpectedly, has some of the same qualities, has never been received with the same appreciation (it is still, as far as I know, unperformed). This is partly due to the chronic problem of translating ancient Greek tragic texts for a modern audience, but as much to the undignified Dionysian mischief Mahon's version generates, with the note struck immediately by the bravura panto-style opening: 'My name is Dionysus, son of Zeus/ and Semele, Cadmus's eldest daughter. Whoosh!' Mahon's Dionysus combines divinity and camp, and it is his mocking spirit which determines the tone of the play, which, with its tendency to snappily witty or bathetic couplets of the type used in the Molière, is engagingly irreverent, revelling in mocking both the 'dignity' of the priggish Pentheus and, I guess, received ideas of Greek tragedy. It certainly makes a stark contrast to Yeats's *Oedipus at Colonus* or, closer to home, Paulin's heavily political *Antigone* or Heaney's solemn *The Cure at Troy*.

When he went on to do his own *Racine's Phaedra* for the Gate Theatre he told an interviewer:

> Working on a translation like this gives you a creative charge –
> a rush as the cokeheads say – and the vicarious thrill that you
> are writing one of the great European plays. I wouldn't be the
> first practitioner to say working for the theatre has a beneficial
> effect: you're working with real voices, you're dealing with the
> world.

He goes on to suggest that working on the Racine translation in New York in the year before *The Hudson Letter* was one of the shaping forces behind his New York poem. He said he had worked himself 'into a straitjacket formally, particularly towards the end of my *Selected Poems*'.[32] Translation was a way out.

3

When *The Hudson Letter* came out in 1995, it heralded a new stage in Mahon's career and life in the wake of a severe breakdown, hospitalisation for his chronic alcohol problem and eventual recovery. The first part of the book originally included a number of translations, including the Ovidean 'Pygmalion and Galatea', 'The Travel Section' after Laforgue's 'Albums', 8 grotesque lyric fragments after Beckett entitled 'Burbles', and 'An Orphan at the Door' from Nuala NÌ Dhomhnaill's Irish. The Beckett are discarded, the Laforgue poem about America incorporated into the title sequence, and 'The Orphan at the Door' placed suggestively between the grimly autobiographical 'Dawn at St Patrick's' and the convalescent 'Noon at St Michael's', a reminder of Mahon's Irish anchorage.

Mahon's third Ovidian adaptation, 'Pygmalion and Galatea', makes a spectacular contrast to Ted Hughes's altogether rougher, more archaic-seeming version of the story in *Tales from Ovid* (1997). Mahon's account of the story is suave, minimal, underplayed. Again he uses octosyllabic lines, with a flexible improvisatory rhyme-scheme, creating an effect of unemphatic conversational pulse – playful fantasy again, perhaps. Though both poets stick quite closely to the Latin, their effects are as antithetical as you might expect. The differences are most marked at the moment of transformation itself, where Hughes's Pygmalion is beside himself with excitement and Hughes's verse gets equally over-excited:

> Pygmalion hurried away home
> To his ivory obsession. He burst in,
> Fevered with deprivation,
> Fell on her, embraced her, and kissed her
> Like one collapsing in a desert
> To drink at a dribble from a rock.
>
> But his hand sprang off her breast
> As if stung. He lowered it again, incredulous
>
> At the softness, the warmth
> Under his fingers. Warm
> And soft as warm soft wax -
> But alive
> With the elastic of life.[33]

Obsession, fever, collapse in the desert, stings, and (a little later) 'hallucination': the emotional temperature of Hughes's tale is pitched characteristically high (so high that it misses the anachronistically elastic implications of 'the elastic of life' which might in this context suggest modern underwear). Mahon's narrative, by contrast, is altogether quicker-footed, concise and emotionally cool (Hughes's three references to 'warmth' are condensed to one, for example):

> Hastening home, the impatient lover
> ran to the maid and, leaning over,
> embraced her there on her chaste couch.
> Her skin seemed warmer to his touch;
> his fingers felt her thighs, at which
> the ivory grew soft between
> his thumbs, as wax melts in the sun
> and, gently worked by loving hands,
> stretches, relaxes and expands,
> responsive even as it responds.

Clearly both poets respond to different invitations in the Ovidian text, working to resurrect it into two very different kinds of poetic life (as well as verse forms). Mahon's touch is lighter, less sweaty and exclamatory: the pathos, absurdity and erotic mystery of the metamorphosis are glanced at in the verbal play of the 'chaste couch', the ivory softening under the two thumbs, the body being 'gently worked' by sculptor and/or lover. Mahon's tone is much more akin to Ben Jonson's Horatian manner or the witty stylisation of cavalier erotic poetry than Hughes's Lawrentian fantasia. If the lover is enraptured by the fulfilment of his wet dream, the poet is drier and more relaxed about it, looking at Pygmalion's obsession from a certain distance. What the lines here capture, though, is the responsiveness of the sculpted body as it 'stretches, relaxes and expands'. For Mahon her responsiveness is all.[34]

All translation reproduces a version of the Pygmalion fantasy, and as Marshall McLuhan talked about hot and cold media, perhaps we could talk of hot and cool translations. In which case there is no doubt as to which Mahon aspires to, even when, as here, the poem is associated with a new poetry of erotic recognition, evident in 'Noon at St Michael's', *The Hudson Letter* and the later Italian translations.

The title poem, Mahon's metropolitan *Winterreise*, is a polyphonic reflection of mid winter in New York, a study of exile and inner and outer dereliction in late twentieth-century Reaganite Manhattan. Translation is not an obvious concern of the sequence as a whole perhaps, though much of it is built out of quotation. Nevertheless several sections engage with textual metamorphosis, and draw upon classical originals to dramatise the poet's alienation in contemporary U.S. culture. Section VIII has an Ovidian epigram and is built around a translation of the Procne and Philomel episode from *Metamorphoses* VI; Section XIII, 'Sappho in "Judith's Room"', draws on translations of the great Greek female poet, to gauge the Irish poet's attitudes towards the contemporary feminism represented by the New York bookstore it's named after; and finally Section XV, 'Domnei', includes and draws on translations from Provençal, the poets Ezra Pound saw as the roots of his 'Spirit of Romance' and the modern Western European lyric tradition, in particular a poem of Macabru with which it ends. All three of these sections hinge on the relationship between culture and the erotic, as he puts it at the end of the Ovid poem as the translation breaks off: 'Never mind the hidden agenda, the sub-text;/ it's not really about male arrogance, "rough sex",/ or vengeful sisterhood, but about art/ and the encoded mysteries of the human heart'.

With its incorporation into *Collected Poems*, *The Hudson Letter*, though largely unchanged, loses 'Sneakers', a study in low-life demotic bar language, and gains 'The Travel Section' instead, an imitation of Laforgue's 'Albums' which Mahon transforms into a satire on American versions of pastoral (complete with 'a new cult of the Golden Age/ with its own code based on holistic books,/ blithe and post-modern for the post-pastoral folks'). Including it in his updated *Waste Land*, this ironic critique of the romance of rural America acquires a different bite. The Ovidian episode, remembering Mahon's earlier 'Ovid in Tomis', is now given a U.S. address and title, 'Ovid on West 4th', suggesting perhaps that Mahon in the big Apple is as exiled as Ovid in barbarian Tomis. T.S. Eliot had momentarily tapped into the same Ovidian tale in *The Waste Land*, where splinters of it break the surface of his London ('So rudely forced. Tereu'). Mahon's engagement is more sustained. Like Eliot's, Mahon's poem excavates into literary tradition, to project its vision of both the breakdown of love on the one hand (in the Ovidian episode) and lyric passion (in the translations of Sappho and Macabru) on the other. In these episodes the sequence dissolves any clear distinction between translating and originating poetry. Till the last four lines, the poem translates Ovid but it captures the horrific sexual and familial violence with grotesque immediacy, possibly suggesting the battle within Mahon's own broken marriage over his children but insisting on the persistence of such primal horrors in the present ('fair Philomela appeared, dripping with gore,/ right in Tereus's face, as he picked at his own young'). Like the other translations it forms an integral part of the New York sequence, with its intertwining of the fate of the modern lyric with the fate of the poetic nightingale invoked in the opening poem, where the poet hears, not Eliot's 'inviolate voice' but 'Respighi's temperate nightingale on WQXR', leading him to invoke 'the nightingale' as a 'Muse'.

'Ovid on West 4th' picks up the gory climax of the tale of Procne, Tereus and Philomela told in *Metamorphoses* Book VI: 'When his wronged wife Procne sat him down to eat/ King Tereus little knew what was on his plate'. Mahon's tone is jauntily jarring, underlining the macabre reality of the cannibal feast by the play on the idiomatic idea of knowing what's on your plate. While not updating the story itself, he re-situates it in a contemporary urban setting '(Afternoon now, some silence in the street/ till released children dash to bus and swing)', compounding its antique horror by setting it amid the routines of modern childhood. Reference to 'genes' and the 'digestive tract' as well as the final commentary about 'the hidden agenda, the sub-text', insist on us reading Ovid's grotesque family drama in current terms. This is very unlike Ted Hughes's portentously mythopoeic rendering of the same scene in *Tales from Ovid* ('His roar tore itself/ Out of every fibre in his body./ He heaved the table aside -/ Shouting for the Furies/ To come up out of hell with their snake-heads').[35] Mahon extracts a kind of black humour and almost childish linguistic bathos out of the account of Tereus: 'forking his own son hot from a covered dish', 'as for the king, he nearly had a seizure', 'howling he overturned the dinner table/ and called the furies from the hobs of Hell', 'with hair on end and furious sword-bill/ turned into a hoopoe and is furious still'.

As so often, Mahon only translates part of the episode. In this case, though the extract acknowledges Procne as 'wronged wife' and has Philomela view Tereus as 'her ravisher', it omits the context for their terrible revenge; the horrible story of Tereus's rape, mutilation and imprisonment of his sister-in-law Philomela and subsequent cover-up (lines 412 to 646). This may give the reader pause at the close in the commentary Mahon adds to Ovid's story (which ends with the metamorphosis of all three protagonists into birds). Mahon says 'it's not really about male arrogance, "rough sex",/ or vengeful sisterhood, but about art/ and the encoded mysteries of the human heart.' This is epigrammatically compelling, and if we read the poem autobiographically, in connection with 'Chinatown' where the poet dines with his son rather than on him, it suggests that the lyric birds of nightingale and swallow convert sex and violence into the winged currency of aesthetic metamorphosis. He adds the resonant transposition of the nightingale to the present in the beautiful lines 'where even today, the nightingale can be heard/ descanting in convent garden and Georgian square'. On the other hand, while the original story is indeed about 'encoded mysteries of the human heart', these mysteries include, as the Ovidian horror story about sexual violence tells us, 'male arrogance,' 'rough sex' and 'vengeful sisterhood', then and now. For all the classical mask, the translation suggests that Mahon, like Tereus, may be furious still – and that the mysteries encoded in art are intimately rooted in the unresolvable passions and injuries that emanate from love. This Ovidian interlude reminds us of the relation between the 'lyric appetite' and less acceptable kinds of appetite, and that the song of the poetic nightingale originates in what Yeats calls 'the foul rag-and-bone shop of the heart'.

If 'Ovid on West 4th' re-situates one of Ovid's metamorphoses in Manhattan, 'Sappho in "Judith's Room"' imagines the 7th century Lesbian poet visiting a women's bookshop in Greenwich Village. If 'Ovid on West 4th' revives a classical picture of female rage in response to male violence, implicitly in dialogue with *The Waste Land*, then 'Sappho in "Judith's Room"', with its symmetrical title, engages via a feminist 'American bookstore' in the West Village with the legacy of the first great woman poet in the classical tradition, offering a corrective daimonic reading of the tradition to that offered in Eavan Boland's vision of lost women poets in 'The Journey', insisting by contrast on the lyric as 'a site of praise and not of grievances' (p. 210). There are multiple dialogues in play here.

Sappho's work only survives in fragments or groups of enigmatic lines and phrases. Early translators turned these into neatly formed, free-standing lyrics in stanzaic form, while post-Poundian modernists like Guy Davenport relish their very fragmentariness. Mahon doesn't take either of these routes. Instead, he incorporates splinters of phrases, surviving fragments and images, within the continuum of the rhymed epistolary pentameter form he uses for *The Hudson Letter* in general, giving Sappho a monologue of her own, as Ovid did in the fifteenth epistle of *The Heroides*.

The reed-voiced nightingale has been my guide,
soft-spoken announcer of spring, whose song I set
against a cult of contention I decried -
except, of course, for the 'fight to be affectionate'.
A corps of men, a list of ships? Give me instead
my non-violent girls – Cydro, Gongula – and particularly
our glamorous Anactoria somewhere over the sea
whose mischievous sparkle remains to me
a finer sight than Homeric bronze; for now
like the moon rising at sunset, casting its glow
on the waves, on evening meadows of brine and dew,
she climbs the night sky, and perhaps out there she hears
the wind among the reeds, and calls, so the soft-petalled ears
of darkness hear her, and the dividing sea.
Aphrodite, weaver of intrigue, revisit my heart
as so often before in your dove-drawn chariot.
Nothing was alien to me, nothing inhuman:
what did I teach but the love of women?
Soon, when the moon and Pleiades have gone
in the vast silence of the night I shall lie alone
or sit, 'Tenth Muse', in this American bookstore
relishing the historical ironies in store
and the 'homeless flow of life' beyond the door.

                                              (*CP* 209)

The nightingale here remembers Keats's and many others in the
poem but also Sappho's. The nightingale figures in many of
Sappho's lyric splinters, but Mahon's opening draws more
particularly on the fragment Davenport translates as 'First news of
springtime,/ the lovesong of the nightingale', linking it to 'Respighi's
temperate nightingale on WQXR' in Section I where its 'radio
serendipity' embodies 'the resilience of our lyric appetite'. (*CP* 187).[37]

In an intriguing weaving together of resilient lyric fragments,
Mahon's Sappho draws her words from many different sources.
From the 5th line, Mahon takes up fragment 16, where in her
modern editor Denys Page's translation Sappho says 'Some say a
host of horsemen, others of infantry, and others of ships, is the
most beautiful thing in this dark earth, but I say it is what you
love', going on to evoke the Homeric story of Helen and Troy
before celebrating Anaktoria, 'her lovely way of walking' and
what Davenport calls 'the smiling brightness of her eyes.'[38]
'Gongula', like Anactoria, is one of the women lovers named by
Sappho, while Cydro is another named by Ovid in his epistle

devoted to her. The description of moon-light 'on evening meadows of brine and dew' brilliantly condenses lines from fragment 96 which Page translates as 'its light extends over the salt sea alike and the field of flowers', while the account of Aphrodite, the Goddess most associated with Sappho, comes from fragment 1, where 'immortal Aphrodite' is described as a 'weaver of wiles', whose 'yoked golden chariot' is pulled by sparrows (not in fact the more usual doves Mahon conjures). From there Mahon modulates into what Guy Davenport calls 'the fragment the whole world knows', but which Edgar Loebel and Denys Page reject as apocryphal. It is translated by Davenport as follows:

> The moon has set, and the Pleiades.
> It is the middle of the night,
> Hour follows hour. I lie alone.[39]

The lines fall uncannily into place in Mahon's couplet, while gaining a completely different resonance and cultural context:

> Soon, when the moon and Pleiades have gone,
> in the vast silence of the night I shall lie alone
> or sit, 'tenth Muse', in this American bookstore
> relishing the historical ironies in store . . .

Mahon's Sappho is untroubled by anachronism and relishes the historical irony of the way she survives in the feminist bookshop of 'Judith's Room' (presumably named after Virginia Woolf's Judith, Shakespeare's sister) among her own 'Sapphic coterie' – an embodiment of the female lyric poet of 'love's *daimonic* character' in contrast to Eavan Boland's in 'The Journey', 'a site of praise and not of grievances.' She also seems singularly un-phased to have her 'stanzas exhumed from the Egyptian sands' re-cycled in Mahon's lines, enjoying a typical after-life in quite 'another form' ('didn't I say we'd live again in another form?'). She quotes Ovid, who in *Tristia* asked 'Lesbia quid docuit Sappho nisi amare puellae' ('what did Sappho teach but how to love girls?'), the *Palatine Anthology* where she is described as 'a tenth Muse' and Terence's 'humani nil a me alienum puto'.[40] Re-incarnated in 90s New York, she also speaks a chattier, more playful idiom than is normally associated with her a poet, as she talks of 'Mytilene of the dirty dances / making eye contact with new acquaintances' as well as her pleasure in 'a place like Judith's Room/ with Djuna, Janis, Gloria, Brooke and Kim'. As in Mahon's earlier 'Ovid In Tomis', translation and re-incarnation are hard to distinguish, as forms of poetic after-life. Ovid's own Sappho in *The Heroides*, is comparably confident of her lyric stature but is nonetheless cast in the role of Pahon's tragically jilted lover. Mahon's has a waspish, feminist wit and stylish well-travelled air. She is not about to cast herself off the Leucadian cliff, and seems happily reincarnated as a literate, erotically sophisticated New Yorker.[41]

The fifteenth poem, 'Domnei', revisits the lyric tradition and its intertwining with the erotic via the idea of *'l'amour courtois'* and Provence, so central to the Poundian tradition of translation and De Rougemont's. In fact it opens with an ironic reflection on the pseudo-sophistication of contemporary culture comparable to *Mauberley's* 'The pianola "replaces"/ Sappho's barbitos'. 'Now that we all get laid and everyone swings', Mahon begins, 'who needs the formal continence of L'*amour/ courtois* and the hang-ups of a provincial clique ...?' The slippage from 'Provençale to 'provincial' is symptomatic of the latterday provinciality being guyed. The poem then conjures up the image of an 'intense troubadour', singing a rondeau which 'rings/ resiliently on the vineyards, streams and rock-/ strewn hillsides of 12th-century Languedoc'. While it raises the modern view that it may have been 'a vicious fiction or a coercive myth', it finally melts into an italicised poetic translation of a Provençale seasonal love poem by Macabru:[42] 'but when the earth renews itself in spring/ and whitethorn flowers to hear the blackbird sing/ I too sing, although she whom I admire/ finds little to her taste in what I write.' The poem's final couplet translates the lines originally given as epigraph in earlier editions of *The Hudson Letter*, Macabru's *'Quan totz lo segles brunzeis/ Delai on ylh es si resplan'*, which Mahon renders as 'and when the world goes dim, as it does tonight,/ I see the house she goes to blaze with light'. As in the other translations of the sequence, the stanzaic structure of the original is recast in the continuous metre of the poem as a whole. As with them, the way the translated is framed insists on the cultural politics of translation, while dramatising the distance between the source culture in medieval France and late twentieth-century America.

The Hudson Letter incorporates translation into Mahon's work as never before. In his next book, *The Yellow Book*, translation plays a comparable, comparative role, in particular from the French. In fact its starting-point is that moment when English culture appropriated – and translated – French. It opens with one of two versions of Baudelaire, another poem cannibalises a translation of Laforgue's 'L'Hiver qui vient' that he had made earlier, while another ('At the Gate') incorporate lines from Mahon's *Racine* translation.[43] Other poems draw on Irish and classical sources.

The Yellow Book begins with 'Landscape', a translation of the first of Baudelaire's *Tableaux Parisiens* in *Les Fleurs du Mal*. Following hard upon an epigraph from Palinurus ('To live in a decadence need not make us despair; it is but one technical problem the more which a writer has to solve'), the translation is unnumbered and printed in italics, giving it a different status to the rest of the poems in the book. We can read it as epigraph and/or prelude to Mahon's late twentieth-century study of decadence. Though the sequence takes its title from the London-based, Paris-influenced periodical that embodied the previous *fin-de-siècle*, Mahon's book might well equally have been entitled *Tableaux Dubliniens* or *Le Spleen du Dublin*. Certainly the evocative translation of Baudelaire's haunted nocturnal cityscape serves to establish the book's specific double-vision – in which the late nineteenth-century Wildean decadence, which was itself haunted by translations from the French by poets such as Arthur Symons and painters such as Whistler, is re-translated into late twentieth-century Dublin, where Mahon in his Georgian attic in centre city sets himself up as a poet dreaming in an 'apartment block' that is also 'ivory tower.'

> Chastely to write these eclogues, I need to lie
> like the astrologers, in an attic next the sky
> where, high among church spires, I can dream and hear
> their grave-winds wind-blown to my ivory tower.

Baudelaire's 'mansarde' 'auprès du ciel' becomes Mahon's attic 'ivory tower'. Baudelaire doesn't of course use the word, but in using it the Irish poet identifies himself with the suspect and attractive culture of late nineteenth-century *Symbolisme* represented by Baudelaire and his successors. 'Ivory tower', now a cliché, is a translation of Rimbaud's 'tour d'ivoire' and its currency in English is a tribute to such works as Symons' *Modern Movement in Literature* and Edmund Wilson's *Axel's Castle* ('Axel's Castle' is the title of the third poem). Baudelaire's use of the term 'eclogues' at the opening to his *Tableaux Parisiens* is ironic, and the irony is as apt in Mahon's sequence, which like Baudelaire's *Fleurs du Mal*, is a late-in-the-day metropolitan work – as remote from the classical eclogue as you can go. Like *Ulysses*, it is conceived in 'the Heart of the Hibernian Metropolis'.

'Landscape' is a spacious, witty adaptation of the French poem to the landscape and ethos of modern Dublin. John Ashbery included a seductive version of the same poem in *A Wave* (1984), but Mahon's is pricklier and denser, freighted with some of the tensions of his much earlier 'Rage for Order'. Like Baudelaire's poem it is written in rhyming couplets, though Mahon's verse moves between full rhymes (such as 'lie' and 'sky') and more discordant pararhymes (such as 'apartment block' and 'talk'), and between romantic reverie ('and dream of love and gardens, blue resorts/ white fountains weeping into marble courts') and more suspect and suspicious self-irony ('birds chirping day night, whatever notion/ excites the infantile imagination'). 'Blue resorts', with its evocation of sunny holiday brochures and even our resort to 'blue' films, is a brilliant condensation and transposition into twentieth-century idiom of the French poet's atmospheric 'horizons bleuâtres' (Ashbery's 'bluish horizons').[44] In the same way 'the infantile imagination' captures our own century's Freudian transformation of Baudelaire's 'tout ce que l'Idylle a de plus enfantin'. Evoking his dream of writerly retreat, Baudelaire conjures up the spectacle of riot ('L' Émeute') beating on the window panes outside ('tempêtant vainement à mon vitre'), combining a fantasy of withdrawal from the storms of winter with memories of the political riots of 1848. Whereas Ashbery de-politicises the weather ('When the storm rattles the window-pane'), Mahon renders it in another key: 'Rattling the window with its riotous squabble/ no mob distracts me from my writing-table'. We are not far away from 'Rage for Order', with its image of a poet indulging his 'semantic scruples' in a world of mob violence outside – though here the 'mob' is a pure mirage, dispelled as soon as evoked. These changes are typical of Mahon's appropriation of Baudelaire for his own vision. This is especially vivid at the close. It converts Baudelaire's poetics of reverie ('Car je serai plongé dans cette volupté/ D'évoquer le Printemps avec ma volonté') into something altogether less sensuous, but altogether Mahonian in its combination of scepticism and sun-light:

> for here I am, up to my usual tricks -
> evoking spring time on the least pretext,
> extracting sunlight as my whims require,
> my thoughts blazing for want of a real fire.

The 'pretext' here is Baudelaire's text, and translation (like the evocation of 'sunlight') is of course one of Mahon's 'usual tricks'. The effect is to make the act and fact of translation part of the subject as well as the trigger for *The Yellow Book* as a whole. In this case, it enables him to extract his fix of sunlight from Baudelaire's French.

The forest of intertextuality Mahon conjures in the book involves quotation, allusion, imitation, the use of trans-historical parallels and translation. In each case the poet stages himself as someone dealing with the new decadence ('the pastiche paradise of the post-modern,' where Dublin has become a 'Georgian theme park') by affirming his anachronistic dedication to an earlier decadence, that of the late nineteenth-century. This is the moment associated with Wilde, Dowson, Symons and Yeats in England and Ireland, and with their mentors – poets like Baudelaire, de Nerval and Laforgue in France:

> Never mind the new world order and the bus tours,
> you can still switch on the fire, kick off your shoes
> and read the symbolists as the season dies:
> *Now for the coughing in school dormitories,*
> *the hot drinks far from home. November brings*
> *statistics, albums, cocoa, medicine, dreams,*
> *windows flung wide on briny balconies*
> *above an ocean of roofs and lighthouse beams;*
> *like a storm lantern the wintry planet swings.*
>
> (*TYB* 13)

Reading the symbolists also involves translating them. The italicised quotation is a condensed translation from the close of Laforgue's 'L'Hiver qui Vient' ('Blocus sentimental! Messageries du Levant'), one of the most dazzling wintry evocations of 'how the season dies' in the canon.[45] Like the Baudelaire poem, Laforgue's is one of the prototypes of the lyric metropolis mapped by the early twentieth-century modernists, and proved an influential model for Eliot and others. Mahon may even be subliminally echoing Eliot's Laforguian mode too, since the overhanging phrase, 'November brings', in the second italicised line brings to mind his 'Fire Sermon' which speaks of 'The sounds of horns and motors, which shall bring/ Sweeney to Mrs. Porter in the spring'.[46] In fact Mahon unobtrusively quotes from Laforgue's poem earlier in 'Night Thoughts' when he depicts the Fitzwilliam Square garden below his attic window:

> dripping in wintry peace, a secret garden
> absorbed since the end of summer in its own
> patient existence, sea-mist under the trees:
> 'Wet seats now, water-logged cobwebs everywhere;
> believe me, it's all over till next year'.

Even though Mahon's poem is topographically anchored in the

precise details of the Dublin square he actually lives in, the
cobwebs, the benches, the announcement of the end of the cycle,
all come from Laforgue ('On ne peut plus s'asseoir, tous les bancs
sont mouillés;/ Crois-moi, c'est bien fini jusqu'à l'année
prochaine'), like the hot drinks, medicine, dreams, balconies, and
coughing in school dormitories later. Mahon relishes the French
poet's lists and miscellaneous mundanity, as well as using them to
recreate a poetry of mute urban phenomena in his own later time
and place. Here in Mahon's 'Night Thoughts' (a title from another
poet and another era) the gap between original creation and
translation, imitation and vision, intermittently acknowledged by
quotation marks and italics, is almost entirely erased.[47] In fact,
Mahon had worked on a complete translation of Laforgue's poem
earlier, and several drafts of 'The Coming of Winter' survive.[48] As
far as I know they didn't result in a complete published version,
but they return to life in this different guise, as part of Mahon's
meditation on Dublin. In the draft translation Mahon works to
capture the syncopated, variable idiom and measure of the French,
where here he is freed up to appropriate Laforgue in his own
yellow, autumnal cadences and resonant rhymes.

The poem stages the poet in the role of a modern reader,
slipping off his shoes, and retreating from the 'new world order
and the bus tours' to read the *Symbolistes* before his electric fire.
But in doing so, it puts his 'ivory tower' in a definitely modern
context (the fire is 'electric', after all), refusing to erase the marks of
the world order it recoils from. In fact translation is not a place of
retreat or escape, it allows the poet to map his own space – both
his flat in central Dublin and the garden square outside. Laforgue's
improvisatory syncopated poem, constantly 'changeant de ton',
and shape-shifting in metrical form, is very different from
Mahon's, and Mahon only snatches fragments from it, but its
inventories ('Mais, lainages, caoutchoucs, pharmacie, rêvé') not
only offer him translation material ('statistics, albums, cocoa,
medicine, dreams') but a model that he transforms later in the
poem in his own eclectic yellow pages listings in XI ('At the
Chelsea Arts Club').

The Yellow Book absorbs Laforgue and Baudelaire into its own
milieu, taking the Symbolists up into its own compositely ironic
mundane idiom, which owes as much to the metropolitan neo-
classical satirists of eighteenth-century English poetry, Swift and
Pope, as to nineteenth-century France. *The Yellow Book*, with
eclectic *élan*, like them, draws on classical satire, this time in the
guise of yet another 'imitation' of Juvenal's tenth Satire like

Johnson's *Vanity of Human Wishes* (though the idea of emulating Johnson's poem may itself be one of the vainer human wishes), an extended allusion to Racine's severe recreation of classical tragedy in Jansenist guise, 'Phaedra at the Gate', and a modernisation of the eighteenth-century Irish 'The Yellow Bittern'. Literary models from other places and times become templates for recording and resisting the Dublin present.

Section VII of *The Yellow Book* ('An Bonnán Buí') takes its title from the famous drinking poem by the Irish poet Cathal Buidhe Mac Giolla Ghunna, and, while not strictly a translation, is both an update and autobiographical commentary on the Gaelic poet's ode about being on and off the bottle (Mahon's *Sphere Book of Modern Irish Poetry* included translations of it by both Thomas McDonagh and Tom MacIntyre).[49] Mahon's poem is as openly dependent as a Lowellian 'imitation', but it could also be described as a sequel or revision of Mac Giolla Ghunna's great lyric, composed in his own late twentieth-century urbane mode, and grafting his own reflections onto the original (in much the same way as he had done in 'I am Raftery'). His predecessor's poem offers a model and mirror for his own experience of alcoholism ('for mine is the same story'), providing him with a way of mapping out his own predicament, rather in the way James Simmons made use of translations in his *From the Irish*, with 'the ghosts of great originals' challenging him to find contemporary 'equivalents'.[50] The first 21 lines or so are built around Mac Giolla Ghunna's, though moved from stanzaic form into Mahon's more continuously discursive pentameters, and from Mac Giolla Ghunna's time to the idiom of Mahon's day. Contrast Thomas MacDonagh's:

> It's not for the common birds that I mourn,
>> The blackbird, the corncrake or the crane,
> But for the bittern that's shy and apart
>> And drinks in the marsh from the lone bog-drain.
> Oh! If I had known your were near your death,
>> While my breath held out I would have run to you . . .

with Mahon's adaptation of the same lines:

> Others have perished – heron, blackbird, thrushes -
> and lie shivering like you under the whin-bushes;
> but I mourn only the bittern, withdrawn and solitary,
> who used to carouse alone among the rushes
> and sleep rough in the star-glimmering bog-drain.

> It used to be, with characters like us,
> they'd let us wander the roads in wind and rain
> or lock us up and throw away the key -
> but now they have a cure for these psychoses . . .

(The bittern here was originally described as a 'high-brow with a hunched gait and quick forensic eye', a vivid metamorphic incarnation of the bird MacDonagh terms 'shy and apart', sadly cut in this revised and much abbreviated text). After sticking closely to the template of the original for 5 lines, the poet takes off to ponder the changed cultural attitudes to alcohol and alcoholism between the earlier Irish poet's time and Mahon's. The yellowness of the bittern consorts easily with the design of *The Yellow Book*, but the Irish poem, like the French nineteenth-century poets on which he also draws, acts as a springboard for the larger drama of cultural self-questioning in the book as a whole and for the poet's autobiographical reflections on social conformity and decadence.

'At the Gate Theatre' (poem IX) is a tribute to the contemporary Irish actress Dearbhla Molloy in her role as Phaedra and begins by implicitly quoting from her interpretation of the role at the Gate Theatre. However the lines quoted are quotations in other ways too; they quote Racine in Mahon's own translation (drawing verbatim on the text of Mahon's own adaptation of Racine's tragic play).[51] The poem pays tribute to the actor as interpreter, and interprets her in turn. Yet it also draws into the composite language of *The Yellow Book* his own theatrical translation of Racine performed at Dublin's Gate Theatre – insisting on the 'technical problem' of living in a decadence, and the analogous problems of translator and interpreter in recreating the ethos of another age, in this case the tragic vision of the Jansenist tragedian from the court of Louis Quatorze in the idiom of late twentieth-century Ireland. The cultural difference embodied in translation, as with 'The Yellow Bittern' version, is the subject as well as medium here. Racine's lines, and Dearbhla Murphy's performance of Mahon's verse translation, dramatise the disturbing anachronism of Racine's intransigent Jansenist version of classical passion in modern-day Dublin.

Mahon figures as poetic translator·in two other poems of the sequence. Poem X is a translation of Juvenal's *Satire X* (the source earlier of Johnson's *Vanity of Human Wishes* and Lowell's) and Poem XIII ('Dusk') is a version of another of Baudelaire's *Tableaux*, 'Le Crépuscule du Soir'. The Juvenal ('The Idiocy of Human

Aspiration') starts in mid-line, presenting itself explicitly as only a
fragement of the original Latin, but fragment or not it allows the
poet a classical mask to voice his hostility to 'our modern Rome'
(his modern Dublin), and as Juvenal did in his time and Samuel
Johnson in his, satirise the cynicism of the current age of greed
symbolised most abjectly by the greed of old age. There's a touch
of the preacher's voice in Mahon's Juvenal, a voice Mahon had
ironised long ago in 'Ecclesiastes' ('All anyone does now is fuck
and shit;/ instant gratification, "entertainment", longevity/ we
ask, but mumbling age comes even so'). Here, though, the irony is
all at others' expenditure, none at its own (Eliot thought Pound's
vision of hell suspect because he could only imagine a hell
reserved for others). This makes it one of the less rewarding, and
most monolithic poems in the sequence: 'all pursue riches in our
modern Rome', 'all anyone does now is fuck and shit'. All. . .?
Even allowing for some Juvenalian overstatement, this is O.T.T.
Though Mahon manages to steer clear of the authoritative
dispensation of Johnson's great 'Augustan' version, it doesn't
inhabit the complexity of the modern Irish capital in the way that
Johnson's does eighteenth-century London, and it simply doesn't
have the tonal variety or cultural responsiveness of most of
the other poems of the sequence. There are a few moments
when Juvenalian diatribe and modern mores come together
convincingly in Mahon's version: 'What use to you the glittering
décolletages,/ the best box in the house above the stage/ when you
are blind and deaf?' or 'Subdued/ by protocol, and the fear of
solitude/ you wed in haste and now repent at leisure'. Despite
such hits, the translation feels like an archaic interloper from an
earlier moral and poetic epoch, not quite able, even satirically, to
engage with the horrors or 'the delights of modern life'.

'Dusk' is altogether better attuned to both the original (in this
case Baudelaire's French) and to the contemporary city. Though
its view of the city is not unlike Juvenal's, the language of the
poem soaks up the savour of the city's unsavoury night-life in
Daumier-like detail: 'Under the lamplight that the wind teases/
the whores light up outside the whorehouses' while thieves are
'privily forcing bureau-drawer and strong-box/ to stuff their face
and clothe their mistress' backs.' Mahon's couplets capture
something of the worldly satirical gusto of Swift. Unlike the other
poem, this one is as alive to the vulnerability and poignancy of
workers, thinkers and outcasts as it is to the world of petty
criminals and tarts. So Baudelaire's 'Le savant obstiné dont le
front s'alourdit/ Et l'ouvrier courbé qui regagne son lit' find

convincing realised equivalents in Mahon's 'driven thinker with ashen face,/ and cleaning-woman who can know release'. Mahon paints a compelling version of Baudelaire's grim final tableau, with its vision of the 'gouffre commun' and 'l'hôpital' that await the sick, far from what he calls 'la douceur du foyer' (and Mahon calls 'the relief/ of house and hearth')

> Night takes them by the throat; their struggles cease
> as one by one they head for the great gulf;
> the wards fill with their cries, who soon enough
> will come no more to sup the fragrant broth
> with a loved one, at dusk, by a known hearth -
> for some of us have never known the relief
> of house and hearth, being outcast in this life.

This vision of the outcasts of the city is close to that of *The Hudson Letter* – though in general, Mahon does not identify as strongly with the 'outcast' in Dublin as when down-and-out in New York. Baudelaire sponsors a kind of shocked social compassion in the poem that Mahon the cultural commentator and aesthete doesn't give us much of in his own persona. The 'Some of us' invoked at the close may include the poet in his rented Georgian attic, but the poem's world is always social, inhabiting a larger habitat and, as always, hoping to be alert to what 'Glengormley' calls 'the unreconciled in their metaphysical pain.'

Among its many pleasures, *The Yellow Book* allows us an intimate view of Mahon as translator. The first poem establishes a kind of common ground between Mahon and Baudelaire as satirical painters of modern city life. 'Night Thoughts', the second, stages the poet as a reader of Laforgue in modern Dublin, kicking off his shoes in his attic to read the symbolists, but also using fragments of Laforgue as a template to capture his sense of autumn in the contemporary city. Translation establishes a kind of historical solidarity between poets, but is also an instrument of enquiry into the poet's own modernity. 'An Bonnán Buí' is a haunting rewriting of an elegiac Irish drinking poem from an earlier century. Beginning as recast translation, however, it then, without any palpable shift in tone or mode, becomes something else – a searching and witty meditation in time of sobriety on the poet's own alcoholism and enforced sobriety. Similarly in 'The Idiocy of Human Aspirations' and 'Dusk', through translation Mahon internalises and modernises the ferocious metropolitan critiques of Juvenal and Baudelaire, turning the full glare of their satire on the rampant consumerism of contemporary urban life. In a different way 'At the Gate Theatre', which begins by quoting his own stage adaptation of Racine's *Phèdre*, meditates on the difficulty of translation, of theatrical performance of Racine's play, and, in almost Steinerian mode, laments not only the absence of actors able to 'impersonate/ the great ones of the tragic repertoire' but 'the death of tragedy' and 'the tragic sense of life'. It is a meditation of the impossibility of recreating an idiom – an attempt to grapple with the cultural issues involved in translating Racine to the page and stage in our time.

Wilde's argument in *The Decay of Lying* that nature imitates art is integral to everything in *The Yellow Book*. Translation, of course, is always explicitly an 'imitation', and in Mahon's case imitation is everywhere. His own self-conscious culture of mimicry draws upon exemplary figures and artistic performances from the past to reactivate them in the cultural present which is locked in the grip of a different kind of mimicry (in 'The Chelsea Arts Club' for example). He cannot always avoid dressing up his own particular nostalgias (for Dublin in the sixties, say) as a cause for a cultural Jeremiad against the present of the *'o tempora, o mores'* variety. All the same, insisting on the book, if only in tribute to a magazine with the name of a book (and Mahon described himself as a 'mag junkie' in one of his letters from New York for the *Irish Times*), is central to the eloquently bookish solo performance of *The Yellow Book*, a tribute to the 'incurable ache of art' which is always, in a Wildean and Baudelairean sense, produced in dialogue with other art.

4

In the final pages of the *Collected Poems*, Mahon draws on his engagement with a quite different cultural world, that of the Italy Shelley calls the 'paradise of exiles'. Mahon's *Italienreise* figures in a series of new poems – 'Ghosts', 'A Dirge' and the atmospheric Roman sequence, *Roman Script* – but here too original poems are interwoven with translations from Italian authors, from the Renaissance poets Ariosto and Michelangelo, and from the twentieth-century poets Saba and Pasolini. Italy is a new stamping ground for Mahon, and *Roman Script*, originally published by Gallery, sponges up texts and films from and about Italy, particularly from Pasolini who provides the profoundly Mahonian epigraph. *Roman Script* closes with what is described as 'A Rewrite', a version of Metastasio's self-reflexive sonnet 'Nel comporre l'Olympiad' which becomes incorporated into Mahon's reflection on the 'virtuality' of modern Rome, the degree to which the poet's experience is shaped and mediated and fictionalised by art.[52] Metastasio's 'tutto e menzogna, e delirando io vivo' (which literally translated means 'all is falsehood, and I live deleriously') becomes 'and I live in a virtual fever of creation'- a brilliant translation of the earlier poet's idea of fiction into postmodern terms. In translation, of course, a different kind of virtuality is in play than the 'film-set, Cinecitta, a cinema city/ where life is a waking dream in broad daylight'. Nonetheless, translation offers a form of virtual originality to Mahon, even as he comments on it in this brilliant satire upon modern fictions.

Pasolini is one of the presiding spirits of *Roman Script*, so that the translated extract from 'Gramsci's Ashes' that precedes it is intimately linked to it.[53] In fact the tenth stanza is a condensation of Pasolini's vision of Rome: it is he whom Mahon invokes when he speaks of the 'poet of poverty, ash on the night wind, starlight and tower blocks on waste ground,/ peripheral rubbish-dumps' – and 'whose corpse turned up at the beach at Ostia'. The translation offers only the opening section of Pasolini's elegy for the Marxist philosopher Gramsci, the fierce critique of postwar Italy that established him as a major Italian poet. But in Mahon's hands, while staying remarkably faithful to the Italian, it acquires a new resonance as it engages with his deepest political and poetic preoccupations.

The other Italian translations are altogether less specific, less topical and topographical. 'Night and Day' is one of several poems of erotic companionship (compare the wonderful line in 'St Patrick's Day' which speaks of 'our whole existence, one erogenous zone'), but, like Mahon's earlier 'Ovid in Love' and 'Pygmalion and Galatea', the task – or mask – of translation helps licence a vein of playful, worldly and affectionate eroticism. The Italian original, Ariosto's 'Capitolo VIII', is a virtuosic Renaissance inventory not only of the woman's body parts but all the props and surroundings of the love act. Written in *terza rima*, it takes the form of a series of exclamatory playfully formal addresses to the night, stars, door, mind, hands, embraces, mouth, breath, and bed, all of which form part of the choreography of the lovers' love-making. Mahon follows the outline of the Renaissance poem remarkably faithfully, but gives it a definitely modern inflection (the almost inaudible door of the Italian has a 'squeak/ audible only to the intent sex maniac', for example, or reference to 'pre-coital fever and post-coital peace/ consensual chiaroscuro and thumping heart'), and entirely recasts its grammar and tonality.

> I'm still not sure if I'm imagining things
> when your hands guide me to a secret spot
> where hips and thighs like vines reticulate,
> I quench my thirst in your wide-open mouth,
> we gasp the quick rush and exchange of breath
> and tremble in the metaphysical love-fight.

Though most of the images are triggered by the Italian, they are also metamorphosed. The repeated embraces are likened to the twinings of ivy or acanthus ('l'edere o acanto'), and this becomes a place where 'vines reticulate', drawing together the oral eroticism of the kissing mouths with the pleasures of the vine. The 'metaphysical love fight' is entirely Mahon's invention – an intertwining of the Italian poem with the English 'metaphysical' style of Donne, remembering the conjoining of English lyric and Italian lyric in the sixteenth century. Celebrating the pleasures of seeing his lover, the Italian simply itemises her divine eyes, forehead and ivory breast, her brow and hair of curling gold, rose lips and so on, all very much a standard line. Mahon, by contrast, varies and individuates the gaze which now rests 'on gaze, flesh tones and cherishable breast, the speaking ears, the flickering and the moist/ and the rose-petal lips unknown to thorn.' 'Cherishable breast' and 'speaking ears' have an affectionate, quasi-humorous quality, where sexiness and familiarity are combined. Though at the close he can mock himself as her 'dozy lover', the mockery doesn't dispel the unabashed wishfulness of the last question: 'can we not live in a world of love for ever?'

The two Michelangelo sonnets that follow also dwell on the will towards immortality – aesthetic and human. Mahon's idiom here doesn't have quite the same individuating personal signature – in particular in the second poem, which despite its pungent Wyatt-like opening, 'Certain of death, though not yet of the hour', falls rather flat. Its not clear how to find an equivalence for Michelangelo's lament that 'l tristo esempio ancora/ Vince e sommerge ogni perfetta usanza', but Mahon's 'The world is blind, and profit-driven verbiage/ silences any superior thought' sets up a facile opposition between 'superior' thinking and the market-place, which though of our time, succumbs to one of its clichés rather than confronting it. By contrast, the opening of the first sonnet genuinely modernises the poet sculptor's affirmation that 'più dura/ L'immagin viva in pietra alpestra e dura/ Che 'l suo fattor' ('the live figure lasts longer in the hard mountain stone than its maker'):

> How can it be, as long experience shows,
> the image present in the calcium carbonate
> lasts longer, lady, than the artist does
> who turns to dust again as at the start?

The scientific redescription of Michelangelo's marble gives what has become, after Shakespeare, something of a cliché, a new lease of relative immortality and draws the poem into the orbit of the poetry of obsolescence in which Mahon specialises. He also transforms the rhyme scheme of his sonnet from the Petrarchan Italian form to the Shakespearean English one, consummated in a final couplet. Oddly, the familiar bravado of the claim to permanence, couched in the breezy idiom of Mahon's version, makes the self-congratulatory Shakespearean sentiment of the final couplet almost suspect ('so people centuries after we have gone/ will see your beauty and my wretched plight/ and know in loving you I got it right').

By contrast, 'A Siren' recreates the poignant sexual recognition of Saba's poem about an older man's love for a younger woman in a supple and relaxed conversational idiom ('your friends, young like yourself, crowd round/ and make a noise in the bar'). Mahon gives a mythological title to Saba's 'Swimming Champion' (or 'Campionessa di Nuoto'), but otherwise, while he characteristically regularises the metre, sticks faithfully to its story of an awed, erotic epiphany.[54] 'Anyone watching you in the water would think: "A siren!"', it begins, in genial colloquial style, then modulates fluidly to the arrestingly full-throated cantabile of the closing pentameter ('and joins your rising to my own setting sun'), its rhyme and diurnal rhythm matching the closing couplet of the Italian: 't'incurvò della bella bocca altera,/ che sposò la tua aurora alla mia sera'. Here, as not I think in the Michelangelo, Mahon's translation speaks the same poetic language as his own, with something of the same oblique intimacy we find in the Italian touring poem, 'Ghosts', that follows, with its funny, far-reaching opening line, 'We live the lives our parents never knew/ when they sang "Come Back to Sorento"' as well as the wonderful new 'A Swim in Co. Wicklow'. Here, translations and originals converge, as past and present do when 'white curtains blew like ghosts into the room'. For the poet of 'Afterlives', it may be that his translations offer a distinctive kind of afterlife – materialised ghosts of foreign poems, surfacing in another tongue.

'I live in a virtual fever of creation', Mahon says in the

Metastasian 'Rewrite' that concludes *Roman Script*. We could also say that he lives in a virtual fever of re-creation (in all senses). Much of his *oeuvre* takes the form of re-writing. Translation, for Mahon, is only a special case, I want to argue, of this creative process of recreation and adaptation. As much as poems from paintings such as 'Courtyards in Delft' or 'The Hunt by Night', or poems built up out of prose like 'Hunger' or 'Death and the Sun' (now 'Camus in Ulster'), 'Gramsci's Ashes' and 'Landscape', 'Ovid in West 4th' and 'The Travel Section', are Mahon poems that take their bearings from earlier cultural artefacts, in this case poems by Pasolini, Baudelaire, Ovid and Laforgue. It is not that they have been done over in the manner of cavalier Lowellian imitation so much as converted osmotically into new lyrics now bearing Mahon's signature.

Mahon may not be thought of as one of the finest verse translators of our time, but the *Collected Poems* shows that he is not only one of the most compelling poets writing today, but that translation, generated out of dialogue with a linguistic and historical 'Elsewhere', is integral to the way his poetry tests and contests the idiom of the day.

DEREK MAHON: COMING IN FROM THE COLD

FRANK SEWELL

> While those who enjoyed *The Hudson Letter* will enjoy this new volume, those who value Mahon for something other than his role as another talking head in the gallery of eminent Irish men of letters will experience again a familiar disappointment.[1]

What is all too familiar and disappointing about Peter McDonald's review of *The Yellow Book* is its tone of knowingness and use of the word 'Irish' as a pejorative adjective suggestive of self-promotion, bombasticism, scoundrelly patriotism, and 'Oirishness' as a form of anti-art. For example, while insisting that Mahon 'is the author of some of the best lyric poetry in English which our end of century has produced', McDonald bitterly regrets that 'for the time being, [he] seems to have chosen to work hard at sounding like an Irish poet. This is a lesser thing, and it is everybody's loss'.[2]

Ironically, it was Kavanagh in his enthusiasm for Auden who famously designated Irishness as a form of anti-art but he did so only for passing reasons: the frustrated Monaghan poet was desperately attempting to drag Irish poetry out from under the shadow of Yeats and of his indomitable influence. Obviously, it is too much of a simplification to claim that Irishness *per se* is a form of anti-art but it may, in the light of such comments, be worth considering if and when 'Irishness' possibly *could* become counter-productive to art.

Seán Ó Ríordáin, a generation before Mahon, believed that if 'nativeness / dúchas' was assumed or put on rather than lived or left alone to look after itself,[3] it could prevent a person from 'going' (in Hopkins' formula) him or her-self, and could furthermore mislead that person into a state of non-self, anti-self or false selfhood:

Maidir le bheith dúchasach is i ngan fhios duit féin nó, más maith
leat, ded lom-dheargainneoin a bheir dúchasach. Bí, agus beir
dúchasach. Ach maidir le bheith ag iarraidh a bheith dúchasach,
mar a bhíonn a lán den aicme ghlórach a bhíonn ag plé le Gaeilge,
sí seo an riail: Bí dúchasach agus ní bheir dúchasach, ná ní bheir.
Tá an dúchas préamhaithe sa bheatha. Ní cóta mór é ná filleadh
beag.[4]

McDonald appears to be arguing that, latterly, Derek Mahon has
been trying to *go* 'native',[5] to sound 'more like an Irish poet' by,
for example, becoming noticeably more sympathetic to the Irish
and less so to the British, Unionist and/or imperialist,[6] and that in
the process he has turned into 'another talking head in the gallery
of eminent Irish men of letters'.[7] The allegedly greener Mahon, we
are told, sounds, therefore, less like himself or, rather, his old self;
less like *a* poet or, rather, McDonald's suspect ideal of a politically
non-aligned (on the national question) poet. But does Mahon
really sound less like himself and more like an 'Irish poet' these
days?

Ireland, in Mahon's 'The Joycentenary Ode' (*SP* 145), is
'Ourland' – his, included; the place 'we cmome to' even if it has
seemed to him at times to be 'beyond cumminity'. Kavanagh,
however, once asked 'shall we be thus forever?', and if Mahon,
after all his travels, has decided that 'cumminity' is preferable to
ending up 'on the edge of everything' (*SP* 97), that only reflects
the humanity of the 'humane perspective' which he inherited from
Louis MacNeice, his openness to change and to 'fragile, solving
ambiguity' (*SP* 11). For example, looking back to Ireland from the
'modern Rome' of New York, Mahon re-imagines

> . . . that land of the real I left in '91,
> of Jennifer Johnston and Seosaimhín Ní Ghabhráin;
> I can see a united Ireland from the air,
> its meteorological gaiety and despair,
> some evidence of light industry and agriculture,
> familiar contours, turf-smoke on field and town;
> I can even hear the cabin crew's soft '*fáilte*'
> and the strains of 'My Lagan Love' as we touch down.
> A recovering Ulster Protestant like you from Co. Down [. . .]
>   ('The Hudson Letter' XVII, *THL* 72)

Here, contemporary Ireland is cited in one short, shared line as the
land of 'Jennifer Johnston and Seosaimhín Ní Ghabhráin', names
suggestive of Planter and Gael, (perhaps) Protestant and Catholic,

not separated by any line-break or stanza-break but co-existing in the egalitarian manner which much women's writing and feminist criticism claims is possible. Ireland itself is seen as one entity (or 'one place only' (*SP* 153) when viewed from an aerial distance – a bitterly ironic fact in the light or dark, for example, of Northern Ireland television weather-maps which until recently omitted the 26 counties of 'southern' Ireland or else painted them a different colour from the north with a thick dark line to denote and underline the border. Such exclusivity is countered by Mahon's many combinations of contrasting but co-existing elements: the 'meteorological gaiety and despair', light industry and agriculture, field and town, Irish and English languages and names, Ulster (9 counties, after all) and the rest of Ireland . . . Moreover, Aer Lingus cabin crews really do welcome passengers to Dublin with a 'soft *"fáilte"*' (the 't' softened to a 'che' sound) and to the simultaneous *strains* of the Belfast air 'My Lagan Love'. Partition and other historical and linguistic divides may render these facts ironic but not necessarily contradictory or untrue. Seeing and saying so makes Mahon, in his own words, seem like a 'recovering Ulster Protestant' – not in the sick sense in which this has been interpreted but suggesting that part of this poet's project is to recover, repossess or *retrieve* some of the magic, karma and poetic possibility that 'the Protestant ethic has made it its business to dispel' and that 'bad Protestants over the years have removed'.[9]

Heaney reflects that

> Mahon, like MacNeice, like Longley, cannot totally identify with the pieties and refusals of the group they were all three born into, those Northern Unionists bonded by heritage into political solidarity, unconceding custodians of civic power and unyielding refusers of an Irish dimension to their lives. These poets, who share an origin in the Northern Unionist majority, are in natural communion with that Irish culture of which the Unionist ideology is chronically if understandably suspicious. As poets, they comprehend both the solidarities of their own group and the need to subvert them. They could not possibly devote themselves to a project of writing a political Ulster into being on the terms which the dominant Unionist ideology would prescribe, since the only possible imaginative equivalent of the Unionist slogans 'Not an Inch' and 'No Surrender' would be a rigor and imperviousness of which they are incapable.[10]

Mahon himself has regretted Longley's *past* refusals to enjoy the 'benefits of the "Irishness" at [his] disposal':

Longley and Simmons consult neither 'the plain people of Ireland' nor

> 'The people of Burke and of Grattan
> Who gave though free to refuse,'

but a diffuse and fortuitous assembly of Irish, British and American models, not necessarily in that order. In this they are true to their dissociated sensibilities ... although one could wish that, though free to refuse, they might not deprive themselves so completely of the benefits of the 'Irishness' at their disposal. But there, one cannot prescribe.[11]

One certainly cannot prescribe for others but Mahon, from early on, made just such a prescription for himself. From poems dating as far back as 'Teaching in Belfast' (*P* 31) and 'I am Raftery' (*P* 50), it has been evident that the Irish writing tradition (both in English and translated from the Irish) has provided one essential and enabling source for Mahon in his efforts to find the metaphors, rhythms and words to express his own personal situation and concerns. In this sense, the 'home' tradition has continued to fuel Mahon's 'autobiographical modes'[12] of writing in a manner similar to that described by Ní Dhomhnaill who has highlighted two essential and interdependent elements in her work: firstly, 'an ionspioráid phearsanta'[13]/ personal inspiration and, secondly, béaloideas – the store of ancient oral lore and learning. 'Tá nascadh mar sin', she has written, 'idir mo thrioblóid féin agus gach a thagann anuas chugam trí mheán na teanga agus trí mheán an bhéaloidis'.[14] For example, the central metaphor and image of the poem 'Eitleán' / 'Flight' comes from an old Irish riddle which enabled Ní Dhomhnaill to articulate a grief that might otherwise have left her, as they say, 'balbh le brón' / dumb with sorrow, frozen. Through such articulations, finding in béaloideas objective co-relatives, words and images for her own situation, Ní Dhomhnaill hoped from early on in her career to achieve what she has described as 'forbairt ar an traidisiúin trína phearsanú, agus saibhriú an duine trí mheán an traidisiúin'.[15] She uses béaloideas, then, as other writers use myth, or as Derek Mahon himself uses the *literary* traditions of several countries, including Ireland: that is, as a source and springboard for his own translations and answering poems which in turn extend the tradition of 'cosmopolitan-and-Irish'[16] poetry.

In 'I am Raftery' (*P* 50), for example, Mahon – identifiable with the poet-speaker – surfaces from a state of boredom and disillusion as a present-day Raftery taking to the roads with ballads and poems; a writer in temporary residence in East Anglia where he feels like a northern fish out of water and who, should it 'kill' him, is compelled for his own sake to keep in 'touch' with Joyce. The literary tradition into which he taps –

> I have traded-in the 'simplistic maunderings'
> that made me famous, for a wry dissimulation,
> an imagery of adventitious ambiguity dredged
> from God knows what polluted underground spring

– may no longer be pure but surely that is what gives such work as this the zesty, bitter-sweet tang which readers identify with Mahon.[17]

Often, in Mahon's poetry, there are allusions to certain key images from the Irish literary tradition but which he always redeploys in his own ironic, tangential manner. 'Teaching in Belfast' (*P* 31), for example, begins with one of the most famous images from the *aisling* poetry of Aogán Ó Rathaille. It may be that the latter's 'Gile na Gile' / 'Brightness of Brightness' was the subject of the class which prompted or provoked this poem but what is important is that Mahon succeeds in making the old image seem very new and, in a different light, contemporary. To paraphrase Ní Dhomhnaill, the tradition is developed or extended through personalisation while the poet's, or speaker's, present situation and current circumstances are vividly brought to light via an earlier poet's 'glimmer' of hope and artistry. Interestingly, although the speaker of Mahon's poem is, in an ironic inversion, an authority figure, a teacher and confiscator of pen-knives, he is also subject – in a much lighter sense – to some of the confinement and oppression noted by Ó Rathaille, and longs – in a modern northern Irish twist – to escape grim Belfast's 'footfall echoes of jails and hospitals', to forsake the grey skies of the dark north for the blue skies of the wildly 'glittering west', and to make off with a lady-companion 'long since lost' who may – naughtily – personify a fallen Caitlín Ní hUallacháin.

Another Mahon poem, 'Achill' (*SP* 180), contains an epigraph from Piaras Féiritéar (1600–1653): 'im chaoinaí uaigneach nach mór go bhfeicim an lá' / 'a desolate waif scarce seeing the light of day' – yet another Mahon reference to the struggle and longing for light and remote intimacy in the midst (and 'mist') of a dark confinement and isolation. This type of poetry verbally reaches out from speaker to subject in a way that comforts if not actually, physically, connects. Thus it makes for, and stands as, a light of its own – 'I think of my son . . . I think of my daughter' – illuminating the void just as, formally, the poem itself is ringed or haloed with light from first to last line:

> I lie and imagine a first light gleam in the bay . . .
> As I glance through a few thin pages and switch off the light.

The last word, 'light', mentioned in almost *every* Mahon poem, lingers like 'the glow of the sun through mist' despite the solitude, showers, 'sloe-black patches' and sullen graft which, combined, give good reason for the epigraph from Féiritéar, hanging like one of Mahon's glow-worms against the dark background of the poem.

These examples show that to an important extent, Mahon has often in the past sounded like an Irish poet, reacting to, re-activating and extending the tradition of his country's writing. However, I am in no way suggesting that this poet has ever been prone to the monocular vision of an Eire-phone meathead or Cyclops if such a beast has ever existed. On the contrary, Mahon draws thoughts, words and images from the well of world language and literature, including the Russian, French, Japanese, Greek, Roman and American, *as well as* the Irish. The end-result has not been a parochial-and-therefore-universal voice in the manner of Kavanagh but rather the internationalist cosmopolitanism (including a strong Irish dimension) which characterises Mahon's work.

The clearest example is the poem 'Beyond Howth Head' (*P* 51) whose *dinnseanchas* (place-lore) spans Long Island, Cape Cod, the Twelve Pins/Carraroe, Dublin Bay, Birnam Wood, Cork, Spain, Denmark, 'celestial globes of words', Ward's pub, Seaford, Cushendun, Monkstown, North Wales, Blackpool, Merseyside, Clare, Belfast, Greece, the Holyland, Clonmacnoise, Toyama, Kyoto, the universe, Butt Bridge and Howth Head . . . The very diction of the poem, even if ironically at times, spans six languages – English, Irish, Latin, French, German and Japanese – and its literary references are particularly revealing as they provide an important clue to the poet's eclectic range of mentors and influences. The poem's pace and rhyme scheme, meanwhile, suggest a similar Joycean stream of consciousness and of free association to that found in the later, longer couplets of *The Hudson Letter* and *The Yellow Book*.

Other touchstones for Mahon in this poem are Shakespeare, Beckett, Spenser, *aisling* poetry, Yeats, Dylan Thomas, the saga of 'The children of Lír', Greek poetry and mythology, the Old

Testament, earlier Irish language poetry as in the sly reference to
the foxes that have 'quit Clonmacnoise', Chomei, Thoreau, and
Margaret Fuller ... Here, significantly, Mahon sets specifically
Irish references and allusions side by side with a varied array of
ready-to-hand, world-wide bricolage. The inclusion of Irish
material is certainly not part of any patriotic or chauvinistic
strategy, rather, it represents a naturally occurring aspect or
dimension of work by an Irish poet 'free to refuse' but willing to
partake of 'the benefits of the "Irishness" at [his] disposal'.

From the Irish

In the two most recent collections of his own poetry, Mahon has
elected to translate a poem from the Irish language. The first, 'An
Orphan at the Door', is a translation of 'Chomh Leochaileach le
Sliogáin' (literally, 'As Fragile as a Shell') by Nuala Ní
Dhomhnaill. Mahon's switching of the title for a line that occurs
much later in the poem is curious but considered. Keenly aware of
his own very limited knowledge of Irish, Mahon was only enticed
to translate this poem by Ní Dhomhnaill's habit of providing what
she calls a 'crib' – usually a very accurate and carefully-worded
version in English. Significantly, however, Mahon's retitling of his
translated version and his choice of this particular poem beg to be
interpreted as a symbol of how the poet himself feels he stands in
relation to the 'native' tradition: that is, that he remains on the
doorstep or threshold, an outsider orphaned by the politics of past
refusals but now willing, anxious even, to enter into a dialogue
even though he acknowledges or regrets that

> It's only in the soul
> that the miracles take place
> of love, forgiveness and grace;
> it's only in dream-truth
> that the sun and moon shine
> together in a bright sky
> while day dawns on them both.
> (*THL* 17)

For many readers, a kind of miracle did take place when Ní
Dhomhnaill's bilingual *Pharaoh's Daughter* first appeared and the
'sun and moon', Irish and English versions of her selected poems,
including this one, first appeared side by side, inside the one
bookcover.

What Kinsella has called 'the two-tongued Irish tradition' with
'two linguistic entities in dynamic interaction'[21] has continued to

channel its way between, to and from, Mahon and Ní Dhomhnaill. The latter chose Mahon's 'Antarctica' as one of her all-time favourite poems because it powerfully evokes the Goddess Durga, 'the Snow Queen, mistress of the cold, impenetrable regions of the psyche, that inner tundra'.[22] Under Mahon's influence, Ní Dhomhnaill herself explores the same tundra and evokes the same Goddess in 'Beanríon an tSneachta' / 'The Snow Queen'.[23] Mahon has also had a considerable influence on the Donegal poet Cathal Ó Searcaigh. Living in London in the 1970s, Ó Searcaigh was inspired to trace his own long and winding *Bealach 'na Bhaile* / *Homecoming* partly in the light of his fellow Ulster poet's word-journeys in *Lives* and *The Snow Party*, attracted in particular by the possibility – mooted in 'Afterlives' – of learning 'what is meant by home' (*SP* 51).

Thus if Mahon's persona is often that of 'an orphan at the door', standing at the doorstep,[24] waiting to 'come in from the cold' (*SP* 33), it is clear that his work has received a soft but significant *fáilte* / welcome from his peers in Irish. 'Aesthetics', Mahon once described as

> Neither the tearful taper
> nor the withered wick
> that sickly crowd.
>
> But the single bright
> landing light
> ghosting an iodine cloud.[25]

Something of that bright landing light glows in Mahon's cheering and warming transformation of the Irish tradition's taper or candle in his modern re-mix of 'An Bonnán Buí' / 'The Yellow Bittern' (*TYB* 26). This is another extraordinary example of the extension of tradition through personalisation and extension of the person's / artist's field of possibility and play through the evocation and re-activation of tradition. Only the first half of the poem reads anything like a translation of Fermanagh-man Cathal Buí Mac Giolla Ghunna's poem before Mahon gives free reign to his own current preoccupations, together with the associations and identifications he can make with this 'classic' case – no less a 'standard' or 'classic' than Juvenal's 10th a few pages later. Mahon's updating of Mac Giolla Ghunna's famous and often translated poem is performed with enough humour, élan and bitter-ess to answer and update the original:

> What do psychiatrists *want*? – An age of prose . . .
> for ours is an age of reflection, circumspection,
> a time for grief-work and polite sex.

And what do we want?

> Do we choose peace to please some foreign power,
> war-like itself elsewhere, or do we prefer
> the intransigence, bittern, of our native Ulster,
> the bigots shrieking for their beleaguered 'culture'?

Peter McDonald, revealingly, finds the political outlook here to be extremely one-sided even though the 'bigots' could be on either. Mahon, however, is one who knows his song well before he starts singing. Any exclusivist 'culture' such as that espoused presently by the Ulster-Scots Language Society, for example, cannot but be beleaguered by, and because of, its own bigotry: 'areas in Antrim and Down have been "Germanic" speaking since Viking and Medieval times'.[28] Here Germanic is stressed to portray (Ulster) Scots as being 'distinct' from Gaelic and untainted – despite the 'throughother' / 'trína chéile' loan words – by any Celtic influence or overlap. Mahon, on the contrary, though free to refuse the helping hand of a word, image or co-relative from the Irish tradition, chooses to highlight the fact that a poem from the latter, 'An Bonnán Buí', belongs to the world tradition of 'lyrical madness' which one associates with Romantic poets such as Coleridge, de Nerval and, later, Yeats. Mahon's plummet-measured, concluding couplet, in this case, follows the same world-wide tradition by fusing dream-life[29] with reality:

> Waving and drowning, the restored spirit floats
> in blue water, the rising tide that lifts some boats.

Mahon's conclusion is that while both waving and drowning are inevitable, *some* spirits can be restored or, as Marina Warner claimed in another post-colonial context,

> from submersion, from engulfment, the images can return, the drowned can rise, the devoured be pieced together and the cannibalised past be heard, telling its stories.[30]

This optimistic view is revolutionary; it is noticeable that Mahon, however, significantly dilutes such optimism by stressing that, as history has shown, only some boats or spirits can survive or be 'restored'. Throughout *The Yellow Book*, meanwhile, Mahon chooses to urge such boats / spirits onto the shore, symbolically at Kinsale (*TYB* 57), a site of previous defeat for the Irish but through an imaginative act of wishful thinking, a place perhaps of new possibilities not unrelated to the *liberté, égalité, fraternité* of the *United* Irishmen and women of two centuries ago. Such politics and aesthetics may make Mahon sound 'like an Irish poet' but, in fact, he always has, both in his 'breaking bread'[31] with the dead ('Once more, as before, I remember not to forget' (*P* 4)) and also in his longing to escape such memories so as to be through with history (*P* 64) and with his country's ghosts, 'unreconciled, in their metaphysical pain' (*P* 1).

Ghosts of heroes, saints, earlier writers, relatives, girls, etc. have haunted and inhabited Mahon's poetry from the start although his tone on the subject, as in 'Death in Bangor' (*TYB* 51), has often been 'ambiguous':

> I should rather praise
> A worldly time under this worldly sky -
> The terrier-taming, garden-watering days
> Those heroes pictured as they struggled through
> The quick noose of their finite being. By
> Necessity, if not choice, I live here too.
>   ('Glengormley', *SP* 12)

What, for example, does the poet mean by the word 'should'? That he 'ought to' but doesn't, that he 'would' or 'will' make himself praise these things in the future? Note, too, the unexpected reappearance of the 'heroes' in the list of things to be praised. Their sad names linger not only in the histories but 'live here too' in the memories and lives of many descendants, colouring, in particular, this modern poet's experience and apprehension of place both at home ('Rathlin', *SP* 122) and abroad:

> From famine, pestilence and persecution
> Those gaunt forefathers shipped abroad to find
> Rough stone of heaven beyond the western ocean,
> And staked their claim, and pinned their faith.
> Tonight their children whistle through the dark.
>   ('Canadian Pacific', *SP* 24)

Anywhere but
Dinnseanchas, which refers to the poetry and lore of places and their names, is another recurring traditional Irish feature of Mahon's work. Characteristically, he takes a bird's eye view of

locations from Yarmouth to Massachusetts, Toronto to Delft, on
and beyond but always returning to Ireland:

> We might be anywhere but are in one place only,
> One of the milestones of earth-residence
> Unique in each particular, the thinly
> Peopled hinterland serenely tense -
> Not in the hope of a resplendent future
> But with a sure sense of its intrinsic nature.
> ('A Garage in Co. Cork', *SP* 152)

As in the poem 'A Lighthouse in Maine' (*SP* 142), the phrase
'might be anywhere' highlights the universality, or place in the
universal scheme, of a particular location, while the second half of
the phrase 'but are in one place only' or 'but it is in Maine', insists
on the particularity of each unique milestone. One such milestone
in Mahon's work which interests me is the 'Coleraine triangle' and
the whole north-east of Ireland which, apart from Belfast ('neither
beau nor *bien habité*'), Mahon has described as 'un beau pays, mal
habité'. Is the north as black as Mahon paints it in 'The Last
Resort'?

> Salad-and-sand sandwiches
> And dead gulls on the beach;
> Ice-cream in the Arcadia,
> Rain lashing the windows;
> Dull days in the harbour,
> Sunday mornings in church . . .
>
> Yet the place really existed
> And still can crack a smile
> Should a sunbeam pick out
> Your grimy plastic cup
> And consecrate your vile
> Bun with its parting light.
> ('Autobiographies', *SP* 85–89)

What is delightful and darkly amusing about such Mahon poems
is not simply the combination of Larkinesque glumness with lark-
like singing lines, cadences and rhythms but the ('choosing my
words with care', *SP* p. 157) diction, the 'quick forensic eye' (*TYB*
p. 26) and accuracy that are his trademark.

One witnesses the sharpness or sharpening of Mahon's
technique even in the revisions to his work: for example, the
earlier and looser 'one *lost* July fortnight' has been honed to one

that is 'hot' both sexually and politically because the fortnight in question spans no doubt the twelfth of July and its 'unrelaxing scenes of sectarian strife' which each summer distance 'the last resort' from the imagined centre of 'Great' Britain and its former empire. 'Empire News', Mahon implies, is not necessarily good. The 'Jews blinking in shocked sunlight' may have been eventually released but the reason, for example, why 'frozen armies trembled at the gates of Leningrad' in the first place was that Hitler wanted Russia to be, as he put it, his 'India'. The 'male child in a garden / clutching the *Empire News*' grows up – an 'ironic heir of a threadbare colonialism'[33] – to learn such disturbing adult facts.

Observations of this kind are invited by the ingenious selectivity of Mahon's memories included in such autobiographical poems and by their juxtapositions within each line, stanza or section. For example, 'oranges and bananas' set side by side in a single line bring with them connotations of 'orange' Ulster and 'banana' republic, while 'the last ration coupons' may hint at the beginning-of-the-end-of-empire but, for Irish readers, might also provide the faintest of historical echoes of the Famine. Such associations may seem far-fetched or far-flung were it not for other post-colonial references to 'complaining about the natives', distance 'from an imagined centre' and the whole poem's revolutionary resolution in which the poet-schoolboy grows into a Flann O'Brienite hybrid of half-boy half-bike, a transgressor of all borders, including that of time:

> It [the bike] went with me to Dublin
> Where I sold it the same winter;
> But its wheels still sing
> In the memory, stars that turn
> About an eternal centre,
> The bright spokes glittering.
>   *(SP* p. 89)

It was once put to Mahon that his poems about Ireland – especially the north – 'use an imagery of loneliness and desolation, bleak landscapes, images of lonely milk bottles on steps at dawn'. The poet's reply was:

> I love all that stuff! Yes, well that's what Beckett in his appendix to *Watt* calls 'soul landscape' and my soul landscape is Irish and there's no getting away from that.[34]

Beckett himself was inspired by Charlie Chaplin, a caricaturist but also a Communist who, in *The Worker* and other films, sought to amuse but also to convey, like Beckett, some dark and troubling soul truths. Mahon's absorption of Beckett's influence[35] leads him at times, I believe, to paint a comically grotesque and exaggerated picture of the north of Ireland. In 'Songs of Praise', for example, he revisits 'the desolate headland' *(SP* 54) where 'a lost tribe is singing "Abide with Me"':

> Tonight, their simple church grown glamorous,
> The proud parishioners of the outlying parts
> Lift up their hymn-books and their hearts
> To please the outside-broadcast cameras.
> The darkness deepens; day draws to a close;
> A well-bred sixth-former yawns with her nose.
>
> Outside, the hymn dies among rocks and dunes.
> Conflicting rhythms of the incurious sea,
> Not even contemptuous of these tiny tunes,
> Take over where our thin ascriptions fail.
> Down there the silence of the laboratory,
> Trombone dispatches of the beleaguered whale.
>
> ('Songs of Praise', *SP* 119)

Notably, while he enjoys the irony, the vanity of human wishes, the poet is not contemptuous since it is 'our' thin ascriptions which fail, including a writer's own constructs which he has elsewhere written off as 'an eddy of semantic scruples / in an unstructurable sea' (*P* 44).

A less comically grotesque image of the lost tribe and, by extension, of northerners in general, perhaps, is to be found in 'Going Home', a poem dedicated to the 'planter' poet, habitué of the Antrim Glens and champion of Ulster regionalism, John Hewitt. This poem contrasts the leafy glades of southern England with the great Irish forests prior to colonisation[36] and with what Mahon, unlike Hewitt, sees as the 'last stubborn growth' of today:

> Battered by constant rain
> And twisted by the sea-wind
>
> With nothing to recommend it
> But its harsh tenacity . . .
> As if its very existence
> Were a reason to continue . . .

> Its worn fingers scrabbling
> at a torn sky, it stands
> On the edge of everything
> Like a burnt-out angel
> Raising petitionary hands.
>
> Grotesque by day, at twilight
> An almost tragic figure
> Of anguish and despair,
> It merges into the funeral
> Cloud-continent of night
> As if it belongs there.
>   *(SP* p. 97)

No Ulster renaissance seems imminent in Mahon's view according to these lines which contain more of the despair than the humour of Beckett.

One thing, however, that Mahon and Hewitt do share, whether they feel as if they belong or not, is an ear for the song of a certain Lagan blackbird.[37] The difference is that Hewitt gets bogged down with the nationality of the bird, the language of its song and the 'difficulty' of translating it. Mahon simply transposes it, keeping the song going in the post-war, post-industrial, some say post-colonial, era:

> No sound of machinery anywhere,
> When from a bramble bush a hidden
> Blackbird suddenly gave tongue,
> Its diffident, resilient song
> Breaking the silence of the seas.
>   *(SP* p. 101)

Curiously, Mahon mixes the 'woodnotes, whin-/gold, sudden' of the blackbird with the English tradition ('One morning in the month of June') and with his own contrasting polysyllables[38] ('diffident, resilient').

Yet, Irish history is such – in Joyce's words – a nightmare that Mahon picks up not only songs and chords from the past but screams and discords. This is because poetry is a forum where even the unspeakable is sometimes registered and a poet's antennae,[39] when randomly stirred, sensitive as a seismograph:

> A long time since the last scream cut short -
> Then an unnatural silence; and then

> A natural silence, slowly broken . . .
> ('Rathlin', *SP* 122)

In 'Memory of Brother Michael', Kavanagh mused that 'when
Drake was winning seas for England / We sailed in puddles of the
past'.[40] From a more recent, further north perspective afforded by
Rathlin Island where Drake was implicated in massacre, Mahon
observes that 'bombs doze in the housing estates / but here they
are through with history'. His broad historical vision may leave
the poet wondering 'whether the future lies before us or behind'
but generally his recourse is to home in on the present moment for
a penetrating existentialist insight snatched out of time or history.
In 'Derry Morning', for example, the facing poem in *Selected
Poems*, Mahon notes that

> Smoke from a thousand chimneys strains
> One way beneath the returning rains
> That shroud the bomb-sites, while the fog
> Of time receives the ideologue.
> (*SP* 123)

For the moment, however, neither the city nor the poem escape
being wrapped up in the 'gloom' with which Mahon associates
this 'benighted' northern coast and tends to block or blot it out: 'a
Russian freighter bound for home / Mourns to the city in its
gloom'.

Yet – a favourite word of Mahon's – there are lighter moments
when the poet's vision extends to scan and span those visions and
vistas when the night and the dark let up:

> Yet there are mornings when,
> Even in midwinter, sunlight
> Flares, and a rare stillness
> Lies upon roof and garden-
> Each object eldritch-bright,
> The sea scarred but at peace.
> ('North Wind: Portrush', *SP* 124)

and when the wild wind 'choirs' unforgettably. The poet's
tongue, however, remains as cutting as that North Wind when
it comes to describing – himself included, usually[41] – northern
folk:

> The wrapped-up bourgeoisie
> Hardened by wind and sea . . .

Our hearts starred with frost
Through countless generations . . .

Here only the stricken souls
No spring can unperturb.
                                    (SP 125)

Mahon echoes Larkin in suggesting that it is not the place's fault
but that of the people:

Portstewart, Portrush, Portballintrae -
Un beau pays mal habité,
Policed by rednecks in dark cloth
And roving gangs of tartan youth.
No place for a gentleman like you.
The good, the beautiful and the true
Have a tough time of it; and yet
There is that rather obvious sunset
                                    (P 110)

and the hope, too, of sunrise, a new dawn or spring of which 'we
scarcely dare to dream':

                . . . The ideal future
Shines out of our better nature,
Dimly visible from afar:
'The sun is but a morning star'.
                                    (P 113)

It is significant and poignant that the poem, 'The Sea in Winter',
and the collection, *Poems 1962–1978*, end with an only half-made
wish that, trailing off in so-called 'points of omission', opts for
silence rather than simplification and avoids placing the poet-
speaker in the distrusted, if not detested, role of preacher:

                . . . and if the dawn
That wakes us now should also find us
Cured of our ancient colour-blindness . . .
I who know nothing go to teach
While a new day crawls up the beach.
                                    (P 114)

Fittingly, the three points of omission above offer a space that
invites readers to make their own wish, imagine their own ideal
future or pray for their own special intention. This is craftily
appropriate since it is up to readers, especially Irish readers, to

first imagine an alternative to the 'given' life in order to make change or improvement possible: for example, in Mahon's view the war in the north of Ireland is, largely,

> between the fluidity of a possible life (poetry is a great lubricant) and the *rigor mortis* of archaic postures, political and cultural. The poets themselves have taken no part in political events, but they have contributed to that possible life, or to the possibility of that possible life.[42]

Some of the fluidity and also the *rigor mortis* of which Mahon writes above is evident in his lullaby, selected and translated from Corbière, to 'Old Roscoff' (*SP* 128). The poet invites the town to 'sleep', as it has done, 'with [its] one watchful eye / On England these three hundred years', and notes a certain irony in the archaic posture of the town's cannon, silent in their own state of *rigor mortis*:

> Your cannon, swept by wintry rain,
> Lie prostrate on their beds of mud.
> Their mouths will never speak again;
> They sleep the long sleep of the dead,
> Their only roar the adenoidal
> Echoes of equinoctial snores
> From the cold muzzles pointing still
> At England, trailing a few wild flowers.

Notably, when Mahon himself trains his eye on Ireland, he avoids any risk of 'narcissistic provincialism' by ensuring that his writing 'has something to say beyond the shores of Ireland';[43] equally, however, as in the above example, whenever he turns his eye to places other than Ireland, he casts an Irish eye upon them – that is, an eye which selects or focuses on features of foreign places in a way that reverberates both for himself and for other Irish readers back home. For this reason, Mahon tends to view other countries in the light of his own experience of Ireland ('Thinking of Inishere in Cambridge, Massachusetts', (*P* 27)) and of Ireland's experience, comparing, for example, the 'clobbering' of John Burgoyne with that of the O'Neill, and contrasting the independence of America with the colonisation of Ireland (*THL* 28–29).

Likewise, when Mahon turns to other writers for inspiration, he freely chooses from abroad but repeatedly returns to a core of – for him – essential influences who happen to be Irish and whose influence on him is widely acknowledged, not least by the poet himself. These influences include Joyce, Beckett and MacNeice –

all of whom he genuinely admires and with whom, I believe, he identifies – but also Yeats whom he likewise admires but with whom he tends to be in dispute (*SP* 133). For me, however, Mahon is like Keith Douglas in that he is 'one of those in whom man and poet are close',[44] one whose style of living translates into and, to some extent, dictates his style of writing. For example, Mahon brings Yeats down to earth with a belting – or below the belt – blow, one which Mahon himself seems to have felt in encountering and experiencing some of the harsher realities:

> One fortunate in both would have us choose
> 'Perfection of the life or of the work'.
> Nonsense, you work best on a full stomach
> As everybody over thirty knows -
> For who, unbreakfasted, will love the lark?
> Prepare your protein-fed epiphanies,
> Your heavenly mansions blazing in the dark.
>
> (*SP* 133)

Such an outlook is completely consistent with Mahon's re-occurring poems focusing on outsiders such as the 'Gypsies' (*SP* 43) and, more recently, the homeless of 'Alien Nation':

> We are all far from home, be our home still
> a Chicago slum, a house under the Cave Hill
> or a caravan parked in a field above Cushendun.
> Clutching our bits and pieces, arrogant in dereliction . . .
>
> (*THL* 62)

The last line is a democratisation of Eliot's famous 'fragments *I* have shored against *my* ruins' – for which, of course, some shore underfoot and shelter overhead is necessary.[45]

Coming in from the cold

A wild wind continues to whisk and choir through Mahon's poetry, driving him homelessly onward in the journey which he knows 'is never done' (*THL* 77); and that is how some critics like to image this poet. Mahon, however, with his 'humane perspective' all too humanly keeps coming back 'knocking late', 'rappin' till the break of dawn' at the door of a home he scarcely believes in[46] but which, through felt experience, he recognises as a 'lost' but no less necessary, warm – even, in some ways, appealing and welcoming – domain: 'When does the thaw begin? / We have been too long in the cold. – Take us in; take us in!' (*THL* 77).

In such poems, Mahon word-paints his own Dutch interior:

> So take us in where we set out long ago,
> the magic garden in the lost domain, the vigilant lamplight
> glimpsed through teeming rain,
> the house, the stove in the kitchen, the warm bed,
> the hearth, *vrai lieu*, ranged crockery overhead-
> 'felicitous space' lost to the tribes.
>
>   ('The Small Rain', *THL* 75–77)

This scene of nostalgic warmth and intimacy is at once familial and familiar as in some of Mahon's early work, including the poem 'A Tolerable Wisdom':

> You've heard the gravel at the window, seen
> A lost figure unmanned by closing time.
> More honour to you that you took him in,
> Fed buns and cocoa, sweetness, the sought dream
> Of warmth and light against your listening skin
> And rocked him to a tolerable wisdom.
>
>   *(SP* 33)

Such homecomings could be negatively interpreted as rather sentimental, especially, it seems, when the lady or home that the poet comes home to turns out, later on, to be Éire / Ireland. McDonald, for example, complains of 'inert romanticism' and even atavism in Mahon's most recent southward circlings towards Dublin and Kinsale which conclude *The Yellow Book*: 'one might almost say that Mahon has gone native'.[47] In my view, however, it has taken MacNeicean honesty, as well as remarkable courage and skill for the philosophical, ironical, and semi-detached Mr. cosmopolitan Mahon to write so intimately and entertainingly, so 'seeriously and truly' to 'felt experience' (*THL* 30). In doing so, he has given of himself and drawn from 'the given life' (*P* 114) a poetry where not only thoughts *(SP* 62) but paradoxes (*THL* 30) grow – not least of which is that the wanderer wondering what is meant by home (*SP* 51) has hit home to the many. For the more Mahon has sounded himself out, the more Irish he has sounded; and the more Irish he has sounded, the more his poetry has chimed and choired with the 'global village' of which he is a citizen and where, yes, lightning really does strike twice (*THL* 42).

'THE SOUL OF SILENCE': DEREK MAHON'S MASCULINITIES

JOHN GOODBY

Left completely to his own devices, the bachelor's idea of interior decoration is a pyramid of empty beer-cans on a window-sill.
– P.J. O'Rourke, *The Bachelor Home Companion* (epigraph to *The Hudson Letter*)

A near-consensus exists, or existed until the recent publication of *The Hudson Letter* and *The Yellow Book*, on the status of Derek Mahon's poetry. This critical certitude – lacking, to anything like the same degree, for other Northern Irish poets – rested to some extent on the high quality and relative slenderness of the Mahon *oeuvre*. But it was also a function of an assumed 'universal' quality, Mahon being distinctive among Northern Irish poets in appealing to a dimension beyond the Northern crisis (or his own personal crises), to cosmic cataclysms, eco-deaths, the universal as the entropic rundown of the universe. This form of universalism contrasted sharply with that of his contemporaries, which was grounded in a liberal humanist appeal to common humanity, and it was one which can be said to have frequently saved Mahon's work from blandness and platitude. The *sub specie aeternitatis* viewpoint was, in any case, never merely an escape from the historical and social, just as the commitment to the 'well-made' lyric was problematised almost from the first by a Beckettian fascination with modernist alienation, withdrawal and minimalism.[1] Yet to highlight the tension between a desire to be 'through with history' and its simultaneous urgent presence in *Lives* and *The Snow Party* was, arguably, to approach the poetry in a necessarily reductive way, one which saw text and context as fundamentally separate, however much the former could be made to 'comment' on the latter. A more thoroughly intertextual sense of Mahon's poetry, I would claim, was available in areas most critics tended to overlook – those of class, and more particularly, gender – which suggested that its habitually universalist and metaphysical frames of reference mediated the social in a more complex manner. Put another way, it should be seen as a judgement on the masculinist critical paradigms habitually applied to Northern poetry that the phrase 'middle class cunts' in 'Lives' – in a poem addressed to the obstreperously plebeian James Simmons – was never interrogated for what it might reveal about class or gender, or for whether its animus might inform the poetry more generally.[2] Taking this as a cue might suggest that the usual aestheticist and historicist approaches to Mahon's work might be fruitfully considered in terms of one category which brings both together, namely its uncompromising maleness.

Mahon and Men's Studies

In terms of general public debate the idea that maleness constitutes a specific *problem* – visible in educational under-performance, social maladjustment, ill health and so on – is a relatively new one. An article such as that by Anthony Clare, which appeared in *The Independent* a year ago – 'Idle, sad and baffled by sex. What's wrong with men?' – could be fairly said to represent, in its title, the level the debate has reached to date.[3] The idea of masculinity as a special object of literary-critical scrutiny, however, is rather less recent than this public and still somewhat sensationalist investigation, developing as it has from explorations of the cultural meaning of 'maleness'; that is, the ways in which masculinity is constructed and by which it operates. Indeed, Men's Studies developed as a psycho-sociological discipline as long ago as the 1970s in response to the emergence of the Women's Movement and feminism. Yet its origins point to the fact that the trail from, say, R.W. Connell's *Masculinities* (1995)[4] back to *The Snow Party* is not necessarily a clear one; in particular, the disciplinary sources of Men's Studies make for models which initially at least allowed little room for nuanced (con)textual approaches. However, more subtle approaches to the specifically literary implications of masculinity have emerged over the last decade; moreover, it is of some significance that it was precisely with Mahon's own generation – with those men raised in the immediate postwar period – that Men's Studies originated.[5] In terms of Mahon's work, of course, the importance of notions of masculinity, even in a crudely thematic sense, is apparent as soon as its working-class family background, scarcity of female figures (as opposed to male exemplars) and modernist-influenced conceptions of artistic activity are considered. Yet more than this, I shall argue, the centrality to Mahon's work of silence and absence, key categories in studies of masculinity, point to a deeper implication of the poetry in the specifics of the construction of male selfhood. These features are, of course, frequently attributed to a taste for historical pathos – the 'unsayable' of the Ulster Protestant liberal experience – but they are also traceable to the experience of postwar fathering and resultant masculine forms of emotional witholding. Both aspects acquire in Mahon's writing an inflection from the more general hypermasculinity of Unionist/Loyalist culture which he ostensibly rejects.

The point is not just that the poems tend to use only male, often assertively self-sufficient personae, nor that they assume a male reader (consider the phrase 'woman-inquisition' in 'Ecclesiastes', for example). Nor is it even that they flatter to deceive female addressees or subjects in the manner of the epigraph to 'The Globe in North Carolina', taken from Voznesensky ('There are no religions, no revelations; there are women'). To state this would be to state the obvious and to court banality. Conversely, it would be an insensitive critic who, for the sake of a reductive political correctness, failed to warm to Mahon's account of his and Michael Longley's male consociation as students in Dublin; devouring poetry, 'smoking and drinking too much', they shared 'a malodorous basement flat in Merrion Square', where 'after I'd worn a shirt for about a month I'd carefully fold it and put it away in a bottom drawer until it was clean again'.[6] Rather, it is more to recall Seamus Heaney's 1965 *New Statesman* review of Nell Dunn's *Talking to Women*: 'Here in Ireland this old thing of the equality of the sexes has long been seen for the cant it is'.[7] The point is not what a sexist Heaney (or Mahon) was (or is), but the way our experience of gender – its relationships, language and representations – change; and, in turn, that this, as Rita Felski puts it in *The Gender of Modernity*, is evidence of 'the profoundly historical nature of private feelings'.[8] Mahon's work reveals shifting attitudes to gender over three decades but, unlike those of Heaney, they have been ignored by critics. Male Catholic / Nationalist-background poets have received a great deal of (usually negative) attention for their representation of women. But the lack of any obvious equivalent representations by Protestant-background poets (there are no Bog Queens in Michael Longley) has meant nobody has asked just what attitudes to women and gender are found in their work, even though it would seem obvious that these might, if nothing else, yield some clues concerning the failure of any accomplished Protestant *woman* poet to emerge in Northern Ireland in the last thirty years. (The differing social and civil status of women in Protestant and Catholic communities needs to be noted at this point since these structure male assumptions and attitudes; it may be, for example, that a belief in the comparative freedom of women in the civil sphere complicates the process by which they might reject their community for would-be Protestant women writers. For Catholic women writers, as we know, the sway the Church exercises over their bodies and private lives constrains and shapes both self-perception and what is permitted and taboo in poetic discourse. Perhaps most important, mariology – despite the Virgin's function in ultimately confirming the subordination of women – contrasts with the unrelieved masculinity, in symbolic terms at least, of Protestantism. Similarly, the gendering of the national territory as female, the use of the *aisling* genre and so on in the Nationalist / Catholic tradition at least recognise a female dimension to human experience, albeit one which has to be challenged or transmuted.) The main point, of course, is that in a polarised sectarian society different versions of patriarchy reinforce each other, an aspect of self- and social formation remarked in poetry as early as 1932 by Louis MacNeice in the chilling final stanza of 'Belfast':

> Over [this] country of cowled and haunted faces
> The sun goes down with a banging of Orange drums
> While the male kind murders each its woman
> To whose prayer for oblivion answers no Madonna.[9]

'Forgive us, this is our way'
A set of interlinked assumptions inform Mahon's first three collections, *Night-Crossing* (1968), *Lives* (1972), *The Snow Party* (1975). These are that certain values (the notion of 'genius', professionalism, detachment and autonomy, asceticism) – seen as productive of the highest artistic achievement – are available only to men. The implication, visible in the poems themselves, is that women are a threat to the integral, creative male self embarked on an artistic quest. (This is not to say that Mahon doesn't recognise a value in what is conventionally meant by 'the feminine' – 'these hills are hard / As nails, yet soft and feminine in their turn' (*SP* 11) – merely that the 'feminine' takes its 'turn', is a subordinate, contrastive term in the male / female pairing.) This has been noted by Eavan Boland: 'I think it has limited his work . . . that he preserved maleness as a sort of caste-system within the poem. It has taken initiatives in other genres – the recent film *The Crying*

Game is one example – to suggest the power of sexual disaffection to act as a commentary on historic disorder'.[10] The quality of distance seen by many as a tactic of disengagement appears, for Boland, to be a more wilful masculine withdrawal from full engagement with the external world. If this rather basic engagement / disengagement model recalls Seamus Deane's argument in *Celtic Revivals* that Mahon became a better poet when he started to 'engage' more with history, it nevertheless draws attention to the extent to which, for example, the gender implications of the personae of the poetry has been overlooked. These are almost invariably versions of the male *poète maudit*, members of the aesthetic (rather than Calvinist) elect, sometimes ironic, often aloof, always misunderstood, ultimately damned but going down in glory. They include van Gogh, Beckett, 'Dowson & Co.', Flann O'Brien, de Nerval, Rimbaud, Malcolm Lowry, Villon and de Quincey, all exemplars not simply of artistic achievement but of a rebellion which can be related to Mahon's projection of himself as the grit within the Welfare State oyster, a product of, but inassimilable by, postwar prosperity.[11] It's no coincidence, either, that these figures are so often also spectacular substance abusers, epitomising that self-possession on the verge of self-disintegration which is the hallmark of a specifically masculine bohemianism. Thus, alcohol is seen not merely as granting insight; in 'A Tolerable Wisdom', where the speaker turns up late at night to be sheltered by a woman who 'took . . . in' 'A lost figure *unmanned* by closing time' (*SP* 33; my emphasis), it bestows bohemian scapegrace potency only to undo it. 'Take in', of course, is ambiguously sexual; and masculine unpredictability is celebrated even as the housebound, available woman is honoured. The point, however, is that 'unmanned' identifies a masculinity which is endorsed by a capacity for drink, but which also, and more commonly, functions paradoxically as a *substitute* for sexual encounters through which potency might be validated, as a substitute for engagement which nevertheless ratifies this particular artistic variant on the standard type of manliness. I shall say more on this point later; for now, I merely note that at every opportunity masculine extremism is made the precondition for exemplary suffering and creativity.

The terms of Mahon's poetry can in part be seen as part of the widespread concern with paternity and fathers found in much postwar British mens' writing, from John Osborne and Philip Larkin to Amis (*père* and *fils*) and Michael Hofmann. Certainly, Mahon defines the familial in terms of males; the relations his

early poetry celebrate include a grandfather, a not-so-wicked
uncle and a father-in-law. They, like Mahon's artistic heroes,
refuse to be 'pinned down' to commitment, the ordinary or the
domestic. The paradoxical transcendence of the quotidian
available to them is summed up in 'Grandfather', of whom we are
told 'Nothing escapes him; he escapes us all' (*SP* 13). 'My Wicked
Uncle', similarly, deals in a laddishness subversive of
commonsense: 'something about him / Demanded that you
picture the surprise / Of the Chairman of the Board, when to /
"What will you have with your whiskey?" my uncle replies, /
"Another whiskey please"' (*P* 6). Like these two, 'Father-in-Law'
is a poet in his way: 'When you lost your balance like Li Po / They
found unfinished poems in your sea-chest' (*SP* 55). Edna Longley
has touched on the prevalence of the tendency in Northern Irish
writing, noting the 'amazing popularity of [the father] as motif',
and it is possible to view this popularity as structured by anxiety
over the Britain-as-father, Northern-Ireland-as-child troping of the
political relationship (although Longley does not make this point
herself).[12] Pointedly, Mahon's male artistic band and family
figures are all notably father substitutes, not his actual – biological,
historical – father at all. Proud as he claims to be of the shipyard
forebears which include his father, Mahon never refers to him in
his poetry. Jonathan Rutherford, in *Men's Silences: Predicaments in
Masculinity* (1992) sets the ambivalence towards fathers in a
specific social and historical context, arguing that masculinity is
overly dependent for its coherence upon external public
discourses and that, as a consequence, 'men experience periods of
social and cultural transition as a disturbance to their identities'.[13]
Conventional postwar masculinities (which Rutherford and others
see as formative of their fathers' generation, and so of their own)
centred on the awkward transition to peace overshadowed, for
British men, by National Service and war. This transition was
played out in struggles over domesticity and fatherhood, the
shifting balance of power within the home, and was reflected in
popular cultural genres, such as the 1950s Western (thus, while a
film like *Shane* clearly allegorises the decline and death of
undomesticated masculinity, those by John Ford address an
anxiety about the absent father and the power of the mother). In
literary terms this is at the heart of Osborne's *Look Back in Anger*,
for example, and in Jimmy Porter's suggestion that Allison
personifies the state of the nation: soft, possessive, with no 'great
causes' left to fight for: 'No, there's nothing for it, me boy, but to
let yourself be butchered by the women', he tells Cliff. Perhaps

most influential, for a poet, was Larkin's strategy of ironic misogyny and withdrawal from marriage, domesticity, and the entire postwar social paradigm.[14] Rutherford argues, convincingly, that men of the postwar generation suffered both from an obsession with absent, unavailable fathers, and an identification with mothers which took the form of a contradictory longing for, and vehement struggle to be free from them. This, in turn, took the form of a silence concerning the mother because of anxieties about becoming a father.

'Looking for some such panacea'

Yet in its very masculinity, of course, Mahon's poetry is fated to undermine its extreme positions, as the ambiguous (un)manning by drink in 'A Tolerable Wisdom' hints. 'Hypermasculinity' – like any discursive system attempting to foreclose alternatives – continually betrays itself into its opposite. The logical consequences of the 'manly' denigration of, or silence concerning women may, of course, be an 'unmanly' male bonding, even homoeroticism and homosexuality. This is precisely the insight of Tom Paulin's figuring of Protestant Ulster as 'masculine Islam, the rule of the just', where men hold hands in a 'buggered shade' (a recent popular-cultural version of the same double-bind is contained in the Rab C. Nesbitt one-liner: 'This is Glasgow. Here they think you're a poof if you fall in love with a woman'.[15]) Mahon's own form of hypermasculinity, however, is too asexual and ascetic, too socially detached, for this issue to be raised in such a concentratedly parodic manner. Rather, the absent female occasionally figures, nostalgically and conventionally, the loss which drives the artist. Thus, 'De Quincey in Later Life' focuses throughout on the mature writer, in the last lines pulling back to reveal the woman against whom De Quincey has defined himself. 'Anne' is offered both as solution for the problems of his maleness and the sign of his lack, a craving filled by the addiction which has consumed him in her absence:

> . . . the restless thunder of London —
> Where he had gone in his eighteenth year
> And walked the embankments after dark
> With Anne, looking for some such panacea.
> (SP 15)

Like the sean-nós singer of 'Aran', the male artist requires a female presence to 'earth' him, but only in order that with his 'free hand' (the adjective 'free' a telling comment on the constraints Mahon sees as inevitable in male-female relationships) he can listen 'to his own rendition, / Singing the darkness into the light' (*SP* 31). Presence of the female Other validates the artistic quest, the women providing an audience, a witness; yet at the same time, her absence is a crucial precondition of creativity. Occasionally female marginality is seen to yield an ambiguous quasi-mythic wisdom, like the old woman in 'Jail Journal', the poet's 'reasonable' *alter ego*, who sits 'in the window opposite ... / Talking to no-one. I shout. / Either she is deaf or / She has reason' (*P* 16). Beckettian detachment is one form of evading the female in early Mahon (the Beckettian provenance of this figure can be detected in the last line's deliberately literal translation of a French idiom: 'Elle a de raison'); however, it is largely because this figure is aged, and therefore sexless, that she can be permitted an appearance.

More complicated is 'An Unborn Child', whose speaker confesses he imagines his mother as a 'city', complete with 'sewers'; he himself is another metaphor for the isolated poet capable only of isolated imagining. The mother is associated with flesh, the carrying off of waste. Comparisons with, say, MacNeice's 'Prayer Before Birth' (or Dylan Thomas's 'If my head hurt a hair's foot') show the increased alienation of child from mother in Mahon's poem and, by implication, the sense of her body as constraining and corrupting. Nevertheless, as in 'Jail Journal', the limitations of the speaker are apparent in his admission of egocentricity. The one woman in Mahon's male pantheon of artist-martyrs appears in 'The Death of Marilyn Monroe'. Monroe joins Mahon's artistic pantheon as a result of her exemplary, self-punishing, scapegoated death, which makes her (ironically) an honorary male for the purposes of the poem. This allows her mythicisation in terms of the price of her fame (the insider's badge of excess is provided by 'her little bottle of barbiturate'), and though it emphasises her 'final ... Stark-nakedness', it insists it is 'desolate' rather than fuel for prurient speculation (*P* 7). Beginning as a rare successful creative use of Dylan Thomas, the poem's conclusion halts at the 'immovable' (rather than irresistible) 'body', and registers ambivalence towards the romanticisation of Monroe as a cultural fetish.

A rather different form of ambivalence is seen in two poems which specifically address the 'silence' referred to in the title of this essay. The first, 'A Mythological Figure', describes an imaginary Cassandra-like figure only able to sing, never to speak, when she opens her mouth. Her songs would be 'without words'

> Or the words without meaning —
> Like the cries of love or the cries of mourning.
>
> (*P* 10)

Song supplants speech, female emotion overrides masculine reason; Mahon's figure is given the noises which accompany origins ('love') and ends ('mourning'), but at the cost of female articulacy, agency, self-representation, of words with meaning. She is inescapable but – in the strict sense of the word – meaningless. This could be seen as the kind of double-edged tribute which finally puts women more firmly in their traditional place, and while that would be a limited interpretation it is one, I think, most readers would accept (Tom Paulin, the only critic to single the poem out, misses this aspect with his vague claim that 'only a rare and extraordinary imagination would invent such a figure'.[16]) Another 'silence' poem addressed to a female figure provides an interesting, non-mythological, contrast. 'Preface to a Love Poem' also sets the beloved in the realm of the inexpressible and transcendental. Female otherness is identified with the condition to which the poem aspires, even though its condition is that inexpressibility: this saying is 'a way of airing my distraught / Love of your silence; you are the soul of silence . . .'. But it is male self-indulgence ('to say "I love you" out of indolence') which is explored here, male inarticulacy – the speaker's distance and abstraction – which is scrutinised, his poem 'at one remove, a substitute / For final answers', a 'night-cry, neither here nor there'. The idea of relinquishing poetic male powers and not simply yielding in the face of the sublime is aired here for the first time in Mahon, the poem as (male) construct, the poet controlled by, rather than imperiously commanding language:

> A form of words, compact and compromise,
> Prepared in the false dawn of the half-true . . .
>
> Words never choosing but the words choose them . . .
>
> (*SP* 14)

Masculinities and Modernisms: 'Stiff with rhetoric'
Steven Clark, in *Sordid Images: the Poetry of Masculine Desire* (1994), claims that misogynistic language in poetry, or texts generally, cannot be sexist in the way a direct enunciation can because the process of reading forces language to undergo a process of distantiation: 'certain institutional usages may be made of it but in

itself it escapes the specificity of context in which the authority of
masculine speech resides'. For Clark, this isn't to exculpate
misogynistic poetry so much as to note that 'The difference
between the sexist statement and the misogynistic text is one of
formal coherence and disengagement from an empirical rationale'.
Thus, it is premature to read misogynist texts simply as

> instruments of consolation, reassurance or cultural reinforcement
> ... These poems [he deals *inter alia* with Larkin, Eliot and
> Rochester] seem more designed to promote than alleviate anxiety,
> to disrupt and disorientate rather than to naturalise ... Their
> attraction lies not in the way they assert control but in the way
> they threaten it. The complexity of the mechanisms of ascription
> and reattribution in these texts should not be underestimated.[17]

There is a danger – acknowledged by Clark – of special pleading
in this. Yet at the same time there is a good deal that requires
consideration if the threat of moralism in reading Mahon in the
terms I propose is to be avoided. Clark's challenge is not only that
we look directly at misogyny but also acknowledge that the
apparent antithesis between misogynistic and the culturally
endorsed form of the love poem is just that, and that the latter
'contains within itself not merely a capacity for potential
emotional reversal, but also an implicit reinforcement of a
communal masculinity'.[18] This can be linked to my earlier point
about the dubiousness of 'male bonding', but also usefully
questions the very notion of 'misogyny' as a simple, binary male-
female relation. Eve Kosofsky Sedgwick, in *Between Men: English
Literature and Male Homosocial Desire* (1985), suggests a more
radical source for Clarke's point about 'communal masculinity'.
For Sedgwick, desire is everywhere mediated, and that despite its
apparently binary forms, it is structured by a triangular and
largely masculine relationship of rivalry. If, among three people
(call them A, B and C for convenience), if A desires B we normally
assume that this is because A desires B because B is desirable. For
Sedgwick, however, it is more likely that A desires B because B is
desired by C. Love stories in fiction frequently concern the rivalry
of two men (A and C) for a woman (B), with the great novelists
revealing the imitative nature of desire and exposing the lie of
spontaneous desire (Sedgwick deals largely with the novel,
following the work of the critic René Girard). Indeed, this rivalry
itself frequently becomes more important than actual desire for
the woman. In Sedgwick's work this insight is pushed further;
Western culture in general, for her, is structured by a crisis of

homo / heterosexual definition, with relationships as presented in culture most commonly configured in terms of what she calls 'homosocial desire', which is not to be confused with homosexuality. Rather than literature being full of unconscious homosexuals waiting to be outed, for Sedgwick homosocial desire is central to the understanding of what we might like to think of as simply 'heterosexual' writing (*Hamlet* and *Wuthering Heights* are only two of the most obvious examples). The hidden conflicts of homosocial desire generate much of the violence and power of such texts.[19] Importantly, Sedgwick provides a way of thinking Northern Irish constructions of masculinity which does not rely on stereotypical homo/heterosexual binary oppositions. In Mahon's case Sedgwick's conflictual relationships are present in literary terms at once 'communal' and agonistic, while central to the 'anxiety' detected by Clarke in 'misogynistic' poetry is his relationship to modernism. As Suzanne Clark has noted, the concepts privileged by modernist writers and critics already exist in specifically masculine terms,[20] while Rutherford notes that silence on the mother in male writing 'maintain[s] the myth that the male is ontologically for himself and his masculinity derived from his own being and authority'.[21] Embracing modernism is part of the process by which Mahon silences his biological parents within his work – again, the difference between him and other Northern Irish poets is striking – to claim a literary origin. 'Death and the Sun', in which 'while you [Camus] lay in the *mairie*, / I pedalled home from Bab-el-Oued / To my mother silently making tea . . .', juxtaposes the eloquence in death of Camus with the death-in-life taciturnity of Mahon's mother; like many modernist writers, this one is fascinated by the possibility of self-authoring (*SP* 192). As 'The Hudson Letter' has it,

> We are all lost boys, or so we like to imagine -
> each sprung, like Gatsby, from his own self-conception;
> whereas, of course, there's not much you can do
> about the odd parents who conceived of you . . .
>   (*THL* 59)

He has, of course, always had a particular regard for that most thoroughly male and self-created group of poets, the French Symbolistes, variously victimised by mother (Rimbaud), wife (Verlaine), or lovers (Gèrard de Nerval and Tristan Corbière). Both Rimbaud and Corbière were in the list of five for whom the term 'Les poètes maudits' was coined by Verlaine in 1884, and Mahon has written poems for (or versioned) both of them, although it is de Nerval, coolly and brilliantly translated in *The Chimeras*, who means most to him.[22] These 'palaeomodernists', to use Frank Kermode's term – modernist in content, but not in form – point to the complex links between Mahon and modernism, the incompleteness of his affiliation, with both early Yeats and Beckett at different ends of a modernist continuum running roughly from 1880 to 1940. Mahon is highly conscious of this inheritance, and his preference for traditional metrics and minimalism over high modernist experimentalism is his ironic (if ultimately constricting) framing of modernism's pretensions. Nevertheless, as Boland points out, he has been more than half in love with élitism:

> The crisis as far as Modernism was concerned, was the authority of the poet. For all the disruption of style and approach, this was unfinished business. Unlike Larkin, who flamboyantly disassembled that authority, Derek remained fascinated by it. In some of his best poems ... there is a rigorous investigation of the power of witness and voyeurism, together with an underlying longing that the old legend of the poet's power be true and verifiable.[23]

The dalliance with modernism is consummated in 'A Kensington Notebook', where high modernism is presented, as it presented itself (as an aesthetic as well as in its *cadre*), in supremely masculine terms. This is a poem about 'The Men of 1914', and in the modernism of these artists – Pound, Lewis, Eliot, Ford, Gaudier-Brezska – as Peter Nicholls points out, 'the recurrent trope of Woman transfigured (and displaced) by Art occupied a central place. Through this transfiguration and displacement, according to Nicholls, their art sought an escape from mimesis, or realism: 'The critical writings of Pound, Eliot and Lewis thus contains a sort of self-narration which associates formal experiment with a history of self-narration: the Modernist comes of age through his emergence from both the "womanish introspection" which Yeats, for example, discerned in his own early work, and from the habits of imitation on which contemporary democracy depends'.[24] Mahon's own 'self-narration', of course, does not rely on formal experiment; rather, what he offers in 'A Kensington Notebook' is a historicised modernism – modernism as period piece – while his work as a whole feeds off a tension between his refusal of experiment and his exploitation of modernist tropes and attitudes. The trope of 'Woman transfigured (and displaced) by Art' is thus not as central to Mahon's work as it is to that of the modernists; indeed, the echoing of Hugh Selwyn Mauberley's 'porcelain revery' in the 'cold dream / of . . . A palace of porcelain' in 'The Last of the Fire Kings' acts as something of a rebuke to it (the 'Fire King' as modernist artist, it may be). Nevertheless the trope is present, usually in the form of 'displacement' rather than 'transfiguration'. 'A Kensington Notebook' cleverly pastiches the metrical conservatism of Pound's Mauberley poems – one of the few formal points of entry to modernism for Mahon – foregrounding and thematizing this strategy. Ford Madox Ford is the most humanly attractive of the artistic company on parade, his suffragism and socialism alluded to, but via the banality of a calculated *double entendre*, in the lines 'A man could stand up / Then, and a woman too'. Mahon's treatment of Pound is ambiguous; 'Romance' is seen as flowering equally in his Vorticist London years as when, later,

> Confucius of the dooryard,
> Prophet of Γσ Χαλον,
> He drawls treason into
> A Roman microphone.
> (*SP* 92)

The following section on Wyndham Lewis notes that 'Aesthetic bombardiering / Prefigures the real thing'; high explosives and artillery called down by toying with pearl-handled revolvers and 'Vitriol versus cocoa' (and in the process recalling the cocoa of 'A Tolerable Wisdom'). Yet Mahon is ultimately forgiving, signing off with an image of Pound 'Poling his profile toward / What farther shore?' Mahon leaves the ultimate revenge on modernist presumption to time; but if he colludes with, by resorting to, the depthlessness of pastiche – for Frederic Jameson the period style of postmodernism – he also leaves himself elegiacally diminished along with Ford, Pound and Lewis by the 'Anxious and vehement' yet drained and low-key present.

'Remembering the Nineties': the later poetry
Mahon's poetry consistently reveals the contradictions inherent in any writing which assumes masculinity as normative. The very intensity of male exclusivity forces an awareness of the reliance on women, a resentment and (more rarely) an acknowledgement of it. Moreover, this form of masculinity is an inherently unstable construction: the perfection seen as the proper achievement of the unhampered, undistracted male artist becomes sterile, unable to reproduce itself, a dead end, almost a kind of public lavatory (the chill 'palace of porcelain'), where only the boys may hang out.

Although not self-consciously 'feminist', the predicament presented has its elements of similarity with feminist critiques of male subjectivity.[25] As with any complicatedly self-aware poet, there has always been, in Mahon, an awareness of the alternatives to stereotyping, an awareness undoubtedly increased by his outsider, anti-communal sense, his agreement with Cyril Connolly's famous claim, after World War Two, that 'It is closing time in the gardens of the West and from now on an artist will be measured by the quality of his solitude' (a comment which suggests links between postwar apocalypticism and the *fin-de-siècle* tone of much of Mahon's poetry). Yet one of the differences between a prewar aestheticism and its contemporary equivalent is the latter's coincidence with ecologism and opposition to technologism, associated with maleness – as opposed to femaleness – since the Enlightenment. Post-nuclear scenarios may not be associated with the relaxation of the boundaries of masculine selfhood, but apocalypse may be the only way of justifying such abandonment. It is worth noting, moreover, that Seidler – in emphasising the centrality of control of emotion and denial of sexuality in the construction of masculinity – connects both to the exaltation of abstract reason in the Western intellectual tradition.[26] In 'The Antigone Riddle' such hyperrationalism is indicted, non-violently, by a kind of Green proto-feminism which opposes abstract 'progress':

> Elocution, logic, political science,
> Antibiotics, do-it-yourself,
> And a plover flops in his oil slick.
>
> Shy minerals contract at the sound of his voice,
> Cod point in silence when his bombers pass,
> And the windfall waits
> In silence for his departure
> Before it drops in
> Silence to the long grass.
>
>   (*P* 67)

His 'voice'; *his* 'bombers'; *his* 'departure': a different kind of 'progress' is proposed here, as the Mahonesque virtue of 'silence' is switched from the (male) artist's necessary reserve to a (female) Nature's rebuke of the military-industrial complex with which he may be complicit.

By the time of *Lives*' title poem, Mahon had shown an interest in exploring multiple personae and viewpoints, not just as a succession of historical characters but as a mutating single sensibility. This procedure, developed against the historical-archaeological narratives of Heaney (to whom 'Lives' is ironically dedicated) is, like the ecological thematics of a poem such as 'The Antigone Riddle', inherently subversive of the fixed subject positions associated with masculine certitude. The period after *The Snow Party* (1975), seen by many critics as the end of one phase of Mahon's development, saw this being thematised in *Poems 1962–1978, Courtyards in Delft* (1980) and *The Hunt By Night* (1982). In the late 1970s a more discursive, relaxed Mahon is revealed and the cultivation of a more laid-back, childhood-discussing, rural, generally intimate and 'feminine' subject position is clear in 'Surrey Poems', 'Autobiographies' and 'Light Music'.[27] It's as much a sign of the male-dominated nature of Northern Irish poetry criticism that these poems were criticised at the time for showing a falling-away of his powers; it might be more accurate to detect a relinquishing of some of the hieratic pose of the earlier work (what John Constable calls 'the reduction of the poet's debate to a single ... proposition' is a criticism of Mahon for giving up his power of coolly witholding judgement and the true, ambiguous poise of the (male) poet – although, of course, that ambiguousness is generally contained within an ironic frame which limits its potential for subversion of masculine certitude, as I shall argue).[28] This is one direction in which, it seems to me, 'A Disused Shed in Co. Wicklow' points – the rights to representation of those marginalised in the 'Indian compounds' (as of those earlier in 'the kitchen houses' of the 'desperate city'), rather than those of the elect. The historical pathos of the poem, eerily juggling 'light meter', unnerving anthropomorphism and genocidal horror ('Lost people of Treblinka'), stems from its unstable generic blend of seemingly incompatible allegorical and symbolist modes; even the painful sincerity of the mushrooms' pleas is not wholly immune from the essential absurdity of the conception.

Might this change in Mahon's poetry be connected in any way with its historical moment? The shift is, undoubtedly, ultimately the result of an inner logic of stylistic development; but it can, nevertheless, be tentatively associated with the mediation of wider cultural trends, and in particular those associated with the emergence of the postmodern. For all that John Constable speaks of the 'factitiousness' of the poems in *The Hunt by Night*, for example, its title piece seems to me to present very well a modernist-influenced writer's querying of the ludic superficiality which, in one form of postmodernism, characterises all artistic activity (that is, as 'some elaborate / Spectacle put on for fun . . .') (*HBN* 31). But in Northern Ireland, this form of change also coincided, roughly speaking, with the 'Ulsterization' of the Troubles from the mid-1970s. This was the point at which realisation dawned that the conflict wasn't going to be 'solved' in the near future. The effects of an awareness of such a normalisation, as of elements of the postmodern cultural 'dominant', can be traced in the work of Tom Paulin, Paul Muldoon and Medbh McGuckian, whose first work began to appear at this time, and which displays a suspicion of the opposition between public and private worlds accepted by poets of Mahon's generation. For Mahon, as for Michael Longley and Seamus Heaney, the realm of the poem was the personal world of the lyric self under threat, one infected by, and implicated in, the violence, but not essentially shaped by it. Violence was seen, in other words, as an 'unnatural' irruption into pre-existing normality. The younger poets reinterpreted this relationship between public and private, inner and outer, reading the self as to a far greater degree constituted by the Troubles, with a much weaker sense of some prelapsarian, 'natural' self. The real comparison for Mahon, however, is with Heaney, and the distance between *North* (1975) and *Station Island* (1983). Mahon's equivalent is his development between *The Snow Party* and *The Hunt by Night*, a development dramatized in 'Courtyards in Delft', with its extra now-you-see-it-now-you-don't fifth verse, added after the publication of the original four-verse version in 1980. That original version had ended, in typical understated fashion, with the links between imperialism and a cleanliness-is-next-to-godliness work ethic hinted rather than directly pointed. The obliquity is gone in the additional verse:

> For the pale light of that provincial town
> Will spread itself, like ink or oil,
> Over the not yet accurate linen
> Map of the world which occupies one wall
> And punish nature in the name of God.
> If only, now, the Maenads, as of right,
> Came smashing crockery, with fire and sword,
> We could sleep easier in our beds at night.
>   (*HBN* 10)

This, of course, creates a real problem of interpretation if ambiguity is seen as the essence of Mahon's poetry. As I've tried to suggest, however, ambiguity – as a form of male witholding or silence – can itself be valorised to the extent that it becomes a form of didacticism. There is enough information to make Mahon's point in the first four verses, but the poet may know better than his critics what he is up to here; arguably, the new element isn't so much the explicitness of the argument as the female presence of the Maenads. In this reading, what is outraged – and what the poem attempts to appease – is a kind of female principle, overrun by masculine, bourgeois instrumental reason and now revenging itself. The guilt of the speaker is that of a man as well as of a displaced Ulster Protestant, both complicit in 'punish[ing] nature in the name of God' and both undergoing an apocalyptic trashing which brilliantly mixes the end of civilisation with the close of an evening in a Greek restaurant (like the joint symbolic and allegorical modes in 'A Disused Shed', this may be an example of the 'heterogeneous' qualities to which John Redmond has objected in Mahon's work.)[29]

If this is correct, the poetry of the 1980s and 1990s qualifies, to some extent, the male vision of art which incurs the wrath of the Maenads, in personal as well as more public and aesthetic terms. The bruised ruefulness of poems like 'Craigvara House' and 'Dawn at St. Patrick's' might be taken to bear this out, although up to *Antarctica* (1985) this desire is offset by the increasing sense of being trapped by form (this is the true significance of the sprawling verse epistle adopted in *The Hudson Letter*). One 'feminising' literary influence of the 1980s is that of Paul Durcan, and what Edna Longley calls his 'outraged feminine sensibility'. Fascinatingly, Mahon has written a pastiche Durcan poem, 'Poet Arrested for Distributing Daffodils in Castlebar', and in the essay 'Orpheus Ascending' he quotes Durcan on the break-up of his marriage, calling him, in *Daddy, Daddy*, 'more of a feminist than ever. (Perhaps "womanist" would be better) . . . [Orpheus did] look back . . . and Euridice was lost forever; after which he turned gay and was killed by the Maenads. Durcan has not, to my knowledge, turned gay, and he is in no danger from the Maenads'.[30] Mahon's appraisal of the not-really imitable Durcan is a stage on the road towards reconfiguring his own poetic procedures in *The Hudson Letter* (1995) and *The Yellow Book* (1997), although the casual allusion to the 'gayness' of Orpheus reflects the way, for men, the threat to the boundaries of gender may easily be experienced as a threat to identity itself. (It's also worth noting in this connection the dramatic adaptations of Molière by Mahon in the 1980s, *High Time* (1985) and *The School for Wives* (1986).[31]

Of Hudson and Yellow

Mahon's two collections of the 1990s read, in part, as palinodes. Stylistic tightness is relaxed, the dreck of the modern world is more openly admitted, the tone is confessional. Attitudes from the earlier poetry are, at least implicitly, corrected. Mahon's daughter, son and new love (or loves) – the family and relationships which appeared only intermittently in the earlier poetry – now loom large – so large, indeed, that it can be at the expense of the poem, as in 'The Hudson Letter' itself. Mahon's daughter and the new female presence are crucial here, since Mahon's mother is an absence before *The Yellow Book* (and his ex-wife never really makes an appearance). Thus, Katie is described, approvingly, as 'a precocious feminist, already at the age of five / contemptuous of your raggedy dolls', while the partner 're-reads Yeats in a feminist light' in 'Noon at St. Michael's' (*THL* 54). Female claims on masculine isolation, introspection and selfishness are not only established, but their justice is openly acknowledged.

The most extended exploration of this new area of interest occurs in 'Sappho in "Judith's Room"', which takes the form of a monologue by a collection of Sappho's poetry in a women's writing bookshop in New York. An interesting conceit – cousin to the speaking objects of *Lives* and *The Snow Party* – this poem also sets limits to Mahon's concessions to feminism. This is clear in the intertextual material, which includes Sappho citing both Eavan Boland's 'The Journey' and Mahon's own early 'Girls in Their Seasons', from *Night-Crossing*. In the first case she quotes Boland's line, part of a description of an imaginary underworld of women and children 'in their extremities', which lists the pre-twentieth century child-killing diseases ('Cholera, typhus, croup, diphtheria'), but argues that this misery can only be of marginal significance to her own work: 'beyond speech and the most inclusive song, / my theme is love and love's *daimonic* character, / a site of praise and not of grievances / whatever the torment' (*THL*, 64). In what is perhaps the most audacious move, the final lines of Mahon's own poem are addressed by the lesbian Sappho to her lovers: 'Girls all, be with me now and keep me warm – / didn't I say we'd live again in another form?'. The point I want to make here – without implying that there is any 'correct' position attitude or one which Mahon should necessarily adopt – is the extent to which, despite making the right noises, the disruption of gender stereotypes confines itself to thematics.

At one level we can see this in the way Mahon appears to be not so much reinventing as repeating himself. The use of 'Girls in their

Seasons' is, cited above, one example; another comes in 'The Small Rain' section of 'The Hudson Letter', which is framed by a reworking of the lines from 'A Tolerable Wisdom' quoted earlier:

> Once upon a time it was let me out and let me go -
> the night flight over deserts, amid cloud,
> a dream of discipline and fit solitude.
> Now, drifters, loners, harsh and disconsolate,
> inane and unappeased . . .
> . . . it's take me back and take me in.
> We have been too long in the cold. – Take us in; take us in!
>
> (*THL*, 77)

This sounds like a recantation, but it doesn't tell us anything we didn't already know. The feeling is obliquely confirmed if we look at the way 'The Small Rain' deals with another charged aspect of US life, that of race. In this case the same problem – of representing otherness with which there is no real engagement – is made more acute in the unfortunate attempts at black speech. 'Hey, man, they got us niggas by the nuts, / Gotta get with the program move our butts' (*THL* 76) is not so much rap as an embarrassing, middle-aged white approximation of it; or, as 'Sneakers' puts it, 'Do you want to be patronized by those sons of bitches? (*THL* 50). There is, perhaps, a link to be made here with the formal restrictions of Mahon's poetry I referred to in the discussion of 'A Kensington Notebook', since throughout *The Hudson Letter* the attempt to represent contemporary New York in a more general sense leads to unconvincing passages of collage – or, rather, of news material which in a modernist poem proper would be presented in collage form ('INSIDER TRADING REPORTS ARE LINKED TO PRICE OF BONDS / NO SOLUTION AT HAND WHILE NUCLEAR WASTE PILES UP' (*THL* 47)). Mahon's habitual problems with popular culture (as opposed to junk proper), and in relating it to 'high' art, are exacerbated by his location. The modernist canon, to which he has always been committed, sits uneasily with the willed slices of US life; revealingly, the poems often begin with a New York scene but appeal, in seeking fit closure, to the likes of Glenn Gould, George Herbert, Confucius and Racine. The irony is all at the expense of the present. US postmodernity, as 'America Deserta' in *The Yellow Book* shows, can only be dealt with in aesthetic terms by Mahon when its subordination to past culture is made explicit; simple juxtaposition does less than justice to either the present or to Mahon's cultural touchstones. A similar problem applies to the concessions to feminism and female presences in both *The Hudson Letter* and *The Yellow Book*; indeed, 'At the Chelsea Arts Club' suggests that feminism is simply an aspect of modernity which Mahon chooses, almost arbitrarily, to accommodate rather than reject.[32] The reasons for this, however, are as much aesthetic as personal-political and based on a belief that while some relaxation of his defences is possible, even desirable, the maintenance of his poetic relies on the preservation of a space beyond gender – or any – oppositions. This transcendent, conflict-resolving aspect of the poetry is a legacy Mahon shares with other members of his generation of Northern Irish poets, and is spelt out most clearly in *The Hudson Letter*'s version of the story of Tereus and Philomela. The final lines unconvincingly try to persuade us that the tale is

> ... not really about male arrogance, 'rough sex'
> or vengeful sisterhood, but about art
> and the encoded mysteries of the human heart.
>   (*THL* 52)

The trouble is, as this poem and 'Sappho in "Judith's Room"' show, that the preservation of lyric autonomy is not a neutral matter, but is predicated on specific kinds of male selfhood. Traditionally the Western lyric tradition is a masculine one built on the idealisation (and concomitant silencing) of women. In 'Domnei' the datedness of this 'formal continence' is admitted, as is the objection that 'this was a deplorable thing, / a vicious fiction or a coercive myth', only to be overridden in a lyrically resonant, 'solving' closing passage ('... when the world dims, as it does tonight, / I see the house she goes to blaze with light').[33]

Mahon's dilemma in the 1990s poetry, then, could be said to lie in the (heroically) incomplete nature of his adjustment to change. His impulse to self-disclosure has increased, as has the amplitude of his forms, but the generic and aesthetic terms of the older poetry remain in place. Like Heaney and Longley he remains a lyricist with all that implies in terms of desire for closure and aesthetic resolution, symbolic transcendence of social conflict and traditionally gendered poetic discourse. Within this discourse there are generally only thematic and local compensations for the masculinist control it embodies and the 'silences' – male and female – upon which it rests. These, given Mahon's ability, are sometimes substantial; nevertheless, the danger is of increased self-awareness producing a soggy valedictory humanism, avoidance of which lent the earlier poetry much of its distinctiveness. Thus, Mahon – rightly – has been identified with

Beckett, MacNeice, Francis Stuart, Bowen and O'Brien, Irish writers who discomfit a 'sectarian sociology', and subject the metaphysics of identity on which so much Irish writing and criticism rests to an intensely sceptical scrutiny. He understands, that is, that over-insistence on a fixed self and the integrity of texts may feed a politicised aesthetics in which such things amount to a political apology for the statelet of Northern Ireland. Nevertheless this scepticism towards the self and towards identitarian literary politics is limited by an inability to extend understanding of the untenable nature of the integral self to constructions of masculinity.

'Knowing nods': Protestant masculinity?

Throughout this essay, two main narratives have offered themselves, one psychoanalytic, the other more or less sociological. Both are too 'abstract' for the taste of an empiricist criticism centred on stable self / statehood, and need to be brought together in order to properly assess the significance of Mahon's masculinities. In the psychoanalytic reading, the telling silence is that which has been preserved until recently on family relationships. In *The Hudson Letter*'s 'Chinatown' Mahon tells his son:

> I need hardly speak to you in praise of women
> since you grew up among them. (So did I
> but there's a tale will keep indefinitely.)
>   (*THL* 59)

Here the father whose absence means his son grows up among women is Mahon himself, apparently repeating his own father's behaviour. Tellingly the 'praise' turns, in looking to his own past, into something more negative (Seidler's claim that men are often brought up to be strangers to themselves is another way of saying that they are brought up to be strangers to their fathers). 'Praise' is produced here, ambiguously, as self-exculpation by the inadequate father praising his ex-wife; this is consistent with the penitential, supplicatory attitudes of the later poetry, but more telling is the silence concerning his own experience, and in reality the 'tale' doesn't 'keep'. By *The Yellow Book*, following his mother's death, Mahon seems to feel free to bare the core of his resentment in his latest and strongest repudiation of Northern Protestant culture, 'Death in Bangor'. There is a point in 'Rage for Order', a poem in *The Snow Party* twenty years before, where Mahon briefly ditches Camus, one of the touchstones of his work (in, for example, 'Death and the Sun' in *Antarctica*). He does so by alluding to Sartre's dismissal of Camus' support for the French government in its colonial war in Algeria as 'talk of justice and his mother', talk which Camus justified on the grounds that he would put his mother above any political principle. Of course, the speaker is himself a subject of suspicion, being one of those responsible for 'the scorched gable and the burnt-out buses' even as he scorns the poet's 'grandiloquent and deprecating' posture, the 'rhetorical device / of an etiolated emperor – / Nero if you prefer, no mother there' (although he finally concludes that he will also need the poet's 'desperate ironies' (*P* 44)). Looking back from the later poem, it is possible to speculate that Mahon may have been siding with Sartre out of his resentment of a mother whom he later describes as obsessed with 'appearances', pious philistinism personified. In 'Death in Bangor', his mother's death ends a long silence and produces one of Mahon's most blatant acts of repudiation: thus, he speaks of 'your frantic kitsch decor designed for you / by thick industrialists and twisted ministers' and, revisiting 'Rage for Order' again, dubs her 'a kind of artist, a rage-for-order freak' (*TYB* 51). (It is also a kind of self-description, as 'Matthew V. 29–30' and incessant revision – rages for order so radical that they destabilise or erase the security they seek – show.) As Mahon admits, it amounts to a 'cold epitaph from your only son', the claim that the 'wish [is] genuine if the tone [is] ambiguous' embodied with a vengeance in the assertion that 'I can love you now that you're dead and gone' (*TYB* 53). Unlike Muldoon, returning to similar memories in 'Yarrow', Mahon cannot accept the instruction that he should 'meet excess of love with excess of love'.[34]

In reading the later poetry for self-revelation and for its own re-reading of the earlier poetry, it is certainly possible to match Mahon to Rutherford's account of obsession with unavailable fathers, identification with mothers (taking the form of a contradictory longing for and vehement struggle to escape them). Subsequent silence concerning the mother because of anxieties about becoming a father also matches what we can make out of Mahon's relationship to his family. But precisely because Mahon's own scepticism concerning identity does not permit us to say – what psychoanalytic criticism often does say – that the 'Mahon' of 'Chinatown' (or 'Death in Bangor') is the historical personage Derek Mahon, this kind of criticism remains inadequate. An awareness of the ways in which Freud's family romance is shaped by external forces is essential; as Cornell puts it, masculinity must be understood as an aspect of large-scale social structures and processes. In 'Death in Bangor', rage against the mother leads to a critique of Northern Irish culture and points south of the border. In this sense the silences of the work are not merely those internalised by a male as a response to socialisation within the family, but are also those which shadow them in the larger 'family' of Unionism, the outcomes of its ideological complexity and contradiction. This may seem perverse; just how 'complex' is Unionism, or its more virulent form, Loyalism? To put it like this, however, is to confuse political predictability with ideological simplicity; and it is precisely a refusal to acknowledge complexity which has produced critical silences to date.

One place to begin looking at this ambivalent rejectionism, the prodigal son aspect of Mahon's stance, might be with the recognition of the inadequacy of nationalist paradigms.[35] As Desmond Bell claims

> Ulster Protestant identity ... has displayed a particularly refractory character to the usual perspectives and concepts of political science. At the heart of this lies the complex relation of Ulster Protestants as a social group to the politics of nation and ideology of nationalism usually seen as central to understanding the political mobilisation and ethnic sensibilities of the Catholic population in Ireland. We live in a world of nations and rightly regard nationalism as a major mobilising ideology in the post-colonial era. Yet within the effusive discourse of nation and nationalism the Protestants of Ulster have remained strangely silent. Indeed, if they were to speak in such terms and proclaim as the prime object of their political loyalty a real or imagined sovereign state of 'Ulster', we would find their political attitudes and behaviour much easier to understand. But by and large ... they do not.[36]

In opposing both the 'one nation' and 'two nation' nationalist theorisations of Protestant ideology, Bell cites David Miller's *Queen's Rebels*, in which it is argued that for Loyalists no community – Britain, the UK, 'Ulster' or Ireland – has attained all the characteristics possessed by a nation in the modern world, and that their political ideology is thus located outside of the force field of nationalism as such.[37] Historically viewing its relationship with Britain as contractarian, rather than in terms of membership of a British nation, Protestants see themselves as frontiersmen and women, representatives of imperial power and Protestant interest. Loyalty is conditional on Britain safeguarding that interest, and is contracted with the Crown rather than with Parliament. The privileges of British citizenship are thus seen as *exclusive entitlements* bequested to Protestants *qua* Protestants by the crown rather than as *inclusive rights* afforded to every member of the country by Parliament, as is the liberal-democratic norm. Catholics, by definition, can thus never be full citizens. Loyalism is divided between an explicit *conditional* obligation to the external sovereign power and an implicit unconditional obligation to the internal Protestant community, which sees itself as perpetually beleaguered. Although to put it purely in these terms lays undue emphasis on the historical influence of an idealist discourse – the 'effectivity of Loyalist ideology' resides elsewhere than in such abstract distinctions – there is no doubt about the contradiction between intra-presbytery democracy and extra-presbytery authoritarianism. This contradiction makes for the smothering of internal difference – of class and gender, for example – and, like all contradictions, can only be naturalised through a process of silencing. The effect of this has been described by W.J. McCormack who has written of the way in which even those who eschew the old slogans or the Union flag may appeal nevertheless to self-definition in terms of '"an inward deep feeling which I do not think can be described in words" ... Refusing to articulate its position, Unionism renders it unassailable ...'. The ideology of Unionism / Loyalism requires suppression of its contradictions, which are made all the more acute by the relatively transparent attitudes to citizenship (and identity) within the larger state to which Unionists so fervently claim to belong. McCormack continues:

> [the] merging of the pathological and the sacramental, symptoms and inward grace, as an expression of the inexpressible unwittingly unveils a nexus of projected guilt and transcendental security. Such thinking is difficult terrain for critics, and the various strategies of northern poets with Protestant antecedents – Derek Mahon and Michael Longley being the most notable – seek to overcome this valorized inarticulacy, and yet also to minimize ... this overblown degenerate metaphysic ... [38]

Mahon's dissent from his 'antecedents' is well known (indeed, his current mild Nationalism explains the accusations of Lundyism in some reviews of *The Yellow Book*); yet his poetry, as I have attempted to show, is shaped by a secularised form of the specifically masculine and 'sacramental' silences which structure Unionist culture, aestheticising them from 'The Spring Vacation's

'knowing nod' and 'sullen silence' onwards. In Mahon's latest
work the hoped-for place 'through with history', 'a lost heaven'
where our alternative lives may flourish, has little of the room it
once had for 'the lost tribe' which 'sing[s] "Abide With Me"',
tinged as it is by its embrace of the postmodern and Nationalism.
This remains bound to aestheticised gender idealisations, and the
attempt to 'overcome' a 'degenerate metaphysic' which is bound
to 'minimize' it, given that that metaphysic is unavoidably a
masculine space, one riven by its contradictions but nevertheless
shaped by the pattern of silences which are so constitutive of 'the
male personality'.

'RESIDENT ALIEN': AMERICA IN THE POETRY OF DEREK MAHON

NEIL CORCORAN

The Ulster writer, says Hewitt, 'must be a *rooted* man. He must carry the native tang of his idiom like the native dust on his sleeve; otherwise he is an airy internationalist, thistledown, a twig in a stream . . . He must know where he comes from and where he is; otherwise how can he tell where he wishes to go?' This is a bit tough on thistledown; and, speaking as a twig in a stream, I feel there's a certain harshness, a dogmatism, at work there. What of the free-floating imagination, Keats's 'negative capability', Yeats's 'lonely impulse of delight'? Literature, surely, is more than a branch of ethics. What about humour, mischief, wickedness? 'Send war in our time, O Lord!'

Derek Mahon, Journalism

The passport picture is perhaps the most egregious little modernism.

Paul Fussell, Abroad

1.

The most interesting and inward criticism of Derek Mahon has always made a point of the peculiar status of place in his work. Although numerous place-names figure in it, it always appears, nevertheless, profoundly unsettled or displaced. A contemporary poetry of departures, one of its characteristic locations is the seashore; and that, as John Kerrigan has persuasively shown, is a location haunted – at least at the back of this poetry's mind – by the exile's lament in Ovid's *Tristia*.[1] At the same time, however, the poetry has little truck with the tropes of exile familiar from a great deal of modern Irish literature. Because an effort of detachment seems the very spirit in which many of Mahon's poems are written, the nostalgia consequent on exilic attachments is, for an Irish poet, singularly lacking; and this despite the fact that some of the poems appear to make play, even in their titles, with exactly such tropes: witness 'Thinking of Inis Oírr in Cambridge, Mass.', for instance. If this poem is, on one level, a contemporary companion for the Romantic yearning of Yeats's 'The Lake Isle of Innisfree', it substitutes for that too a more convinced, and therefore modernist, sense of the fictionality of all the locations of such longing: the poem's 'dream of limestone in sea-light' may be a scale for the measurement of all subsequent experience but, admittedly oneiric, it makes Inis Oírr acknowledgedly an imaginative construction, rather than an actually existent place in an idealised Irish West. When Mahon remembers Inis Oírr in Cambridge, Mass., that is to say, it is with a Proustian kind of memory which understands how 'les vrais paradis sont les paradis qu' on a perdu'.

This nimble avoidance of rhetorical cliché no doubt has something to do with Mahon's origins as a Belfast Protestant, although to labour this point might well be to fall into other sorts of cliché, as Seamus Deane does when he observes that Mahon's urbanity 'helps him to fend off the forces of atavism, ignorance and oppression which are part of his Northern Protestant heritage'.[2] It may well be that it is precisely this kind of unsubtle and embattled version of a 'heritage', and the frozen discourses of identity which have surrounded much contemporary Irish cultural debate, that the displacements or strange placelessness of Mahon's work is designed to avoid or even, at an obliquely sophisticated level, to impugn. Remembering how Seamus Heaney works to establish place in poems like 'Anahorish' and 'Broagh' and how even Paul Muldoon, a poet in many ways Heaney's subverter, establishes the Moy in place in his earlier poems, it is remarkable to be told by Peter Denman, in a lively and revealing study of Mahon's notorious revisions, that in successive versions of some poems, place-names get substituted, becoming, Denman memorably says, 'equivalents in the gazetteer of anywheres'.[3] Places in Mahon, John Kerrigan observes in a nice paradox, 'are more important than where they are';[4] and in fact some poems can hardly bring themselves to admit that places are actually where they are. Of 'A Lighthouse in Maine', for instance, the poem says: 'It might be anywhere – / Hokkaido, Mayo, Maine; / But it is in Maine', where the rhythm teeters towards uncertainty even as it attempts to establish assurance, and where in any case the pass has been sold by the conditional, which suggests the irrelevance of the whole attempt at such topographical clarification. Very frequently in the poems, reinforcing such displacements, one place is viewed from another, often in a destabilisingly ironic topographical or historical perspective: Inis Oírr from Cambridge, as we have seen; Belfast from London in 'Afterlives'; Kinsale from Penshurst in 'Penshurst Place'; the relatively treeless North of Ireland from a pastoral English woodland in 'Going Home'; the Belfast of Mahon's childhood from seventeenth-century Holland in 'Courtyards in Delft'; Treblinka and Pompeii from 'A Disused Shed in Co. Wexford'.

Such displacements have their consonance with a set of personal and cultural assumptions in Mahon, in which he famously celebrates what others have derogated as Louis MacNeice's being a 'tourist in his own country'; and Hugh Haughton is surely right to read into this Mahon's self-identification with the condition of the modem *déraciné* intellectual, and against a common, predominantly nationalist, credo of Irish poetic stability or rootedness.[5] But these displacements in the poetry also appear to carry the burden of some less voluntary displacements in Irish historical experience. In 'A Garage in Co. Cork', contemplating the 'picturesque abandon' of the eponymous deserted garage, and making a poignantly belated little Ovidian myth out of it, the poet wonders of its inhabitants, 'Where did they go? South Boston? Cricklewood?'; and the almost unwilled purposelessness of their leaving for these interchangeable American and English locations, which nevertheless constitutes their fate, becomes another lesson in how 'We might be anywhere but are in one place only', and this is in turn a Cavafy-like lesson, for those who are confined to such places, in the 'intrinsic nature' of any future likely to be available to them. In Mahon's best-known poem, 'A Disused Shed in Co. Wexford', which is indebted to J.G. Farrell's novel *Troubles* (1970), the pitiful, clamorous, supplicating mushrooms represent, in part, the class or caste of the Anglo-Irish which fell, or was finally pushed, out of power and history in the 1920s, even though they may also figure other types of endangered species too, such as the contemporary Protestants of Northern Ireland. It could well be that such specifically social and cultural disappearances and terminations lie behind the finely-tuned and frequently-invoked apocalypticism of Mahon's work, in which displacements and unsettlings of this kind are caught up into the largest potential unsettling of all, that of nuclear catastrophe; but they also surely restore by the back door – the back door of that disused shed, maybe, into which the poet-photographer intrudes his 'light meter' – and in an imaginatively renewed form, the familiar Irish trope of exile. These poems implicitly refuse what Mahon has called, again in relation to MacNeice, 'the histrionic and approximate sense in which the word is used in Ireland';[6] but their inwardness with *émigré* and *déraciné* Irish experience makes it not sentimental of her for Edna Longley to have said of Mahon that 'he receives a defenceless spirit into the protectorate of poetry',[7] even if one ought to modify this by observing that it is in fact defenceless bodies, as well as a defenceless spirit, to which his poems give sanctuary or succour.

2.

These various kinds of displacement put their pressures on the ways in which America is perceived in his work, and perceived in relation to Ireland, as it frequently is, particularly latterly. In the introduction to the anthology he co-edited with Peter Fallon, the *Penguin Book of Contemporary Irish Poetry* (1990), Mahon draws America into the radius of Irish poetry when he drily observes that the countries are 'determined ... by transatlantic neigh-bourhood'; and I leave out of account here the question of which editor actually wrote this introduction (which has been the subject of some speculation), since both are actually signatories to it.[8] This three-thousand-miles-apart 'determination' is, we must assume, in fact not so much geographical as historical: Mahon is presumably alluding here to the presence of Irish America as a determinant in modern and contemporary transatlantic aesthetic and cultural relations, and also to what his 'Joycentenary Ode' calls, in its pastiche Finneganese, 'the gineral californucation' which has 'revolationized / Ourland beyond raggednition'; but the anthologist's insistence on the wide narrowness of the Atlantic Ocean supplies a self-referential rationale for some of his own littoral locations, and it also offers what we might regard as an epigraph to one of his finest poems, 'The Globe in North Carolina', which closes *The Hunt by Night* (1982).

Hugh Haughton has described the way this poem inherits and transforms one of the stock tropes of seventeenth-century metaphysical poetry, that of the globe, and how, further, it is formally indebted to Andrew Marvell.[9] Mahon's variant octosyllabics, which he employs in other poems too, may well share in what T.S. Eliot famously characterised as a 'tough reasonableness beneath the slight lyric grace'[10] of Marvell's poems: they supply a nimble, alert, dexterous mode for meditation and self-reflection, for an apparently reasoned effort towards clarification. Yet, as Haughton also recognises, these are Marvellian octosyllabics very much read through the use Robert Lowell makes of the form in *Near the Ocean* (1967), and crucially in 'Waking Early Sunday Morning' and 'Fourth of July in Maine', those tensely exacerbated combinations of private reflection and political speculation. Any consideration of Hiberno-American literary relations in the 1970s and 1980s must centrally involve Lowell, who also figures prominently in Seamus Heaney. Whereas, however, the Heaney of *Field Work* (1979), and perhaps to some extent of the earlier volume *North* (1975), is indebted primarily to the iconoclastically and conversationally free-verse Lowell of *Life Studies* and *For the Union Dead*, and to the aggressive lyric disruptions of his later blank-verse sonnets, Mahon's sophisticated urbanity is drawn to what we might regard as the effort towards an existentially negative sublime in the Lowell of *Near the Ocean* (whose very title, indeed, defines the locale of many of Mahon's poems). In Mahon, as in Lowell, that is to say, the tough reasonableness of Marvell's civilities – which was itself won out of an imagination of civil war – is disturbed and distressed by things unamenable to reason; and in both, the octosyllabics are the formal representation of the only momentary resolution of almost ungovernable anxieties which the poem makes possible. In Lowell and then in Mahon the ruffled poise of the octosyllabic couplet is a form bruised or even mauled by an apocalyptic sense of history which may well, in Mahon's case, take its initial inspiration or impulse from his own contemporary imagination of civil strife in Ireland. As elsewhere in both poets, therefore, irony becomes a principle of form, discrepancy a fundamental mode of historical perception.

In Lowell's 'Waking Early Sunday Morning', mid-sixties America and the Vietnam war are the source of the ultimate anxiety, and the poem advances, in its final stanza, a negative sublime that is climactically and chillingly self-definitive:

> Pity the planet, all joy gone
> from this sweet volcanic cone;
> peace to our children when they fall
> in small war on the heels of small
> war – until the end of time
> to police the earth, a ghost
> orbiting forever lost
> in our monotonous sublime.

In Mahon's 'The Globe in North Carolina', as in many of his

poems, the ultimate distress is ecological, the poet fearing that a
characteristic 'scepticism / And irony' might 'be dumb'

> Before the new thing that must come
> Out of the scrunched Budweiser can
> To make us sadder, wiser men.

The Coleridgean allusion there makes this poem too a kind of
survivor's tale; and, just as 'Waking Early Sunday Morning'
moves in conclusion to a perspective beyond the great globe itself,
Mahon's poem also takes what it calls, neologistically, the
'theoptic' view, as the globe which spins to the poet's finger-tips in
the poem's opening lines – 'The earth spins to my finger-tips
and / Pauses beneath my outstretched hand' – eventually
metamorphoses into 'our peripheral / Night garden in the glory-
hole / Of space, a home from home'. Seamus Heaney's
'Alphabets' in *The Haw Lantern* plots a not dissimilar trajectory,
and it is feasible that the long perspectives taken in a number of
the contemporary poems of Northern Ireland may well have a
cultural or political dimension, as Heaney has also observed in *The
Place of Writing*.[11] They register both the exacerbations and the
desires of poets unwilling to bow to factional interest; and indeed
when Mahon imagines himself returning to Ireland from America
in Part XVII of 'The Hudson Letter', the theoptic becomes political
too, in however ironised a form: 'I can see a united Ireland from
the air'. In 'The Globe in North Carolina', however, the imperative
is more manifestly metaphysical. The poet as astronomer at the
beginning of the poem develops a 'theoptic' view until, in a self-
reflexive image of the kind Christopher Ricks long ago identified
as characteristic of some Northern Irish poetry, and which it
shares with English metaphysical verse, 'America is its own night-
sky',[12]

> Its own celestial fruit, on which
> Sidereal forms appear, their rich
> Clusters and vague attenuations
> Miming galactic dispositions.
> Hesperus is a lighthouse, Mars
> An air-force base; molecular cars
> Arrowing the turnpikes become
> Lost meteorites in search of home.
>
> No doubt we could go on like this
> For decades yet; but nemesis

Awaits our furious make-believe,
Our harsh refusal to conceive
A world so different from our own
We wouldn't know it were we shown.
Who, in its halcyon days, imagined
Carthage a ballroom for the wind?

These remarkable lines have somewhere behind them, I think, the description in the 'Ithaca' episode of *Ulysses* – that other, and celebrated, long perspective taken in modern Irish literature – of the Dublin night sky as a 'heaventree of stars hung with humid nightblue fruit'; but they require, too, the slight exoticism of their transatlantic location for the startlingly vertiginous play they make with their contemporary revision of medieval and renaissance concepts of microcosm and macrocosm. It is, in part, as though Mahon's witty lexical refinement is searching for a form that will allow him to combine, without undue attention or stress, the almost self-parodying precisions or pedanticisms of the words 'sidereal', 'attenuations', 'nemesis' and 'halcyon' with the word 'turnpikes', that most routine vocabulary of American topography which nevertheless strikes the unAmerican ear with an open-road, empty-space, freewheeling attractiveness. And, indeed, the word 'America' itself figures in the poem with an aura of the exotic or the glamorous about it too, as it does in the work of some other cisatlantic poets who grew up in places and periods of utter noncalifornucation: a notable recent example being the Ted Hughes of *Birthday Letters*, in which, to a marked degree, Sylvia Plath when he first meets her is his America, his newfound-land.[13]

It may seem heavy-handed and contrary to the spirit of Mahon's poem, with its suave, if 'salt', astringency, to insist that its premonition of ecological catastrophe is neither narcissistic nor merely glamorously nihilistic, as his intimations of apocalypse have sometimes been accused of being, but that in fact it secretes an ethics or a politics: since to remind us that nemesis awaits the make-believe of self-interested ignorance, our 'era-provincial self-regard', has its corrective impulse. This is why the extraordinary conception of the Earth itself as only a 'home from home' is followed by the annotation of the 'Devotion we can bring to it', a devotion which may be – and this is the poem's own phrase – 'true / Redemption'. Yet, as if himself turning wilfully from the possible sententiousness of this underlying theme, Mahon ends 'The Globe in North Carolina' by veering away from a conclusion in some version of the anticipated sublime, the kind of

emotionally and argumentatively appropriate conclusion to which
Lowell comes in 'Waking Early Sunday Morning'. Instead, he
bravely and surprisingly digresses by opening his final stanzas,
and then closing them, with those marks of ellipsis characteristic
of a later Lowellian manner:

> . . . You lie, an ocean to the east,
> Your limbs composed, your mind at rest,
> Asleep in a sunrise which will be
> Your mid-day when it reaches me;
> And what misgivings I might have
> About the true importance of
> The 'merely human' pales before
> The mere fact of your being there.
>
> Five miles away a south-bound freight
> Sings its euphoria to the state
> And passes on; unfinished work
> Awaits me in the scented dark.
> The halved globe, slowly turning, hugs
> Its silence, while the lightning bugs
> Are quiet beneath the open window,
> Listening to that lonesome whistle blow . . .

   The drifting ellipses which announce the sudden veering away
from a poem of social and cosmic meditation towards a love
poem here destabilise the Lowellian sublimity with what might
appear an almost auto-deconstructive dissonance, one that diverts
climactic closure into something more like irresolution or
incompletion; and this is, we may take it, the ultimate importance
of elsewhere in Derek Mahon. 'America' may provide the
exoticism of the theoptic view, and may establish the Earth itself
as only a home from home unnervingly, but also in a way that
existentially adapts a Christian metaphysics – but there is an
elsewhere, 'an ocean to the east', which is itself a closer home for
the displaced poet. It is at this point, returning to the image of the
globe on the desk with which the poem began, that Mahon most
clearly inherits the timbre of the seventeenth-century metaphysical love lyric. Indeed, the effectiveness of these stanzas
is of a kind that opens a negotiation with the wistfulness of
pastiche, which it nevertheless forecloses immediately by citing
the alternative wistfulness of that staple 'lonesome whistle' of
American country-and-western music, a kind entirely appropriate, of course, to this North Carolina location. That this poem

finds its form by returning finally to an opening image, but returning there only in an unpredictable digression, may be regarded as one of the strongest instances in Mahon of that stylish combination of composure and discomposure, of finish and process, *brio* and melancholy, which holds so many of his poems in profitably unresolved tension. The combination may, indeed, be written in little into that elegant lexical move from the derogatorily quoted phrase 'the "merely human"' to the bravura assurance of the *propria persona* phrase 'the mere fact of your being here', where the move, which is that made by the whole poem, is from misgiving dismay to a steadying resolve, and is enacted by the restoration of a vanished etymology to the word 'mere', so that its use in the second phrase is suddenly vibrantly and piquantly Shakespeare's: 'absolute, entire, sheer, perfect, downright', as the OED tells us.

What the lines also do, however, is to introduce to the poem in a complex way the issue of gender which has already been raised by the epigraph from Voznesensky. When 'The Globe in North Carolina' takes the theoptic view, it includes a theme familiar from many of Mahon's poems, the death but possible further life, or afterlife, of the gods, the quasi-Stevensian attempt to locate in consciousness some form of transcendence in a post-Christian period and in a post-religious sensibility. This leads to the poet's apostrophe to the moon mythologised as Selene:

> Great mother, now the gods have gone
> We place our faith in you alone,
> Inverting the procedures which
> Knelt us to things beyond our reach.

This continues in the vocative until immediately preceding the ellipsis before the final two stanzas which I have already quoted; and that ellipsis, as we have seen, introduces the apostrophe 'You lie . . .'. There is a gnomic, riddling element in some of Mahon's work which has not, strangely, been much picked up on by his critics, but which may well be connected with his obsessive revisionism; and here it consists, for the first-time reader of this poem, in an uncertainty about whether the 'You' being addressed here, after the ellipsis, is still the moon, the 'Great mother'. The effect, that is to say, is to have the prominently gendered moon goddess waver or warp across the dissolve of the ellipsis into the less prominently gendered but (we assume) also female lover of the poet as she lies composed in sleep. The poem shares an element of its imagery with 'Courtyards in Delft', which opens the volume *The Hunt by Night* which 'The Globe in North Carolina' closes: in the former poem, 'the pale light of that provincial town / Will spread itself, like ink or oil. . .', and in the latter, 'Night spreads like ink on the unhedged / Tobacco fields and clucking lakes'. The similes in both cases are, of course, self-reflexive in ways entirely appropriate to their preoccupations, foregrounding the activity of painter and poet in poems which are, in part, inquiries into the sources and value of artistic and poetic composition or representation: significantly, at the end of 'The Globe in North Carolina' the poet reminds himself, and us, that 'unfinished work / Awaits me in the scented dark'. The sharing of that simile, however, may alert us to the fact that not only seventeenth-century poetry but seventeenth-century painting too may be involved in 'The Globe in North Carolina', as it is in 'Courtyards in Delft', in a volume which makes other references to paintings and takes its title from a work by Uccello, to which 'The Globe in North Carolina' itself also makes reference. I am suggesting that it is conceivable that behind the image that opens the poem there lies Vermeer's painting in the Louvre known as 'The Astronomer', one of the very few Vermeers to represent only a male figure, in which the eponymous astronomer leans forward to touch his globe as light pours onto it from the window in front. But even if no such specific allusion is being made, I still think that we can interpret the poem's move from an apostrophe to the mother to one to the lover in something of the way in which Edward Snow, in his book on Vermeer, conceives of what he calls the 'intricate relation' between three Vermeer paintings, 'The Astronomer', the similarly male representation of 'The Geographer', and the much better-known female representation of 'Woman Holding a Balance':

> The male figures reach out through consciousness in an attempt to map, to encompass the limits of their world, to grasp the realm beyond as thought or image or microcosm; yet in doing so they instinctively tighten their grip on the material dimension that supports their speculations. The woman locates more intuitively (both in her measuring and by virtue of her presence) the center, the balance point, and, suspending it, gently touches down.[14]

Snow also reads that gentle touching down as a benediction; and, in turn, reading that against the quoted painting of the Last Judgement before which the woman stands in the intricately allusive Vermeer, he says that 'There could scarcely be a greater contrast between this gesture and that of the Christ in the background of "Woman Holding a Balance", whose upraised arms preside over the apocalyptic destruction of everything that is graced by, and abides in, Vermeer's art'.[15] The image of the female lover composed, and in repose, at the end of 'The Globe in North Carolina' is similarly positioned against apocalyptic destruction, and indeed the poem's images of microcosmic and macrocosmic America are prominently gendered as masculine: the 'hardware in the heavens'; the phallic lighthouse of Hesperus; the air-force base of Mars; and the equally phallic cars 'Arrowing the turnpikes'. I am not of course suggesting that Mahon's work is collusive with seventeenth-century stereotypes of masculine exploration and feminine intuitive balance. What I am suggesting, however, is that 'The Globe in North Carolina' finds its ultimate elsewhere in the difference of gender, and that in the calm repose of that recognition, as it terminates a poem fraught with the deepest global anxieties, it offers its own constructive celebration of what might be opposed to the cosmic destructiveness whose possibility it also conjures. 'No doubt we could go on like this / For decades yet', the poem says, where 'go on' carries the colloquial sense 'talk to little purpose or effect' as well as the stronger sense of 'proceed'; but not, the implication must be, if 'The mere fact of your being there' convinces us of the devotion that should attend on the mere fact of being.

3.

Among various others of Mahon's poems in octosyllabics are the verse letters, 'Beyond Howth Head' and 'The Sea in Winter', written in the 1970s. Both have named addressees, like Auden's 'Letter to Lord Byron' and 'New Year Letter'. The form was, for Auden, 'light verse', but both of his letters have, nevertheless, serious concerns, even if these are indeed managed with a certain levity of tone. In Mahon, as in Auden, 'light verse' is an effort to open solitude or even solipsism into sociability, since the letter assumes that it has at least one auditor or correspondent, just as it also assumes, although in a different way, what, as we have seen, many of Mahon's poems do: the co-existence of at least two places and two times being brought into significant relation; verse letters, in this, following ordinary letters in what Charles Lamb in his essay 'Distant Correspondents' (which is itself in the form of a letter) calls 'this grand solecism of *two presents*' in which '*my Now*' encounters '*your Now*'. In 'Letter to Lord Byron', Auden, setting an ambition for himself, tells his addressee, 'You are the master of the airy manner'. Nothing in Derek Mahon's octosyllabic letters is ever quite so airborne, however, that it does not aspire to a further negative sublime; and both of his verse letters climax in chilly declensions – 'I who know nothing go to teach / While a new day crawls up the beach' in 'The Sea in Winter', and 'I put out the light / on Mailer's *Armies of the Night*' in 'Beyond Howth Head'.[16] The poems are wry, disaffected, 'less deceived', with a kind of icy celebration of contingency and débris made in the face of an obvious melancholy, dejection or morose apocalypticism and, in the case of 'The Sea in Winter', in the face of an anatomisation of the political culture of the North of Ireland to which Mahon has temporarily returned – 'Portstewart, Portrush, Portballintrae – / *Un beau pays mal habité*' – which perhaps matches Lowell's state of the union poems in *Near the Ocean* with its own state of the Union address.

Despite these poems, and the fact that Mahon subsequently wrote a series of prose letters from New York for the *Irish Times*, it was quite unpredictable that his return to poetry after a ten-year gap between the interim collection *Antarctica* (1985) and *The Hudson Letter* (1995) should be prominently, in 'The Yaddo Letter' and the lengthy title sequence itself, via the verse letter, now newly constituted formally in irregularly rhyming loose pentameters, rather than octosyllabics, although the form does occasionally permit a short run of tetrameters; and part of the unpredictability of such a thing for Mahon is the fact that, unlike other prominent modern Irish poets, he had not previously employed anything resembling the long poem or sequence. In relation to the earlier work, Seamus Deane observes that the general mood of elegy is 'no more than an inflection away from satire',[17] and the forms adopted in 'The Hudson Letter', with their faint but distinct echoes of the eighteenth-century heroic couplet, inflect these poems further in that direction, although we should also note that satire is traditionally itself an element of elegy (as it is, for instance, in 'Lycidas'), and also that the Horatian verse epistle and the Juvenalian verse satire are audible classical precedents. At the same time, these are very capacious discursive forms in which the poet's self-presentation is more straight-forwardly sociable and apparently autobiographical than any-thing previously in Mahon, and more open to the contingent and the provisional. In fact, the initiation of the form in 'The Yaddo Letter' serves as the vehicle for Mahon's address, from a writer's colony in upper New York State, to the children in England whom, as a divorced father, he rarely sees (Parts IX and

XI of 'The Hudson Letter' are also addresses to his daughter and son). 'The Yaddo Letter', it may be, stays only just on the right side of the maudlin and the sententious, if indeed it always does, and in Part XI of 'The Hudson Letter' the poet satirises himself as a 'Polonius of the twilight zone' and actually quotes that prolix and preposterous Shakespearean father at several points. If the maudlin and the sententious are tones occasionally at least at the edge of earshot in the sequence, however, this kind of familial intimacy also serves to anchor it in the frayed anxieties, exacerbations, self-doubts and guilts of the quotidian in a way that wilfully distresses the poised, melancholy perfectionism of earlier Mahon which, however much one might admire it (and this critic admires it immensely), could hardly be expected, itself alone, to maintain viability throughout an entire career, even if the volume's predominantly negative or indifferent reviewers have thought otherwise. The element of routine ongoingness in the sequence is also carried by its intermittent address to a 'you' who appears to be a lover offering a possible alternative to the more immediate personal distresses also alluded to during the poems.

'The Hudson Letter' is a lengthy, eighteen-part verse letter sent from the banks of the Hudson river in New York City, where this poet now displaced into American exile establishes one further maritime location as his *mise-en-scène*: 'a rented "studio apartment" in New York / five blocks from the river', on the island of Manhattan. The poet who admires Louis MacNeice for being a tourist in his own country now becomes, as he says in Part VI, 'an undesirable "resident alien" on this shore', enjoying that official status in which one is not a citizen but has 'lawful permanent residency' in the United States. The sense of a temporarily anchored rootlessness which the official legal phrase conveys is, it could be said, the condition to which all Mahon's work aspires; and this passport identity provides the impulse for an unpredictable extension to, and variation of, the Mahon lyric, an ironically alert and adroit representation of the solitary poet among his predicaments. Indeed, 'The Hudson Letter' may be regarded as one in a long line of Mahon's poems about poets, some of them about poetes maudits, except that this is now a self-portrait as poet, and one taken, as it were, from the inside.

If tonal variety and the representation of a discursive subjectivity distinguish 'The Hudson Letter' from Mahon's earlier work, however, the sequence shares with it, and outdoes it in, an intense literary and cultural allusiveness. Its eighteen sections are prefaced with epigraphs from a wide range of writers, including Camus,

MacNeice, de Nerval, Eugene O'Neill, Woody Allen, Scott Fitgerald, Susan Sontag, J.M. Barrie and Oscar Wilde, and these convey the strong sense of a cultured writer riffling through his bookshelves, living among and in his texts. In addition, the poem contains all sorts of other quotations from, and allusions to, poems and poets, including other famous poet-visitors to, and residers in, New York, such as Lorca, Dylan Thomas, MacNeice, Auden and Hart Crane. It also refers extensively to novels, philosophical texts, movies, plays and music. In addition, it is interspersed with upper-case citations of the texts prominent on the streets of the New York which the poet walks as a latter-day *flâneur*: advertising hoardings, newspaper headlines, neon signs, graffiti. It also contains some less identifiable quotations from, I imagine, sources such as gazetteers, *National Geographic*-type journals, and newspapers; embedded quotations from the titles of other texts (Paul Tillich's *The Courage to Be*, John MacCormack's 'I Hear You Calling Me', Saint Exupéry's *Vol de Nuit* (*Night Flight*), and Alain-Fournier's *Le Grand Meaulnes* (*The Lost Domain*), for instance); identified quotations which make sections of the poem read like wittily and engagingly raconteurial conversation – as when Part XIV, for instance, reports Noel Coward's opinion that King Kong clutches Fay Wray 'like a suppository'; and joke or phoney citations which send up the whole idea of citation, as when Part II offers a self-image of the poet-professor grading papers 'with the radio low / as Pascal said we should'. And it includes too that more invisible kind of quotation which is translation, version and pastiche: Part II, 'Last Night', is a poem resembling Hitchcock's *Rear Window*, which is itself alluded to in Part XIV (a section on *King Kong*, watched on video, dedicated to Fay Wray); Part V, '"To Mrs. Moore at Inishshannon"', is what I take to be a pastiche letter from a late nineteenth-century emigrant from Cork to New York; Part VII, 'Sneaker's"', is a kind of 'found poem' constructed exclusively from snippets of bar-room conversation and monologue; Part VIII is a version of the Tereus and Philomela story from Ovid, intercut with reflection and critical commentary, and including a draft cancellation; Part XIII, 'Sappho in "Judith's Room"', is a monologue by Sappho in contemporary New York which includes translations from her poems; and Part XIV, 'Beauty and the Beast', begins as an excellent pastiche of the camply insouciant pretend-aimlessness of the Frank O'Hara of such poems as 'The Day Lady Died':

> I go nightshopping like Frank O'Hara,
> I go bopping up Bleecker for juice, croissants, Perrier, ice-cream

and Gitanes *filtre*, pick up the laundry, get back
to five (5!) messages on the answering machine . . .

The element of the bravura in these performances, which makes
the poem virtually a compendium of citation, evidences a zest
which is not now compounded with melancholy, as it is in the
earlier Mahon; and the sense of the writer performing himself in a
stable and viable solitude, of the contemporary intellectual
constructing an existence from the cultural representations
available to him, and available as sustenance and delight, is
intense in the sequence. The proliferating referentiality is also,
however, an insistence that, even though this letter has its
dedicatees, it is, in the end and indeed even in its inception,
primarily a letter from the self to the self: the poem is a
compellingly inward demonstration of the contemporary ways in
which solitude can be managed without self-pity. Its dense
textuality is also, of course, as it makes explicit every so often,
testimony to the way a contemporary, postmodern consciousness
is itself a textualised subjectivity, already written as well as
writing; and indeed, in this regard, it is perhaps not too fanciful to
see the sequence as secreting a series of references to that ur-poem
of modernist textuality, *The Waste Land*. It contains, as *The Waste
Land* does, a pub scene; the mythical material of Tereus and
Philomela; many drifting megalopolitan crowds; as we have seen,
an immense amount of literary reference, quotation and pastiche;
and, in the persona of the poet himself, a character, like some of
those in Eliot, in a state of nervous extremity ('O show me how to
recover my lost nerve!' he says in the opening section). The Derek
Mahon who, in his earlier sequence 'A Kensington Notebook' – in
a form which brilliantly pastiches the quatrains of 'Hugh Selwyn
Mauberley' – offers a view and a critique of Ezra Pound in
London before the First World War at work on the enterprise of
international Modernism, here places himself as the
knowledgeable inheritor of the already-writtenness of that literary
Modernism, although one who has made the opposite
transatlantic crossing. Citation in Eliot and Pound sometimes
takes on the aspect of nightmare, however, where the fragments,
for all that they might shore one against ruin, nevertheless
emphasise the ruin too, whereas in Mahon it is more manifestly
ballast, part of the effort of pleasurable self-recuperation, and
entirely at ease with its own cultural pluralism and non-
differentiation ('Thank God for the VCR'). For all that, however,
its knowledge that pastiche is the virtually inevitable magnetic

pole to which a sophisticated modern, or postmodern, style will always veer is as radical as Eliot's, and this is a knowledge at once of formation and of deformation: echoic, whimsical at times, buoyed by its own losses.

In addition to the local epigraphs and references, the whole poem is itself prefaced by three further epigraphs, one of which is the stanza from Keats's 'Ode to a Nightingale' in which the nightingale's song is invoked as the great Romantic figure for a permanent imaginative solace: 'the self-same song that found a path / Through the sad heart of Ruth when, sick for home, / she stood in tears amid the alien corn'. Keats's poem is alluded to several times in the sequence itself, and its symbolic nightingale appears, along with a range of other birds, at various further points within it, acting as a little *leit-motif* in this otherwise apparently random poetic structure; indeed, rather as birds and birdsong also figure in *The Waste Land*. The Keatsian epigraph is intended, presumably, to introduce the trope of exile, emigration, alienation, even as it deflects the 'histrionic and approximate' Irish sense with which the word has been used into a remembering of its provenance in Romantic and post-Romantic literature more generally. The point of the epigraph would tally with the sense of the Earth itself as a 'home from home' in 'The Globe in North Carolina': that is, it offers a conception of exile as a fundamental human pattern and predicament, rather than a too readily available national appropriation.

This does not prevent the poem, however, from presenting, in several of its sections, specific situatings of Irish emigrant experience: that of the late nineteenth-century Bridget Moore in the pastiche letter to her mother which forms Part V, and, in Part XVII, that of Yeats's father, the painter John B. Yeats, who moved to New York late in life, never to return to Ireland. These specific Irish-American instances are complemented, however, by vivid considerations of the actual contemporary homeless and dispossessed, those who sleep in cardboard boxes in New York City, and who are given a section to themselves, Part XII, the punningly entitled 'Alien Nation'; and Mahon identifies with these in the radical sense that, as he says there, 'I too have been homeless and in detox'. This is, obviously, the personal experience which yawns as a chasm below the perilously achieved lucidity and stability of the steadying rhythms of 'The Hudson Letter' and which, we must assume, accounts for the ten-year gap in Mahon's writing career. Just as Mahon as poetic self-portraitist in the sequence inherits the figure of the poet from previous poems of his own, so in this respect too he himself becomes one of those derelicts, down-and-outs, beggars and tramps, one of the outsiders and the alienated who figure frequently in his own earlier work. In this way, it might be said that 'The Hudson Letter' receives the defenceless spirit of its own poet into the protectorate of his poetry, to very poignant effect and without the self-exacerbating theatricality which can sometimes accompany such kinds of revelation in more straightforwardly 'confessional' modes of modern writing.

If the Keatsian nightingale supplies Mahon's poem with an epigraph offering one of the most conventional of all Romantic analogies for the utterance of the poet, the poem itself, in its various representations of birds, transforms that inherited symbol into a figure which embraces this once apparently destitute poet and his companions in dereliction when Part VI explores an image of exotic ornithological species escaped during a storm in New York whose chances of survival 'are less than fair':

> . . . On ledge and rail they sit, Inca tern and Andean gull, who
> fled their storm-wrecked cage in the Bronx Zoo
> and now flap in exhilaration and growing fear
> above Yonkers, New Rochelle, Bay Ridge, the whole 'tri-state area',
> a transmigration of souls, crazy-eyed as they peer
> through mutant cloud-cover and air thick with snow-dust,
> toxic aerosol dazzle and invasive car-exhaust,
> or perch forlorn on gargoyle and asbestos roof,
> fine-featured, ruffled, attentive, almost too high to hear
> the plaintive, desolate cab-horns on Madison and Fifth:
> like Daisy's Cunard nightingale, they belong in another life.[18]

As an image of displacement, and as an emblem for the almost hopeless attempt to survive in a world choked by pollution, these lines inherit a great deal from Mahon's earlier work, and the plangency of their long perspective forms a memorable addition to the range of his 'theoptic' views. What is newly poignant in them, however, is the implicit human relevance and empathy: this 'transmigration of souls' does duty for the numerous other human transmigrations in the poem too.

This unillusioned but resilient universalist's theoptic view appreciates, in Part X, named 'Auden on St. Mark's Place', the resolve of that other exile and poetic aerialist ('as the hawk sees it or the helmeted airman'): 'in the darkest hours / of holocaust and apocalypse, cheap music and singles bars, / you remind us of what the examined life involves'. 'The Hudson Letter' too is testimony to a well-examined life: confessional in acknowledging its poet's own distresses, yet seeking neither sympathy nor forgiveness. There is no autocratic Yeatsian casting out of remorse here: on the contrary, the poem is instructive in its capacity to cope, to endure, and to empathise; and it is exemplary in the quality of its unsentimental but deep affections. It is entirely appropriate, then, that the Yeats to whom allegiance is given in the sequence is Yeats *père*, the improvident man but affectionate father in his letters to his son, and the bravely resilient recommender of the virtues of being, in his own cited words, 'an exile and a stranger'. John B. Yeats is, elsewhere in that section, discovered making his own empathetic response to a young Irish exile; and 'The Hudson Letter' concludes in Part XVIII, 'The Small Rain', with a universalisation of affectionate sympathy and involvement made while contemplating 'the moon's exilic glare', that ultimate elsewhere always visible from wherever one is at night time. This is a climactic long and inclusive perspective, one further theoptic view, and, finally, a secular, humanist prayer. Coming at the end of this complex, many-layered poem in which this poet has found a mode of unsentimentally direct address, its cadence of sympathetic renewal has great resonance, particularly when we remember that it inherits that of the mushrooms' plea from 'A Disused Shed in Co. Wexford' ('"Save us, save us," they seem to say'):

> I think of the homeless, no rm. at the inn;
> far off, the gaseous planets where they spin,
> the star-lit towers of Ninevah and Babylon,
> the secret voice of nightingale and dolphin,
> fish crowding the Verrazano Bridge; and see,
> even in the icy heart of February,
> primrose and gentian. When does the thaw begin?
> We have been too long in the cold. – Take us in; take us in!

THE TWILIGHT OF THE CITIES: DEREK MAHON'S DARK CINEMA

STAN SMITH

1. Dark Origins

The commonest word in Derek Mahon's *Poems 1962–1978* is 'light'. It occurs sixty times, together with four 'lights', twelve 'sunlight', and one 'dawnlight'. After an intervenient 'seals' (singular and plural together, sixty-one instances), 'light' is followed by 'dark', with forty-five occurrences, plus ten 'darkness', two 'darker', one 'darken', and one 'darkening'. Thereafter, the most frequent word is 'night/s', with thirty-nine singular and ten plural instances, one 'nightfall', eight 'midnight', and, more dubiously relevant, six 'tonight', two 'nightly', and two 'nightmare/s'. 'Day' is almost as frequent, with thirty-four singular and seventeen plural instances, two 'daylight', and one 'daylong'. Even if based only on the three volumes, *Night-Crossing* (1968), *Lives* (1972), and *The Snow Party* (1975), that went to make up this selection from Mahon's early writings, this is a striking assemblage of frequencies. A non-electronic scan of the expanded *Selected Poems* (1991) tends to confirm the impression. Leaving aside the perambulations of *The Hudson Letter* (1995), with its very different ethos and themes, the play of light and dark seems to be at the heart of Mahon's poetic project.[1]

One might infer from this that Mahon's is a chiaroscuro vision, operating through strong contrasts of light and dark, and proceed to generalise about the poetry's reflection of a rigidly antithetical Northern Irish culture – what the poem 'Ecclesiastes' calls Ulster's 'bleak / afflatus', to which, it suggests, his own bosom returns a ready echo, as a 'God-fearing, God- / chosen purist little puritan', capable himself of standing on 'a corner stiff / with rhetoric, promising nothing under the sun'. The black and white statistics of a concordance can, however, deceive. Setting aside that small number of instances where 'light' refers to weight rather than illumination, a high proportion of the contexts in which 'light' is used in the main sense indicates a much more equivocal picture, one hinted at by that cluster of variants on 'dawn', and by the comparative stress of 'darker', 'darken' and 'darkening'.

Equivocation, indeed, is the very element in which light and dark meet in Mahon's poetry. Their characteristic encounter is not in the sharp contrasts of bright sunlight and shade, but in the play of shadow and half light, the gradations of dawn and dusk. As the little poem 'Spring' suggests, it is in a 'Dawnlight pearling the branches' that Mahon finds an apter insight into the human condition. Besides that single 'dawnlight', 'dawn' itself occurs twenty-two times in *Poems 1962–1978*, and 'dawns' once, always either as nouns or, twice, epithet nouns. 'Twilight' occurs five times in the volume, and in two further instances is generalised, in the plural, into a recurrent state of things, while 'shadow/s' (eleven and five respectively) and two instances of 'shadowy', reinforce the suggestions of a rather different and more ambiguous agenda. That fine elegy at the grave of his agnostic Northern Protestant mentor, Louis MacNeice, 'In Carrowdore Churchyard', insists that the 'play of shadow' offers a 'humane perspective', which (addressing both himself and the dead poet in a playful paronomasia) 'Suits you down to the ground', its 'ironical' incongruities offering, in 'Each fragile, solving ambiguity', an image of 'how we ought to live'.

It is in what 'The Studio' calls 'the play / Of light and shadow (shadow mostly)' that Mahon's mental universe is constituted. In his poetry, as in Beckett's bleaker cosmos, 'we are running out of light / And love', as 'Girls in their Seasons' puts it. But this itself is a not unambiguous condition, for, repeatedly, Mahon's poetic evinces what his 'Epitaph for Robert Flaherty' speaks of as

> The relief to be out of the sun,
> To have come north once more
> To my islands of dark ore
> Where winter is so long
> Only a little light
> Gets through, and that perfect.

'The Spring Vacation' deploys a similar imagery to describe how one makes one's accommodations in a divided North, addressing a Michael Longley equally in the know, likewise able to

> . . . yield instead to the humorous formulae,
> The hidden menace in the knowing nod . . .

> . . . keep sullen silence in light and shade,
> Rehearsing our astute salvations under
> The cold gaze of a sanctimonious God

This 'sullen silence', 'Waking among my own. . . / In a tide of sunlight between shower and shower', is seen as the resumption of 'an old conspiracy' with the givens of a fallen world. Mahon's poems inhabit that 'quivering silence' where, 'The Studio' says, 'day by day, the play / Of light and shadow (shadow mostly) / Repeats itself, though never exactly'. Such repetition without exactitude is as much a feature of Mahon's as of Beckett's universe, taking on a metaphysical significance intimately linked, as here, to the play of halflights. Confronting a world that lives only in repetition, 'The Studio' yearns for an apocalyptic return to origins, in the imagined destruction of the present and actual which links the primal chaos with more recent states of political anarchy and disintegrative violence. The image recalls the weirdly beautiful slo-mo explosion of a hotel at the climax of Antonioni's 1970 film *Zabriskie Point*:

> You would think with so much going on outside
> The deal table would make for the window,
> The ranged crockery freak and wail
> Remembering its dark origins, the frail
> Oilcloth, in a fury of recognitions,
> Disperse in a thousand directions . . .
>   . . . But it
> Never happens like that.

In Mahon's universe, however, such apocalyptic prospects remain unrealised. Instead, the apocalyptic dwindles, as in Beckett, into the endless repetitive attrition of things in which the world wears down, for ever. The Beckett comparison is one that Mahon not only invites but openly acknowledges, writing, in 'An Image from Beckett', for example, of being 'haunted' by a northern landscape of houses huddled by a shore, a place of 'hard boards / And darkness once again', interrupted for an instant by a flash of 'sweetness and light', in which one spends one's time imagining not only 'grave / Cities' (another pun), but also the emergence of new civilizations from the humus they deposit. Life may be a 'Biblical span', 'good while it lasted', which ends in a Beckettian 'drop six feet / Through a glitter of wintry light', but the poem closes with the speaker imagining those who come after him:

    To whom in my will,

    This, I have left my will.
    I hope they have time,
    And light enough, to read it

In a parodic repetition of Yeats's performative utterance in 'The
Tower' ('It is time that I wrote my will'), the poem itself
becomes both the will and the thing willed, accompanied by the
equally wilful hope with which both conclude, in a tenebrous
echo of the self-inscribing double-takes of *Molloy* and *Malone
Dies*. In eschewing the metaphysical in the name of the material,
Mahon resumes, reinvents a metaphysics, repeating, in a
residual poetry of life's residues, what 'Beyond Howth Head'
identifies as 'Beckett's bleak *reductio*'. It is characteristic of
Mahon's lightly-worn intertextuality that his profound
imaginative debt to that paradoxical nihilist should be
acknowledged in a poem which purports to be no more than a
gloss on and reiteration of 'An Image from Beckett'.

   The fourth and final poem of 'Breton Walks' (renamed 'Four
Walks in the Country Near Saint Brieuc' in *Selected Poems*) is
called 'Exit Molloy', in a self-consciously stagey stage-direction
which situates its eponymous speaker, 'Now at the end' of
things, 'wintering' in a 'dark ditch' – Yeats's drunken beggar
transformed into Beckett's lugubrious derelict, smelling spring,
while only a mile away the little town nestles 'Happy and
fatuous in the light of day'. This multiply interstitial location
(between winter and spring, dark and light, earth and air, rural
and urban, Yeats and Beckett) is existentially double also, since
the speaker observes that 'I am not important and I have to die',
only immediately to concede that 'Strictly speaking I am
already dead'. The second poem in the sequence had spoken of
birds watching, as they have always done, 'The shadowy
ingress of mankind', while the third poem, 'After Midnight',
had evoked a 'self-made man', surrounded in the dark by
hostile creatures of the field, 'Their slit-eyes glittering
everywhere'. But it is the first poem of the sequence, 'Early
Morning', which most centrally recalls Beckett, amidst rumours
of Yeats's mad old women, while evoking a scene which is
quintessentially Mahon.

   The poem opens with the typology of the creation myth from
Genesis. This, however, is no big bang but rather a process of
gradual emergence which is as much the slow reverse rewind of

an endless attrition, so that the renewing light of each dawn seems more like a running down of darkness:

> No doubt the creation was something like this -
> A cold day breaking on silent stones,
> Slower than time, spectacular only in size.
> First there is darkness, then somehow light;
> We call this day and the other night,
> And watch in vain for the second of sunrise.

Such a separation is not the categorical demarcation of light and dark of the original creation. No divine *fiat* marks out this universe into antithetical principles. Indeed, the observer is baffled by his inability to spot what seems more like a trick of prestidigitation than act of creation, as that helpless 'somehow' suggests. Such watching in vain implies a general *vanitas vanitatum* in the rising and going down of suns. *Ecclesiastes*, after all, provides title and imagery for that fierce denunciation of Northern Protestantism quoted above, in a poem which combines self-denunciation (casting his love of the liminal world of January rain darkening already dark doorsteps as a compromising, complicitous vulnerability) with an extrojected *contemptus mundi* for a world steeped in a rhetoric which promises 'nothing under the sun' – a dry echo of *Ecclesiastes'* reflections on the tedium of earthly repetition: 'There is nothing new under the sun.'

In 'Early Morning' boundaries and divisions are arbitrary human impositions on the indeterminacies of a cosmos bored by repetition. The old woman suddenly apprehended with the click of her wooden shoe may be a Beckettian creature, but she also appears out of the 'primeval shapes' of dawn as a figure of the *Unheimlich* like the witches in *Macbeth*. The image, however, resists Yeatsian romanticisation. This is no Crazy Jane. Instead, she is seen at once, in another, dignifying Shakespearian idiom, as 'Abroad in the field of light, sombrely dressed', a this-worldly figure, capable of human discriminations, who 'calls good-day, since there are bad days too', and casts her eyes down politely after greeting. Indeed, the old woman stands as an antidote to all myth-making *in extremis* of the Yeatsian variety, even as location and idiom recall the mythic scenarios of Ted Hughes's 'Pibroch':

> She has seen perhaps
> Ten thousand dawns like this, and is not impressed

The fantasy of origins envisaged in the poem's opening is replaced in its close by one of stale recurrence, the same of which a disabused Macbeth, victim of the witches' equivocations, came to speak, lamenting a 'Tomorrow and tomorrow and tomorrow' that 'Creeps in this petty pace from day to day, / To the last syllable of recorded time'. But there are other, more unlikely intertexts at work here.

What the poem explores, in this apparently primal scene, is precisely those 'Ghostlier demarcations, keener / Sounds' of which Wallace Stevens wrote in 'The Idea of Order at Key West'. Mahon quotes Stevens's phrase, relocating the line break, in the *Poems 1963–1978* text of his verse epistle to Desmond O'Grady, 'The Sea in Winter', though the passage is dropped from subsequent versions. (The poem actually called 'Rage for Order' is also dropped from the later volume.) 'The Sea in Winter' opens with a contrast between the 'blue nights' of O'Grady's Greek island and the thinner, colder air of Mahon's Portstewart, where, recalling Matthew Arnold's contrast of Sophocles' Aegean and his own 'distant northern sea', Mahon gestures towards the burden of 'Dover Beach': that the Sea of Faith has ebbed, leaving the human subject stranded on the shore in postmodern disenchantment. In 'A Portrait of the Artist' Mahon had van Gogh speak of himself as moving like a glow-worm among the caged Belgian miners, 'And the light on my forehead / Is the dying light of faith', in which, he says, 'God gutters down to metaphor'. But this secular nihilism, for Arnold partially redeemed by the ersatz transcendences of art, 'The Sea in Winter' presents, in a recursive embedding of allusions, as nothing new. Centuries before Mahon, Arnold, or even Sophocles, the poet of *Ecclesiastes* had reached the same conclusion:

> Meanwhile the given life goes on;
> There is nothing new under the sun.

'It all happened before' says the blasé speaker of 'One of these Nights', while another poem that nods in Stevens's direction, 'Another Sunday Morning', speaks wearily of 'so many empires come and gone', all essentially the same, so as to put the speaker in his generic place as a cultural item, suffering 'the strife / And strain of the late-bourgeois life'. Mahon's verse epistle is prefaced by an epigraph from Rimbaud: 'Nous ne sommes pas au monde; / la vraie vie est absente ' ('We are not in the world; the true life is absent'). Sometimes, the epistle says, 'rounding the cliff top / at dusk' – the enjambement suggesting its own little drama of thresholds crossed – and finding the town lit up as if for a festival, 'I pretend not to be here at all'. The given life is not the real life, but a shadow existence, always alluding to but never disclosing the authentic being whose shadow it is, pretending to be itself, but with pretensions elsewhere, remembering its dark origins.

2. False Dawns

The allusion to Stevens's 'Idea of Order' in the earlier version of 'The Sea in Winter' is complexly ambivalent. Mahon describes himself here as returned, like the prodigal son in Ibsen's *Ghosts*, to 'the grim, arthritic coasts / of the cold north', finding himself 'unnerved, his talents on the shelf', 'while light dies in the choral hills', or again, like Theseus, knowing the fear of 'chthonic echoes'. This self-subverting stance can be explained in part by reference to the account of the archetypal poet in the poem 'Rage for Order', irresponsibly 'indulging / his wretched rage for order' while Rome – or Ulster – burns. 'Somewhere beyond the scorched gable-end and burnt-out buses', the poet in the latter poem is 'far from his people', framed in 'the fitful glare of his high window', which is contrasted with 'our scattered glass', down in the historical and chaotic street. His 'dying art' is no more than 'an eddy of semantic scruples / in an unstructurable sea', giving the lie to Stevens's eloquent vision of a redemptive poetic making on the linguistic thresholds of mind and world:

> The maker's rage to order words of the sea,
> Words of the fragrant portals, dimly-starred,
> And of ourselves and of our origins,
> In ghostlier demarcations, keener sounds.

In Mahon's poem the artistic posture is not 'blessed' but 'grandiloquent and deprecating', and 'his talk of justice and his mother / the rhetorical device / of an etiolated emperor' – closer, that is, to Stevens's 'Emperor of Ice Cream', a poem in which the death of the mother evacuates the universe of significance, so that 'be', mere facticity, becomes the 'finale of seem'. But the poem then turns the tables on this contempt for the poetic maker, as its reproachful speaker is revealed not as the poet at all but as some self-styled maker of history, a politico contemptuous of poets, but admitting at last that his 'desperate love', which claims to tear down in order to build up, will before long have need of the poet's 'desperate ironies'.

The play between the history-maker's singular and 'desperate love' and the poet's plurally 'desperate ironies' is a key one in Mahon's perception of the relation of art to politics. Ovid in exile, the subject of a whole poem, 'Ovid in Tomis', in *Selected Poems*, is the

figure behind the poet of 'The Sea in Winter', a poem important
enough for Mahon to place it last in *Poems 1962–1978*. But here, exile
to the margins of significance is not contingent, a chance expulsion,
but essential: it comes with the territory. What the poem calls the
poet's 'curious sense / Of working on the circumference', is
something shared by both the letter writer and his addressee. For
while the writer envies his addressee's white island in the south,
with all its sensual charms, each is alike in exile, moping in the
linguistic margins of the real, 'trapped ... / In (his) own idiom' as
much as those whose shouts, as of 'souls in torment round the town',
can be heard from the street outside. Seeking the 'Elusive dawn
epiphany, / Faith that the trivia doodled here / Will bear their fruit
sometime, somewhere', each knows in his own way that those
indeterminate sometimes and somewheres are the true location of
the real, which words can never access. In the order of discourse, as
in the material world, 'morning scatters down the strand / Relics of
last night's gale-force wind', while 'Far out', the Atlantic of the real
'faintly breaks'. The world of consciousness, constructed in language,
is always necessarily at a remove, and the poet's self-reproach –

> Why am I always staring out
> Of windows, preferably from a height?

– is not just an indictment of patronising liberal abstentionism, but
defines, rather, an ontological condition. Such voyeurism is not a
twentieth century invention but, the poem suggests, the perennial
condition of the human subject, forever deluded by its desire to
enter into some unmediated rapport with the real, but always
frustrated, cast out of an Edenic imaginary of real presence which
can be envisaged only through the language of lack, abjection,
exile. For that fullness of self-presence, the complete union with
the world's body, the delusory ambition of Romantic cults of the
Sublime, was seen in the very origins of western philosophy, long
before Christianity, as the fantasy of a soul cast out from the
divine harmony of the Forms. Mahon's anguish at the alienation
of the subject from its object world may be couched in the
phenomenology of Wordsworth or Coleridge, or in the politics of
twentieth-century social-democracy, but its ancient lineage is
indicated in the recognition that the 'Elusive dawn epiphany' he
desires is of necessity a second-hand construct, shaped by
consciousness out of 'relics' of a reality which is always, by
definition, elsewhere: the true life is absent.

All art shares in the peculiar mix of fraudulence and
authenticity represented by van Meegeren, the brilliant forger of

Old Masters, in 'The Forger'. Selling fake Vermeers to Goering, van Meegeren found himself cast at the end of the war arraigned by war-crimes tribunals as a collaborator, giving comfort to the enemy. (It is an added irony that such defrauding of top Nazis should be classified as 'collaboration'.) van Meegeren sees himself as heroically 'working beyond criticism / And better than the best' – in part because, as long as the forgeries remained undiscovered, it was his originals who would be the objects of criticism, but also because his fakes surpassed critical analysis: the only way to judge them properly would be to evaluate them as genuine works of forgery. In not spotting his fakes, and in uttering self-justifying 'claptrap' after they were disclosed, it was the art critics who were the real frauds, he says. There is a sense in which the forger is better than, not only the critics, but also the painters whose work he simulated. van Meegeren is confident that his 'genius will live on ... even at one remove', because 'The thing I meant was love'. From his 'obscurity and derision', his deceits cast on reality 'A light to transform the world'. In a universe where the multiplication of traces, echoes, reflections is the truth of things, the authentic fake may be the truly original.

'At one remove' is a resonant phrase in Mahon's poetry. It recurs in, for example, 'Preface to a Love Poem', in the same context of disenchantment about the meretriciousness of art. The immediate ancestor of Mahon's poem is W.H Auden's *Dichtung und Wahrheit* ('Poetry and Truth'), a prose meditation pointedly subtitled 'An Unwritten Poem', which argues that 'love poetry' is an oxymoron, since a true lover does not expend his spirit on artful words, and all poems which do are merely deceitful feignings, literary artifices whose real intention is the production of a work of literature. (Elsewhere, Auden said roughly the same about literature that addressed the atrocities of modern history: in so far as the intention was to produce a lasting work of art, the work simply exploited, parasitically, the atrocities it lamented or protested.) In a similar vein, Mahon's lines are merely a preface to poetry, an apology for not writing the 'true' love poem which by definition cannot be written. This poem, then, as its first line tells us, is merely a provisional approximation, a fallen simulacrum of the *echt* poem he wants to write, 'a circling of itself and you',

> A form of words, compact and compromise,
>   Prepared in the false dawn of the half-true
> Beyond which the shapes of truth materialize.
>   This is a blind with sunlight filtering through.

As such, the insufficient text is multiply displaced, shut out from
its true identity like the desiring lover himself, 'a night-cry, neither
here nor there, / A ghostly echo from the clamorous dead' – a
dead which includes such poets as Shakespeare who, as the poem
reminds us without giving him name, famously promised to write
a love poem 'Outlasting stone and bronze'. The poem, then, like
all its predecessors (which themselves become prefaces, in the
tradition, to this latest variant of the genre) is necessarily 'at one
remove, a substitute / for final answers'. The wise man may know
'To cleave to the one living absolute / beyond paraphrase'; but
this poem can only offer inadequate paraphrase of its own
inexpressible desire, the words 'aching in their own pursuit' (that
other meditation on beauty and truth, Keats's 'Grecian Urn' ode, is
recalled here) 'To say "I love you" out of indolence'. It is again the
image of the sea, as deployed by Stevens and by Auden in *The Sea
and the Mirror* and *The Enchanted Flood* as metaphor for the
inexpressible historical world, which Mahon deploys here, in the
subjunctive, to define that realm of the really real which art can
only dissimulate,

> As one might speak at sea without forethought
> Drifting inconsequently among islands.

In the end, this apology for a poem is left simply airing its
distraught love of the beloved's silence. As for Auden, it is as 'the
soul of silence' that the loved one embodies the desired but
unachievable authenticity of self-presence, totally consonant with
itself. As Auden wrote in his critical study *Secondary Worlds*,
himself deploying the Platonic simile, 'One might say that for
Truth the word silence is the least inadequate metaphor, and that
words can only bear witness as shadows bear witness to light'
(1968, p. 136).

Behind such an attitude lies, of course, that ancient
philosophical lineage which originates with Plato. But neoplatonism has always had two main inflexions. The positive
inflexion concedes that the things of this fallen world are mere
copies of eternal, ideal Forms, but takes consolation from the
existence of those Forms: somewhere, they really exist, sustaining,
casting their shadows onto, the fallen world of mortality. The
extreme version of such optimism is Sir Philip Sidney's assertion,
in *An Apologie for Poetrie*, that art in general and poetry in
particular offer truer versions of the ideal Forms than our
transient time-bound histories permit, offering, in his memorable
phrase, 'a golden world for nature's world of brass'. The

pessimistic strand of neoplatonism, however, represented in our own time perhaps by Jacques Derrida, insists with melancholy frequency that the world we know is unreal, a phantasma, or, in Baudrillard's idiom, a mere 'simulacrum' of the true, which we can never apprehend, so that we are permanently exiled among *disjecta membra* which are the relics, in the empirical world, of those ideal and inapprehensible Forms. Mahon's forger as image of the poetic maker then wittily and ironically works the changes on both lineages of neoplatonism, while remaining at one remove from the struggle, just as 'Preface to a Love Poem' epitomises poetry's notorious ability to have it both ways (for, as Auden put it in the title of a poem which retreaded Shakespeare, 'The Truest Poetry is the Most Feigning'). In Mahon's poetry, however, it is the material world itself which, in a Kantian variation on the neoplatonic motif, constitutes the unknowable reality of which consciousness produces fake and factititious copies, and it is among these and with these that we must make our peace, find our accommodation and accommodations, amidst the false dawns of the half-true.

3. Traces

Whereas for Auden it is the creations of art that are 'secondary worlds', for the epistemologically sceptical Mahon it is consciousness itself which is condemned to secondariness and dependency. 'Preface to a Love Poem' situates the subject as prefatory to experience. Mahon's poetry repeatedly seems to be remembering the future, as if what is yet-to-be is already past-and-gone. Anticipation is converted into a peculiar kind of dispossession and nostalgia for an always-already absconded reality. 'Afterlives', for example, opens with the speaker waking in a dark flat, to find in the morning light a premonition of that future in which, lit by a 'bright / Reason', the 'long-term solutions' will have put an end to the orators' yap and the sound of gunfire, 'And the dark places [will] be / Ablaze with love and poetry'. But the poem shifts at once to self-indictment, contrasting 'our privileged ideals' with our actual 'dim / Forms', kneeling in abjection, before moving, in its second part, to a familiar pattern of return to origins in which 'I am going home by sea' to a dawn-lit world of memories and regrets. Enjambement may allow both 'Reason' and 'Forms' to be ambiguously capitalised, but the poem closes (on the repeated word 'home'), with a sense of loss and exclusion, in a fallen world felt to be unreal, a repetition of memoried places and faces, in the dim light of a Belfast which is already historical, living in its own and his past. Mahon's poems are haunted by the idea that the lives we have are already – a repeated motif – 'afterlives': second-hand, ghostly imitations and repetitions of some lost original. 'Leaves', recalling a passage in *Godot*, speculates that 'Somewhere there is an afterlife / Of dead leaves', a stadium filled with an infinite rustling and sighing, and goes on to distinguish the supposedly 'real' 'lives we might have lived', 'Somewhere in the heaven / Of lost futures', from the lives we have actually led, the future becoming a peculiar past-future subjunctive. 'Beyond Howth Head' writes of offering one's life as a 'forfeiture' to 'a phantom future', 'Our afterlives a coming true / Of perfect worlds we never knew'.

The first poem to be called 'Going Home', addressed to Douglas Dunn, discerns, in the Humber estuary's daylong 'indigestible / Dawn mist', that 'ours is the afterlife / Of the unjudgeable', and speaks of the self in the past tense, as if already posthumous:

> Extraordinary people
> We were in our time,
> How we lived in our time
>
> As if blindfold
> Or not wholly serious
> Inventing names for things
>
> To propitiate silence.

'Going home', of course, is a proverbial euphemism for things which have outworn their use, and for dying. The poem sees those 'shift workers' crossing on the river ferry, associating Humber and Acheron, as figures of us all, who will likewise 'vanish for ever' under the same 'cindery sky' that 'broke the hearts / Of the foundered legionaries'. Each life is a repetition of other lives, and we are all transient spirits under the same 'pale light' that 'wanes'

> As if to guide us home
>
> To the blank Elysium
> Predicated on our
> Eschewal of metaphysics . . .

A rotting barge in the mud then becomes an omen, set there to discredit 'A residual poetry of / Leavetaking and homecoming', for the last homecoming is precisely to this universal residuary dereliction.

Those who report on the transitoriness of human cultures, whether poets, as here, or 'The Early Anthropologists', in the poem of that name, are themselves part of the story they tell, shiftwork signifiers circulating what is finally not signification but insignificance, signifying nothing. In a characteristic bracketing, Mahon casts the anthropologists as themselves the stuff of anthropology, who have

> Left traces of their
> Lives everywhere -
> Gibbering tapes
> Nobody can decipher,
> Photographs of their ancestors
> Shaking spears at the camera . . .

But such 'traces' are ambiguous in their very texture, either indecipherable or misinterpreted, since only fancifully could the photographs they took of Trobriand Islander or Inuit be seen as those of the anthropologists' ancestors. The anthropologists have been appropriated by the objects of their study, misinterpreted by posterity as the progeny of the alien people whose lives they transcribed. But that posterity (ourselves) will in turn be misinterpreted by 'Those who come after / Bearing fruit through the ruins', in an endlessly embedded recursion which recalls Vladimir's song of the dog at the start of Act II of *Waiting For Godot*:

> Once it [anthropology] studied man,
> Now it studies the study of man,
> Soon it will study . . .
> Like the baking-soda tin inside
> The baking-soda tin.

With every recension, the dark origins recede further and further into framing discourses, traces of traces of traces.

But the shadows are also cast forward, as the tanka-like poem 'Rory' suggests:

> He leads me into
> a grainy twilight
> of old photographs.
>
> The sun is behind us,
> his shadow in mine.

This 'grainy twilight' is, in fact, the true address of the human, where we all live. As a shared dedicatee of both verse selections, Rory, one presumes, is Mahon's son, which allows a punning play on 'sun'. But, here, both son and father are united in the shadow cast by the originary sun of remote ancestors, those ideal forms who lurk in the grainy twilight of family photograph albums. For, as Hardy put it in 'The Family Face', the individual perishes, but the family face – for a later generation, the genetic profile – lives on, a ghostly paradigm investing the real.

In 'Glengormley', the world has been made safe for the children, the inheritors, 'safe from monsters, and the giants. . . / Can worry us no more': 'Only words can hurt us now'. But this means also that a postulated holy and heroic age of authentic being has been replaced by the simulacra of a time in which life resides in a second-hand textuality, so that the heirs are simultaneously dispossessed of their rightful inheritance. Now 'no saint or hero. . . brings dangerous tokens to the new era – / Their sad names linger in the histories'. If, as the poet says, he would 'rather praise / A worldly time under this worldly sky', because, 'By / Necessity, if not choice, I live here too', that last conditional is all-important, for it is the sense of loss, rather than achievement, which gives the poem a mellow melancholy not totally disguised by its surface jolliness. The worldliness of this world retreats into wordiness the more it is examined. The present we inhabit is a fallen age, a mere simulacrum of the 'real time' that preceded us. Even, 'Kinsale' laments, 'The kind of rain we knew is a thing of the past'. As 'Girls on the Bridge' says, 'We live / These days as on a different planet', dreaming of some lost originary moment which was really real, some

> Lost evening when
>   Our grandmothers, if grand
> Mothers we had, stood at the edge
> Of womanhood on a country bridge
>   And gazed at a still pond
>   And knew no pain.

Even the reality of those grandmothers may be in dispute, that 'if' suggests, in what is a characteristic grammatico-rhetorical strategy. For, as 'His Song' confesses, self-consciously deploying the neoplatonic topos:

> I shall never know them again
> but still your bright shadow
> puts out its shadow, daylight, on
> the shadows I lie with now.

The little poem 'Rocks', itself 'after' the Breton poet Guillevic, calls up a world where the real has everywhere been turned into traces of itself:

> The rocks would never recognize
> The image of themselves
> These lovers entertain,
> Lying in their shadows
> In the last traces of time.

The reality of 'the thing itself', the Kantian *Ding-an-sich*, defers to the consciousness which reads it out from its traces. The lovers who 'entertain' these rocks in consciousness (there are echoes here of Hardy's 'At Castle Boterel' perhaps), may be evanescent, just passing through, but since they are – for the present at least – the present, they also constitute the 'last traces of time' in reading time's traces. Similarly 'The Banished Gods', in hiding in the margins of existence, 'Lost in a reverie of their own natures', depend for their survival on those who come after, who read their traces in the half light. Only the itinerant tourist's 'flash-bulb firing squad', in the words of 'A Disused Shed in Co. Wexford' restores the 'feverish forms' of the actual, 'Grown beyond nature now', to a human world in which they have meaning The concept of the ghost, an afterlife which is simply the trace of some original presence, is pervasive in Mahon's poetry, and this *unheimlich*, fake 'presence' is repeatedly associated with a textuality which reruns the always absent original event, whether it is the 'restless ghost' of 'The Poet in Residence' (*'after'* Corbière'), who 'dreamed his life, his dream the tide that flows / Rattling among the stones, the tide that ebbs', listening, 'Up there on the exposed / Roof of himself', for, perhaps, 'his own lost / Contumacious spirit'; or Captain Oates, in 'Antarctica', 'Goading his ghost into the howling snow', in his numb self-sacrifice a figure of ludic heroism amidst 'the earthly pantomime', disclosing 'At the heart of the ridiculous, the sublime'; or the 'curious ghost' of 'Father-in-Law', who stares from the photograph on the mantelpiece, a sea-captain who 'lost (his) balance like Li Po', leaving 'unfinished poems in [his] sea-chest', speaking, thus, to the 'lyric lunacy' of his son-in-law.

Mahon's seas are frequently haunted, by the ghosts of the real and of literature alike. In 'Beyond Howth Head', for example, the Irish Sea is 'the troubled / Channel between us and North Wales / Where Lycid's ghost for ever sails', where such ghosts clearly have much to do with the historic 'troubles' of Britain and Ireland. This is a poem full of intertextual hauntings, linking, *inter alia*, Yeats's

Celtic twilight with Spengler's Germanic one (a wind out of 'A Prayer for my Daughter' banging in from the Atlantic to hammer on 'Dark doors of the declining west'), seeing TV aerials moved about to catch BBC signals as 'Our heliotropic Birnam Wood', and imagining that Spenserian world of armadas and massacres when '"Lewde libertie"('s) midnight work / Disturbed the peace of Co. Cork'. Summoning up ghosts from the vasty deep, like Milton or Shakespeare's Glendower, Mahon's late-night epistle invites that spirit to 'Come back and be with us again!', but in a more congenial form, flashing 'an *aisling*, through the dawn / Where Yeats's hill-men still break stone'. But this last echo of Yeats's disenchantment with Irish independence, in the epigrammatic two-liner, 'Parnell', suggests that such ghostly repetitions are just that: mere compulsion-repetitions of a paradigmatic act which never finds outcome or egress, perpetually fixed in the unreality of its endless replay, as, in 'Antarctica', the recycled lines of the villanelle form mock that original act in which Oates sought to break the closed circle of event. In the same way, in 'After the Titanic', the captain who escaped from his sinking ship goes down every night in his dreams 'with all those dim / Lost faces'. In a world perpetually reinscribed under the rubric of recurrence, as 'Lives' admits, 'It all seems / A little unreal to me now', for 'I know too much / To be anything any more'. Nevertheless, as its paired poem 'Deaths' responds, we must 'Fight now for our / Fourth lives with an / informed, articulate / Fury...'

4. *Earthed*

'The Golden Bough', its title playfully alluding to Sir James Frazer's study in anthropological relativism, fluctuates between the diurnal and the apocalyptic, to speak of 'The twilight of cities' and of a return to origins among 'the soft / Vegetables where our / Politics were conceived'. But Mahon is clear that, though history is repetition, you can't go home again, either politically or personally, in a world inscribed under the banner of mutability. 'Heraclitus on Rivers' nominates one philosophical source of this sceptical vision, which may hold terror or reassurance according to the inclination of the observer. Certainly, the poem says, nobody steps into the same river twice, and 'your changing metabolism / Means that you are no longer you'. But if the cells die, and the 'precise / Configuration' of the heavens when she said she loved you won't come again in this lifetime, what abides, at least for the moment, is the memory that this happened. Monuments of bronze will disappear too, for even bronze is perishable; but, taking on Shakespeare's famous sonnet about poetic immortality, words too will also disappear, finally, 'All these things will pass away in time', not only your best poem, but the language in which it's written, and even the idea of language itself.

In 'The Return', renamed 'Going Home' in *Selected Poems*, Mahon fancifully imagines being rooted in one place by turning into a tree, 'Like somebody in Ovid'. But the tree with which he really identifies is one twisted by the sea-wind, which has 'nothing to recommend it / But its harsh tenacity', significant only in its liminal situation between windows and sea, 'On the edge of everything', like, he says, 'a burnt-out angel / Raising petitionary hands'. An 'almost tragic figure' of anguish and despair at twilight, it merges into night's 'Cloud-continent', in the last words of the poem, 'As if it belongs there'. Even a tree's rootedness is merely provisional. He too, now moving on, had behaved here 'As if I owned the place'. This delusion of ownership may be a necessary human conceit, but it is revealed as pure fabrication in the moment of transit, which compels him to recognise the *hubris* of acting 'As if the trees responded / To my ignorant admiration / Before dawn when the branches / Glitter at first light'. The only home this poem acknowledges is the provisional one of half-light and marginality. Yet the peripatetic self yearns towards a lost *Heimlichkeit*, a rootedness in which it might be earthed for ever.

'The Studio', discussed above, projects the speaker's frustration in a finely imagined empathy with 'the simple bulb in the ceiling':

> ...honed
> By death to a worm of pain, to a hair
> Of heat, to a light snowflake laid
> In a dark river at night – and wearied
> Above all by the life-price of time
> And the failure by only a few tenths
> Of an inch but completely and for ever
> Of the ends of a carefully drawn equator
> To meet, sing and be one.

The bulb's filament, in a series of amplificatory analogies which have a Blakean vividness, is seen as inadequate, a worm of pain, a hair of heat, a light snowflake in a dark river, because its glowing arc never reaches the completeness of a circle (unlike the earth's equator). But this is of course deliberately to misunderstand the nature of electricity. If the filament were a completed circle (that traditional Platonic image of perfection) it would not give light:

the current would simply pass through and beyond. The light cast is a product of the filament's imperfection, its failure to be united with itself in a closed circuit. Such frustrated yearning for completeness, 'completely and for ever', ought to compel the bulb to 'Roar into the floor', as the poet himself is tempted to do. But it doesn't happen like that. On the contrary, the very precondition of singing is the failure to make ends meet.

Mahon's elaborate metaphysical conceit here recalls a similarly complex playing with fire and electricity in 'In the Aran Islands' (later, 'Aran'), where the folksinger in the pub seems to be united with, 'earthed' to his culture, his art, his girlfriend, in a way the poet envies but cannot emulate:

> He is earthed to his girl, one hand fastened
> In hers, and with his free hand listens,
> An earphone, to his own rendition,
> Singing the darkness into the light.

Suffering jealousy at the success of the 'Hand-clasping, echo-prolonging poet! // Scorched with a fearful admiration':

> I dream myself to that tradition,
> Fifty winters off the land -
> One hand to an ear for the vibration,
> The far wires, the reverberation
> Down light-years of the imagination
> And, in the other hand, your hand.
> The long glow leaps from the dark soil, however -
> No marsh-light holds a candle to this.

The conceit doggedly chews the bone of the poet's dilemma, wanting himself to sing the darkness of origins into the light of the mind. Unable to return unequivocally to his own dark origins, racked by all that implied distrust of any *nostalgie de la boue*, the metaphor mutates through that of domestic national economy (electrification of the countryside was a fairly recent event in rural Ireland when the poem was written) to a cosmic vision, speaking of the 'light-years of the imagination' in which time becomes space, before returning, to close, with that homely yet also *unheimlich* image of the marsh gas bubbling up from dark soil, with all its Gothic associations of death, ghosts and vampirism. Drawn to the dark origins of his art, the poet finds only reflections and repetitions, the ghostly echoes of other, played-out stories and folk-tales. That strange adjective 'scorched', used to describe how admiration affects the singer, but ambiguously poised between speaker and singer, suggests a scorched earth policy in which any such return is bound to be scotched, in which the prolonging of echoes is also a loss of substance, presence, in a welter of vibrations and reverberations, second-hand handholdings, a burning bush of delusory fantasies, offering only a will-o'-the-wisp enlightenment. If Mahon's folk-singer imagines himself 'earthed' to the chthonic powers of his native Ireland, we are all truly earthed in a rather different sense, one more keenly apprehended by the archaeologist who prises the *disjecta membra* of human remains from their 'organic relation' to the earth in which they are buried

5. Terminal Lights

It is in what 'North Sea' calls 'The terminal light of beaches', with 'old tins at the tide-line', that Mahon's poetry feels most at home, treading the margins among the residual bric-à-brac of the real. And it is among such bric-à-brac that it posits a kind of survival. 'The Apotheosis of Tins' situates Mahon's nostalgia for the present in terms which merge the 'retarded pathos' of origins with the sophistication of an idiom that puts them in their place. The discarded tins welcome their abjection, 'Having spent the night in a sewer of precognition, / consoled by moon-glow', a half-light which offers refuge:

> Deprived of use, we are safe now
> from the historical nightmare
> and may give our attention at last
> to things of the spirit.

In this 'terminal democracy' of flotsam, where 'It is always rush-hour', a pointless ebbing and flowing of rubbish, 'If we have learnt one thing from our desertion', the tins say:

> it is the value of self-definition.
> No one, not even the poet
> whose shadow halts above us after
> dawn and before dark
> will have our trust.
> We resist your patronage, your reflective leisure.

Such flotsam is everything that history casts aside as of little value, the mere spindrift of Stephen Dedalus's 'historical nightmare'. Yet the tins have immortal longings, too, imagining themselves not only eternal in their returns on the tide, but also as somehow elevated above the status they have been given:

> Promoted artifacts by the dereliction
> of our creator, and greater now
> than the sum of his skills,
> we shall be with you while there are beaches.

Proudly, they define themselves as 'Imperishable by-products of the perishable will', out-hamming Hamlet, lying – an apposite pun – 'like skulls / in the hands of soliloquists'. In due course, they will be resurrected as the carriers of ancient messages from the dawn of things, for whom

> The longest queues in the science museum
> will form at our last homes
> saying, 'Think now,
> what an organic relation
> of art to life
> in the dawn; what saintly
> devotion to the notion of permanence
> in the flux of sensation
> and crisis, perhaps
> we can learn from them'.

The folk-singer of 'Aran' represents one version of art as something organically 'earthed' in its community, though Mahon even there hints at the factitious, secondary quality of that relation, as a form of cultural revivalism, which makes the singer not simply the antithesis of van Meegeren in 'The Forger'. Furthermore, the latter, like any 'genuine' Romantic artist, has suffered obscurity and derision, 'And sheltered in my heart of hearts / A light to transform the world'. Both figures raise the question of authenticity, in conflict with the neoplatonic idea of art as a copy of a copy, only ever a shadow of the real thing on the walls of the human cave. These cans, in their *hubris*, however, represent another possibility. Having lost their function as objects of use, they are apotheosised, in the museums of the future, into self-sufficient works of art, just as so many artefacts from ancient or alien cultures are thus converted in the museums of the present.

Thinking of the 'new night' of the coming era in 'The Globe in North Carolina', Mahon predicts that it will be, 'As before, a partial dark / stage-lit by a mysterious glow / As in the *Night Hunt* by Uccello'. This painting clearly has a special significance for him, one indicated in the poem called 'The Hunt by Night', which uses the Platonic myth of the cave to focus on the changing function of art, its historical transformation from utility to entertainment. Resituating Uccello's sophisticated artwork and the Platonic myth amidst the Stone Age origins of image-making, and then linking them all to the still active terrors of the modern nursery, the poem itself enacts the transmutation of the primal cave's 'Flickering shades' into 'pleasant mysteries', 'Tamed and framed to courtly uses' – by implication mere child's play:

> Swift flights of bisons in a cave
>   Where man the maker killed to live;
>   But neolithic bush became
>   The midnight woods
>
>   Of nursery walls,
>   The ancient fears mutated
>   To play, horses to rocking-horses
> Tamed and framed to courtly uses . . .
>
>   As if our hunt by night
>   So very tense,
>
>   So long pursued,
>   In what dark cave begun
>   And not yet done, were not the great
> Adventure we suppose but some elaborate
>   Spectacle put on for fun
>   And not for food.

Art now, in its self-contained aesthetic autonomy, is representation, 're-presentation', not the thing itself, unlike those images painted on the walls of the Magdalenian caves as direct, practical interventions in the magico-economic strategies of the hunt. Far from elevating art, this descent could be seen as a degeneration, a falling away from an 'original' authenticity, creating simulacra which are mere copies of copies. But Mahon is not here espousing a fashionable primitivism, as is indicated by that suggestion that 'our hunt by night', so tense and 'long pursued', is a continuing presence, not only in our dreams, but in the dark unconscious of human motivations. The twilight of the cities is always with us, and we have never, in truth, escaped from 'the soft / Vegetables where our / Politics were conceived', into an existential rootlessness.

Mahon's elegiac memoir of Albert Camus, 'Death and the Sun', placed last in the *Selected Poems*, invites the reader to

> Imagine Plato's neolithic troglodyte
> Released from his dark cinema, released even
> From the fire proper, so that he stands at last,
> Absurd and anxious, out in the open air
> And gazes, shading his eyes, at the world there -
> Tangible fact ablaze in a clear light
> That casts no shadow, where the vast
> Sun gongs its lenity from a brazen heaven
> Listening in silence to his rich despair.

The men in the Belfast dole queues, quietly 'roll(ing) their own', are Sisyphus' descendants, 'briefly content'. Camus in *The Myth of Sisyphus*, writing in postwar disillusion with the murderous utopianism of a Soviet-style Communism, had argued that human history was an endless Sisyphean struggle to roll an intransigent real to the top of the hill, only to have it roll down the other side. Reading Camus as a teenage existentialist, Mahon confides, he numbered himself among the 'Wee shadows fighting in a smoky cave / Who would be one day brought to light', and found a model in 'the artist who refused suicide' as an answer to absurdity. 'We too knew the familiar foe', he says, in allusion to the small animosities of Irish history, but, in the cold Ulster night, 'never imagined the plague to come, / So long had it crouched there in the dark'.

In 'The Globe in North Carolina', Mahon had observed that,

> Here as elsewhere, I recognize
> A wood invisible for its trees
> Where everything must change except
> The fact of change; our scepticism
> And irony, grown trite, be dumb
> Before the new thing that must come . . .

– even if that new thing is simply the old thing in a new guise. Mahon's poetry repeatedly returns to those commonplaces of the neoplatonic tradition, seeing the generic paradigms that underlie, and presume to render unreal, all passing and particular human experience. But his obvious strength as a poet lies in his ability to see each tree in turn in all its particularity, without forgetting the wood. 'A Garage in Co. Cork' lovingly anatomises this place he thinks he may have passed through once before, in his nomadic youth. At first it seems unreal, ephemeral, and, 'Like a frontier store-front in an old western / It might have nothing behind it but thin air'. The poem speculates on all the disappearances and departures which have left this place in its semi-abandoned state. But, in the end, what impresses him is its quiet confidence in its own abidingness, its rootedness in itself: 'We might be anywhere, but are in one place only'. This is 'One of the milestones of earthresidence / Unique in each particular', even as it embodies a generic pattern, living, not in the hope of any resplendent future, but in a serene present tense, with 'a sure sense of its intrinsic nature'. Such a scene is paradigmatic one in Mahon's poetry, its unique particularity itself polemically and paradoxically constituting its representativeness.

The unremitting, pitiless sunlight of a desert without shadow evoked at the end of 'Death and the Sun' is no place for the human being: 'One cannot look for long at death or the sun'. Confronting the wide glare of the absolutist's heaven, that clear and brazen light which casts no shadow, the oxymoron with which *Selected Poems* closes ushers the human back into the dark cinema from which it had thought, foolishly, to escape.

APOCALYPSE NOW AND THEN: *THE YELLOW BOOK*

PATRICK CROTTY

Derek Mahon published no full collection of new poems between *The Hunt by Night* in 1982 and *The Hudson Letter* in 1995. A mere two years after the appearance of the latter volume came the career's first attempt at a book-length poem, *The Yellow Book*. Two years later again, *Collected Poems* appeared, featuring a large selection of the published poetry along with twenty-three pages of material apparently post-dating the 1997 sequence. These statistics suggest that Mahon has found a new lease of creative life, at least where the quantity of his output is concerned. 'Oh, show me how to recover my lost nerve!', the speaker of the opening section of *The Hudson Letter* had pleaded (CP 186), and if that cry is interpreted as evidence of a crisis of creative confidence by a poet who had produced only the pamphlet *Antarctica* and the poems collected in Part One of *The Hudson Letter* in a thirteen year span, the spate of utterance inaugurated by the title sequence of *The Hudson Letter* might be said to constitute its resolution: well over a third of *Collected Poems* is given over to verse published from 1995 on. (Mahon had not been idle during what was in poetic terms a relatively fallow period. Two Molière plays, Euripides's *Bacchae*, a Penguin edition of the poems of Philippe Jaccottet and a stage version of Racine's *Phaedra* eventually published in 1996 – reveal the extent to which his energies were given over to translation in the decade leading up to *The Hudson Letter*. *The Penguin Book of Contemporary Irish Poetry* (1990), which he edited with Peter Fallon, also derives from this time, as do all but thirteen of the fifty-seven pieces collected in *Journalism: Selected Prose* (1970–1995.)

The Yellow Book* is not a particularly long work – at forty-seven text pages it runs to just half a dozen pages more than the title sequence of *The Hudson Letter* – but it demands to be addressed as an integral unit by virtue not only of its filling a separate volume but of the physical properties of that volume. With the vivid, almost garish yellow of its front and back covers and spine, the poem comprised a very yellow book indeed on its first appearance. The cover might of course be a joke, like the reproduction of Hogarth's 'The Distrest Poet' on the front of *Journalism*, but the book's arrival in the world was implicated in temporal as well as spatial contingencies, and both categories of contingency make it necessary for this essay to concentrate on the original text of 1997 rather than on the revised and in some respects greatly improved version which appeared two years later in *Collected Poems*. (The revisions will be examined in the course of my concluding remarks.) It was obviously appropriate that a poetic sequence meditating on the end of the century and of the millennium should make its appearance in the late 1990s – one can say as much without endorsing John Lyon's observation that '*The Yellow Book* writes. . . its own application for admission to the Millennium Dome'[1] – but the specific year of the sequence's publication is significant. 1997 marked the centenary of the demise of the celebrated journal whose name Mahon's poem borrows, the yellow-bound periodical launched by Henry Harland and John Lane in London in 1894. It is an important part of Mahon's purpose that the original *Yellow Book* – albeit unjustly – became a by-word for decadence. (The periodical was considered shocking and indecent by some sections of late Victorian opinion, though the particular accusations of decadence made against it pertained only to the first issue. W.B. Yeats and Henry James, along with Arnold Bennett and H.G. Wells, were leading contributors to subsequent issues, and among the remarkable texts by less celebrated writers published in *The Yellow Book* was John Davidson's 'Thirty Bob A Week', a minor masterpiece of vigorous demotic admired by T.S. Eliot which, whatever the subsequent vicissitudes of its unfortunate author, falls wide of the most resourcefully capacious definition of decadence.) It would be difficult to overstate the symbolic importance of the precise dating of Mahon's *Yellow Book* in relation to its nineteenth century predecessor in terms of the overall trajectory of his career. Not only does it dramatise the sense of the cyclical recurrence of eras of decadence adumbrated at a number of points in the text; more importantly, it advertises the sequence's status as an intervention in historic time. That is to say, it highlights the radical difference between this text and the most admired and commented upon of Mahon's lyrics of the 1970s, which, as critic after critic has noted, cultivate a fastidious refusal of the pressures of history and politics. *The Yellow Book* is continuous with Mahon's greatest lyrics in its sense of catastrophe and apocalypse, a sense which now takes on the burden of specificity; it is discontinuous with them in its embrace of the historical moment and in its presentation of the poet as a representative figure, who, if he is in some respects no less solitary and alienated than the speakers of the earlier works, feels free at key junctures to give witness to communal and even – unthinkably for the Mahon of old – national experience. The speaker in 'The Last of the Fire Kings' (*CP* 64) had declared himself '(t)hrough with history'. The speaker of *The Yellow Book*, conversely, feels that history itself may be through – there had been much journalistic and academic chatter in the intervening years about the End of History – but if so he is an interested participant who wishes to have his say on its demise.

   The Yellow Book and *The Hudson Letter* title poem between them bring to the fullness of its development a tendency which had been evident in Mahon's work at least since 1990, when 'Dawn at St Patrick's' (*CP* 169) was included in the Gallery Press *Selected Poems*. The 'I' of this poem represents the poet in his personal and social being to a far greater and more explicit degree than the 'I' of earlier poems with apparently autobiographical starting points such as 'Beyond Howth Head' (*CP* 52) and 'Afterlives' (*CP* 58). Does the placing of 'Dawn at St Patrick's' in *Selected Poems* before the group of lyrics first printed at the end of *Poems 1962–1978* imply that it was composed in the late seventies? (It is reproduced after the *Antarctica* lyrics in *Collected Poems*, a position that honours its date of first publication.) At any rate the poem is the first of the poet's works to communicate the sort of rueful, almost embarrassed self-consciousness which distinguishes the pose of the poems of the nineties from Mahon's classic manner. 'They don't lock the razors here / as in Bowditch Hall' he observes, as if to suggest that there is something ridiculous in this indulgence in confessionalism by comparison with the poetry of Lowell's *Life Studies*. The line 'I sit on my Protestant bed, a make-believe existentialist' evinces a weakly comic bewilderment as it wheedles towards the reader to whom no concessions whatever were made in Mahon's earlier lyrics. (It does not occur to us to question the authenticity of the existential anguish of poems such as 'Rage for Order' (*CP* 47) or 'The Last of the Fire Kings'. It may, however, have occurred to the poet to do so.) When this confessional note is struck again, in 'The Yaddo Letter' (*CP* 182), the lyrical mode itself has been given up in favour of the epistolary style which will be carried over into 'The Hudson Letter' and – stripped of epistolary context – *The Yellow Book*. 'The Yaddo Letter', dated April-May 1990[2] and addressed from the famous upstate New York artists' retreat to the poet's children in London, provides a possible gloss on the shift in Mahon's approach to his art:

> I'd hoped to be more fun and try to write
> you something entertaining as I often try to do;
> but this time round I wanted to be *seerious* and true
> to felt experience.
>
> (*CP* 185)

Arguments about aesthetic quality frequently take on a moral character, with stylistic and formal austerity being interpreted as guarantors of an underlying seriousness of purpose. Thus Seamus Deane has observed, in the course of one of the most acute critical readings Mahon's early poetry has received: 'The formal control of his poems is an expression of a kind of moral stoicism, a mark of endurance under pressure'.[3] The lines from 'The Yaddo Letter' might be said to turn this argument on its head and to propose, albeit by implication, that the stance of aesthetic aloofness which so impressed admirers of the earlier poems had involved the poet in a sort of dishonesty, a misrepresentation of the conditions in which life actually has to be lived. The beauty of the lyrics – however dessicated and cheerless their vision, it seems appropriate to refer in Keatsian terms to poems which set so much store by poise and delicacy of expression – is now rejected in favour of the sometimes almost banal truth of the discursive verse. This model of Mahon's development would see the later poetry's very inelegance as an earnest of its attempt to be '*seerious* and true / to felt experience'. Indeed Mahon's abjuration of the aloof panache of his early poetry might be said to be no less emphatically 'protestant' than his elaboration of that pose was in the first instance.[4] There may be a parallel here with the poetic development of W.H. Auden, and in particular with Auden's mature attitude to admired passages in his poetry up to 1939 which he dropped or drastically amended in later editions of his work, refusing to sacrifice his sense of the truth of things to considerations of aesthetic decorum. (The related question of Mahon's attitude to the texts of his earlier poems is matter for a longer essay than this one.) Indeed mention of one poet of the 1930s brings to mind another paradigm of the evolution of Mahon's poetic practice. The work up to 1982 might be said to exemplify 'pure poetry', and the writing from 1995 an 'impure poetry', as discussed in Louis MacNeice's early critical writings.[5]

The affinities between *The Yellow Book* and *Autumn Journal* are not far to seek.

While there is disagreement as to the quality of Mahon's recent work, it seems to me unfair to suggest, as a number of hostile critics have done, that it represents no more than a degraded version of the poet's classic manner.[6] Tropes and obsessions familiar from the earlier achievement are reformulated in *The Yellow Book*, it is true, and well-known lines and phrases of young and early middle-aged Mahon are cited here and there – indeed a whole short poem, 'Dejection Ode' (*CP* 164), is recycled at the beginning of Section XV. This writing is so different in kind from the spryly ironic lyric formalism which first brought Mahon to critical attention, however, that it deserves to be judged on its own merits – if not on its own terms – rather than measured by its failure to repeat at their characteristic intensity the characteristic effects of the poetry from *Night Crossing* to *The Hunt by Night*. It is probably more accurate to speak of the refusal rather than of the failure of the recent work to reproduce those effects. With its loping lines, its chatty mode of address, its movement between autobiographical reflection and cultural commentary, and its laid-back if by no means low-brow literary allusiveness, the writing in *The Hudson Letter* and *The Yellow Book* marks one of the most determined attempts at self-reinvention in recent Irish or British poetry. It might even be argued that such an attempt was timely in Mahon's case, given that his work had begun to look in some degree repetitive – the most successful poems in *The Hunt by Night* (1982), after all, restate positions sketched as early as *Lives* (1972) if not indeed *Night-Crossing* (1968).

There are many precedents for the reluctance or inability of a poet to continue to give his or her readers the kind of verse they admire and have come to expect as of right. The prototype of the lost poetic leader was William Wordsworth, whose abandonment of an aesthetically and politically radical poetics in favour of a species of Anglican moralizing continues to be a matter of dismay and debate two hundred years after the appearance of his first great poems. Arthur Rimbaud's choice of African silence over European articulacy offers a scarcely less notorious example of the phenomenon. In the twentieth century, Hugh MacDiarmid moved from a Scots lyricism of extreme semantic compression and aural delicacy to an encyclopaedic and frequently hectoring English verse which, whatever else may be said for it, is devoid of the virtues of concentration and musical subtlety once seen as synonymous with him.

The more recent if less celebrated case of John Berryman provides a suggestive parallel with the course of Mahon's development in the 1990s. The voice of *Love & Fame* (1970), the last volume of his verse to appear in Berryman's lifetime, has a plainness, and the versification a deadness, which came as a severe disappointment to admirers of the rhetorical resource and figurative and metrical invention of *The Dream Songs* of the 1960s. The speaker of *Love & Fame* is a scarcely inflected version of the dried-out poet *in propria persona*. (It is instructive to read the collection alongside Berryman's posthumously published novel *Recovery*.) Fragile and reflective, he lacks the hilarious unpredictability and abandon of the *Dream Songs'* Henry. Both works are strongly autobiographical, but in *Love & Fame* the authorial *id* gives way as protagonist to the authorial *superego*,[7] with an inevitable loss of heroics. The composition of *The Dream Songs* had been fuelled by the very alcoholic excesses this deeply sober later poetry deplores and which had reduced Berryman's personal life to chaos. Dried-out poets may find themselves reduced – for a time at least – to dried-out poetry. While I would not wish to push the analogy between the careers of these two poets too far, it may be fruitful to think of Mahon's recent work as belonging, like the later prose and poetry of Berryman, to the literature of alcoholic recovery. This is clearly a delicate matter, but one which it is legitimate to raise in view of the increasingly frank references in his writing from 'Dawn at St Patrick's' to *The Yellow Book* to the poet's successful struggle against alcoholism. (While 'Dawn at St Patrick's' is not explicit with regard to the reasons for the speaker's confinement, phrases like 'a snifter of Lucozade', 'We have remained upright' and 'a sobering thought' hint at an alcoholic rest-cure. In 'The Hudson Letter' Mahon describes himself as 'a recovering Ulster Protestant' (*CP* 218), a phrase which works as a joke only if we expect the noun qualified by 'recovering' to be 'alcoholic'. *The Yellow Book* is much more forthright. 'Once you would wake up shaking at this hour', the speaker tells himself on page 12, while in the course of his address to the yellow bittern in Section VII he describes himself as

> At peace in my patch of sunlit convalescence
> with vitamin pills and a bottle of mineral water,
> forced on the dry. . .
>
> (*TYB* 26–7)

(Later, on page 44, tobacco is presented as a less dangerous drug for the speaker than alcohol: 'Sold / on sobriety, I turn to the idea of nicotine'.) Mahon's earlier work is not so wild as *The Dream Songs*, nor his later so tame as *Love & Fame*. Yet his poetry of the sixties and seventies is unusually rich (in the post-war Irish context perhaps uniquely rich) in sudden, epiphanic bursts of lyric *frisson*, and such moments are rare almost to the point of non-existence in *The Hudson Letter* and *The Yellow Book*. Lines like

> a subliminal batsqueak
> of reflex lamentation
>> ('An Image from Beckett', *CP* 40)

> a dying art,
> An eddy of semantic scruple
> In an unstructurable sea
>> ('Rage for Order', *CP* 47)

and

> It is time for the nymphs
> a glimpse of skin in the woods
>> ('Light Music', *CP* 71)

come to mind almost at random as examples of the verbal lightning we value so much in the earlier work and which it is possible to see as a kind of lyric inebriety. These points of intensity may be said to comprise poetic instances of that thrilling deliverance from the quotidian recovering alcoholics are counselled against aspiring to as they learn fealty to the dull rhythms of everydayness. The psychology of recovery, that is to suggest, may have made it necessary for Mahon's poetry to abjure, for the moment, its former excitements. (Mahon's own recourse to the lightning figure in 'The Hudson Letter', where he describes himself as 'exposed in thunderstorms, as once before, / and hoping to draw voltage one more time' (*CP* 191), might be adduced to counter this view.) To dwell on the absence of moments of verbal *frisson* from the discursive poems is to paint the difference between early and late Mahon in negative terms. There are positive differences as well, and some of these, too, may be related to the material conditions of the more recent work's production. The length of the two discursive sequences and indeed of the individual lines which make them up may reflect a newfound calmness of lifestyle. While I do not wish to imply that the mainly brief, short-lined lyrics were grabbed by a toper from encroaching darkness, there is certainly a sense in which the larger forms of 'The Hudson Letter' and *The Yellow Book* appear to have been meditated at his ease and executed in his unhurried leisure by a man who has come through.

Reading *The Yellow Book*, we can be forgiven for feeling that the relaxation in the poet's personal circumstances has carried over rather too smoothly into the procedures of his poetry. Indeed at certain – or rather uncertain – points, it appears that Mahon's days of redemption are paradoxically also his dog-days, those languorous times when, as Auden describes them in 'Under Sirius', the 'Sibyl utters / A gush of table chat'[8] While my ultimate aim in this essay is to establish that there is much to admire in *The Yellow Book*, I see little point in denying that some sections of the sequence are slack in conception, and many, intermittently at least, slacker again in execution. The sequence proper is prefaced by one of the book's weaker passages, 'Landscape', a translation of Baudelaire's 'Paysage':

> Chastely to write these eclogues I need to lie,
> like the astrologers, in an attic next the sky
> where, high among church spires, I can dream and hear
> their grave hymns wind-blown to my ivory tower.
> Chin in hand, up here in my apartment block,
> I can see workshops full of noise and talk,
> cranes and masts of the ocean-going city,
> vast cloud formations dreaming about eternity.
>
> (*TYB* 11]

These opening lines move along competently enough until the clumsy, stress-displacing chime of 'city'/'eternity' , but there is worse to come – the clichés of 'azure' sky and of the moon 'dispensing its mysterious influence', the (unintentionally?) dissonant 'tricks'/'pretext' rhyme of the penultimate couplet, the failure of the last line to fully articulate its antithesis of literal and metaphorical fire:

> I watch a foggy star glitter and shine
> in the azure sky, a lamp at a window-pane,
> smoke rising into the firmament like incense,
> the moon dispensing its mysterious influence.
> . . .
> [F]or here I am, up to my usual tricks -
> evoking spring-time on the least pretext,
> extracting sunlight as my whims require,
> my thoughts blazing for want of a real fire.
>
> (*TYB* 11)

Clearly the jadedness of posture here may call for an illustrative jadedness of language, but so indecisive is the process of ironisation of cliché that Mahon's translation provides less a dramatisation than an incidence of tiredness. The identification between the poet generally seen as the immediate forebear of late nineteenth century French poetic decadence and his Belfast-born, Dublin-based translator seems a little too coy, and the changes made to confirm and complicate the connection – Paris's chimneys giving way to Dublin's cranes, the note of self-deprecation introduced by the 'ivory tower' cliché – fail to add up to the sort of reinvention of a text from another language Mahon will brilliantly execute in relation to Cathal Buí Mac Giolla Ghunna's 'An Bonnán Buí' later in the sequence.

If Mahon sees fit to mistranslate some details in order to adapt the French original to the requirements of its new Irish context, why does he stop the process short and retain the term *eclogues*? One reviewer, John Lyon, has taken him at his – or rather Baudelaire's – word and concluded that *The Yellow Book* is intended as a collection of eclogues.[9] But this seems most unlikely. Eclogue is a pastoral form, and there is no trace here of the Arcadian paraphernalia Louis MacNeice was careful to retain when he bent the eclogue to his sardonic purposes in some of his best-known early poems. The mode of *The Yellow Book* has a more plausible classical prototype in the Latin elegy of Tibullus and Catullus. This form is not elegiac in the later and by now customary threnodic sense of that term, but consists rather of relaxed meditation essayed in alternating dactylic hexameters and pentameters. Though Mahon is generally content with loose pentameters in *The Yellow Book*, here and there he comes very close to the classical elegiac distich, as in the following lines from Section II, 'Axel's Castle':

> Coleridge. Only at dusk Minerva's owl will fly;
> only at dusk does wisdom return to the park.
>
> (*TYB* 14)

Coincidentally or not, it was Coleridge who described elegy as the form of poetry 'natural to a reflective mind'.[10] In European literatures it has not been considered necessary for an elegist to attempt to reproduce the classical metre – Donne's elegies, for instance, are in pentameters. One of the best-known post-Renaissance examples of the form in English is Edward Young's nine-volume *The Complaint, or, Night Thoughts on Life, Death and Immortality* (1742–46), a work usually known by the shorter title

Night Thoughts which it shares, perhaps significantly, with Section
I of *The Yellow Book*. There are to my knowledge only a handful of
instances in twentieth century poetry where the term *elegy* is
applied in its older sense – Rainer Maria Rilke's *Duino Elegies*, Ezra
Pound's *Homage to Sextus Propertius* (extra-textually) and the New
Zealand-born Scots poet Sydney Goodsir Smith's *Under the Eildon
Tree* (1948). The latter work, a raffish, wittily allusive mock
classical meditation on love and poetry, bears the subtitle *A Poem
in XXIV Elegies*.[11] A research student might profitably be directed
to explore the generic parallels between Goodsir Smith's and
Mahon's book-length poems.

To what extent is it legitimate to speak of *The Yellow Book* as a
'poem'? Mahon takes considerable pains to make his sequence
integral. His three main unifying strategies relate to subject
matter, imagery and what might loosely be called rhetoric. Firstly,
the book exhibits a pervasive thematic concern with dacadence,
whereby the confused pre-millenial culture of the present, as
viewed from Mahon's apartment in Dublin's Fitzwilliam Square,
is brought into relationship with the last *fin de siècle* in Dublin
and London, and with a number of other times and places
characterised by a sense of civilisational decline. Secondly, the
visual imagery of the volume dwells repeatedly on the colour
yellow, in homage to the *Yellow Book* of the 1890s. Thirdly, an
effort to knit the fabric of the verse together can be discerned in
the repetition of phrases, tropes and details of description from
section to section. Some of the myriad allusions in what Section
VIII calls the book's 'forest of intertextuality' (*TYB* 29) are of
similar type or to the same writers, adding a further sense of warp
and weft to Mahon's discourse. While in the comments which
follow I will attempt in so far as possible to disentangle these three
skeins for the purposes of critical clarity, it is hardly necessary to
say that in the best stretches of *The Yellow Book* they work in close
mutual support.

As a number of contributors to the present volume note,
Mahon's poems typically bring *here* into relationship with *there*,
the city of Nagoya where the Snow Party takes place with the
elsewhere where witches are burned (*CP* 63), for instance, or the
New York of 'The Hudson Letter''s composition with the various
theres to which it is sent, the Tomis of Ovid's exile (in 'Ovid in
Tomis', *CP* 157) with the Rome he pines for etc. *The Yellow Book*
plays a temporal variation on the characteristic spatial bilocation
of the earlier poetry. The end of the twentieth century is compared
to the end of the nineteenth, but also to the stylish 1940s of

Elizabeth Bowen and Cyril Connolly, the Gaelic twilight of the early eighteenth century when Cathal Buí Mac Giolla Ghunna drank and wrote his songs, the last days of the Earl of Tyrone's power at the turn of the sixteenth and seventeenth centuries, the ancient Rome of Petronius and Juvenal, and innocent 1960s Dublin of Austin Clarke (of which Mahon himself had some direct experience in his undergraduate days at Trinity College). The concern with decadence, and in particular with the closing years of the nineteenth century, builds on a long-standing interest of the poet's. One of the very fine early lyrics he has suppressed, 'The Poets of the Nineties' (originally published in *Lives* and last glimpsed on page 2 of 1979s *Poems 1962–1978*), was the first of many of his poems to concern alienated, marginalised or otherwise desperate artists. It also introduced the nature *vs* art theme which is sounded repeatedly through *The Yellow Book*. In all of the periods cited in the 1997 sequence, cultures, classes or coteries were on the point of extinction, but each had its writers who brought a stylistic flourish to their witness of decay even if they did not necessarily work out a *modus vivendi* to enable them to adapt to the demise of their accustomed conditions. Mahon presents himself in the 1990s as a poet caught in a similar civilisational breakdown and offers *The Yellow Book* as his testament to the times. A self-deprecating and at times almost facetious knowingness saves the analogy between the speaker and his distinguished forebears from portentousness, but it can leave *The Yellow Book*'s treatment of history looking distinctly glib. The past may be another country for Mahon, but it is one in which things are done much the same as in the present. If history has ended so many times before, it seems no great matter that it is about to do so again. Indeed the most recent decadences identified by the poet – the era of Bowen and Connolly, the Dublin of Clarke – coincided with earlier phases of his own life, and given that he emerged from those bothers unscathed he may not have too much to fear from the current situation. Perhaps such a comment reflects a reductive, overly literal reading of Mahon's concern with history – there is after all a sense in which World War Two did bring the gracious milieu of Bowen and Connolly to an end, and in which the Ireland of the 1960s genuinely represented the dying phase of a theocratic but in some respects comfortable and homely political order. Nonetheless it can seem at times as if too much fuss is being made about the end of civilisation, perhaps because relatively few of the proliferating examples of cultural twilight represent genuinely cataclysmic declensions of power, privilege or sensibility. In the last section, set in his favourite Irish holiday locale of Kinsale in County Cork, site of the defeat of O'Neill and O'Donnell which served as a prelude to the Plantation of Ulster, the poet asks

> Does history, exhausted, come full cycle?

going on to observe that

> It ended here at a previous *fin de siècle* . . .
>   (*TYB* 57)

This neatly brings the end of the old Gaelic order into relationship with what Mahon sees as the eclipse of his own unlamented (by him) Ulster Protestant tribe, a subterranean theme of the later stages of *The Yellow Book*, but if the main reference is to the dominant theme of the volume there would appear to be a manifest disproportion between the terms of the comparison. To parallel the destruction of the Gaelic world to the confusions of postmodernity, surely, is to overdramatise the contemporary crisis. And yet elsewhere in the book – in Section VIII, 'Remembering the 90s' – our millennial dilemma is presented as more serious than any earlier period of deliquescence in that literature itself, which survived previous cultural breakdowns to bequeathe us an invaluable record of decay, seems threatened with extinction:

>   in the known future
> new books will be rarities in techno-culture,
> a forest of intertextuality like this,
> each one a rare book and what few we have
> written for prize-money and not for love,
> while the real books like vintage wines survive
> among the antiquities, each yellowing page
> known only to the astrologer and mage
> where blind librarians study as on a keyboard
> gnomic encryptions, secrets of the word,
> a lost knowledge; and all the rest is lit(t)erature.
>   (*TYB* 29)

The reader who searches over nine lines to find a companion rhyme ('techno-culture') for 'lit(t)erature', the last word of the section, can be forgiven for concluding that one of the ways in which the present decadence differs from its predecessors is that its literary witness has manifestly less regard for style than Juvenal, Wilde and the other heroes of *The Yellow Book* (though to say this is not to deny the charm of the last line's bracketted jibe against postmodernist critical idiom). A not inconsiderable proportion of the volume is given over to loosely versified whining and opining about the drift of things, about pop music, fax machines, microtechnology, the internet, the whole 'pastiche paradise of the post-modern' (*TYB* 19), as Mahon calls it in Section IV, in one of the irritatingly journalistic phrases which pack the latter half of many poems which begin brightly. When, in Section XI, 'At the Chelsea Arts Club', he adapts Pater's famous dictum to assert that 'Everything aspires to the condition of rock music' (*TYB* 35) one can laugh at the joke while at the same time feeling that the poet is being snobbish now as well as curmudgeonly. A good deal of rock music, after all, not only aspires to but achieves a more continent artistry than is on display in those passages of *The Yellow Book* where Mahon lays about him with lists of the deficiencies of the present age. In such passages, indeed, the poet may be said to reverse the career trajectory of his early *alter-ego* Raftery by trading in the 'wry dissimulation' which made him famous for 'simplistic maunderings' ('I Am Raftery', *CP* 51). Doubtless it is these weaker stretches which have led Mahon's detractors to see *The Yellow Book* itself in relation to his earlier practice as an example of what Section VIII calls 'the deliquescence of each rigorous thing' (*TYB* 28).

The sequence is characterised by a sense of place as well as a sense of time, however, and the firmness with which Mahon renders location in *The Yellow Book* goes some way towards making good any lack of architectonic coherence deriving from the volume's handling of temporal relationships. If there is no reference to this aspect of the work in the very hostile reviews of Peter McDonald and John Lyon, that is not entirely the fault of the reviewers, as the poet does little to flag his effort to turn environment to symbol, an effort which, if rudimentary by the standards of Yeats's mythologising of his surroundings in *The Tower* and *The Winding Stair*, lends considerable resonance to key passages. The nearest Mahon comes to drawing attention to *The Yellow Book*'s procedure in this regard is his choice of an observation by George Moore – 'A mature artist takes the material closest to hand' – as epigraph for Section II (*TYB* 14) and his absorption of Moore's words into his own discourse two-thirds of the way through the section. Mahon lives in a top-floor apartment in Fitzwilliam Street, which forms the south-east boundary of Fitzwilliam Square, one of the most elegant of Dublin's Georgian Squares, just off Baggot Street in the still fashionable quarter of the

city between St Stephen's Green and Ballsbridge. Fitzwilliam
Square like the rest of Georgian Dublin was once the preserve of
the Anglo-Irish, a class whose political and cultural pre-eminence
came to an end almost within living memory. (Indeed the last
days of their power coincided with the *Yellow Book* era in London.)
The very stones among which Mahon passes his days, that is to
say, breathe of historical eclipse, the sequence's dominant theme.
'My attic window under the shining slates was once', as he
observes in 'Night Thoughts', 'where maids slept in the days of
Wilde and Yeats' (*TYB* 12) – a line amended, presumably on
grounds of historical accuracy but with happy consequences for
the figurative texture of the sequence, to 'where children slept in
the days of Wilde and Yeats' in *Collected Poems* (*CP* 224). On the
floor immediately beneath the poet's apartment are the Dublin
consulting rooms of Anthony Clare, a fact which presumably
accounts for the guest appearance of the famous psychiatrist in
Section VII (*TYB* 27). The loudspeakers on the tour buses which
draw up beneath the poet's window several times a day announce
that the square is no longer inhabited, all its houses being entirely
given over to legal, medical and accountancy practices: it is
understandable that such false news so insistently repeated might
make the auditor feel at times as if he belongs to a threatened
species. In the centre of the square stands a large garden, closed to
the public, and with its well-maintained interior largely hidden
from view by the trees and bushes which run along the inside of
the perimeter railing. This is 'the secret garden' of 'Night
Thoughts', the 'locked park' (*TYB* 12) to which the poet, in his
capacity as one of the last residents of the square, holds a key
(there is a wicket gate midway along each side of the square). The
lines conflating Wallace Stevens's and Richard Wilbur's snowman
(or snow man) poems with Oscar Wilde's 'The Selfish Giant' in
Section VIII, 'Remembering the 90s', take on an existential urgency
when one appreciates the extreme specificity of the scene, the
relationship of apartment window, 'square' and 'garden' to each
other, and in particular the fact that the children are playing in a
garden from which the watching ex-child is, for the moment at
least, literally as well as metaphorically outcast :

> The snow-man infants from the nursery school
> devised from the first fall of January
> stares back from the far corner of the square -
> a selfish giant made to freeze and rule
> the garden as if self-generated there,

> his abstract mien and cold, bituminous eye
> proclaiming a different order of reality
> from the bright children who gave rise to him.
> When they go there to play at mid-morning
> their primary colours seem to prefigure spring,
> the deliquescence of each rigorous thing;
> but the ex-child at the window watching them,
> specs on his nose and winter in his eyes,
> knows himself outcast from the continuum
> and draws his curtain against darkening skies . . .
>
> (*TYB* 28)

Mahon's decision to include a version of forty-eight lines from the opening of the famous tenth satire of Juvenal is at first sight puzzling. Why challenge such mighty forebears as Dr Johnson and Robert Lowell? Johnson substituted well-known English and European writers and statesmen for Juvenal's Romans in his magisterial 1749 version of the poem, 'The Vanity of Human Wishes'. Lowell borrowed Johnson's title but left many of the Roman details of the original intact. By carefully positioning his version among more explicitly public poems of his own in his 1967 collection *Near the Ocean*, however, he endowed it with significant power as a tacit commentary on the excesses of the post-Kennedy era. Mahon's title, 'The Idiocy of Human Aspiration', has a misanthropic edge we may recognise as characteristic, but his use of Juvenal is justified less by that than by the details which give the poem a Georgian Dublin setting of small apartments and of parks which, even though locked and supposedly private, can be frightening places after nightfall:

> You're better off to sit tight in your room,
> Take change if you go out walking after dark
> and keep your wits about you in the park
> where a knife gleams behind each shadowy tree.
>
> (*TYB* 33)

The book's yellow motif, though almost stridently brought to the reader's attention through the title and cover, may ultimately contribute less to the cohesion of Mahon's discourse than the quietly pervasive sense of locale discussed above. With one triumphant exception, the 'yellows' in the text occur arbitrarily and more or less incidentally. We have already encountered the phrase 'each yellowing page' in the description of disregarded books at the dystopian conclusion of Section VIII. Section XI conjures the smoking room of the Chelsea Arts Club:

> Best in the afternoon when the bar is shut,
> the smoking room, an empty Chekhov set,
> stained ochre, yields to silence, buttery light,
> euphoria and nostalgia; so let me write
> in praise of yellow while it is still bright . . .
>
> *(TYB* 36)

The triteness of the triplet underscores the arbitrariness of this instance of the colour. Addressing the shade of Oscar Wilde in Section XIV, 'Rue des Beaux-Arts', Mahon quotes him appositely:

> As you said, a yellow-journalism survivor
> has no need to fear the yellow fever . . .
>
> *(TYB* 41)

Elsewhere there are references to 'Elysian yellows' (Section XV, *TYB* 45) and, in the lines evoking J.G. Farrell's novel *Troubles* in Section XVII (*TYB* 49), to 'a yellow vintage "motor" in the garage'.

Somewhat perversely, the one occurrence of yellow in a section title is visible only to those who know the Irish language. Section VII is called 'An Bonnán Buí' after the famous song by Cathal Buí MacGiolla Ghunna, a song so admired by Mahon that he included not one but two translations of it in his *Sphere Book of Modern Irish Poetry*.[12] The original 'An Bonnán Buí' ('The Yellow Bittern') offers a sort of prototype of the tonalities of *The Yellow Book* in what Seán Ó Tuama and Thomas Kinsella call its 'finely judged blend of pathos and humour'.[13] Nowhere in his sequence does Mahon blend those qualities as subtly as in the first twenty or so lines of this section, in a passage which pursues the yellow theme with something of the energy and precision of his best lyrics. The Irish original playfully exploits the shared yellowness of bird and bard – Cathal Buí means Yellow Cathal, in reference, according to tradition, to the poet's drink-induced complexion. (MacGiolla Ghunna was born in Fermanagh c1680 and buried in Donaghmoyne, Co Monaghan c1756. The fact that he is said to have been an unfrocked priest might make him another of *The Yellow Book*'s disgraced visionaries.) MacGiolla Ghunna addresses a bittern found dead by a frozen pond, his beak in the unbroken ice, and muses on the dangers of not·drinking. Among the many fine translations of the song is one by Seamus Heaney published in *The School Bag* more or less contemporaneously with *The Yellow Book*.[14] Mahon's 'An Bonnán Buí' is not so much a translation as a fantasia based on selected details of the original, some of them adapted to the post-alcoholic context of his sequence ('A sobering thought'). There is perhaps even a reference to Mahon's declared fear that he may have lost his poetic nerve in 'your voice stilled by enforced sobriety'. The Hiberno-English idiom which can sound like Paddywhackery in some sections of *The Yellow Book* is here perfectly matched to subject and situation ('the whole unfortunate country frozen over'):

> A sobering thought, the idea of you stretched there,
> bittern, under a dark sky, your exposed bones
> yellow too in a ditch among cold stones,
> ice glittering everywhere on bog and river,
> the whole unfortunate country frozen over
> and your voice stilled by enforced sobriety -
> a thought more wrenching than the fall of Troy
> because more intimate; for we'd hear your shout
> of delight from a pale patch of watery sunlight
> out on the mud there as you took your first
> drink of the day and now, destroyed by thirst,
> you lie in brambles while the rats rotate.
>
> > (*TYB* 26)

The source drawn upon by these lines is probably Kinsella's translation, which I quote in the parentheses below. (The best known version, MacDonagh's, reduces the poem from five to four stanzas and elides some of the particulars turned to account by Mahon.) The lines on the fall of Troy rebuke the extravagance of the original ('I feel it worse than the ruin of Troy / to see you stretched on the naked stones'), inserting a note of more desperate sympathy. 'While the rats rotate' adds a grim mechanical determinism to the scene ('and the big rats travelling toward your wake'). Later Mahon yanks up the comedy of the situation, transforming the bird ('so like myself in face and hue') into the type of the dipsomaniacal *poète maudit*:

> but I mourn only the bittern, withdrawn and solitary,
> a highbrow with a hunched gait and quick forensic eye
> who used to carouse alone among the rushes
> and sleep rough in the star-glimmering bog-drain.
>
> > (*TYB* 26)

The joke is anticipated in the section epigraph from *Guide to Irish Birds*, with its stress on the crepuscular habits of the bittern: 'A heron-like species, rare visitors, most recent records referring to winter months . . . very active at dusk'.

At once exuberant and exacting, this intertextual *divertissement* exemplifies the rhetoric of *The Yellow Book* at its best. The writing in the generality of the sequence is rather less taut. Mahon's method is to offer relaxed meditations on a small number of inter-related topics – decadence (alike in its politico-cultural and moral senses), solitude, addiction, art and nature, the lost secret garden of childhood, the transformation of places to tourist destinations – which through rehearsal in different combinations lend a sense of orchestration and even of complexity to the proceedings. Details recur from section to section. The 'darkened convoys' (*TYB* 16) of Section III, 'At the Shelbourne', for instance, link Elizabeth Bowen to the poet, who in Section I remembers 'navies aglow off Bangor and Whitehead' (*TYB* 12), while another World War Two detail – 'huge transport planes thundering overhead' (*TYB* 12) – connects him to Schopenhauer, the remnants of whose world are destroyed by Allied bombers at the conclusion of Section V. The 'cranes' of 'Landscape' (*TYB* 11) and the 'crane-light' of Section I (*TYB* 12) point up the similarities between Baudelaire's and Mahon's attic eyries. The sequence's many complaints about tourism are cheerfully ironized by Section XII's portrait of the artist as a holiday-maker in Greece. The solitude, tourism and addiction motifs are brought together by the play of 'ivory tower' and 'lighthouse' references on pages 12, 44 and 55, the last one nicely neutralizing the cliché in the first of these terms by employing it as a synonym for the second (i.e. the lighthouse becomes an actual, three-dimensional ivory tower):

> Now the ivory towers will be visitor centres.

Proliferating allusions to other literary works add a further element of richness to the rhetoric of *The Yellow Book*. Indeed the sequence is less 'a forest of intertextuality' than a mosaic of quotations and echoes. Some of these can strike the reader as pointless and even self-indulgent. The allusions to Larkin's 'High Windows' in Section II (*TYB* 15) and MacNeice's *Autumn Journal* and 'Bagpipe Music' in Section IX (*TYB* 31), for instance, add little weight to the lines in which they occur. Other intertextual connections, however, contribute centrally to the wit of *The Yellow Book*, and significantly deepen the resonance of initially slight-seeming passages. The ghost of Marvell's line about Cromwell ruining the great work of time[15] in Mahon's comment about McAlpine's fusiliers who, with their *'site hats* (my emphasis) and brick dust' ... 'ruin the work of years', casts the poet as a melancholy cavalier helpless before the depredations of roundhead modernity. The references to 'nymphs', 'apple core' and 'white sock' in Section 14, 'Aphrodite's Pool' (*TYB* 37), conflate details from Chapters 1 and 14 of Nabokov s *Lolita* to present the speaker as a harmless, touristic version of the pentapod monster Humbert Humbert. The myriad allusions to the poetry of Austin Clarke in Section IV, '"shiver in your tenement"', are a matter not only of verbal echoes but of imitation of such favourite Clarke devices as homonymic ('censors' . . . 'censers', *TYB* 18) and assonantal ('heart' . . . 'artistry', *TYB* 19) rhyme and of puns on 'Clarke', 'clerk' and 'clerical'. (It might be objected that Mahon's title drains the humanitarian rage from the famous 'green pagoda. . . . Go da/ And shiver in your tenement' conclusion of 'New Liberty Hall'[16] by converting the overcrowded rooms of the urban poor to the lonely attics of aesthetes.) *The Yellow Book* exploits political as well as literary allusions. The concluding line of Section VII, for instance, plays a disconsolate variation on Seán Lemass's remark, in relation to economic expansion, that 'a rising tide lifts all boats'. Section XVIII, 'Death in Bangor', closes on the phrase 'blue skies of the republic', which mixes the political (the UVF slogan, 'We will never trade the blue skies of Ulster for the grey skies of an Irish republic') with the literary (the ante-penultimate paragraph of *The Great Gatsby*, with its evocation of 'the dark fields of the republic'[17]).

The stance of *The Yellow Book* in relation to a particular republic – the southern Irish state of the author's domicile – highlights like nothing else the extent to which Mahon has shifted poetic ground over the decades. The poet who observed in 1974 that 'The time is coming . . . when the question "Is So-and-So really an *Irish* writer?" will clear a room in seconds' (*J* 21) now writes out of what appears to be a deep though unreflective sense of affiliation to the Irish Republic and its informing nationalist ideology. References to 'our noble birthright' (*TYB* 47) and 'our proper dark' (*TYB* 44) remain unironized, as if to flaunt Mahon's membership of a wider community of 'We Irish' than any dreamed of by Berkeley or Yeats. If in one sense this espousal of a southern Irish identity is at odds with the earlier poetry's distaste for engagement with history and for any species of communal belonging, in another – its repudiation of the poet's politico-cultural origins in Northern Ireland – it is continuous with it. 'Death in Bangor', the unlamenting requiem for the poet's mother which comprises the eighteenth section, implies that Mahon has been driven by his quarrel with the longer surviving of his Ulster Protestant parents to identify with the land frequently if inadvertently alluded to in her hummed 'South of the Border' (*TYB* 52). Insofar as *The Yellow Book* continues the quarrel after her death by valorizing a southern nationalist perspective and offering a scornful, reductive portrait of unionist culture – see the lines beginning 'I thought of the plain Protestant fatalism of home' (*TYB* 52) – it might be said to court the sort of angry northern response Peter McDonald's review has duly supplied.[18]

In Section IV Mahon numbers 'solitude' among 'things of the past' (*TYB* 19). Tonally, where his own work is concerned, it should certainly be so counted: the eremetical *hauteur* of the earlier poems gives way in *The Yellow Book* to something far more chummy. One of the oddest things about the sequence is that while it is centrally concerned with loneliness and isolation, it voices its alienated themes in a sociable and at times almost clubbable manner. The first person plural into which a number of passages modulate, having begun in the first or second singular, can speak for the poet and like-minded marginalised artists (most wittily in Section XV, 'Smoke', with its company of nicotine-addicted notables) but it can as readily air the views the Plain People of Ireland:

> (A)t home now with the ersatz, the pop, the phony
> we seldom see a real nun, a copy of *An Phoblacht*
> or love and hate, as once, with a full heart.
> Those were the days . . . .
>
> (*TYB* 19)

Whence this newfound joy in collectivism? And are we – it seems appropriate to have recourse to the first person plural here – really to lament the disappearance of the Sinn Féin paper? At junctures like this the reader appears to be in the presence of a species of nostalgic populism so unexamined as to deserve the customary epithet 'mindless'. Or perhaps the poet is having fun at the expense alike of adherents of the anti-republican, anti-clerical consensus among the liberal intelligentsia in the south of Ireland, and of unionists in the north. One of Mahon's favourite writers, Albert Camus, wrote in a late story of an artist who collapses, exhausted, leaving a long laboured over canvas blank except for a tiny word which can be construed either as *solitary* or the adjectival form of *solidarity*.[19] *The Yellow Book* may be an extremely busy canvas but it is one – if we may animate the metaphor – which shimmers bafflingly between homage to solitude on the one hand and to solidarity on the other.

No account of *The Yellow Book* would be complete without an acknowledgement of how closely worked the end of the sequence is by comparison with what has gone before. The last three sections build towards what is in its downbeat way something of a grand conclusion. Section XVIII, 'Death in Bangor', sketches the failure of the poet's native culture to imaginatively sustain him and hints at his reasons for moving south; Section XIX, 'On the Automation of the Irish Lights', set for the most part at the Old Head of Kinsale, in the far south, finds an inspired figurative correlative for the sequence's sense of progressive depersonalisation (and supplies a suggestive description of its procedures – 'a routine enlightenment, bright but abandoned', *TYB* 54); Section XX, 'Christmas in Kinsale', voiced from the end of the year and the end of the millennium, is set in the same locale, the place where Gaelic power met its *nemesis* – an event in which the Protestant Ulster consigned to history in Section XVIII had its origins. The closing lines, like such early poems as 'The Apotheosis of Tins' (*CP* 69) and 'The Mute Phenomena' (*CP* 82), focus on civilisations as producers of rubbish:

> Holed up here in the cold gardens of the west
> I take out at mid-morning my Christmas rubbish.
> Sphere-music, the morning stars consort together
> in a fine blaze of anticyclone weather
> hallowing the calm inner and the rough outer harbour,
> the silence of frost and crow on telephone lines,
> the wet and dry, the garbage and the trash
> remains of rib and chop, warm cinders, ash,
> bags, boxes, bulbs and batteries, bathroom waste,
> carcases, tinfoil, leaves, crumbs, scraps and bones -
> if this were summer there would be crowds of flies
> buzzing for joy around the rubbish bins.
> The harsh will dies here among snails and peonies,
> its grave an iridescence in the sea-breeze,
> a bucket of water where the rainbow ends.
> Elsewhere the cutting edge, the tough cities,
> the nuclear wind from Windscale, derelict zones;
> here the triumph of carnival, rinds and skins,
> mud-wrestling organisms in post-historical phase
> and the fuzzy vegetable glow of origins.
> A cock crows good-morning from an oil-drum
> like a peacock on a rain-barrel in Byzantium,
> soap-bubbles foam in a drainpipe and life begins.

> I dreamed last night of a blue Cycladic dawn,
> a lone figure pointing to the horizon,
> again the white islands shouting, 'Come on; come on!' ...
>   (*TYB* 57)

'In the refuse of the world a new world is born', observed Pier
Paolo Pasolini, in a comment glossed by this climactic passage
from *The Yellow Book* and also by *Roman Script* (*CP* 273), the
longest of Mahon's new poems. These lines, their redundant
reference to garbage *and* trash notwithstanding, come close to the
quality of the opening of the 'Bonnán Buí' section and contain
perhaps the two brightest images in the entire sequence, the
bucket of water which makes do for a crock of gold and the
gloriously anti-Yeatsian cock on the oildrum. Mahon has sung
throughout *The Yellow Book* of what is past or passing; his oily bird
– not such a form as Grecian goldsmiths make – sings raucously of
what is to come, the new order which will emerge from the
wreckage and refuse of the cultures whose demise is lamented
throughout the sequence. '"Come on; Come on! ..."', the lone
Cycladic figure's invitation to the future, links *The Yellow Book*, in
the larger architecture of Mahon's *oeuvre*, to the plaintive climax of
'The Hudson Letter', '"Take us in; Take us in!"'

The version of *The Yellow Book* published in *Collected Poems* (*CP*
223–65) is different in no fewer than one hundred and thirty
details from the original. Lines and sequences of lines have been
dropped, replaced or recast. Section epigraphs have been excised
or replaced, and particulars of punctuation, capitalisation and
individual word choice have been altered. Groups of two or three
new lines have been interpolated at many points in the sequence.
Section VIII, 'Remembering the 90s', is now called 'Hangover
Square' and the title of Section XVIII has been toned down from
'Death in Bangor' to 'A Bangor Requiem'. Anthony Clare is no
longer mentioned by name, and the fourth and fifth lines of
Section II have lost their resemblance to an elegiac distich. The
poet is now projected as a less relentlessly solitary creature,
having been joined in Section II by 'a foxy lady' who 'slips into her
shoes / and leaves me words of wisdom' (*CP* 226). The general
impact of these revisions is to make the sequence more taut than
the version published in 1997, sometimes significantly so. A
number of the textual changes bear upon matters discussed in this
essay. The stylistic quality of the preamble, now called simply
'(*Context: Baudelaire*)', has been greatly enhanced by a handful of
emendations.

(V)ast cloud formations dreaming about eternity

gives way to

vast cloud-pack photographs of eternity

which is not only more semantically compressed than the original but rhythmically much kinder to the 'city'/'eternity' rhyme. The substitution of 'writing desk' for 'writing-table' provides a near full rhyme for 'pretext', subtly muting the dissonance with 'tricks'. The star now 'opens freshly' instead of glittering predictably. The fountains 'splash' where they had earlier – rather puzzlingly – 'wept'. These changes have an impact on the unchanged phrases objected to above ('azure sky', 'mysterious influence'): in their new, more alert context they seem less slack. Two of the weakest closing passages, from sections VII and VIII (the lines about the demise of 'lit(t)erature') have disappeared. Section VII, 'An Bonnán Buí', may still not sustain the outstanding quality of its opening movement, but the fourteen new lines which replace the discarded thirty-one introduce a third Ulster poet, Patrick Kavanagh, to the original duo of MacGiolla Ghunna and Mahon, and play almost as expert a variation on some of his most famous lines as the opening does on the song to the Yellow Bittern. The fact that Kavanagh had made the area around Pembroke Road and the Grand Canal, within walking distance of Fitzwilliam Square, his poetic territory in the 1950s adds a further degree of appropriateness to his presence at this point in the proceedings. Here are the last thirteen of the new lines (There is a bronze statue of Kavanagh on the banks of the canal):

> She says I'm done for if I drink again;
> so now, relieved of dangerous stimuli,
> at peace with my plastic bottle of H_2O
> and the slack strings of insouciance, I sit
> with bronze Kavanagh on his canal-bank seat,
> not in the tremendous silence of mid-July
> but the fast bright zing of a winter afternoon
> dizzy with head-set, flash-bulb and digifone,
> to learn the *tao* he once claimed as his own
> and share with him the moor-hen and the swan,
> the thoughtless lyric of a cloud in the sky
> and the play of light and shadow on the slow
> commemorative waters; relax, go with the flow.
> (*CP* 237–8)

The twelve new lyrics printed at the end of *Collected Poems* triumphantly confirm the recovery of poetic nerve suggested by the more vigorous passages of *The Yellow Book*. Some of them are thematically continuous with the sequence. 'Night and Day *(after Ariosto)*' (*CP* 266), a much more spirited performance than either version of Baudelaire's 'Paysage', extends Mahon's interest in crepuscular atmospherics, while the first of the two Michelangelo sonnets translated on page 267 reformulates the art *vs* nature motif. 'Shapes and Shadows' (*CP* 278) offers a less problematic model of communal affiliation than '"shiver in your tenement"', and demonstrates – along with 'A Swim in County Wicklow' (*CP* 280) – that the poet is capable of communicating a mood of relaxed acceptance in a disciplined, non-discursive lyrical idiom which moves its argument along by means of sharply realised images. These poems should not, however, be used as sticks with which to beat *The Yellow Book*. Mahon's sequence, for all its unevenness and occasional lapses of tone, stands on its merits as one of the most rewarding and entertaining poetic productions of the twilight years of the twentieth century.

NOTES

INTRODUCTION: THE CRITICAL CONTEXT

ELMER KENNEDY-ANDREWS

1. See also the preface to *The Sphere Book of Modern Irish Poetry*, where Mahon refers to 'the metaphysical unease in which all poetry of lasting value has its source' (London, Sphere, 1972), p. 12.
2. Derek Mahon, *The Irish Times*, 16th July, 1987. Quoted by Hugh Haughton in Clíodhna Ní Anluain (ed.), *Reading the Future: Irish Writers in Conversation with Mike Murphy* (Dublin, Lilliput Press, 2000), p. 163. Also quoted by Gerald Dawe in his essay in this volume, p. 24.
3. In an interview, Mahon has said: 'I think the Protestant ethic has made it its business to dispel any karma that there might have been. In so far as I have written about the North . . . I may have been trying to put back in some of the karma that bad Protestants over the generations have removed' (*Poetry Ireland Review*, 14 (Autumn 1985), p. 14.
4. Michael Longley, *Tuppeny Stung: Autobiographical Chapters* (Belfast, Lagan Press, 1994), p. 38.
5. Edna Longley, 'Derek Mahon: Extreme Religion of Art', in Michael Kenneally (ed.), *Poetry in Contemporary Irish Literature* (Gerrards Cross, Colin Smythe, 1995), pp. 280–303, p. 287.
6. Brian Donnelly, 'Introduction', *Irish University Review, Derek Mahon Special Number*, 24, 1 (1994), p. 1.
7. Derek Mahon (ed.), *The Sphere Book of Modern Irish Poetry*, pp. 13–14.
8. Eavan Boland, 'Compact and Compromise: Derek Mahon as a Young Poet', *Irish University Review, Derek Mahon Special Number*, 24, 1 (1994), pp. 61–6, p. 63.
9. *Ibid.*, p. 61.
10. Derek Mahon, 'Poetry in Northern Ireland', *Twentieth Century Studies*, November 1970, pp. 89–93, p. 90.
11. *Ibid.*, p. 92.
12. Edna Longley, 'From Cathleen to Anorexia: The Breakdown of Irelands', in *The Living Stream* (Newcastle-upon-Tyne, Bloodaxe, 1994), pp. 173–195, p. 195.
13. Derek Mahon (ed.), *The Sphere Book of Modern Irish Poetry* (London,

Sphere, 1972), pp. 13–14.

14. Derek Mahon and Peter Fallon (eds.), 'Introduction', *The Penguin Book of Contemporary Irish Poetry* (Harmondsworth, Penguin, 1990), pp. xvi-xxii, pp. xix-xx.
15. Peter Porter, *Observer*, 19 December 1992.
16. Declan Kiberd, *Inventing Irelands: The Literature of the Modern Nation* (London, Vintage, 1996), p. 599.
17. 'Introduction', *Faber Book of Modern Irish Verse*, ed. Paul Muldoon (London, Faber, 1986), p. 18.
18. Seamus Heaney, 'The Pre-Natal Mountain: Vision and Irony in Recent Irish Poetry', in *The Place of Writing*, Emory Studies in the Humanities (Atlanta, Scholars Press, 1989), pp. 36–53, p. 47.
19. *Ibid.*, p. 42.
20. *Ibid.*, pp. 48–9.
21. Edna Longley, 'The Singing Line: Form in Derek Mahon's Poetry', in *Poetry in the Wars* (Newcastle-upon-Tyne, Bloodaxe, 1986), pp. 170–184, p. 172.
22. Kiberd, p. 378.
23. Boland, p. 66.
24. Stan Smith, *Inviolable Voice: History and 20th Century Poetry* (Dublin, Gill and Macmillan, 1982), p. 189.
25. Seamus Deane, 'Unhappy and at Home', interview with Seamus Heaney, *The Crane Bag*, 1, 1 (1977), pp. 61–7, p. 61.
26. Seamus Deane, 'Derek Mahon: Freedom from History', in *Celtic Revivals* (London, Faber, 1985), pp. 156–65, p. 158.
27. *Ibid.*, p. 162.
28. Seamus Deane, 'Seamus Heaney: The Timorous and the Bold', in *Celtic Revivals*, pp. 174–186, pp. 180–1.
29. Deane, *Celtic Revivals*, p. 156.
30. *Ibid.*, p. 159.
31. *Ibid.*, p. 162.
32. *Ibid.*, p. 160.
33. *Ibid.*, p. 162.
34. Edna Longley, 'Introduction: Revising "Irish Literature"', in *The Living Stream*, pp. 9–68, p. 39.
35. Edna Longley, 'Poetry and Politics in Northern Ireland', in *Poetry in the Wars*, p. 185.
36. Derek Mahon, 'Poetry in Northern Ireland', *Twentieth Century Studies*, November 1970, p. 93.
37. Mark Patrick Hederman, 'Poetry and the Fifth Province', *The Crane Bag*, 9, 1 (1985), pp. 110–19, p. 111.
38. Edna Longley, 'Derek Mahon: Extreme Religion of Art', in *Poetry in Contemporary Irish Literature*, p. 296.
39. *Ibid.*, p. 296.
40. *Ibid.*, p. 297.
41. Deane, *Celtic Revivals*, p. 163.
42. *Ibid.*, p. 163.

43. Edna Longley, 'Derek Mahon: Extreme Religion of Art', in *Poetry in Contemporary Irish Literature*, p. 299.
44. *Ibid.*, p. 301.
45. *Ibid.*, p. 292.
46. Brendan Kennelly, 'Derek Mahon's Humane Perspective', in Terence Brown and Nicholas Grene (eds.), *Tradition and Influence in Anglo-Irish Poetry* (Basingstoke, Macmillan, 1989), pp. 143–52, p. 143.
47. *Ibid.*, p. 143.
48. *Ibid.*, p 144.
49. *Ibid.*, p. 143.
50. *Ibid.*, p. 146.
51. Peter McDonald, *Mistaken Identities: Poetry and Northern Ireland* (Oxford, Clarendon, 1997), p. 6.
52. *Ibid.*, p. 87.
53. *Ibid.*, p. 95.
54. Edna Longley, '"Defending Ireland's Soul": Protestant Writers and Irish Nationalism after Independence', in *The Living Stream*, pp. 130–149, p. 149.
55. W.J. McCormack, *The Battle of the Books: Two Decades of Irish Cultural Debate* (Mullingar, Lilliput Press, 1986), p. 65.
56. Gerald Dawe, '"Icon and Lares": Derek Mahon and Michael Longley', in Gerald Dawe and Edna Longley (eds.), *Across a Roaring Hill: The Protestant Imagination in Modern Ireland* (Belfast, Blackstaff Press, 1985), pp. 218–35, p. 218.
57. *Ibid.*, pp. 218–9.
58. This is to indicate a MacNeicean balance which Seamus Deane has also noted: 'The blends of vocabulary and of tone in Mahon's poetry shift the reader's attention from specific detail to general conditions. There is no dwelling in the sensuous and no concentration on abstractions. He is neither conceptual nor sensual: his sensibility is equidistant from both but is alert to the attractions of each'. (Deane, *Celtic Revivals*, p. 159).
59. Timothy Kearney, The Poetry of the North: A Post-modernist Perspective', *The Crane Bag*, 3 2 (1979), pp. 45–53, p. 45.
60. Quoted by Kiberd, p. 40.

LOOKING BACK FROM *THE YELLOW BOOK*

Edna Longley

1. W.B. Yeats, *Essays and Introductions* (London: Macmillan, 1961),94, 522.
2. Eric Warner and Graham Hough (eds.), *Strangeness and Beauty: An Anthology of Aesthetic Criticism 1840–1910* (Cambridge: Cambridge University Press), p. 2.

3. Derek Mahon interviewed by Eamon Grennan, *Paris Review* (Spring 2000), pp. 151–78, (pp. 165–6) – the interview took place in 1991.
4. *Ibid.*, p. 171
5. Bill Tinley, '"Harmonies and Disharmonies": Derek Mahon's Francophile Poetics', *Irish University Review*: Special Issue: Derek Mahon, 24, 1 (Spring-Summer 1994), pp. 80–96 (p. 82).
6. Graham Robb, *Rimbaud* (London, Picador, 2000), p. 59.
7. Tinley, pp. 86–7.
8. Mahon interview, p, 173.
9. John Redmond, 'Wilful Inconsistency: Derek Mahon's Verse-Letters', *Irish University Review*, 24, 1 (Spring-Summer 1994), pp. 96–116 (p. 96).
10. Peter McDonald, 'Incurable Ache', review of *The Yellow Book*, *Poetry Ireland Review* 56 (Spring 1998), pp. 117–19 (p. 117).
11. Mahon interview, p. 163.
12. See Edna Longley, '"Atlantic's Premises": American Influences on Northern Irish Poetry in the 1960s', in Longley, *Poetry & Posterity* (Tarset, Northumberland: Bloodaxe Books, 2000), 259–79.
13. Derek Mahon, 'Poetry in Northern Ireland', *Twentieth Century Studies*, 4 (November 1970), pp. 89–93 (p. 91).
14. Philippe Jaccottet, *Selected Poems with Translations by Derek Mahon* (London, Penguin 1998), p. 13
15. Mahon interview, p. 167.
16. *Ibid.*, p. 156.
17. *Ibid.*, p. 163.
18. *Ibid.*, p. 162.
19. *Ibid.*, pp. 160–1.
20. *Ibid.*, p. 171.
21. McDonald, 'Incurable Ache', p. 119.
22. Mahon interview, p. 169.
23. See Edna Longley, 'Derek Mahon: Extreme Religion of Art', in Michael Kenneally (ed.), *Poetry in Contemporary Irish Literature* (Gerrards Cross: Colin Smythe, 1995), pp. 280–303 (pp. 297–300).

HEIRS AND GRACES: THE INFLUENCE AND EXAMPLE OF DEREK MAHON

Gerald Dawe

1. Michael Longley, *Tuppeny Stung: Autobiographical Chapters* (Belfast, Lagan Press, 1994), pp. 38–9.
2. Derek Mahon, *The Irish Times*, 16th July, 1987.
3. 'An Interview with Derek Mahon' by Terence Brown, *Poetry Ireland Review*, No 14 (Autumn 1985), pp. 11–19.
4. Peter Porter, 'Privileges of an Irish Poet', *The Sunday Telegraph*, 30th

August, 1998, p. 13.

5. Derek Mahon, 'The Existential Lyric', review of Samuel Beckett, *Collected Poems in English and French*, in Derek Mahon, *Journalism* (Oldcastle, Gallery Press, 1996), p. 56.

6. Peter Ansorge, *From Liverpool to Los Angeles: On Writing for Theatre, Film and Television* (London, Faber and Faber, 1997), p. 140.

'SOLVING AMBIGUITY': THE SECULAR MYSTICISM OF DEREK MAHON

Bruce Stewart

1. Margaret Atwood, *Cat's Eye* (London, Bloomsbury, 1989), p. 421.

2. Derek Mahon, 'Poetry in Northern Ireland', *Twentieth Century Studies*, 4 (November 1970).

3. See Eavan Boland, 'Compact and Compromise: Derek Mahon as a Young Poet', *Irish University Review*, 24, 1 (Spring-Summer 1994), pp. 87–120, p. 89.

4. See Gerald Dawe, 'A Question of Imagination: Poetry in Ireland', in *Against Piety: Essays in Irish Poetry* (Belfast, Lagan Press, 1995), pp. 31–43. Dawe speaks of the 'poet's own ironic, *critical* and questioning relationship with the details of his individual experience' together with 'a relative freedom from . . . public conformations and conventions' (p. 41).

5. Colm Tóibín, 'New Ways to Kill Your Father: Historical Revisionism', in Karl-Heinz Westarp and Michael Boss (eds.), *Ireland: Towards New Identities?* (Aarhus University Press, 1998), pp. 28–36, p. 31. Strictly speaking, Irish revisionism is a movement associated with historians such as T.W. Moody, F.S.L. Lyons and R.F. Foster who challenged the nationalist consensus on the past.

6. The latter a 'misconception' that he subsequently challenged: 'First of all, I am not sophisticated, I am not cosmopolitan . . . ' (Interview, *Irish Literary Supplement*, Fall 1991, p. 28).

7. Edna Longley, 'Poetry and Politics in Northern Ireland', in *The Crane Bag*, 9, 1 (1985), pp. 26–40, p. 35; rep. in *Poetry in the Wars* (Newcastle-upon-Tyne, Bloodaxe, 1986), pp. 185–210. See also Mark Patrick Hederman, 'Poetry and the Fifth Province', *The Crane Bag*, 9, 1 (1985), pp. 110–19.

8. Seamus Deane, 'Derek Mahon: Freedom from History', in *Celtic Revivals: Essays in Modern Irish Literature 1880–1980* (London, Faber and Faber, 1985), pp. 156–65, p. 156.

9. Seamus Heaney, 'The Sense of Place', in *Preoccupations: Selected Prose 1968–1978* (London, Faber and Faber, 1980), pp. 131–49. The essay was given as a lecture at the Ulster Museum in 1977.

10. *Ibid.*, p. 148.

11. Seamus Heaney, 'Place and Displacement: Recent Poetry of Northern Ireland' [1985], rep. in Elmer Andrews (ed.), *Contemporary Irish Poetry: A Collection of Critical Essays* (London, Macmillan, 1996), pp. 124–44, p. 135. Heaney adds: 'I do not want to reduce Derek Mahon's poems to this single theme of alienated distance, for his work also abounds in poems where the social voice is up and away on the back of Pegasus ... but I would nevertheless insist that I am not forcing his work to fit a thesis'. (*Idem.*)

12. Seamus Heaney, *Preoccupations*, p. 145. Heaney modified his welcome on a subsequent occasion when he accused Hewitt of being 'Nelson-eyed' in relation to Irish culture. ('The Frontiers of Writing', in *Redress of Poetry*, London, Faber and Faber, 1995, pp. 195–98, p. 196.)

13. Willie Kelly, 'Each Poem for me is a New Beginning' (interview with Derek Mahon), *Cork Review*, 2 (1981), pp. 10–12 (p. 11).

14. Quoted in John Constable, 'Derek Mahon's Development', *Agenda*, 22, 3/4 (Autumn-Winter 1984–5), pp. 107–18, p. 107.

15. Seamus Heaney, 'Place and Displacement: Recent Poetry of Northern Ireland' [rep. in] Andrews, p. 131.

16. 'Bogland' was collected in *Door Into the Dark* (London, Faber and Faber, 1969); 'The Tollund Man' appeared first in *Threshold* (Summer 1970) and was collected in *Wintering Out* (London, Faber and Faber, 1972).

17. Brian O'Doherty, *The Irish Imagination 1959–1971* [Rosc Catalogue] (Dublin 1971), p. 58.

18. Seamus Heaney, 'Feeling into Words', in *Preoccupations* , pp. 41–60, pp. 54–55.

19. Ciaran Carson, '"Escaped from the Massacre"', *The Honest Ulsterman*, 50 (Winter 1975), pp. 184–85.

20. Viz., 'A Stone Age Figure Far Below' in *Poems, 1962–1978* (1979), pp. 46–47 and *Collected Poems* (1999), p. 12.

21. Elmer Andrews, 'The Poetry of Derek Mahon: "places where a thought might grow"', in Andrews (ed.), *Contemporary Irish Poetry: A Collection of Critical Essays*, pp. 235–63, p. 245.

22. Derek Mahon, Introduction, *Sphere Book of Irish Poetry* (London, Sphere Book, 1972), p. 12.

23. Samuel Beckett, 'Recent Irish Poetry', *Bookman*, 86 (1934); rep. in Michael Smith (ed.), *The Lace Curtain* (1971), p. 59.

24. Andrews, p. 241.

25. Richard York has compared de Nerval's original and Mahon's translation: 'Homme, libre penseur! Te crois-tu seul pensant / Dans ce monde où la vie éclate en toute chose?'; 'Your great mistake is to disregard the satire / Bandied among the mute phenomena'. ('Derek Mahon as Translator', in *Rivista Alicantian de Estudios Ingleses*, 5 (1992), pp. 163–81, p. 167).

26. MacNeice's biographer Jon Stallworthy writes: 'I think of Mahon's 'In Carrowdore Churchyard' as initiating the turn in MacNeice's

reputation. Long before his death he seemed an Irish poet to English readers, while for too many Irish readers he didn't really belong to Ireland. Here, however, was a Irish poet (Mahon) of the next generation claiming kinship not with the imperial Yeats or the rooted Kavanagh, but with a poet who seemed to take his text from Joyce's *Portrait of the Artist as a Young Man*: "I will try to fly those nets"'. ('Fathers and Sons', in *Bullán: A Journal of Irish Studies*, 2, 1 (Summer 1995), pp. 1–15, p. 11).

27. The poet has kindly supplied a photocopy of the original. In the typescript, the phrases 'he is a secular mystic, an explorer of *le vrai lieu* ("the real place")' have been stroked out, while the phrase 'Jaccottet is an intensely visual poet', immediately before 'Nabokov (. . . &c.)' has been omitted by Terence Brown. Also omitted is a telling quotation from Geoffrey Gregory who muses if 'deity and art don't originate in sparkle, glitter, crystal, refracted light, an abstracted portion of the sun, the gravel after rain . . .' (from *Notes from an Odd Country*). Grigson on MacNeice's 'sparkle' and the deep knowledge lies beneath is also quoted with approval on the first page of Edna Longley's full-length study of MacNeice which Mahon reviewed for *The Irish Times* in 1988 (*Journalism*, 1996, pp. 47–49).

28. Terence Brown and Alec Reid (eds.), *Time Was Away: The World of Louis MacNeice* (Dublin, Dolmen, 1974).

29. Terence Brown, *Louis MacNeice: Sceptical Vision* (Dublin, Gill and Macmillan, 1975). See also Louis MacNeice: 'An Anglo-Irish Quest', in *Northern Voices: Poets from Ulster* (Dublin, Gill and Macmillan, 1975): 'MacNeice's poetry presents to us a philosophically sceptical sensibility whose experience is of metaphysical isolation, loneliness, and separation' (p. 106.)

30. Michael Longley, 'My Protestant Education', *New Statesman*, 10 Aug. 1974, p. 219.

31. Adrian Frazier, 'Proper Portion: Derek Mahon's *The Hunt by Night*', [review], in *Éire-Ireland*, 18, 4 (Winter, 1983), pp. 136–43, p. 142. That Frazier is taking his cue from Heaney may be guessed from the allusion to one of the latter's collections: 'But instead of a door out of the dark, the door leading more deeply into the dark takes us out of despair'. (*Idem.*)

32. 'Theoptic eye' appeared as 'panoptic eye' in the 24-page pamphlet publication *Courtyards in Delft* (Oldcastle, Gallery Press, 1980). *Collected Poems* (1999), pp. 68–69, p. 69. An earlier version which places this stanza in parenthesis is printed in *Poems, 1962–1978* (1979), pp. 72–73.

33. Prominent among the sentences that Joyce copied was this: 'The soul is the first entelechy of a naturally organic thing'. (*De anima*, 1.2; cited in Jacques Aubert, *l'Esthetique de James Joyce*, Paris, 1973, p. 129.) In *Ulysses* Stephen Dedalus speaks correspondingly of 'rendering visible not the lay sense but the first entelechy, the structural rhythm' (London, Bodley Head Edn., 1967, p. 564.)

34. In scholastic philosophy God is Pure Being [*ens*] and things are like him insofar as they participate in Being [*esse*].

35. Terence Brown, 'Derek Mahon: The Poet and Painting', in *Irish University Review*, 24, 1 (Spring/Summer, 1994), pp. 38–50, p. 42.

36. See R.F. Foster, 'Protestant Magic', in *Paddy and Mr Punch: Connections in Irish History and English History* (London, Allen Lane/Penguin, 1993) [Chap. 11], pp. 212–32. Bram Stoker's use of the Catholic eucharist to seal up vampires' coffins in *Dracula* (1897) is a case in point.

37. The term is central to Stephen Dedalus's theory of 'aesthetic apprehension' in *A Portrait of the Artist as a Young Man* (1916): 'The radiance [*claritas*] . . . is the scholastic *quidditas*, the whatness of the thing'. (London, Jonathan Cape, 1943 & Edns.), pp. 241–42. Seamus Heaney has rehearsed an aspect of this theory in the title-poem of *Seeing Things* (London, Faber and Faber, 1991), where he invokes the 'dry-eyed Latin word *claritas*'. (See *Opened Ground: Poems 1966–1996*, 1998, p. 339.)

38. Seamus Heaney, 'A Sense of Place', in *Preoccupations*, p. 132.

39. Mahon said of the poem he calls 'Shed': 'The trouble with a performance like that is that you can't do it again, though "A Garage in Co. Cork" earned the accolade of a mention in "Pseud's Corner". (William Scammell, 'Derek Mahon Interviewed', in *Poetry Review*, 81, 2 (Summer 1991), pp. 4–6, p. 6., col. 2.)

40. Andrews, p. 260.

41. Constable, p. 118.

42. Spenser's sojourn at Kilcolman Castle is the subject of the sixth stanza of 'Beyond Howth Head'. There Mahon invites the English poet to 'come and inspire us once again!' but to step beyond his colonial bounds and 'flash, an *aisling*, through the dawn / Where Yeats's hill-men still break stone'. (*CP* 53.)

43. William Wilson, 'A Theoptic Eye: Derek Mahon and the Hunt by Night', in *Éire-Ireland*, 25, 4 (1990), pp. 120–31, p. 122.

44. James A. Murphy, Lucy McDiarmid, and Michael J. Durkan, 'Q & A with Derek Mahon', in *Irish Literary Supplement*, 10, 2 (Fall 1991), pp. 27–28, p. 28.

45. See Brian Moore, *Catholics* (1972; Triad Edn. 1983), p. 61. In the novel, *Unbeliever's Faith* is the title of a work by one Father Janson who argues that 'there can be a future for Christianity, provided it gets rid of God'. (*idem.*)

46. John F. Deane, (ed.), *Irish Poetry of Faith and Doubt: The Cold Heaven* (Dublin, Wolfhound, 1990), p. 14 [Introduction].

47. Louis MacNeice, *The Poetry of W.B. Yeats* (London, Oxford University Press, 1941; rep. 1967), p. 27.

48. MacNeice, *The Strings are False* (1965); quoted in Dawe, 'Anatomist of Melancholia: Louis MacNeice, in *Against Piety: Essays in Irish Poetry* (Belfast: Lagan Press, 1995), pp. 82–87, p. 85.

49. Quoted in Gerald Dawe, *Against Piety*, p. 86.
50. MacNeice, *Poetry of W.B. Yeats*, p. 16.
51. *Idem*.
52. D.B. Moore, *The Poetry of Louis MacNeice* (Leicester University Press, 1972), p. 249.
53. Michael Longley, 'Poetry', in Michael Longley (ed.), *Causeway: The Arts in Ulster* (NI Arts Council, 1971), pp. 95–109, p. 97. Dawe is less complimentary about the 'autobiographical writings': 'What haunts MacNeice's poetry is what is strangely absent from *The Strings are False* – his willingness to find out what lies in the corner of his mind: the dormant, flawed and mysterious feelings that pervade his poems'. (*Against Piety: Essays in Irish Poetry*, p. 82).
54. Terence Brown, 'Louis MacNeice's Ireland', in Brown and Nicholas Grene (eds.), *Tradition and Influence in Anglo-Irish Poetry* (London, Macmillan, 1989), pp. 92–93. See also 'Louis MacNeice, 1907–1963: His Poetry', in *Studies* (Autumn 1970); *Louis MacNeice: Sceptical Vision* (Dublin: Gill and Macmillan, 1975), and *Northern Voices: Poets from Ulster* (Dublin: Gill and Macmillan, 1975), 'Louis MacNeice, An Anglo-Irish Quest', pp. 98–113.
55. The measure of the old man's narrow existence suggests a vaguely superstitious atmosphere: 'if a coat-hanger / Knocked in an open wardrobe / That was a strange event / To be pondered on for hours'. (*CP* 88)
56. Scammell, *op. cit.*
57. Of these, the 1979 version is the most anomalous as containing variant line-breaks and additional inverted commas. It also contains a curious repetition with the phrases 'desperate love' and 'desperate ironies' in the final stanza (*P* 44).
58. Waterman was a member of the English Department of the New University of Ulster while Derek Mahon was writer-in-residence there in 1978–79.
59. Andrew Waterman, '"Somewhere, Out there, Beyond": The Poetry of Seamus Heaney and Derek Mahon', in *PN Review*, 8, 1 (1980), pp. 39–47, p. 42.
60. *Idem*.
61. 'Derek Mahon Interviewed', in *Poetry Review*, 81, 2 (Summer 1991), p. 6, col. 1. The reference appears to be to Douglas Dunn, '"Let God not Abandon Us": On the Poetry of Derek Mahon', *Stone Ferry Review*, 2 (Winter 1978), pp. 7–30.
62. *Idem*.
63. *Idem*.
64. 'A Rage for Order' was inspired by Wallace Stevens' phrase in 'The Idea of Order at Key West' (see Stevens, *Selected Poems*, London, Faber and Faber, 1953), pp. 77–9, p. 79.
65. Derek Mahon, 'Each Poem for me is a New Beginning', *Cork Review*, 2 (1981), p. 11.

DEREK MAHON: HISTORY, MUTE PHENOMENA AND BEYOND

Jerzy Jarniewicz

1. Peter McDonald, 'History and Poetry: Derek Mahon and Tom Paulin', in Elmer Andrews (ed.), *Contemporary Irish Poetry: A Collection of Critical Essays* (London, Macmillan, 1992).
2. Raymond Williams, *Keywords: A Vocabulary of Culture and Society* (London, Fontana, 1984), pp. 146–8.
3. Edna Longley, '"When Did You Last See Your Father?": Perceptions of the Past in Northern Irish Writing 1965–1985', in *The Living Stream: Literature and Revisionism in Ireland* (Newcastle-upon-Tyne, Bloodaxe, 1994), p. 150.
4. 'Rather than exploring the past, Mahon's poems, often apocalyptic as well as expressive of a millenarian yearning, project into the future', from Robert Welch (ed.), *The Oxford Companion to Irish Literature* (Oxford, Oxford University Press, 1996), p. 352.
5. Kenneth McLeish (ed.), *Guide to Human Thought* (London, Bloomsbury, 1993), p. 352.
6. Piotr Sommer, *Zapisy rozmów. Wywiady z poetami brytyjskimi* (Warsaw, Czytelnik, 1985).
7. From: Zbigniew Herbert, *Selected Poems*, trans. Czeslaw Milosz and Peter Dale Scott (Harmondsworth, Penguin, 1968).
8. Trans. Czeslaw Milosz and Peter Dale Scott. *Ibid.*
9. Tom Paulin, Introduction, *Faber Book of Political Verse* (London, Faber and Faber, 1986), p. 17.
10. Philip Hobsbaum, in Tracy Chevalier (ed.), *Contemporary Poets* (Chicago and London, St James Press, 1991), p. 599.
11. Tom Paulin, 'A Terminal Ironist', in *Ireland and the English Crisis* (Newcastle-upon-Tyne, Bloodaxe, 1984).
12. Sean O'Brien, *The Deregulated Muse* (Newcastle-upon-Tyne, Bloodaxe, 1998).
13. Quoted in Peter France (ed.), *The New Oxford Companion to French Literature* (Oxford, Oxford University Press, 1995).

'WEIRD/ HAECCEITY': PLACE IN DEREK MAHON'S POETRY

Eamonn Hughes

1. Derek Mahon, 'The Sea in Winter', *Selected Poems*, pp. 113–118. I will use this volume as the source for Mahon's texts except in those cases where an earlier version of a poem, or a poem which is not reprinted there, makes a substantive difference to the argument. This is not simply a way of avoiding, as much as possible, the vexed issue of Mahon's revisions, but also because *Selected Poems*

summarises the phases of Mahon's writing with which this essay is primarily concerned. Much of what I have to say here applies tangentially, if at all, to the later poetry collected in *The Hudson Letter* and *The Yellow Book*.

2. Bertrand Russell, quoted in Jean-Michel Rabate, *Joyce Upon the Void: the Genesis of Doubt* (London, Macmillan, 1991), p. 3.

3. For further comments on this see Barbara Bender (ed.), *Landscape, Politics and Perspectives* (Providence and Oxford, Berg, 1993); Erica Carter, James Donald and Judith Squires (eds.), *Space and Place: Theories of Identities and Location* (London, Lawrence and Wishart, 1993); Edward Soja, *Postmodern Geographies. The Reassertion of Space in Critical Social Theory* (London, Verso, 1989). For a fuller consideration of how these reconceptualisations might be brought to bear on Northern Irish poetry see Eamonn Hughes, '"Could anyone write it?": Place in Tom Paulin's Poetry', in Colin Graham and Richard Kirkland (eds.), *Ireland and Cultural Theory: The Mechanics of Authenticity* (London, Macmillan, 1999), pp. 162–92, (esp. pp. 162–8).

4. Derek Mahon (ed.), *Modern Irish Poetry* (London, Sphere, 1972), pp. 13, 14.

5. Derek Mahon. 'MacNeice in Ireland and England', *Journalism*, ed. Terence Brown (Oldcastle: The Gallery Press, 1996), pp. 21–29, (p. 21).

6. Peter Fallon and Derek Mahon (eds.), *The Penguin Book of Contemporary Irish Poetry* (London, Penguin, 1990), pp. xvi, xx-xxi, xxii. (Emphasis added.) Questions about the authorship of this Introduction can be set aside on the basis that Mahon's name is on it and on the basis of the remarks I go on to make about it.

7. For the former see Seamus Deane, 'Derek Mahon: Freedom from History', in *Celtic Revivals: Essays in Modern Irish Literature* (London, Faber and Faber, 1985), pp. 156–165; Edna Longley, 'The Singing Line: Form in Derek Mahon's Poetry', *Poetry in the Wars* (Newcastle-upon-Tyne, Bloodaxe, 1986), pp. 170–184; Tim Kendall, 'Leavetakings and Homecomings, Derek Mahon's Belfast', *Eire-Ireland*, 29, 4 (1994), pp. 101–116; for the latter see Bill Tinley, 'Harmonies and Disharmonies – Derek Mahon's Francophile Poetics', *Irish University Review*, 24, 1 (1994), pp. 80–95; Bill Tinley, 'International Perspectives in the Poetry of Derek Mahon', *Irish University Review*, 21, 1 (1991), pp. 106–117; George Watson, 'Landscape in Ulster Poetry', in Gerald Dawe and John Wilson Foster (eds.), *The Poet's Place: Ulster Literature and Society: Essays in Honour of John Hewitt, 1907–1987* (Belfast: Institute of Irish Studies, 1991), pp. 1–16; Elmer Andrews, 'The Poetry of Derek Mahon: "places where a thought might grow"', in Elmer Andrews (ed.), *Contemporary Irish Poetry: A Collection of Critical Essays* (London: Macmillan, 1992), pp. 235–263.

8. This distinction is Edna Longley's made in her 'An ABC of Reading

Contemporary Irish Poetry', *Princeton University Library Chronicle*, LIX, 3 (Spring 1998), pp. 517–545, (p. 540). It is worth noting that while 'Place' does not figure in her lexicon, five items ('Dublin', 'Belfast', 'East', 'Urban/Rural', and 'West') are directly about types of place, and a further two ('Nationalism/Nationality' and 'EXiles/EXpats') dwell on the issue.

9. Mahon's usual colour range is sufficiently limited and confined to muted colours that the 'red bandana' of 'Ecclesiastes' stands out vividly as a mark of rebellion. The gap between the earlier work, with which this essay is concerned, and his more recent work is nowhere better indicated than in *The Yellow Book*.

10. I owe this recognition of the maternal symbolism of the washing line to Edna Longley.

11. See Peter McDonald, 'History and Poetry: Derek Mahon and Tom Paulin', in Andrews, pp. 86–106, (p. 86).

12. Terence Brown, 'Derek Mahon – The Poet and Painting', *Irish University Review*, 24, 1 (1994), pp. 38–50; see also Tim Kendall, 'Leavetakings and Homecomings, Derek Mahon's Belfast' on the ways in which Mahon uses window and other imagery to frame his view, a tendency which reaches a peak in the concrete poem 'The Window', *P* 108.

13. Derek Mahon, 'Christ on the Mount of Olives, II', *The Chimeras. A Version of Les Chimeres by Gerard de Nerval* (Dublin: The Gallery Press, 1982), p. 16. The Beckett connection is strengthened if we remember his use of the Berkeleyan phrase 'esse est percipi'.

14. Hugh Haughton, '"Even now there are places where a thought might grow": Place and Displacement in the Poetry of Derek Mahon', in Neil Corcoran (ed.) *The Chosen Ground: Essays on the Contemporary Poetry of Northern Ireland* (Bridgend, Seren Books, 1992), pp. 87–122, (p. 93). (Emphasis added).

15. Haughton, p. 94; and see Seamus Deane, *Celtic Revivals*, p. 156.

16. Derek Mahon, 'A Tribute to Beckett on his Eightieth Birthday', *Journalism*, p. 61.

17. Elmer Andrews, 'The Poetry of Derek Mahon', p. 244.

18. Kathleen Shields, 'Derek Mahon's Poetry of Belonging', *Irish University Review*, 24, 1 (1994), 67–79, (p. 74).

19. 'Purity', *The Strange Museum* (London, Faber and Faber, 1980), p. 5. I explore W.H. Auden's opposition between the desert and the sea, and his identification of the new attitude to the sea in the Romantic period when 'the voyage' becomes the 'true condition of man' as an Enlightenment concern with equality gives way to a Romantic concern with individuality in '"Could anyone write it?": Place in Tom Paulin's Poetry'. See W.H. Auden, *The Enchafed Flood, or, The Romantic Iconography of the Sea* (London, Faber and Faber, 1951), pp. 23, 55. There is an interesting possible pun on the relation between the sea and sin in 'A Kensington Notebook': The 'dewy-eyed/ Pelagianism of home' ('A Kensington Notebook, 1', *SP* 90) is most

obviously a reference to the doctrine of the denial of original sin, but can also be taken as a reference to sea-dwelling – pelagic – and therefore lack of evolution; if evolution is inevitable, so too is sin, and *vice versa*.

20. See John Kerrigan, 'Ulster Ovids', in Corcoran, pp. 237–69.
21. See Peter Denman, 'Know The One? – Insolent Ontology and Mahon's Revisions', *Irish University Review*, 24, 1 (1994), pp. 27–37, (pp. 28–9).
22. Derek Mahon, *Journalism*, p. 25.
23. Shields, p. 69.
24. Neil Corcoran, *English Poetry Since 1940* (London, Longman, 1993), p. 191.
25. See David Lloyd, '"Pap for the Dispossessed": Seamus Heaney and the Poetics of Identity', in *Anomalous States: Irish Writing and the Post-Colonial Moment* (Dublin, The Lilliput Press, 1993), pp. 13–40, (p. 24) in which, discussing Heaney and nationalism, Lloyd argues that naming is always in the service of 'likeness, never difference'.
26. See Terence Brown, *The Whole Protestant Community* (Derry, Field Day, 1985), p. 17. See also Patricia Horton, 'Romantic Intersections: Romanticism and Contemporary Northern Irish Poetry' (Unpublished Ph.D. Thesis, Queen's University of Belfast, 1996), pp. 59–60.
27. See Haughton, p. 112, on the 'self-inwoven simile' in Mahon's poetry.

RHYTHM AND REVISION IN MAHON'S POETIC DEVELOPMENT

Michael Allen

1. Julia Kristeva, *Revolution in Poetic Language*, tr. Margaret Waller (New York, Columbia University Press, 1984) p. 65.
2. Kristeva, p. 30.
3. Edward Mendelson, Preface, *W. H. Auden: Selected Poems, New Edition* (New York, Vintage, 1989), p. xix. See Mahon's comment on the fiffh stanza added to 'Courtyards in Delft' in *The Hunt by Night* (1982) and removed in *Selected Poems*: 'I tried to be too explicit with a fifth stanza and succeeded only in being inept; so I've now reverted to the original version, which I hope is marginally more ept.' (William Scammell, 'Derek Mahon Interviewed', *Poetry Review*, 81:2 (Summer 1991), p. 6.)
4. Edward Albee, *Who's Afraid of Virginia Woolf?* (Harmondsworth: Penguin, 1989), p. 17.
5. This identification was clear in his introduction to the *Sphere Book of Modern Irish Poetry* in 1972 and is still in evidence in an

interview with Terence Brown in 1985: 'the poet from the North had a new thing to say, a new kind of sound to make, a new texture to create. Looking back an it, there's a sort of inevitability that the new energy should have come from the North.' (*Poetry Ireland Review* 14 (Autumn 1985), p. 73.) He seems to step away from it when editing (jointly with Peter Fallon) the *Penguin Book of Comtemporary Irish Poetry* (Harmondsworth, 1989): 'as ever, poets from the North contribute to a national body of work which, in its turn, belongs to a global community. These poets are tied less to particular places – or parishes – than ever before'. (Introduction, p. xx.)

6. Clair Wills, *Improprieties: Politics and Sexuality in Northern Irish Poetry* (Oxford: Clarendon Press, 1993), p. 37.

7. The 'culture' Mahon speaks for is not the old 'high culture' exactly (witness his enthusiasm in 'The Hudson Letter' XlV for Fay Wray and King Kong) but is not as demotic, either, as the one we might associate with Frank O'Hara (his model in this section of the poem).

8. Simmons and Montague, both of whom Mahon would want to add to this 'Ulster trio' (Interview with Terence Brown, p. 4), belong to a slightly older generation.

9. Edna Longley, 'Where a Thought Might Grow' (Review of *Selected Poems*), *Poetry Review*, 81:2 (Summer 1991), pp. 8–9.

10. Charles Olson, 'Projective Verse', in *Collected Prose*, ed. Donald Allen and Benjamin Friedlander (Berkeley, University of California Press, 1997), p. 239.

11. Robert Duncan, 'Ideas of the Meaning of Form', *A Selected Prose*, ed. R.J. Bertholf (New York, New Directions, 1995), p. 35.

12. Robert Lowell, 'An Interview with Frederick Seidel', in *Paris Review*, xxv, (Winter/Spring 1961), 57–95); repr. Robert Lowell, *Collected Prose*, ed. Robert Giroux (London, Faber, 1987), pp. 242–4.

13. Ezra Pound, Canto LXXXI, *The Cantos of Ezra Pound*, (London: Faber and Faber, 1968) p. 583.

14. See, in particular, the introduction to *Secret Marriages* (Manchester: Phoenix Pamphlet Poets Press, 1968, pp. 2–3). Interviews with Dillon Johnston, ('An Interview with Michael Longley', *Irish Literary Supplement*, (Fall 1986), p. 21) and Robert Johnstone ('The Longley Tapes', *Honest Ulsterman*, No. 78 (Summer 1985), p. 27) confirm retrospectively the relationship between writer's block and rhythmic development.

15. 'Strong poetry is strong only by virtue of a kind of textual usurpation that is analogous to what Marxism encompasses as its social usurpation or Freudianism as its psychic usurpation. A strong poem does not formulate poetic facts any more than strong reading or criticism formulates them, for a strong reading is the only poetic fact, the only revenge against time that endures, that is successful in canonizing one text as opposed to a rival text. There is no textual authority without an act of imposition, a declaration of

property ... Harold Bloom, 'Poetry, Revisionisms, Repression', from *Poetry and Repression: Revisionism from Blake to Stevens* (New Haven and London, Yale University Press, 1976), p. 6.

16. Peter Denman, 'Know the One? Insolent Ontology and Mahon's Revisions', *Irish University Review*, 24, 1 (1994), p. 30.

17. My second example seems to confirm Edna Longley's view that '[t]he urge to revise, however subtle the shifts of ideology, and self-representation, is an urge to rewrite history' ('Where a Thought Might Grow', p. 8) and my own uneasiness with this revision may be shared by Mahon, since he included neither version of the poem in *Selected Poems*. The revision of 'Day Trip. . .', even if it is an attempt to rewrite history (like the other revisions I will discuss) seems to me to result in a different and successful poem (if less interesting than the original). A parallel might be the case of the 'found poem' which is always adjusted by the 'finder'-poet (what Mahon 'found' in this case was a poem written by his earlier self). Edward Mendelson has criticised the view that 'a poet loses his right to revise or reject his work after he publishes it': '[t]his argument', he says, ' presupposes ... that an authentic poem is shaped by its own internal forces rather than by the external effects of craft . . . ' (Preface, *Selected Poems of W.H. Auden*, p. xviii). My own argument would be that shaping from both within and without are involved in the genesis of an authentic poem, but one or the other may predominate.

18. See Thomas Wolfe, *You Can't Go Home Again* (1940).

19.   I wake in a dark flat
       To the soft roar of the world.
       Pigeons neck on the white
       Roofs as I draw the curtains
       And look out over London
       Rain-fresh in the morning light.

       This is our element, the bright
       Reason on which we rely ...
       . . . .
       . . . the dark places
       Ablaze with love and poetry
       When the power of good prevails. . .
       (Lives, 1).

20. See Seamus Heaney, *Place and Displacement: Recent Poetry of Northern Ireland* (Grasmere, Trustees of Dove Cottage, 1984), pp. 12–13.

21. Albee, p. 16.

22. See 'J. P. Donleavy's Dublin' (*Lives* p. 13). Not irrelevantly, the piece was retitled 'Dog Days' in *Poems* and 'Dream Days' in *Selected Poems*.

23. Eamonn Hughes's essay '"weird/ haecceity": Derek Mahon and the sense of place', pp. 67–80) follows standard practice in steadily

referring to *Selected Poems*: it made me realise that the text I had
mentally retained (from *Lives)* was virtually a different poem from
the one he was talking about.

24. Denman, pp. 27–28.
25. Wallace Stevens, 'The Idea of Order at Key West', *Collected Poems*
    (New York, Knopf, 1961), p. 130.
26. 'in reading poetry one responds as if one were making a given kind
    of movement or a given kind of effort . . .' F.R. Leavis, 'Imagery and
    Movement', *A Selection from Scrutiny* (Cambridge: Cambridge
    University Press, 1968), vol 1, p. 235.
27. Steven Tuohy, review of *The Hunt by Night*, *PN Review*, 10, 1 (1983),
    p. 28.
28. See Denman, pp. 29–30.
29. (1) Two stanzas involving religious practices which appear in the
    1972 version of 'Entropy' (*Lives*, pp. 30–3 1) are deleted in the *Poems*
    text. In 1975 they had been incorporated, together with four stanzas
    from 'What Will Remain' (*Lives*, pp. 26–27), into a piece called
    'Thammuz' (*The Snow Party*, pp. 11–12) which does not appear in
    Poems. (2) The human addressee in the 1981 version of 'The Globe in
    North Carolina' (*Courtyards in Delft*, Dublin, Gallery Press, 1981, pp.
    28–29) is assimilated into a consciously religious invocation of
    'mother earth': the connection is broken in the *Hunt by Night*
    version of the poem (1982) and the whole sequence of thought
    considerably secularised.
    (3) 'Courtyards in Delft' which the poet himself says is 'about
    Protestantism' (interview with Terence Brown, p. 6)) has only four
    stanzas in the 1981 volume for which it provides the title: a fifth
    interpretive stanza is added in *The Hunt by Night* (1982), removed in
    Selected Poems (1991) but as Peter Denman points out, retained in
    The Penguin Book of Contemporary Irish Poetry (1990) of which Mahon
    is joint editor. (The American edition of *Selected Poems* also
    appeared in 1990, leaving the text of this poem indeterminate).
    (Denman, pp. 29–30.) But see also Mahon's comment quoted in note
    3 above.
30. Edward Mendelson (ed.), *The English Auden: Poems, Essays and
    Dramatic Writings, 1922–1939* (London, Faber, 1977).
31. Hugh Haughton's description of the *Selected Poems* is not unfair:
    'effectively a drastic self-censoring *Collected Poems*' (*T.L.S.* No 4960,
    24th April 1998, p. 24).
32. Scott Brewster, 'A Residual Poetry: Heaney, Mahon and Hedgehog
    History', *Irish University Review* , 28, 1 (Spring/Summer 1998),
    p. 56.
33. 'Religion is thus here the distorted or symbolic coming to
    consciousness of itself, of the human community, . . . the symbolic
    space in which the collectivity thinks itself and celebrates its own
    unity; so that it does not seem a very difficult next step, if, with

Frye, we see literature as a weaker form of myth or a later stage of ritual, to conclude that in that sense all literature, no matter how weakly, must be informed by what we have called a political unconscious, that all literature must be read as a symbolic meditation on the destiny of community.' Frederic Jameson, *The Political Unconscious: Narrative as a Socially Symbolic Act* (London, Methuen, 1983) p. 70.

34. See 'Lives' and 'Deaths' in *Lives* (1972) and Longley's 'Options' and 'Alibis' in *An Exploded View* (1973).
35. John Ashbery, *The Double Dream of Spring* (New York, Dutton, 1970), p. 24.
36. W.K. Wimsatt and Monroe C. Beardsley, 'The Intentional Fallacy', in W.K. Wimsatt, *The Verbal Icon: Studies in the Meaning of Poetry* (New York, Noonday Press, 1962), p. 5.

DEREK MAHON AND THE VISUAL ARTS

R.A. York

1. Terence Brown, 'Derek Mahon: The Poet and the Painting', *Irish University Review*, 24, 1994, pp. 38–50.
2. For reproductions see: J. Pope-Hennessy, *Paolo Uccello* (London, Phaidon, 1969); P.C. Sutton, *Pieter de Hooch* (Oxford, Phaidon, 1980); T. Messer, *Munch* (New York, Abrams, 1970). I am grateful to my wife Rosemary for help in tracing the works of art referred to.
3. Hugh Haughton, 'Place and Displacement in Derek Mahon', in Neil Corcoran (ed.), *The Chosen Ground* (Bridgend, Seren Books, 1992), p. 104.
4. Hugh Haughton, 'The Purloined Title', in D. Gohrbrandt and B. von Lutz, (eds.), *Seeing and Saying, Self-referentiality in British and American Literature* (Franfurt, Lang, 1998), pp. 89–116.
5. There are some, with a useful essay, in A. Blankert, *Vermeer, the Complete Paintings* (London, Granada, 1981).
6. Vincent van Gogh, *Letters*, ed. M. Ro (London, Fontana, 1963), pp. 124, 114.
7. For a more optimistic view of these two poems, see Elmer Andrews 'The Poetry of Derek Mahon' in Elmer Andrews (ed.), *Contemporary Irish Poetry: A Collection of Critical Essays* (London, Macmillan, 1992), p. 238.
8. *Ibid.*, p. 254.
9. Edna Longley, *Poetry in the Wars* (Newcastle-upon-Tyne, Bloodaxe, 1986), p. 175.
10. Brown, p. 44.
11. *Ibid.*, p. 49.

'THE IMPORTANCE OF ELSEWHERE': MAHON AND
TRANSLATION

Hugh Haughton

1. For earlier accounts of Mahon and translation see Terence Brown, 'Home and Away: Derek Mahon's France', in Barbara Hayley and Christopher Murray (eds.), *Ireland and France, a Bountiful Friendship* (Gerrards Cross, Colin Smythe, 1992); Bill Tinley, 'International Perspectives in the Poetry of Derek Mahon', *Irish University Review*, 21.1 (Spring-Summer 1991) and 'Harmonies and Disharmonies': Mahon's Francophone Poetics', *Irish University Review* 24.1 (Spring-Summer 1996); R.A. York, 'Derek Mahon as Translator', *Revista Alicantina de Estudios Ingleses*, 6 November 1992.

2. Derek Mahon (ed.), *The Sphere Book of Modern Irish Poetry* (London, Sphere, 1972) p. 13. Incidentally Mahon chose as one of the 3 poems representing himself 'I am Raftery.'

3. T.S. Eliot, *Notes Towards the Definition of Culture*, (London, Faber and Faber, 1948), p. 113.

4. For an incisive, informative summary of the history of translation in Ireland, see Michael Cronin, *Translating Ireland: Translation, Languages, Cultures*, (Cork: Cork University Press, 1996).

5. Terence Brown, 'Translating Ireland', in Gerald Dawe and Jonathan Williams (eds.), *Krino 1986–1996: An Anthology of Modern Irish Writing*, (Dublin, Gill and Macmillan, 1996), pp. 138–9.

6. Bill Tinley has written well about 'Mahon's Francophone Poetics' and 'The International Dimension' of Mahon's imagination, but otherwise there has been little about this central strand in his work.

7. Seamus Heaney, 'Place and Displacement in Contemporary Northern Irish Poetry', in Elmer Andrews (ed.), *Contemporary Irish Poetry: A Collection of Critical Essays* (London, Macmillan, 1992), pp. 124–44.

8. Derek Mahon, 'Epitaph, from Tristan Corbière', *Icarus* 37 (June 1962); 'Elevation', *Dubliner* 3.2 (Summer 1964).

9. The Villon survived in revised form in *Poems 1962–1978* and one fragment of Cavafy, 'The Facts of Life, after Cavafy'.

10. Asked by Eamon Grennan whether translation gave him a sense of being part of a 'larger community', Mahon said 'Translation puts me within their context, and invites them into the Irish context.' Draft of *Paris Review* interview, Mahon papers, Emory University.

11. D. Anderson (ed.), *Pound's Calvacanti: An Edition of the Translations, Notes and Essays* (Princeton: Princeton University Press, 1983), p. 251.

12. Derek Mahon, *Words in the Air, A Selection of Poems by Philippe Jaccottet*, with translations and introduction by Derek Mahon (Oldcastle, Gallery, 1998), p. 20.

13. Derek Mahon, *High Time, After Molière* (Oldcastle, Gallery, 1985); *The*

School for Wives, After Molière (Oldcastle, Gallery, 1986); *Racine's Phaedra* (Oldcastle, Gallery, 1996); *The Bacchae, After Euripides* (Oldcastle, Gallery, 1991). His adaptation of Turgenev's *First Love* is entitled 'Summer Lightning' and was broadcast by RTE and Channel 4, 1982/4. Raphaële Billetdoux, *Night Without Day*, translated from the French by Derek Mahon (New York, Viking, 1987).

14. Seamus Heaney's *Opened Ground* is a comparable case. Heaney tended not to be thought of as a translator prior to his recent *Beowulf* but he has of course published many translations, including the Dantean *Ugolino* and Canto 1 of *The Inferno, Sweeney Astray, The Midnight Court* (which brings together a version of Brian Merriman's great satirical poem in Irish and passages of Ovid), *The Cure at Troy* (a version of Sophocles's *Philoctetes* with a distinctly Northern Irish inflection), his jointly translated version of the Polish poet Kolakowsky's great Renaissance elegies *Lamentations*, poems from the Roumanian of Marin Sorescu and Irish of Nuala Ni Dhomhnaill, as well as an English version of Janacek's song cycle, Janacek's *Diary of One Who Disappeared*. None of this creative activity (apart from the *Ugolino* fragment and extracts from *Sweeney Astray*) finds expression in Heaney's Collected Poems.

15. Lawrence Venuti, *The Translator's Invisibility: A History of Translation* (London and New York, Routledge, 1995).

16. These terms are Venuti's.

17. 'Derek Mahon on Lowell', *Phoenix*, No. 2 (Summer 1967), p. 51.

18. Derek Mahon, Introduction, *Racine's Phaedra* (Oldcastle, Gallery Press, 1996).

19. Lowell's defence of his methods in the preface to *Imitations* lays down a case for Mahon's own practice. Lowell admits to having taken drastic liberties with the originals throughout – with Villon 'somewhat stripped', for example, Mallarmé 'unclotted', and more than a third of Rimbaud's 'Le Bateau Ivre' cut: 'I have dropped lines, moved lines, moved stanzas, changed images and altered metre and intent', Lowell announces impenitently. (*Imitations*, London, Faber and Faber, 1962, p. xii.) In this respect, Mahon was to follow him – his own version of Rimbaud is comparably truncated, as is his Juvenal and Corbière..

20. Derek Mahon, 'Pythagorean Lines; Respectful Version', *Cyphers*, 16, (Winter 1981).

21. de Nerval, *Les Chimères*, ed. Norma Rinsler (London, Athone Press, 1973), p. 54.

22. Boris Pasternak, *Dr Zhivago*, trans Max Hayward (London, Fontana, 1958), p. 476.

23. Pasternak, p. 279. It is interesting to compare Mahon's versions with Hayward's in the novel, p. 512 and 533, or with Donald Davie's *Poems of Dr Zhivago* (Manchester: Manchester University Press, 1965).

24. The four versions in the Penguin *Horace in English* all weigh in considerably longer.

25. Louis MacNeice, *Collected Poems*, ed. E.R. Dodds (London, Faber and Faber, 1966), p. 550.

26. Peter McDonald, 'Louis MacNeice's Posterity', *Princeton University Library Chronicle*, vol. LIX, no 3 (Spring 1998), p. 387. McDonald finds the Mahon missing in the very 'zest' it invokes but the critic in his turn misses the tonal and semantic ambiguities lurking in this deceptively low-key poem.

27. John Kerrigan, 'Ulster Ovids', in Neil Corcoran (ed.), *The Chosen Ground: Essays on the Contemporary Poetry of Northern Ireland* (Bridgend: Seren Books, 1992), pp. 237–68.

28. Originally 'statue of me' (*HBN, SP*).

29. See Sarah Anne Brown, *The Metamorphosis of Ovid From Chaucer to Ted Hughes* (London, Duckworth, 1999).

30. These are respectively 1.5 (one of those translated by Marlowe) and 2.1 of Ovid's collection, and the second of them was chosen by Christopher Martin for his *Ovid in English*, Penguin, 1998. Mahon's version of the Galatea story was first published in *After Ovid*, eds. Michael Hofmann and James Lasdun (1994), pp. 237–9.

31. Asked by Eamon Grennan about his motives for translation, he said they varied, and then said: 'Well ... with Pasternak, when I read a version of "White Nights" in an anthology, I thought, "Hold on, that's a Mahon poem."' Mahon Papers, Emory University.

32. Medbh Ruane, 'The summoning of Everymahon', *The Sunday Times*, 11 February 1996, p. 24.

33. Ted Hughes, *Tales from Ovid* (London, Faber and Faber, 1997), p. 149.

34. Michael Longley has done his own idiosyncratic version, 'Water and Ivory'.

35. Ted Hughes, p. 244.

36. Ovid, *The Heroides and Amores*, ed. Grant Showerman (London, Heinemann, 1914), pp. 180 ff.

37. Guy Davenport, *Archilocus, Sappho, Alkman: Three Lyric Poets of the Seventh Century B.C.* translated, with an introduction by Guy Davenport (Berkeley and London, University of California Press, 1980), p. 103; Edgar Loebel and Denys Page, *Poetarum Lesbiorum Fragmenta* (Oxford: Oxford University Press, 1963), Fragment 136.

38. Denys Page, *Sappho and Alcaeus: An Introduction to the Study of Ancient Lesbian Poetry* (Oxford, Clarendon, 1955), pp. 52–3. Davenport, pp. 86–7.

39. Davenport, p. 133. Denys Page, *Poetae Melici Graecae* (Oxford, Clarendon, 1962), Fragment adespotum 976.

40. See 'Life of Sappho' in *Lyra Graeca* trans. J.M. Edmonds (London, Heinemann, 1922), vol 1, pp. 140–181.

41. Drafts of a poem called 'Sappho's Lyre' survive, made up of 'The One you Love' and 'Even in Sardis'. These are translations in

stanzaic form of Sapphic fragments, quite unlike the way Mahon handles the same material here. Mahon Papers, Emory University.

42. Pound partially translates another Macabru poem, 'L'autrier jost'un sebissa' in *The Spirit of Romance* (New York, New Directions, 1952), pp. 62–3. In the Gallery and Wake Forest editions of *The Hudson Letter* there were no italics to mark the move into translation.
43. Mahon paper, Emory University.
44. Charles Baudelaire, *Oeuvres Complètes*, ed Claude Pichois (Paris, Gallimard, 1961) p. 78. Subsequent French quotations from Baudelaire also refer to this edition.
45. See Jules Laforgue, *Poésies Complètes* ed. Pascal Pia (Paris, Livre de Poche, 1970), p. 279 ff.
46. T.S. Eliot, *The Waste Land, Collected Poems 1909–1962* (London, Faber and Faber,1974), p. 70.
47. There is a much earlier uncollected poem alluding to Young's title, 'Night Thought while reading Gibbon', *The Listener*, 29 July, 1971.
48. Mahon Papers, Emory University. Mahon's English publisher, Paul Keegan, had discussed the idea of a book of Laforgue translations with Mahon before the Jaccottet.
49. Derek Mahon, ed., *The Sphere Book of Modern Irish Poetry*, pp. 42 and 188.
50. James Simmons, *From the Irish* (Belfast, Blackstaff Press, 1985), p. x. Simmons's book includes 'For Derek Mahon', a personal tribute to a fellow one-time inhabitant of the Portrush triangle.
51. Derek Mahon, *TYB* 30; *Racine's Phaedra*, p. 52.
52. George Kay (ed.), *Penguin Book of Italian Verse* (Harmondsworth, Penguin, 1965), pp. 232–3.
53. The translation had been provisionally ear-marked to form part of *The Yellow Book*, as the Mahon papers at Emory show.
54. Saba, *Tutte le Poesie*, ed. Mario Lavagetto (Milan, Mondadori, 1988), p. 505.

DEREK MAHON: COMING IN FROM THE COLD

Frank Sewell

1. Peter McDonald, 'Incurable Ache', *Poetry Ireland Review*, No. 56 (Spring 1998), pp. 117–19.
2. *Ibid.*, p. 119.
3. See Louis MacNeice re: 'race-consciousness' in 'Prologue', *The Faber Book of Contemporary Irish Poetry*, (ed.), Paul Muldoon (London, Faber and Faber, 1986), p. 18.
4. 'As for being native, it is without you're knowing it or, if you like, totally in spite of yourself, you'll be native. Just be, and you'll be native. But as for *trying* to be native like a lot of the loud-mouths

who deal with Irish, this is the rule: (try to) be native, and you won't be native, neither will you be. Nativeness is rooted in life. It's not an overcoat or a kilt'. My translation from O Riordain's diary 22nd September 1960. See Seán Ó Coileáin, Sean O Riordain: *Beatha agus Saothar* (BAC: An Clóchomhar Tta, 1982), p. 314.

5. McDonald, p. 119.
6. 'The bugles blow and the Union Jack comes down . . .', *TYB*, p. 50.
7. McDonald, p. 117. Compare to Oscar Wilde's observation that 'we Irish are too poetical to be poets; we are a nation of brilliant failures, but we are the greatest talkers since the Greeks'. See Richard Ellman, *Oscar Wilde* (Harmondsworth, Penguin, 1988), p. 284.
8. McDonald, pp. 118–19.
9. 'An Interview with Derek Mahon' by Terence Brown, *Poetry Ireland Review*, No. 14 (Autumn 1985), pp. 11–9 (p. 14).
10. Seamus Heaney, 'The Pre-Natal Mountain: Vision and Irony in Recent Irish Poetry', *The Place of Writing* (Atlanta, Scholars Press, 1989), pp. 36–53, (pp. 48–9).
11. Derek Mahon, 'Poetry in Northern Ireland', *Twentieth-Century Studies*, No. 4 (November 1970), pp. 89–93 (p. 92).
12. The phrase is used pejoratively by Peter McDonald in 'Incurable Ache', p. 117.
13. See Eoghan Ó Tuairisc (ed.), *Rogha an Fhile/ The Poet's Choice* (Dublin, Goldsmith Press, 1974), pp. 57–8.
14. Nuala Ní Dhomhnaill, 'There is a bond between my own situation and everything that comes down to me through the language and bealoideas', in Ó Tuairisc, (ed.) pp. 57–8.
15. Nuala Ní Dhomhnaill, 'Development of the tradition through personalisation, and enrichment of the person through tradition', in Ó Tuairisc (ed.), p. 58.
16. Theo Durgan, 'Looking Over the Bridge', in Theo Durgan (ed.), *Irish Poetry Since Kavanagh* (Blackrock, Four Courts Press, 1996), pp. 147–58 (p. 156).
17. See, for example, 'Christmas in Kinsale': 'A cock crows good-morning from an oil-drum / like a peacock from a rain-barrel in Byzantium' (*TYB* 57); Mahon's version of 'pylon' poetry?
18. 'Gile na Gile'/ 'Brightness of Brightness', in Seán Ó Tuama and Thomas Kinsella (eds.) *An Duanaire 1600–1900: Poems of the Dispossessed* (Mountrath, Dolmen Press, 1981), pp. 150–3.
19. Mahon, 'Poetry in Northern Ireland', p. 92.
20. Nuala Ní Dhomhnaill, *Pharaoh's Daughter* (Oldcastle, Gallery Press, 1990), p. 84.
21. Thomas Kinsella quoted by Philip O'Leary, in 'An Agile Cormorant: Poetry in Ireland Today', *Eire-Ireland*, No. xxiv, 4 (Winter 1989), pp. 39–53, (pp. 44–5).
22. Niall MacMonagle (ed.), *Lifelines: Letters from Famous People about their Favourite Poem* (Dublin, Town House and Country House, 1995), p. 146.

23. Nuala Ní Dhomhnaill, *Feis* (Maigh Nuad, An Sagart, 1991), p. 21.

24. Seamus Deane writes of Mahon that 'it is remarkable how often the figure in his poems is that of a spectator; or in the love poems is a man brought in from the outside to share a basic warmth . . . Mahon is our true exile – the man who belongs but does not wish to believe so or disbelieves that he must always . . . He is an Irish writer whose Protestantism survives in his uncertainty about Ireland – whether he wishes to belong to it, or whether he would be allowed to belong if he so wished'. Seamus Deane, 'Irish Poetry and Irish Nationalism', in Douglas Dunn (ed.), *Two Decades of Irish Writing: A Critical Survey* (Cheadle, Carcanet Press, 1975), pp. 4–22 (pp. 12–13).

25. Derek Mahon, 'Light Music' Part IX, *Light Music* (Belfast, Ulsterman Publications, 1977), p. 11.

26. Choice of such 'classics' has been criticised as going for the obvious. However, it is a feature of contemporary music, for example, to cover well-known rather than obscure songs. In this sense, however, Mahon is more of a Fugee than a Boyzone-style performer.

27. Bob Dylan, 'A Hard Rain's a-Gonna Fall'.

28. The Ulster-Scotch Leid Society, *Whit wud Ulster-Scotch be?* (A promotional pamphlet/flyer).

29. Geoffrey Brereton, *A Short History of French Literature* (Harmondsworth, Penguin, 1965), p. 28.

30. Marina Warner, *Managing Monsters: Six Myths of Our Time*, The 1994 Reith Lectures (London, Vintage, 1994), p. 79.

31. W.H. Auden, "Let us remember that, though the great artists of the past could not change the course of history it is only through their work that we are able to break bread with the dead, and without communion with the dead a fully human life is impossible'; in W.H. Auden, *Secondary Worlds* (London, Faber and Faber, 1968), p. 141.

32. Derek Mahon, 'Un Beau Pays, Mal Habité: The derivative hedonism and sabbatarian grimness of the Portstewart – Portrush – Coleraine Triangle', in *Magill*, February 1979, pp. 19–22 (p. 22).

33. Mahon, 'Poetry from Northern Ireland', p. 92.

34. 'An Interview with Derek Mahon' by Terence Brown, *Poetry Ireland Review*, No. 14 (Autumn 1985), pp. 11–19 (p. 19).

35. *Ibid.*, p. 18.

36. See 'Cill Chais', in Ó Tuama and Kinsella (eds.), pp. 328–31.

37. See 'The Blackbird of Belfast Lough' quoted by Seamus Heaney, 'The God in the Tree: Early Irish Nature Poetry', in *Preoccupations: Selected Prose 1968–1978* (London, Faber and Faber, 1980), pp. 181–9 (p. 181); John Hewitt, 'Gloss, On the Difficulties of Translation', in Frank Ormsby (ed.), *The Collected Poems of John Hewitt* (Belfast, Blackstaff Press, 1991), p. 129; Derek Mahon, 'The Blackbird', *SP*. p. 101.

38. Seamus Deane, 'His language is surprisingly polysyllabic, given the simple verse forms he favours; yet at his best he can achieve both density and elegance by the combination. In addition, the language

seeks (and actually finds) a cool temperature, the climate of decorum . . .'; in Seamus Deane, 'Irish Poetry and Irish Nationalism', p. 12.

39. See Paul Muldoon, 'Prologue', in *The Faber Book of Contemporary Irish Poetry* (London, Faber and Faber, 1986), pp. 17–8 (p. 18); also Cathal Ó Searcaigh, 'Gréasáin'/'Webs', *Out in the Open* (Indreabhán, Cló Iar-Chonnachta, 1997), pp. 224–7.

40. See Muldoon (ed.), *The Faber Book of Contemporary Irish Poetry*, p. 70.

41. Derek Mahon, 'For I too was young and morose – worse, sinister – in youth/ a frightful little shit, to tell the truth'; in Derek Mahon, 'Chinatown', *THL*, pp. 58–60.

42. Mahon, 'Poetry in Northern Ireland', p. 93.

43. *Ibid.*, p. 92.

44. Ted Hughes, 'Introduction', in Desmond Graham (ed.), *Keith Douglas: Complete Poems* (Oxford: Oxford University Press, 1990), pp. xv-xxvii (p. xvi).

45. See Philip Larkin, 'To put one brick upon another', *Collected Poems* (London, Marvell Press and Faber and Faber, 1990), p. 58.

46. Deane, 'Irish Poetry and Irish Nationalism', pp. 12–3.

47. McDonald, p. 119.

'THE SOUL OF SILENCE': DEREK MAHON'S MASCULINITIES

John Goodby

1. Seamus Deane, 'Derek Mahon: Freedom from History', in *Celtic Revivals: Essays in Modern Irish Literature 1880–1980* (London, Faber and Faber, 1985), pp. 156–65.

2. See my 'Reading Protestant Writing: Representations of the Troubles in the Poetry of Derek Mahon and Glenn Patterson's *Burning Your Own*, in Kathleen Devine (ed.), *Northern Irish Poetry and the Wars* (Gerrards Cross, Colin Smythe, 1999).

3. Anthony Clare, 'The Saturday Essay: Idle, sad and baffled by sex: What's wrong with men?', *The Independent Weekend Review*, 14 November 1998, p. 12.

4. R.W. Connell, *Masculinities* (London, Polity Press, 1995).

5. One literary-critical comparison is with (post)colonial criticism and the rise of new Anglophone literatures from the 1950s onwards, and the way these eventually led to the problematising of 'Englishness'. Mahon's Northern Irishness, of course, means that his work has its relevance to this process also.

6. Eve Patten, 'Translations: an interview with Derek Mahon', *Rhinoceros*, 3 (1986), p. 84. See also Michael Longley, *Tuppeny Stung: Autobiographical Chapters* (Belfast, Lagan Press, 1995), p. 38.

7. Seamus Heaney, *The New Statesman* (1965), p. 848. The piece

concludes: *'Talking to Women* is a good read. But I am just too
smugly male, too dominating and egotistical, to take to a book
where the ladies protest so much. Ladies, I am sure, will like it'.

8. Rita Felski, *The Gender of Modernity* (Cambridge, Mass., Harvard
University Press, 1995), p. 3.

9. Louis MacNeice, *Collected Poems*, ed. E.R. Dodds (London, Faber and
Faber, 1979), p. 17.

10. Eavan Boland, 'Compact and Compromise: Derek Mahon as a
Young Poet', *Irish University Review*, 24, 1 (Spring-Summer 1994), p.
66. Boland intends 'gender', not 'sexual' here, I think, and it's
debatable that it's taken other than literary genres to act as a
'commentary on historic disorder', or that *The Crying Game* is as
subversive as she thinks (for the case that the film is actually
'remarkably conventional' in its political and gender implications,
see Joe Cleary, '"Fork-Tongued on the Border Bit": Partition and the
Politics of Form in Contemporary Narratives of the Northern Irish
Conflict', *South Atlantic Quarterly*, 95, 1 (Winter 1996), pp. 227–76.

11. Mahon's forging of a *cadre* of outsider artist-companions has been
seen as a form of 'male bonding'. This term, which passed into
common use in the early stages of the reaction against the women's
movement, derives from the book *Men in Groups* (1970) by the
appropriately named Lionel Tiger, which argued that such
behaviour results from the 'fact' that *homo sapiens* is a hunting
species. A more or less endocrine theory of masculinity, this is a
good example of an unsophisticated social Darwinism put to the
service of culturally-constructed patriarchal prejudice.

12. Edna Longley, '"When Did You Last See Your Father?": Perceptions
of the Past in Northern Irish Writing 1965–1985', in *The Living
Stream: Literature and Revisionism in Ireland* (Newcastle-upon-Tyne,
Bloodaxe, 1994), p. 12.

13. J. Rutherford, *Men's Silences : Predicaments in Masculinity* (London,
Routledge, 1992).

14. Although Larkin had reached adulthood by the mid-1940s, it is
worth remarking that his mature style evolved in the early 1950s
and is first displayed in *The Less Deceived*, published as late as 1955.
Larkin's belatedness in finding a 'voice' in this sense confirms the
extent to which he drew upon emergent social and cultural
formations of the postwar, rather than prewar, era. Given the
radical conservatism of the sexual politics of his poetry, it may be no
coincidence that this style was fashioned during Larkin's residence
in Belfast between 1950 and 1955.

15. Episode broadcast on BBC1, 11 September 1998.

16. Tom Paulin, 'A Terminal Ironist', in *Ireland and the English Question*
(Newcastle-upon-Tyne, Bloodaxe, 1984), p. 59.

17. Stephen H. Clark, *Sordid Images: The Poetry of Masculine Desire*
(London, Routledge, 1994), p. 256. A different version of the same
point is made by Connell, who points out that belief in an intrinsic

and unchangeable male essence unites both essentialist feminists
and Darwinian misogynists.

18. Clark, p. 3.
19. Eve Kosofsky Sedgwick, *The Epistemology of the Closet* (Hemel
    Hempstead, Harvester/Wheatsheaf, 1991). For the specific usage
    here, see Andrew Bennett and Nicholas Royle, *Introduction to
    Literature, Criticism and Theory* (Hemel Hempstead, Prentice Hall,
    1999), pp. 174–6.
20. Suzanne Clark, *Sentimental Modernism: Women Writers and the
    Revolution of the Word* (Bloomington, Indiana University Press, 1991).
21. Rutherford, p. 21.
22. It was de Nerval who – in Paul Muldon's words – when 'his hopes
    of Adrienne// proved false'
       . . . hanged himself from a lamp-post
    with a length of chain, which made me think

    of something else, then something else again.
    'Something Else', *Meeting the British* (London, Faber and Faber,
    1987), p. 33.
    The poem offers an inarticulable moment, a Mahonesque (male)
    silence or 'something else', which suggests that while one of its
    intertexts is Seamus Heaney's 'Away from it All', another is
    certainly 'Glengormley' with its 'unreconciled . . . hanging from
    lamp-posts in the dawn rain' (*SP* 12).
23. Eavan Boland, p. 65. Again, one might want to query the
    appropriateness of the terminology here: Larkin as 'flamboyant', for
    example, or omission of the point that in 'disassembling' one form
    of authority he was very deliberately constructing another, equally
    influential, based on self-effacement. Nevertheless, as I argue,
    Boland's general point stands.
24. Peter Nicholls, *Modernisms: A Literary Guide* (Basingstoke,
    Macmillan, 1995), pp. 193–4.
25. The male psyche, as Walter J. Ong has argued, is peculiarly
    vulnerable to anxieties about the way in which an overflow of
    passion may be seen as unstable and 'feminine'. Pointing out that
    (contrary to Freud's notion of femininity as a modification of the
    'natural' state of masculinity) nature's primary tendency is to
    produce females, Ong notes that, whether biologically or
    psychologically defined, 'masculinity means becoming something
    different, separation from (maternal) origins, a certain kind of
    getting away, transcendence'. As a result, the 'male's problem is one
    of differentiation. He must prove that he is not . . . female'. Walter J.
    Ong, *Fighting for Life: Contest, Sexuality and Consciousness* (Ithaca,
    New York, 1981), pp. 66, 112.
26. V. Seidler, *Rediscovering Masculinity: Reason, Language and Sexuality*
    (London, Routledge, 1989).
27. What might be called Mahon's eco-feminist aspect can be seen in

'The Globe in North Carolina'. Its first version offers a critique of masculinity on behalf of an earth-mother (or ocean-mother):

Its sex (ocean's) is not in question. What
Man would resolve, so rapt in thought,
With such a grave insouciance?

The revised version of this verse neuters the argument, 'universalising' it:

Redemption lies not in the thrust
Of action only, but the trust
We place in our peripheral
Night-garden in the glory-hole
Of space . . .

The effect is to reinstate gender polarities in crushingly conventional, genitalised terms, 'action' made phallically masculine in 'thrust' and opposed to the female 'glory-hole' of earth.

28. John Constable, 'Derek Mahon's Development', *Agenda*, 22, 3/4 (Autumn-Winter, 1984–5), p. 115.
29. John Redmond, 'Wilful Inconsistency: Derek Mahon's Verse-Letters', *Irish University Review*, vol. 24, no. 1 (Spring-Summer, 1994), pp. 96–116. Redmond's censures on heterogeneity *per se* in poetry are dubious (and have their own revealing gender subtext), but applied to 'The Hudson Letter', they make a useful point: 'at more philosophical moments, the poem abruptly abandons this (casual) style and aims to be "poetic" . . . we turn from hairy-chested heartiness to the "improving" moralism of the maiden aunt as she passes around the home-made cakes . . .', p. 101.
30. Derek Mahon, 'Orpheus Ascending', review of Paul Durcan's *The Berlin Wall Cafe*, in *Journalism* (Oldcastle, Gallery Press, 1996), p. 117.
31. Both, pointedly, are plays which attack male possessiveness and complacency. Archie in *High Time*, is the model here: as he says to the sexist Tom, 'I'm not one of your grisly patriarchs / who makes their children wish them in their box'. Similarly, in an image which seems drawn from the Protestant history which is so significant in the construction of Loyalist masculinity, he warns: 'An ill-used wife's a foe within the gate'.
32. Constituting section XI of *The Yellow Book*, this begins with a diatribe against contemporary Britain in which 'Everything aspires to the condition of rock music', continues with the admission that 'Maybe I'm finally turning into an old fart' (the surprise here clearly in the use of 'finally'), but ambiguously qualifies the mock self-deprecation with an admission that 'I'm in two minds about Tank Girl over there / the Muse in chains, a screw-bolt in one ear,/ the knickers worn over the biking gear . . .'. At this point the confusion of either/or triggered by sexual attraction ('Tank Girls' should be unattractive) provokes a displacement in the form of a virtuosic listing of things Mahon wishes to praise (*TYB*, 35–6).
33. Although it is a sign of Mahon's nervous self-awareness concerning

this procedure that he places this passage within quotation marks.

34. Paul Muldoon, *The Prince of the Quotidian* (London, Faber and Faber, 1994), p. 41.

35. 'Nationalist' in the general rather than the specifically Irish sense, that is. It is worth noting at this point that it is precisely by returning to the sociological-historical – to class, gender and other categories which have tended to be ignored in critical discussion – that a distinction can be made between masculine silences in the work of Protestant-background and Catholic-background poets. While both, that is, are inflected by the cohesion required by their particular ideological monoliths, and while 'the knowing nod' of Mahon has its mirror image in Heaney's 'land of password, handgrip, wink and nod', the gendering of dominant and victim cultures is differentiated in the roles of women, the valorisation of rural as opposed to urban labour, and religious iconography. In this regard, Julia Kristeva's notion of the abject – the immersion in, and self-definition through, victimage – is particularly suggestive.

36. Desmond Bell, 'Contemporary Cultural Studies in Ireland and the "Problem" of Protestant Ideology', *The Crane Bag*, 9, 2 (1985), p. 92.

37. Loyalism's potency as an ideological practice is located, for Bell, not in programmatic self-explanation but in a series of symbolic cultural forms, to which the Orange parade is central, concerned with a public display of the symbols of Protestant identity and territorial demarcation. Neither Miller nor Bell say much about gender; nevertheless hypermasculinism can be seen as central to Loyalist rituals and ethos. See David W. Miller, *Queen's Rebels: Ulster Loyalism in Historical Perspective* (Dublin, Gill and Macmillan, 1978).

38. W.J. McCormack, *The Battle of the Books: Two Decades of Irish Cultural Debate* (Mullingar, Lilliput Press, 1986), p. 71.

RESIDENT ALIEN: AMERICA IN THE POETRY OF DEREK MAHON

Neil Corcoran

1. John Kerrigan, 'Ulster Ovids', in Neil Corcoran (ed.), *The Chosen Ground: Essays on the Contemporary Poetry of Northern Ireland*, (Bridgend, Seren Books, 1992), p. 261.

2. Seamus Deane, *Celtic Revivals* (London, Faber and Faber, 1985), p. 156.

3. Peter Denman, 'Know the One? Insolent Ontology and Mahon's Revisions', *Irish University Review*, vol. 24, no. 1 (Spring-Summer 1994), p. 4. Mahon's sometimes extensive revisions to his poems in subsequent printings are discussed illuminatingly in this essay. I myself find them, as many readers do, deeply irritating, and usually disadvantageous. I have, however, thought it necessary to quote in

this essay from the versions given in *Selected Poems*, apart from the instance I particularise in note 19 below. The poems of *The Hudson Letter* are not (yet) affected by Mahon's revisionary mania.

4. Kerrigan, p. 260.
5 Hugh Haughton, '"Even now there are places where a thought might grow": Place and Displacement in the Poetry of Derek Mahon', in *The Chosen Ground*, pp. 87–120.
6 Derek Mahon, *Journalism: Selected Prose 1970–1995*, ed. Terence Brown (Oldcastle, Gallery Books, 1996), p. 25. His observation here that, in this sense, 'exile . . . was an option available to Joyce and O'Casey, who "belonged" to the people from whom they wished to escape. It was not available, in the same sense, to MacNeice, whose background was a mixture of Anglo-Irish and Ulster Protestant (C of I). Whatever his sympathies, he didn't, by class or religious background. "Belong to the people"' also clearly has relevance to Mahon himself. The mordant fastidiousness of his inverted commas here is less a register of disdain than an indication of his own outsider status in relation to these structures of feeling; although disdain is undoubtedly an element of it.
7. Edna Longley, *Poetry in the Wars* (Newcastle-Upon-Tyne, Bloodaxe Books, 1986), p. 206.
8. Peter Fallon and Derek Mahon (eds.), *The Penguin Book of Contemporary Irish Poetry* Harmondsworth, Penguin Books, 1990), p. xxii. This would undoubtedly seem to Michael Allen a retrospective re-drawing of the transatlantic map, since, in an article on Seamus Heaney and America, he observes that 'Whatever pan-Irish notions [Michael Longley and Mahon] might have picked up as students in Dublin, they were excluded from the outset from a Hiberno-American rapport by their Northern Protestant cultural antecedents'. See 'The Parish and the Dream: Heaney and America, 1969-1987', *The Southern Review*, vol. 31, no. 3 (July 1995), p. 727.
9. Haughton, pp. 111–13.
10. T. S. Eliot, *Selected Essays* (London, Faber and Faber, 1932), p. 293.
11. Seamus Heaney, *The Place of Writing* (Atlanta, Ga., Scholars Press, 1989), p. 42.
12. Christopher Ricks, *The Force of Poetry* (Oxford, Clarendon Press, 1984), pp. 34–59.
13. Michael Allen, loc. cit., p. 732, makes a different, but possibly related, point about the use of the word in Seamus Heaney's 'Elegy' for Robert Lowell: 'The word "America" functions here with the enigmatic, liturgical force it always carries in the literature of the [American] Dream (at the end of *The Adventures of Augie March*, for instance)'.
14. Edward Snow, *A Study of Vermeer*, revised and enlarged edition (Berkeley and London, University of California Press, 1994), p. 163.
15. *Ibid.*, p. 166.
16. I quote here the version published in *Lives* (1972), since that of the

Selected Poems – 'I put out the light / on shadows of the encroaching
night' – is such a disfigurement. It loses the literariness which is so
strong a feature of these poems, and is intensified in this version by
the fact that the Mailer title is derived from Matthew Arnold's
'Dover Beach', which is also referred to in this stanza in its original
form; and, in that loss of allusion, it also loses, it may be, a relatively
oblique reference to the Robert Lowell to whom Mahon is, in part,
indebted for his octosyllabics, since Lowell is prominently featured
in Mailer's book, which deals with the march on Washington in
1967.

17. Deane, p. 157.
18. The allusion in the last line here is to *The Great Gatsby*. In the first
    chapter of the novel Nick Carraway is told that Daisy's husband
    Tom has 'got some woman in New York'; and when Daisy returns
    to the room she says: 'There's a bird on the lawn that I think must be
    a nightingale come over on the Cunard or White Star Line. He's
    singing away . . . It's romantic, isn't it, Tom?' The pathos of Daisy's
    self-identification is of course ironised subsequently by the depth of
    her emotional and financial attachment to Tom. I annotate this
    allusion, which typifies those of the sequence, to indicate something
    of the extent of Mahon's literary memory, since I doubt if many
    even close readers of Gatsby will necessarily remember this tiny
    moment in the book.

THE TWILIGHT OF THE CITIES; DEREK MAHON'S DARK CINEMA

Stan Smith

I   The word counts given here exclude, as is customary, those high-
    frequency function words (prepositions, pronouns, auxiliaries, and
    similar locators) normally omitted from concordances. The
    concordance of *Poems 1962–1978* was made using the program
    devised by R. J. C. Watt, of the Auden Concordance Project, jointly
    directed by Watt and myself from Dundee and Nottingham Trent
    Universities. See Watt's website at www. rjcw. freeserve. co.uk The
    ideal would be a concordance of all Mahon's volumes, together with
    their variant readings, but this was beyond the scope of the present
    essay, which does not address work published after *Selected Poems*
    (1991). Such a concordance might throw some light on, *inter alia*, the
    reasons for the substantial changes, not all for obviously stylistic
    reasons, made to such poems as the verse epistle 'The Sea in Winter'
    between the two volumes, and the possible structural relations
    between the poem called 'Going Home, for Douglas Dunn', in the
    earlier book and that called 'Going Home', dedicated to John
    Hewitt, in the later one, entitled 'The Return' in *Poems 1962–1978*. It

might also give a clue to the reasons for changing the exclamatory disgust of 'Afterlives', 'What middle-class cunts we are' in the earlier volume, into the mild self-irritation of 'middle-class twits' in *Selected Poems*. Far from improving the poem, this diminishes the vigour of its outrage at 'our privileged ideals' amidst the real violence and squalor of the external world. But this is a future project.

APOCALYPSE NOW AND THEN: *THE YELLOW BOOK*

Patrick Crotty

1. John Lyon, 'Early Mahon, and Later', review of *The Yellow Book*, *Thumbscrew* (Oxford), 10 (Spring-Summer 1998), pp. 108–16, p. 113.
2. In the version in *The Hudson Letter*, p. 31 the date, along with the address, has been removed from the *Collected Poems* version.
3. Seamus Deane, 'Derek Mahon: Freedom from History', in *Celtic Revivals: Essays in Modern Irish Literature 1880–1980* (London, Faber and Faber, 1985), p. 165.
4. *Ibid.*, pp. 159–60.
5. See, for example, 'Poetry Today', in Alan Heuser (ed.), *Selected Literary Criticism of Louis MacNeice* (Oxford, Clarendon Press, 1987), pp. 10–44, p. 41; and Louis MacNeice, *Modern Poetry: A Personal Essay* (London, 1938), passim.
6. See Peter McDonald, 'Incurable Ache', *Poetry Ireland Review*, 56 (Spring 1998), pp 117–9. Also Lyon.
7. As Helen Vendler argues in her essay, 'John Berryman: Freudian Cartoons', in *The Given and the Made: Recent American Poets* (London, Faber and Faber, 1995), pp. 31–57.
8. W.H. Auden, *Collected Shorter Poems* (London, Faber and Faber, 1966), p. 243.
9. Lyon, p. 114.
10. Quoted by J.A. Cuddon, *The Penguin Dictionary of Literary Terms and Literary Theory* (London, Penguin, 1992), p. 272.
11. Sydney Goodsir Smith, *Under the Eildon Tree* (Edinburgh, Serif Books, 1948). Reprinted in *Collected Poems* (London, John Calder, 1975).
12. Thomas McDonagh, 'The Yellow Bittern' in Derek Mahon (ed.), *The Sphere Book of Modern Irish Poetry* (London, Sphere, 1972), p. 42; Tom MacIntyre, 'The Yellow Bittern', in *The Sphere Book of Modern Irish Poetry*, p. 188.
13. Seán Ó Tuama and Thomas Kinsella, *An Duanaire 1600–1900: Poems of the Dispossessed* (Montrath, Dolmen, 1981), p. 133.
14. Seamus Heaney and Ted Hughes (eds.), *The School Bag* (London, Faber and Faber, 1997), p. 349.

15. 'An Horatian Ode upon Cromwell's Return from Ireland', Elizabeth Story Donno (ed.), *Andrew Marvell: The Complete Poems* (Harmondsworth, Penguin, 1972), p. 54.
16. Austin Clarke, *Collected Poems* (Dublin, Dolmen, 1974), p. 429.
17. F. Scott Fitzgerald, *The Great Gatsby* (Harmondsworth, Penguin, 1986), p. 171.
18. 'This tone is familiar in even educated circles in the Irish Republic, and Mahon seems to have caught it to a tee when he writes about those "savages / of the harsh north". Yet it seems likely that this is not satirical ventriloquism but the real Irish thing; one might almost say that Mahon has gone native. The poem 'Death in Bangor' 'revisits' Northern Ireland (or 'the north') with a cartload of clichés and prejudices . . .'
    McDonald, p. 119. See also Mahon, 'The Coleraine Triangle', in *Journalism*, p. 216.
19. Albert Camus, 'The Artist at Work', in *Exile and the Kingdom*, trans. Justin O'Brien (Harmondsworth, Penguin, 1962), p. 115. The French *solidaire* is rather unsatisfactorily rendered as *solidary* by O'Brien.

SELECT BIBLIOGRAPHY

WORK BY DEREK MAHON
(Listed chronologically)

COLLECTED VERSE

Twelve Poems (Belfast, Festival Publications, 1965).
Design for a Grecian Urn (Cambridge, Massachusetts, Erato Press, 1966).
Night-Crossing (London, Oxford University Press, 1968).
Beyond Howth Head (Dublin, Dolmen Press, 1970).
Ecclesiastes (Manchester, Phoenix Pamphlet Poets Press, 1970).
Lives (London, Oxford University Press, 1972).
The Snow Party (London and New York, Oxford University Press, 1975).
Light Music (Belfast, Ulsterman Publications, 1977).
In Their Element: A Selection of Poems. With Seamus Heaney (Belfast, Arts
    Council of Northern Ireland, 1977).
The Sea in Winter (Dublin, Gallery Press; Old Deerfield, Massachusetts,
    Deerfield Press, 1979).
Poems 1962–1978 (London, Oxford University Press, 1979).
Courtyards in Delft (Dublin, Gallery Press, 1981).
The Hunt by Night (Oxford, Oxford University Press, 1982; Winston-
    Salem, North Carolina, Wake Forest University Press, 1983).
A Kensington Notebook (London, Anvil Press Poetry, 1984).
Antarctica (Dublin, Gallery Press, 1986).
Selected Poems (Oldcastle, Gallery Press, 1991; Harmondsworth, Penguin
    Books; New York, Viking Penguin, 1991).
The Yaddo Letter (Oldcastle, Gallery Press, 1992).
The Hudson Letter (Oldcastle, Gallery Press, 1995).
The Yellow Book (Oldcastle, Gallery Press, 1997).
Collected Poems (Oldcastle, Gallery Press, 1999).
Roman Script, with drawings by Anne Madden (Oldcastle, Gallery Press,
    2000).

DRAMA

High Time, After Molière (Dublin, Gallery Press, 1985).
The School for Wives, After Molière (Dublin, Gallery Press, 1986).
The Bacchae, After Euripides (Oldcastle, Gallery Press, 1991).
Racine's Phaedra (Oldcastle, Gallery Press, 1996).

TRANSLATIONS

The Chimeras A version of *Les Chimères* by Gerard de Nerval (Dublin, Gallery Press, 1982).
Selected Poems by Phillipe Jaccottet (London, Viking, 1987; Harmondsworth, Penguin, 1988; Winston-Salem, North Carolina, Wake Forest University Press, 1988).
Words in the Air: A Selection of Poems by Philip Jaccottet, with translations and introduction by Derek Mahon (Oldcastle, Gallery Press, 1998).
Night Without Day, translation from the French of Raphaële Billetdoux's novel (New York, Viking, 1987).

ANTHOLOGIES

The Sphere Book of Modern Irish Poetry (London, Sphere, 1972).
The Penguin Book of Contemporary Irish Poetry. With Peter Fallon (London, Penguin, 1990).

LITERARY JOURNALISM

Journalism: Selected Prose 1970–1995, edited by Terence Brown (Oldcastle, Gallery Press, 1996).
'Poetry in Northern Ireland', *Twentieth Century Studies*, 4 (November 1970), pp. 89–93.

TELEVISION ADAPTATIONS

Shadows on our Skin, adapted from the novel by Jennifer Johnston. BBC 1, London, 20 March 1980.
Summer Lightning, adapted from the novel *First Love* by Ivan Turgenev. RTE, Dublin and Channel 4, London, 1982/1984.
How Many Miles to Babylon? adapted from the novel by Jennifer Johnston. BBC 2, London, 26 February 1982.
The Cry, adapted from the short story by John Montague. BBC 1, London, 31 July 1984.
Death of the Heart, adapted from the novel by Elizabeth Bowen. Granada London, 22 December 1985.
Demon Lover, adapted from the novel by Elizabeth Bowen. Granada London, 21 June 1986.

INTERVIEWS AND PROFILES

Battersby, Eileen. 'Made in Belfast', *Sunday Tribune*, 25 August 1990.
'A Very European Poet', *Irish Times*, 10 November 1992.
Boland, Eavan, 'Northern Writers' Crisis of Conscience: 1: Community', *Irish Times*, 12 August 1970.
'Northern Writers' Crisis of Conscience: 2: Crisis', *Irish Times*, 13 August 1970.
'Northern Writers' Crisis of Conscience: 3: Creativity', *Irish Times*, 14 August 1970.
'The Closed Circuit', *Irish Times*, 16 April 1971.
Brown, Terence, 'An Interview with Derek Mahon', *Poetry Ireland*, 14

(Autumn 1985), pp. 11–19.

Cooke, Harriet. 'Harriet Cooke talks to the Poet Derek Mahon', *Irish Times*, 17 January 1973, p. 10.

Gillespie, Elgy, 'Elgy Gillespie talks to Derek Mahon', *Irish Times* 2, December 1978, p. 14.

Grennan, Eamon, 'Interview with Derek Mahon', *Paris Review* (Spring, 2000), pp. 151–78.

Kelly, Willie, 'Each Poem For Me is a New Beginning, *Cork Review*, 2, 3 (June 1986).

'Derek Mahon: An Interview', *Fifth Column* 1 (1986).

Murphy, James J.; McDiarmid, Lucy; Durkan, Michael J., 'Q. & A. with Derek Mahon, *Irish Literary Supplement* 10, 2 (Fall, 1991), p. 28.

Ni Anluain, Clíodhna (ed.), *Reading the Future: Irish Writers in Conversation with Mike Murphy* (Dublin, Lilliput Press, 2000), pp. 157–171.

Patton, Eve, 'Interview with Derek Mahon', *Rhinoceros* 3 (1990).

Scammell, William. 'Derek Mahon Interviewed', *Poetry Review* 81, 2 (Summer 1991), p. 6.

CRITICISM

Boland, Eavan, 'Compact and Compromise: Derek Mahon as a Young Poet', *Irish University Review: Special Issue: Derek Mahon*, 24, 1 (Spring-Summer, 1994), p. 61–6.

Bradley, Anthony, 'Literature and Culture in the North of Ireland', in Michael Kenneally (ed.), *Cultural Contexts and Literary Idioms in Contemporary Irish Literature* (Gerrards Cross, Colin Smythe, 1988).

'The Irishness of Irish Poetry After Yeats', in James D. Brophy and Eamon Grennan (eds.), *New Irish Writing* (Boston, Twayne, 1989).

Brewster, Scott, 'A Residual Poetry: Heaney, Mahon and Hedgehog History', *Irish University Review*, 28, 1 (Spring-Summer, 1998), pp. 50-64.

Brown, Terence, 'Four New Voices: Poets of the Present'. in *Northern Voices* (Dublin, Gill and Macmillan, 1975).

'Home and Away: Derek Mahon's France', in Barbara Hayley and Christopher Murray (eds.), *Ireland and France, A Bountiful Friendship* (Gerrards Cross, Colin Smythe, 1992).

'Derek Mahon: The Poet and Painting', *Irish University Review*: Special Issue: Derek Mahon, 24, 1 (Spring-Summer, 1994), pp. 38–50.

Byrne, John, 'Derek Mahon: A Commitment to Change', *Crane Bag*, 6, 1 (1982).

Clutterbuck, Catriona, '"Elpenor's crumbling oar": Disconnection and Art in Derek Mahon', *Irish University Review*: Special Issue: Derek Mahon, 24, 1 (Spring-Summer, 1994), pp. 6–26.

Craig, Patricia, 'History and its Retrieval in Contemporary Northern Irish Poetry: Paulin, Montague and Others', in Elmer Andrews (ed.), *Contemporary Irish Poetry* (Basingstoke, Macmillan, 1992), pp. 108–24.

Dawe, Gerald, '"Icon and Lares"': Derek Mahon and Michael Longley' in Gerald Dawe and Edna Longley (eds.), *Across a Roaring Hill: The Protestant Imagination in Modern Ireland* (Belfast, Blackstaff Press, 1985), pp. 219–35. 'A Question of Imagination – Poetry in Ireland Today', in Michael Kenneally (ed.), *Cultural Contexts and Literary Idioms in Contemporary Irish Literature* (Gerrards Cross, Colin Smythe, 1988)

Deane, Seamus, 'Irish Poetry and Irish Nationalism', in Douglas Dunn (ed.), *Two Decades of Irish Writing* (Cheadie, Carcanet, 1975), pp. 4–22. 'Derek Mahon: Freedom from History' in *Celtic Revivals* (London, Faber and Faber, 1965), pp. 157–166.

Denman, Peter, 'Know the One? Insolent Ontology and Mahon's Revisions', *Irish University Review*: Special Issue: Derek Mahon, 24, 1 (Spring-Summer, 1994), pp. 27–37.

Donnelly, Brian, 'The Poetry of Derek Mahon', *English Studies* 60, 1 (1979). 'From Nineveh to the Harbour Bar', *Ploughshares* 6.1 (1980).

Dunn, Douglas, 'Let the God not Abandon Us: On the Poetry of Derek Mahon', *Stone Ferry Review* 2 (Winter 1978).

Duytschaever, Joris, 'History in the Poetry of Derek Mahon', in Joris Duytschaever and Geert Lernout (eds.), *History and Violence in Irish Literature*, Costerus, vol. 71 (Amsterdam, Rodopi, 1978), pp. 98–111.

Frazier, Adrian, 'Proper Portion: Derek Mahon's *The Hunt by Night*' (review), *Éire-Ireland*, 18, 4 (Winter, 1983), pp. 136–43.

Garratt, Robert F. 'The Tradition of Discontinuity: A Glance at Recent Ulster Poetry', in *Modern Irish Poetry: Tradition and Continuity from Yeats to Heaney* (Berkeley, University of Califomia Press, 1986).

Goodby, John, 'Reading Protestant Writing: Representations of the Troubles in the Poetry of Derek Mahon and Glenn Patterson's *Burning Your Own*', in Kathleen Devine (ed.), *Modern Irish Writers and the Wars* (Gerrards Cross, Colin Smythe, 1999), pp. 219–244. *Irish Poetry Since 1950: From Stillness into History* (Manchester, Manchester University Press, 2000).

Graham, Colin, 'Derek Mahon's Cultural Marginalia', in Eve Patten (ed.), *Returning to Ourselves, Second Volume of Papers from the John Hewitt International Summer School* (Belfast, Lagan Press, 1995), pp. 240–8.

Grennan, Eamon, '"To the Point of Speech": The Poetry of Derek Mahon', in *Contemporary Irish Writing* (Boston: Twayne, 1983).

Haughton, Hugh, '"Even now there are places where a thought might grow": Place and Displacement in the Poetry of Derek Mahon', in Neil Corcoran (ed.), *The Chosen Ground: Essays on the Contemporary Poetry of Northern Ireland* (Bridgend, Seren Books, 1992) pp. 87–123.

Heaney, Seamus, 'The Pre-Natal Mountain: Vision and Irony in Recent Irish Poetry', in *The Place of Writing* (Atlanta. Scholars Press, 1989), pp. 36–53. 'Place and Displacement: Reflections on Some Recent Poetry from Northern Ireland', in Elmer Andrews (ed.), *Contemporary Irish Poetry* (Basingstoke, Macmillan, 1992), pp. 124–45.

Johnston, Dillon, 'MacNeice & Mahon', in *Irish Poetry After Joyce* (Notre Dame, University of Notre Dame Press, 1985)

Kearney, Richard, 'Myth and Modernity in Irish Poetry', in Elmer Andrews (ed.), *Contemporary Irish Poetry* (Basingstoke, Macmillan, 1992), pp. 41–63.

Kearney, Timothy, 'The Poetry of the North: A Post-Modernist Perspective' *Crane Bag* 3.2 (1979).

Kendall, Tim, 'Leavetakings and Homecomings, Derek Mahon's Belfast', *Eire-Ireland*, 29, 4 (1994), pp. 101–116.

Kennelly, Brendan, 'Lyric Wit', *Irish Times*, 22 December 1979. 'Derek Mahon's Humane Perspective', in Terence Brown and Nicholas Grene (eds.), *Tradition and Influence in Anglo-Irish Poetry* (Basingstoke, Macmillan, 1989), pp. 143–53.

Kerrigan, John, 'Ulster Ovids', in Neil Corcoran (ed.), *The Chosen Ground: Essays on the Contemporary Poetry of Northern Ireland* (Bridgend, Seren Books, 1992), pp. 237–70.

Longley, Edna, 'Stars and Horses, Pigs and Trees', *Crane Bag*, 3, 2 (1979). 'The Writer and Belfast', in Maurice Harmon (ed.), *The Irish Writer and the City*, Irish Literary Studies 18 (Gerrards Cross, Colin Smythe, 1984). 'Poetry and Politics in Northern Ireland' and 'The Singing Line: Form in Derek Mahon's Poetry', in *Poetry in the Wars* (Newcastle-upon-Tyne, Bloodaxe, 1986), pp. 170–184 and 185–210. 'The Aesthetic and the Territorial', in Elmer Andrews (ed.), *Contemporary Irish Poetry* (Basingstoke, Macmillan, 1992), pp. 63–85. 'Derek Mahon: Extreme Religion of Art', in Michael Kenneally (ed.), *Poetry in Contemporary Irish Literature* (Gerrards Cross, Colin Smythe, 195), pp. 280–303. '"A Barbarous Nook": The Writer and Belfast', '"When Did you Last See Your Father?": Perceptions of the Past in Northern Irish Writing 1965–1985'. 'Poetic Forms and Social Malformations', 'No More Poems about Pantings?' and 'The Room Where MacNeice Wrote "Snow"', in *The Living Stream: Literature and Revisionism in Ireland* (Newcastle-upon-Tyne, Bloodaxe, 1994), pp. 86–108, 150–172, 196–226, 227–251, 252–270. '"Atlantic's Premises": American Influences on Northern Irish Poetry in the 1960s', in *Poetry and Posterity* (Tarset, Bloodaxe, 2000), pp. 259–79.

McDonald, Peter, 'Derek Mahon, Tom Paulin, and the Lost Tribe', in *Mistaken Identities: Poetry and Northern Ireland* (Oxford, Clarendon Press, 1997), pp. 81–109. 'Incurable Ache', review of *The Yellow Book*, *Poetry Ireland Review*, 56 (Spring, 1998), pp. 117–9.

Mahony, Christina Hunt, 'Irish Poetry for Our Age', in *Contemporary Irish Literature: Transforming Tradition* (Basingstoke, Macmillan, 1998), pp. 58–65.

Maxwell, D.E.S., 'Contemporary Poetry in the North of Ireland', in Douglas Dunn (ed.), *Two Decades of Irish Writing* (Cheadle, Carcanet, 1975). 'Semantic Scruples: A Rhetoric for Politics in the North', in Peter Connolly (ed.), *Literature and the Changing Ireland* (Gerrards Cross, Colin Smythe, 1982).

Paulin, Tom, 'A Terminal Ironist', in *Ireland and the English Question* (Newcastle-upon-Tyne, Bloodaxe, 1984), pp. 55–9.

Redmond, John, 'Wilful Inconsistency: Derek Mahon's Verse-Letters', *Irish University Review*: Special Issue: Derek Mahon, 24, 1 (Spring-Summer, 1994), pp. 96–116

Redshaw, Thomas D., 'Ri, As in Regional: Three Ulster Poets', *Eire-Ireland* 9.2 (Summer, 1974).

Riordan, Maurice, 'An Urbane Perspective: The Poetry of Derek Mahon', in Maurice Harmon (ed.), *The Irish Writer and the City*. Irish Literary Studies 18 (Gerrards Cross, Colin Smythe, 1984), pp. 169–79.

Shields, Kathleen, 'Derek Mahon's Poetry of Belonging', *Irish University Review*: Special Issue: Derek Mahon, 24, 1 (Spring-Summer, 1994), pp. 67–79.

Smith, Stan, 'Margins of Tolerance: Responses to Post-War Decline', in *Inviolable Voice: History and Twentieth Century Poetry* (Dublin: Gill and Macmillan, 1982), pp. 170–199.

Tinley, Bill, 'International Perspectives in the Poetry of Derek Mahon', *Irish University Review* 21, 1 (Spring/Summer 1991), pp. 106–117. '"Harmonies and Disharmonies": Derek Mahon's Francophile Poetics', *Irish University Review*: Special Issue: Derek Mahon, 24, 1 (Spring-Summer, 1994), pp. 80–95.

Waterman, Andrew, 'Ulsterectomy', *Hibernia* 26 April 1979. '"Somewhere, Out there, Beyond": The Poetry of Seamus Heaney and Derek Mahon', *PN Review*, 8, 1 (1980), pp. 39–47.

Wilson, William A., 'A Theoptic Eye: Derek Mahon's *The Hunt by Night*, *Eire-Ireland*, 25, 4 (Winter, 1990), pp. 120–31.

York, R.A., 'Derek Mahon as Translator', *Revista Alicantina de Estudios Ingleses*, no. 5 (November, 1992), pp. 163–84.

NOTES ON CONTRIBUTORS

MICHAEL ALLEN teaches American and Irish writing and critical theory at Queen's University, Belfast. He has written on American, English and Irish fiction but of late his main interest has been contemporary poetry. He has edited an anthology of critical essays on Seamus Heaney (1999) and is preparing a book on Michael Longley's poetry.

NEIL CORCORAN is Professor of English at the University of St Andrews. His books include *Seamus Heaney* (1986), *The Chosen Ground: Essays on the Contemporary Poetry of Northern Ireland* (1992), *English Poetry Since 1940* (1993) and *After Yeats and Joyce: Reading Modern Irish Literature* (1997). He has contributed regular reviews to such periodicals as the *Times Literary Supplement* and the *London Review of Books*.

PATRICK CROTTY is Head of the English Department at St Patrick's College, Drumcondra. He has published articles, essays and reviews on Irish, British and American poetry in *Études Écossaises*, *The Irish Review*, *The New Welsh Review*, *The Times Literary Supplement*, *Scottish Literary Journal* and elsewhere. He edited *Modern Irish Poetry: An Anthology* (1995). He is joint editor (with Alan Riach) of the forthcoming three-volume, annotated *Complete Collected Poems of Hugh MacDiarmid*.

GERALD DAWE, poet, is lecturer in English and director of the Oscar Wilde Centre for Irish Writing, School of English, Trinity College, Dublin. His poetry collections include *The Lundys Letter* (1985), *Sunday School* (1991), *Heart of Hearts* (1995) and *The Morning Train* (1999). Other publications include *Against Piety: Essays in Irish Poetry* (1995), *The Rest is History: A Critical Memoir* (1998) and *Stray Dogs and Dark Horses: Essays* (2000).

JOHN GOODBY is Lecturer in English at the University of Wales, Swansea. He is the author of *Irish Poetry Since 1950: From Stillness into History* (2000) and *Under the Spelling Wall: The Critical Fates of Dylan Thomas* (2001) and editor (with Chris Wigginton) of the *New*

Casebook title on Dylan Thomas. He has written widely on Irish, English and Welsh poetry and is a member of the ESRC Transnational Communities programme Axial Writing project. His own poetry is published in *A Birmingham Yank* (1998) and he reviews for *Textual Practice, Angel Exhaust, Poetry Review* and the *TLS*.

HUGH HAUGHTON teaches English at the University of York and is completing a study of Derek Mahon.

EAMONN HUGHES lectures in the School of English, Queen's University of Belfast, specialising in Irish writing. He is the editor of *Northern Ireland: Culture and Politics 1960–1990* (1991) and has published widely on Irish literary and cultural studies.

JERZY JARNIEWICZ is a Polish poet, literary critic and translator who lectures in English at the universities of Lodz and Warsaw. He has published *The Uses of the Commonplace in Contemporary British Poetry* (1994) and written extensively on contemporary poetry for various journals, including *Poetry Review, Irish Review, Krino, Arete, Agni* and *Cambridge Review*. He is editor of the literary monthly *Literatura na Swiecie* (Warsaw), and has translated the work of many contemporary poets and novelists including Seamus Heaney, Craig Raine, Christopher Reid, Philip Roth, Nadine Gordimer, Edmund White and Raymond Carver.

EDNA LONGLEY teaches at Queen's University, Belfast. Her most recent publications are a collection of essays, *Poetry and Posterity* (2000), and (as editor) *The Bloodaxe Book of Twentieth Century Poetry from Britain and Ireland* (2000)

FRANK SEWELL is a graduate of Queen's University of Belfast and the University of Ulster, where he now works as a research officer. His poems have been published in *Outside the Walls* (which he edited along with Francis O'Hare), in journals, newspapers and various anthologies. Also a translator, his English language versions of poems in Irish by Cathal Ó Searcaigh, published in *Out in the Open*, were nominated for the Aristeion European Translation prize. He received the University of Ulster McCrea Literary Award for poetry in 1996 and a Literature Award from the Arts Council in 1999. His critical work includes *Modern Irish Poetry: A New Alhambra* (2000), and he is currently co-editing *Artwords: An Ulster Anthology of Contemporary Visual Art and Poetry*.

STAN SMITH has held the Research Chair in Literary Studies at the Nottingham Trent University since 1999. He previously occupied the established Chair of English at Dundee University. His most recent books are *The Origins of Modernism: Eliot, Yeats, Pound and the Rhetorics of Renewal* (1994) and *W.H. Auden* (1997), and he has guest-edited (with Jennifer Birkett) a special issue of the Zaragoza University annual *Miscelánea* (2000). He is currently preparing an edition of Auden's *The Orators* for the Faber/Princeton Variorum edition of Auden's works, and completing two critical studies: *Ruined Boys: Lineages of Modernism from Eliot to Auden and Beyond*; and *Displaced Persons: Topographies of Postmodern Poetry*. He is series editor of *Longman Critical Readers* and *Longman Studies in Twentieth Century Literature*, and a Fellow of the English Association.

BRUCE STEWART lectures in Irish literary history and bibliography at the University of Ulster and serves as Literary Director of the Princess Grace Irish Library in Monaco. He has taught in Ireland, America and the Middle East and publishes widely in Irish literature. He acted as Assistant editor to the *Oxford Companion to Irish Literature* (1996).

RICHARD YORK was educated at Kettering Grammar School, Emmanuel College Cambridge and University College London. He has taught at the University of Ulster since 1969 and is now Professor of European Literature. His publications include *The Poem as Utterance* (1986), *Strangers and Silence* (1994), *The Rules of Time* (1999) and articles on English and European literature.

INDEX